UNEVEN CENTURIES

THE PRINCETON ECONOMIC HISTORY
OF THE WESTERN WORLD

Joel Mokyr, Series Editor

A list of titles in this series appears at the back of the book.

Uneven Centuries

ECONOMIC DEVELOPMENT
OF TURKEY SINCE 1820

ŞEVKET PAMUK

PRINCETON UNIVERSITY PRESS
PRINCETON & OXFORD

Published by Princeton University Press
41 William Street, Princeton, New Jersey 08540
6 Oxford Street, Woodstock, Oxfordshire OX20 1TR

press.princeton.edu

Library of Congress Control Number: 2018949303
ISBN: 9780691166377

British Library Cataloging-in-Publication Data is available

Editorial: Joe Jackson and Samantha Nader
Production Editorial: Leslie Grundfest
Jacket/Cover Credit: Layla MacRory
Production: Jacqueline Poirier
Copyeditor: Karen Verde

This book has been composed in Arno Pro

Printed on acid-free paper. ∞

Printed in the United States of America

10 9 8 7 6 5 4 3 2 1

CONTENTS

Contents

TABLES AND FIGURES

PREFACE

THE INDUSTRIAL REVOLUTION that began in Great Britain in the second half of the eighteenth century had far-reaching consequences not only for Western Europe but also for the rest of the world. Along with industrial capitalism, modern economic growth spread unevenly across the globe since 1820. This book will examine economic growth and human development in Turkey during the last two centuries from a comparative global perspective. I will try to establish in both absolute and relative terms Turkey's record in economic growth and human development and evaluate both the proximate and deeper causes of this record.

In a number of ways this book reflects some of the key trends in economic historiography in recent decades. It was not so long ago that economic historians focused almost exclusively on the past of the developed economies—Western Europe, North America, and Japan. In recent decades, however, they have been focusing increasingly on the history of developing economies. The study of their economic history should provide important insights into the present-day experiences of the developing countries. As part of these efforts, quantitative economic history and more specifically the construction of long-term economic series, especially GDP and GDP per capita series as well as the construction of series on health and education, has been spreading to the developing economies. I have contributed to the construction of these series for Turkey and more generally for the Middle East in recent years, and they have played a key role in my efforts to insert the case of Turkey during the last two centuries into a comparative framework. Even if most of the existing series may be subject to larger margins of error than those on developed countries, it would not have been possible to properly evaluate Turkey's record without these efforts. In addition, economics and the economic history literature have been making an important distinction in recent years between proximate causes and deeper determinants of economic development. While the proximate causes focus on investment, accumulation of inputs, technology, and productivity, the deeper causes relate to the broader environment, including the social and political variables as well as institutions. In this book I will also emphasize this distinction and I will try to address and evaluate these deeper causes in the context of a developing economy.

There are a number of basic reasons why the case of Turkey should offer important insights into the economic history of developing countries as a whole. Turkey is one of the larger developing countries; the economy of the area within its present-day borders has consistently been among the largest twenty economies and largest eight developing economies of the world during the last two centuries. Its population and total GDP have accounted for about 1 percent of the world population and world GDP during the last two centuries. Moreover, during that same time, Turkey's long-term economic performance has been close to both the world and developing-country averages. For this reason, one can argue that in contrast to the more successful and less successful examples, Turkey is a more representative case and offers greater insights into the experiences of a larger set of the developing countries. Yet, in contrast to the more successful cases, Turkey's long-term economic development has not been studied well. An economic history of Turkey during the last two centuries has not been available in any language.

One of the special features of Turkey is that, aside from brief occupation of parts of the country after World War I, it has not experienced colonial rule in history. The area within the present borders of Turkey was part of a large, multiethnic empire until the end of World War I, and modern Turkey emerged as one of the successor states after the end of the Ottoman Empire. As a result, Turkey's institutions and economy have not been subjected to wholesale institutional change by an outside power. Instead, formal institutional changes have been introduced from within, by governments and elites. In addition, Turkey's institutions and economy have received their share of influences from the outside during the last two centuries.

Turkey did not and does not have large mineral resources or oil. Its economy and exports were based mostly on agriculture during the nineteenth century and until the Great Depression. With the rapid increases in the urbanization rate since the end of World War II, share of agriculture has been declining and the shares of industry and especially services in both GDP and employment have been rising. Manufactures have accounted for more than 90 percent of exports in recent decades. Governments in Turkey have experimented with a variety of economic policies during the last two centuries. In fact, in each of the four historical periods I will define and examine, governments in Turkey pursued economic policies that were consistent with the most common strategy of economic development at the time. The country's economic history since the Industrial Revolution may thus serve as a good case study for learning more not only about the patterns of economic growth and human development in developing countries but also their proximate and deeper causes.

Throughout the book, a good deal of quantitative evidence and intertemporal trends will be presented in tables and figures. In order to facilitate intertemporal and international comparisons, all quantitative series in the book including those for population, per capita income, urbanization rate, and foreign trade, as well as the analysis in the text, will be for the area within the present-day borders of Turkey unless otherwise stated.

I benefited from the insights and support of many people as I prepared this manuscript. It is now a pleasure to acknowledge them. I would like to begin by thanking my graduate students at Boğaziçi University and the London School of Economics during the last decade, on whom I tried out many of the ideas presented herein. Nicole Pope expertly translated an early version of the text from Turkish. As I developed and rewrote it, I benefited from the comments of many friends and colleagues who read parts or all of it or discussed particular issues with me. For their valuable insights, I am especially grateful to Daron Acemoğlu, Robert Allen, Yeşim Arat, Steve Broadberry, Yılmaz Esmer, Bishnu Gupta, Ulaş Karakoç, Kıvanç Karaman, Çağlar Keyder, Debin Ma, Nadir Özbek, Patrick O'Brien, Dani Rodrik, Zafer Toprak, and Murat Üçer.

During a one-day meeting at the California Institute of Technology, Philip Hoffman, Jean-Laurent Rosenthal, Metin Coşgel, Reşat Kasaba, and Paul Rhode provided detailed and very helpful comments on an earlier version of the text. At later stages, I was able to present parts of the manuscript and benefit from the discussion at seminars at New York University Abu Dhabi and the University of Oxford. Two anonymous referees read different versions of the manuscript and provided detailed and very useful comments. It was a pleasure to work with editors Joe Jackson and Leslie Grundfest and the members of their team at Princeton University Press as the text was prepared for publication.

I am especially grateful to the series editor, Joel Mokyr, for providing the right mixture of guidance, criticism, and support from the early stages of the manuscript to its completion. Finally, I would like to thank Yeşim and Zeynep for their advice and support at all stages. This book would not have been possible without them.

UNEVEN CENTURIES

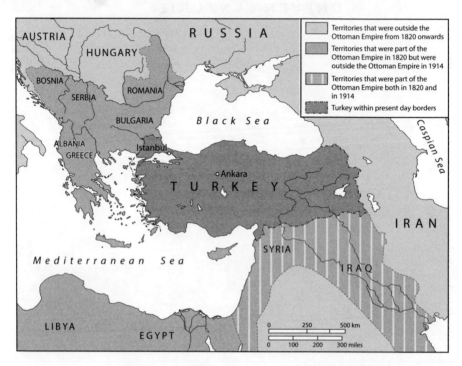

The Ottoman Empire 1820 to 1914 and present-day Turkey

1

Introduction

MOST COUNTRIES AROUND THE WORLD have experienced significant increases in per capita income and improvements in human development during the last two centuries. Turkey's performance in economic growth and human development has been a little above but close to developing-country and world averages. This book aims to establish that record in a global comparative framework for the first time and explore why Turkey's economic performance has remained close to the averages.

The economics and economic history literature has been emphasizing in recent decades that the proximate causes of economic growth, namely the economic variables such as the increases in inputs, land, labor, and capital, and the productivity increases brought on by investments in physical and human capital as well as advances in technology, can provide only a partial explanation. We also need to address the deeper causes for economic growth, particularly the social, political, as well as the historical causes that influence the rate at which inputs and productivity grow. In recent decades, a still developing literature has renewed the argument that for deeper causes, we need to study the institutions defined as written and unwritten rules of a society and their enforcement that affect the incentives to invest and innovate.

Two of Turkey's special features as a developing country are that it has not been subject to colonial rule and that it has experienced waves of top-down institutional changes brought about by its own modernizing elites during the last two centuries. The Ottoman government launched a detailed reform program in 1839. The new nation-state established after World War I continued the secular modernizing reforms in law, administration, education, and elsewhere. Turkey's political system was opened to greater participation and competition after World War II with the transition to a multiparty system which gave greater voice and power to average citizens. Turkey's formal economic institutions and economic policies also experienced a great deal of change during the last two centuries. In each of the four periods I will define herein, governments adopted economic institutions and economic policies that were consistent with the most commonly adopted institutions and policies in the developing countries around the world.

Not all of these changes in formal institutions have supported or enhanced economic growth and development. In fact, some were designed more to support the interests of certain groups than to bring prosperity to all. Nonetheless, many of these institutional changes were designed to and did lead to increases in per capita income and improvements in human development. How did these changes in formal political and economic institutions bring about average rates and why did they not bring about higher rates of economic growth and human development? The answer is not simple and the state of our knowledge is not sufficient for a precise answer. Nonetheless, I will explore the causes in a global comparative framework.

This chapter provides an overview of the book. I will begin by summarizing Turkey's record in economic growth and human development both in absolute and comparative terms. I will then discuss the proximate causes by focusing on investment, accumulation of inputs, technology, and productivity. The deeper causes of Turkey's record in economic development relate to the broader environment, including the social and political environments as well as institutions. I will offer an overview of the recent literature in the role of institutions in long-term economic development and then summarize my argument about the role of institutions and how and in what respects they mattered in the case of Turkey.

Economic Growth and Human Development since 1820

For thousands of years, per capita production and income levels around the world had remained close to subsistence. Even if a society managed to raise per capita incomes, the increases could not be sustained for long. This pattern has changed dramatically in the last two centuries, however. Technological progress began to accelerate in the aftermath of the Industrial Revolution and a higher share of incomes began to be set aside for investments in physical and human capital. Economic growth, defined as lasting increases in per capita production and income, became the fundamental process that determined the wealth or poverty of nations.

Today, most countries in the world have average incomes that are much higher than their levels in 1820. In Britain, the first country to experience the Industrial Revolution, for example, per capita income in 2010 was approximately twelve times that of 1820. Countries or regions did not all grow at the same rate during the past two centuries, however. Countries in Western Europe and North America, which began industrializing early, grew at a faster pace until the middle of the twentieth century. In contrast, the majority of the countries currently referred to as developing experienced limited or no increases in per capita incomes until after World War II, when they began their process of industrialization. Since the end of World War II, a limited number of countries, including Italy, Japan, and South Korea, began to close the gap with high-income countries, thanks to high rates of economic growth. In addition, the pace of economic growth has picked up in the past thirty years in the world's two most populated countries, China and India, and more generally in East and South Asia. Nonetheless, the gap between the early industrializers and developing countries is not smaller today than it was in 1950. In other words, the disparities between the countries, which began industrializing in the nineteenth century and are now developed, and those that started their industrialization later and are currently developing, are much larger today than they were two centuries ago.

Economic growth or increases in per capita income cannot be the only goals or the only measures used to evaluate economic performance. Economists and social scientists argue that in any assessment of long-term economic performance, quality of life, income distribution, health, education, and changing environmental conditions need to be taken into account, as well as production and income. Aside from income or GDP per capita, the measure most widely used to evaluate the development of economies in recent years has been the human development index, which gives equal weight to health and education, in addition to GDP per capita.

The pattern of improvements in health around the world during the last two centuries has also been uneven and followed broadly the pattern of GDP per capita. Life expectancy at birth, the most basic measure of health, first began to rise in Western Europe and the Western offshoots during the nineteenth century while it rose very slowly if at all in the rest of the world. Since the end of World War II, however, along with GDP per capita, life expectancy began to increase rapidly in the developing countries. In fact, a global convergence in life expectancy has emerged since 1950, with life expectancy in most parts of the developing world approaching those of the developed countries.

It is more difficult to develop simple measures of education, the other component of the human development index, but there is a broad correlation between the pattern of GDP per capita and years of schooling of the adult population around the world during the last two centuries. Years of schooling of the adult population rose much more rapidly in Western Europe and North America until World War II, and, as in GDP per capita but unlike life expectancy at birth, there has not been any catch-up, at least in terms of years of schooling, between the early industrializers and the developing countries since.

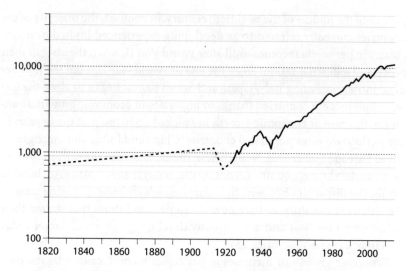

FIGURE 1.1. GDP per Capita in Turkey, 1820–2015 (PPP adjusted and in 1990 US dollars). Sources: Pamuk 2006 for Turkey until 1950; Maddison 2007, pp. 375–86; Bolt and Van Zanden 2014; also see the discussion and sources cited in chapter 2.

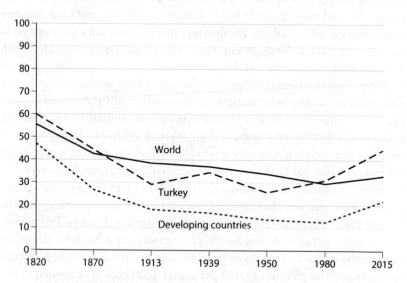

FIGURE 1.2. GDP per Capita in Turkey and the World, 1820–2015 (PPP adjusted and as percentage of Western Europe and the United States). Sources: Pamuk 2006 for Turkey until 1950; Maddison 2007, pp. 375–86; Bolt and Van Zanden 2014; also see the discussion and sources cited in chapter 2.

This book presents for the first time a GDP per capita series for Turkey since the year 1820. This will be an important part of the evidence for evaluating Turkey's absolute and relative economic performance. As I will discuss in greater detail in the next chapter and in the rest of the book, GDP per capita in the area within Turkey's current borders has increased approximately fifteenfold, and Turkey's rates of economic growth have been close to world averages during the last two centuries. Economic growth in Turkey began in the nineteenth century and per capita incomes more than doubled until 1950. However, long-term rates of increase of per capita income remained below 1 percent per year during this period (figure 1.1). Even though Turkey did better than the averages for the developing countries from 1820 until 1950, the gap with developed countries continued to widen. The most basic reason for this pattern was the relatively rapid industrialization in Western Europe and North America while Turkey as well as other developing countries stayed mostly with agriculture. In the case of Turkey, there was a spurt of industrialization and high rates of growth during the 1930s, but those gains were reversed during and after World War II. Per capita incomes in the area within Turkey's current borders declined from 60 percent of average per capita income in Western Europe and the United States in 1820 to 26 percent in 1950 (figure 1.2).

As is the case for most developing countries, long-term growth rates have been significantly higher since the end of World War II. As urbanization and industrialization picked up, annual rate of increase of per capita income rose above 3 percent, and per capita income increased more than sixfold between 1950 and 2015. As a result, per capita incomes in Turkey rose from 26 percent of the per capita income in Western Europe and the United States in 1950 to 31 percent in 1980 and 43 percent in 2015. Between 1950 and 1980, per capita incomes in Turkey have increased at rates slightly higher than the population-weighted averages for the developing countries of Asia, South America, and Africa. Turkey's growth rates continued to be higher than the averages for South America and Africa since 1980. However, the two large developing countries, China and India, and more generally East, Southeast, and most recently South Asia have experienced significantly higher rates of growth than Turkey in recent decades.

Comparisons with four countries with similar populations in southern Europe and the Middle East will provide additional insights into Turkey's long-term trajectory. Early in the nineteenth century Italy and Spain had higher levels of GDP per capita in comparison to Turkey. They began their industrialization during the nineteenth century and achieved higher rates of growth than Turkey during the nineteenth century and the Interwar period primarily because the rates of industrialization were lower in Italy and Spain than in the developed countries. Italy and Spain experienced very high rates of economic growth and were able to converge more significantly than Turkey to the level of the developed countries since the end of World War II. Compared to Turkey, Egypt and Iran had slightly lower levels of GDP per capita early in the nineteenth century and they experienced lower rates of economic growth during the nineteenth century. The GDP per capita levels remained unchanged in Egypt during the Interwar period and the gap with the developed countries widened further until 1950. In contrast, Iran was able to raise its GDP per capita to Turkey's levels in 1950 thanks to large revenues from oil. From the end of World War II until 2015, the GDP per capita gap with Turkey continued to widen. With the support of oil revenues, Iran's GDP per capita remained above that of Turkey until 1980 but has fallen behind since.

A small number of countries in southern Europe like Italy and Spain, and others in East Asia such as Japan and South Korea, as well as Hong Kong and Taiwan, have produced "economic miracles" and were able to significantly close the gap with developed countries since the end of World War II. During each of these catch-up or convergence episodes, annual rates of increase in per capita incomes in these countries remained higher than 5 percent for a period of at least 20–30 years. Turkey's economic growth performance did not come close to the catch-up performances exhibited by these more successful examples. In Turkey, increases in GDP per capita never reached 5 percent during any subperiod in the last two centuries. After falling significantly behind the developed countries during the nineteenth century and until 1950, Turkey's catch-up has been rather limited since. In short, Turkey's long-term growth performance has been close to but slightly higher than the averages for developing countries and close to the averages for the world during the last two centuries.

The pattern of improvements in health and education in Turkey since 1820 is correlated with but not identical to that in GDP per capita. Improvements in health and education in Turkey were also slow in the nineteenth century but they have picked up pace after World War I and especially World War II. Life expectancy at birth in the area within present-day borders increased slowly from about 26–27 years in 1820 to 44 years in 1950. While life expectancy at birth in Turkey remained slightly higher than the averages for the developing countries as a whole, the gap in life expectancy at birth between Turkey and the developed countries increased significantly during the nineteenth century and until 1950. Together with higher rates of economic growth, life expectancy at birth began to increase rapidly after the end of World War II, by almost one year in every two years or by more than 30 years between 1950 and 2015. As a result, the gap with the developed countries in life expectancy at birth closed significantly since the end of World War II for Turkey and for developing countries as a whole.

Turkey's experience with education shows a broadly similar pattern of slow improvement during the nineteenth century and more rapid improvement during the twentieth century, especially since the end of World War II. Despite the education reforms in the nineteenth century, schools and schooling did not spread to rural areas where the great majority of the population lived because of fiscal constraints and because the new schools were not easily accepted by the Muslim population. Literacy rates for the adult population increased slowly during the century and were only slightly above 10 percent on the eve of World War I. In the Interwar period, the overall literacy rate rose faster but educational efforts remained limited mostly to the urban areas and did not reach the rural areas where a majority of the population lived. The overall literacy rate stood at 33 percent in 1950 but rose to 68 percent in 1980 and 95 percent in 2015. Progress was even slower among women.

Since literacy rates from the early periods are not easily available for most developing countries, for international comparisons we need to turn to another basic indicator. Average years of schooling for the adult population over age 15 remained well below 1 year during the nineteenth century and edged up to 1.5 years by 1950. It has since risen to more than 7 years. Data from other regions indicate that in this basic education indicator, Turkey has lagged behind not only the world averages but also the averages for the developing countries as well as the countries with similar levels of GDP per capita for most if not all of the last two centuries. One important cause of this poor performance is the existence of large and persistent gender inequalities. Turkey's low rankings in health and education are also a result of the large regional inequalities and low levels of health and education as well as per capita income in the southeast region, where the majority of the Kurdish population live.

Proximate Causes and Deeper Determinants

For a long time, economists have focused on the proximate causes of economic growth, namely the increases in productivity brought on by investments in physical and human capital as well as advances in technology and organizational efficiency. In recent decades, however, the focus has been shifting from the proximate causes toward the deeper determinants. The latter refer to aspects of the social, political, and economic environments that support and bring about these investments and at the same time determine the extent to which they are productive. The growing recognition that rates of investment and rates of productivity growth are not exogenous but are determined by a variety of factors, both economic and non-economic, has supported the search for deeper determinants. Evidence has been building up in recent years that some part of the international variation in per capita income is explained by the fact that long-term causes such as resource endowments and geography, culture, education, and institutions that interact with each other impact economic growth as a result of deeply interlinked historical processes. Consequently, it has been very difficult to disentangle them and treat the impact of each of these causes separately.

In recent decades a diverse and still developing literature has renewed the argument that institutions, defined as written and unwritten rules of a society and their enforcement, play key roles in promoting economic development. According to this literature, more complex and advanced forms and innovations that lead to increases in productivity can only emerge if institutions or rules and their enforcement in a society encourage and support activities to that effect. Laws supporting production and investment and their enforcement, equality before law, and opening the economy to broader sections will encourage the formation of new partnerships and they will encourage individuals from different sections of society to develop their talents and engage in economic activity.

While research on institutions is still in its early stages, institutions are increasingly seen as more fundamental determinants of economic development and of long-term differences in per capita GDP between countries than rates of physical and human capital accumulation or research and development themselves. Recent studies also suggest not only that rates of physical and human capital accumulation are higher and new technologies are developed in countries with better institutions but also that the existing physical and human capital stock are used more efficiently and the productivity of the existing physical and human capital stock is higher in those countries with better institutions. In other words, differences in the quality of institutions are also seen as the main cause behind the intercountry differences in human capital formation and total factor productivity.

Included among institutions are the written or formal rules or laws legislated from the top down that facilitate economic exchanges by enforcing contracts, protecting property rights, and monitoring all parties to ensure that they adhere to their commitments. Formal institutions did not all originate with states, however. Family, kinship and ethnic ties, religious networks, patronage networks, coalitions, business partnerships, guilds, and foundations are all examples of informal arrangements that began as small-scale, bottom-up efforts in order to regulate and reduce uncertainty in economic life and to develop cooperation between different individuals and groups. Over time, many of these institutions began to be enforced at least partly by the state. The developing literature emphasizes the key role played by political institutions.

The distribution of political power and interests as well as the formation of alliances and coalitions among the elite will influence the choice of political and economic institutions.

Institutions are not limited to formal rules enforced by the state. Large numbers of informal institutions are self-enforced or enforced by non-state actors. These privately organized arrangements, typically built from the bottom up within communities and rooted in social networks, usually do not work by themselves but interact or work together with constellations of other informal and formal institutions. In fact, informal institutions are often necessary for formal arrangements to work properly. In order to understand the role of institutions, it is necessary to understand how the formal and informal institutions interact and create pressures for institutional configurations that may contribute to or prevent growth. In the longer term, for the emergence of economic transactions, cooperation, and partnerships involving larger numbers of people and more complex organizations, some but not necessarily all of the private order or informal institutions need to be replaced by more universalistic and formal arrangements.

External forces have also played important roles in shaping the institutions of a given society. The cases of colonies or formal colonies in which an outside power shapes formal institutions are examples of recent and direct external influence. Equally important during the last two centuries has been the influence of international or global rules such as free trade, the gold standard, and the Bretton Woods system of rules and organizations that were shaped after World War II. More recently, the Washington Consensus principles such as reliance on markets, trade liberalization, and privatization which are often enforced either by the leading global powers or international agencies have influenced formal economic institutions including policies.

There is growing consensus in the literature that the role of the state in economic development is not limited to providing external and internal security, protecting property rights, and enforcing contracts. The state also plays a key role in the formation and enforcement of institutions as well as their development and evolution over time. Historically, the relations between competing elites and their relations to the state have been critical in the formation of the state and state policies. Reaching an understanding if not consensus between elites and harnessing the different powers and capacities of the various elites was a key aspect of state formation and state policies. When the distribution of benefits from an existing institution or a new institution was not consistent with the existing distribution of power in society, the various elites could mobilize, bargain, and put pressure on others as well as the state to try to bring formal and informal institutions back into line. In other words, the extent to which formal institutions could be enforced or to which rule of law prevails often depended on the relations and the degree of understanding between the various groups as well as their elites and the state.

The experience of Britain and the later industrializers in Europe both during the early modern era and the nineteenth century shows that states played key roles in economic development not only by providing security and enforcing laws and contracts, but also by supporting markets and long-distance trade, and in most cases protecting domestic production against foreign competition. States in today's developing world had limited capacity and played limited roles in economic development during the nineteenth century. Since the 1930s and especially after World War II, state interventionism in the economy spread rapidly and states in some developing countries, most notably in East Asia, played key roles in industrialization. The existence of such examples does not mean, however, that state interventionism will always produce results that favor economic development and industrialization. As the results of attempts to replicate the East Asian experience with industrialization confirm, even if the same formal institutions and the same economic policies are adopted, the outcomes can be very different because new institutions interact with other existing institutions as well as the existing social structure and distribution of power.

While the new and growing literature has provided both a theoretical framework and empirical evidence that institutions matter for long-term economic development, it also has some significant limitations. For one thing, how economic institutions are shaped and why they vary across countries is not well understood. The literature has so far not examined in detail the mechanisms through which they shape economic and political outcomes. Similarly, the recent literature has not addressed adequately how institutions may change in the longer term. Here, more attention needs to be paid to the role of agency, the role of different groups in bringing about institutional change. In other words, while evidence is growing that institutions matter, we need to learn more about how they are shaped, how they work, how they persist, and how they change.

At its broadest, the new literature is an attempt to shed light on how economic behavior and outcomes are mediated by the institutional setting in which they take place. The interaction between institutions and economic change, technology, politics, social structure, distribution of power, beliefs, ideologies, and expectations also work both ways. Institutions influence the others but are also influenced by them. Similarly, institutions shape behavior and relations among the various actors and, in turn, are shaped by them. Institutions thus influence behavior, but they are not the sole cause of outcomes. While it may be easier to isolate the effect of institutions on economic development if we believe that institutions evolve independently of the path of economic development, it will not be easy to do so if the other variables also influence the evolution of institutions. The analysis of the role of institutions is more complicated and the case for attributing economic growth to institutions alone is weaker if institutions are endogenous and are influenced by economic change as well as the other variables. Nonetheless, to acknowledge that institutions are influenced by the other variables does not imply that institutions do not matter or that they have only limited impact on economic performance.

Turkey's performance in economic growth and human development has been close to developing-country and world averages. I will argue in the rest of the book that this pattern cannot be satisfactorily explained with reference only to the proximate causes such as rates of investment in physical and human capital and productivity growth. In order to better understand this record, it is also necessary to analyze the deeper causes, most important among them Turkey's institutions, including policies and their evolution. I will argue that while institutions are not the only thing that matters, it is essential to understand their role in order to evaluate Turkey's economic growth and human development performance during the last two centuries. In the following overview I aim to illustrate this distinction regarding the causes of economic growth in the case of Turkey.

Proximate Causes for Turkey since 1820

The basic proximate cause of the growing gap between Western Europe and much of the rest of the world during the nineteenth century was the very different rates of adoption of the new technologies. The steam-powered engines of the Industrial Revolution and other new technologies that followed were introduced first in Western Europe and North America. As investments in these technologies spread, productivity increased sharply in industry, transport, and to a lesser extent in agriculture. Conversely, in Turkey and in most developing countries, industrialization remained limited and the adoption of the steam engine and other new technologies occurred slowly and mostly in transport during the nineteenth century.

Population of the area within Turkey's current borders increased from about 10 million in 1820 to 17 million in 1914. Close to half of this increase was due to immigration. A large part of the slow increases in per capita GDP and incomes in Turkey during the same period were achieved by the expansion of agricultural production for domestic and export markets owing to the improvements in maritime shipping and the construction of railroads. These changes enabled rural households to specialize more in agriculture by increasing their labor time and cultivating more land to produce more cash crops for markets. Technological change in agriculture was slow, however. Mechanization in agriculture remained limited to small pockets of export-oriented production. Rates of aggregate investment were not higher than 5–6 percent of GDP for most of the century and rose to as much as 8 percent during the decades before World War I. As much as one-third of the investments in fixed capital after 1880 were undertaken by European companies that concentrated in railroad construction, infrastructure for foreign trade, and urban utilities. Low rates of investment, slow spread of the new technologies, and slow increases in productivity in agriculture and to a lesser extent in trade are the leading proximate causes of the low but positive rates of economic growth before World War I. Rising but low levels of state expenditures as well as the slow diffusion of new technologies also led to slow improvements in health and education (figure 1.3).

Turkey's population decreased by 20 percent during and after World War I. The large declines in the numbers of Greeks and Armenians, as well as Muslims, had long-term economic as well as political and social consequences. After the disintegration of the Ottoman Empire and the emergence of a new nation-state following World War I, Turkey gained the right to establish its own tariffs beginning in 1929. In response to the Great Depression and the collapse of agricultural prices, an important shift took place in economic strategy. Industrialization was embraced as the new engine of economic growth and protectionism was adopted as the key economic policy for this purpose. Rates of investment mostly in manufacturing and more generally in the urban economy, financed almost entirely with domestic savings, averaged 10 percent of GDP during the 1930s (figure 1.3). The new technologies began to spread in the urban economy. However, agriculture, which continued to employ close to 80 percent of the population, turned inward and remained mostly insulated until after World War II.

Turkey's population increased from 21 million in 1950 to 44 million in 1980 and 79 million in 2015. Urbanization was slow during the nineteenth century and the shift of labor from agriculture to the urban sector accelerated only after World War II. As some of those previously engaged in agriculture began migrating to urban areas to work in industry and services which, on the whole, used more advanced technologies, average labor productivity began to grow more rapidly. Estimates indicate that more than a third of all the increases in labor productivity and per capita income achieved in Turkey since 1950 have been due to the shift of labor from the low-productivity agricultural sector to the more productive urban economy. Share of agriculture in total employment declined from 75–80 percent in 1950 to 50 percent in 1980 to less than 20 percent in 2015, while share of the urban economy in employment increased

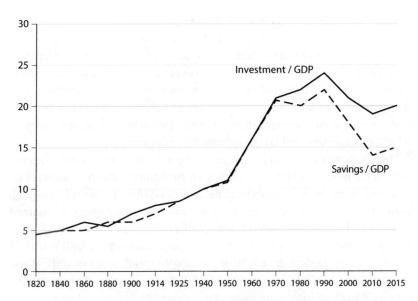

FIGURE 1.3. Savings and Investment Rates in Turkey, 1820–2015 (as percentage of GDP). Sources: Author's estimates until 1913 and official series from Turkey, Turkish Statistical Institute 2014 and Turkey, Ministry of Development 2017 for the period since 1923.

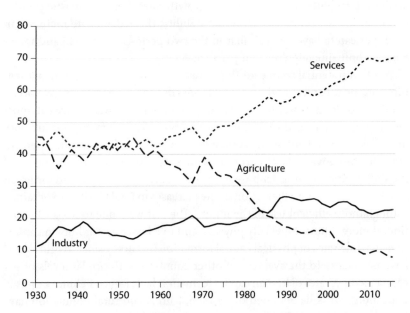

FIGURE 1.4. Changing Sectoral Shares in Turkey, 1930–2015 (three-year moving averages as percentage of GDP). Source: Based on the national income accounts in Turkey, Turkish Statistical Institute 2014.

from 20–25 percent in 1950 to more than 80 percent in 2015. The share of the urban economy in GDP also increased from about 58 percent in 1950 to 75 percent in 1980 and to 92 percent in 2015. Rates of growth of manufacturing industry averaged more than 8 percent per year and the share of manufacturing in total labor force edged upward between 1950 and 1980. However, rates of growth of manufacturing industry slowed to about 5 percent per year and its share in total employment stagnated since 1980 while the share of services in both employment and GDP continued to rise (figure 1.4).

Higher incomes allowed for higher savings rates and higher rates of investment in the more productive technologies. Investment rates rose from 11 percent of GDP in the early 1950s to 22 percent of GDP in the 1970s (figure 1.3). Most of these investments were financed with domestic savings. In contrast to the period before World War I, foreign direct investment remained limited during the Interwar period and also during the decades after World War II. In the more recent period since 1980, the aggregate investment rate did not rise any further and averaged 21 percent of GDP. As the savings rate began to decline after 1998, an increasing share of investments was financed with foreign capital inflows, mostly short and medium term. The resulting current account deficits and stop-go cycles associated with foreign capital inflows have emerged as a serious source of instability for the economy. While there were medium-term fluctuations in average growth rates due to domestic politics and their impact on macroeconomic stability, the average rate increases in GDP per capita have been similar in the two periods, 1950–1980 and 1980–2015, at approximately 3 percent per year.

Another potential source for the increases in productivity in both agriculture and the urban economy was the more efficient use of existing resources, in other words, increases in total factor productivity. As was the case in most developing countries during this period, however, total factor productivity increases remained limited in Turkey since World War II, at around 1 percent annually. Moreover, a large part of this increase was due to urbanization and the shift of labor from agriculture to the urban economy mentioned earlier. In other words, only a small fraction of the increases in total GDP were obtained through more efficient use of the inputs. The rest were due to the accumulation of more inputs, especially physical and to a lesser extent human capital. In fact, while rates of physical capital formation in Turkey since World War II have been close to the averages of other countries with similar levels of per capita income, rates of human capital formation have lagged behind. Levels of education and skills obtained by women, Kurds, and rural population have lagged even further behind.

Broadly speaking, then, with the exception of a spurt in the 1930s, rates of investment remained low and rates of increase of GDP per capita remained below 1 percent from 1820 to 1950. Rates of investment increased and rates of increase of GDP per capita averaged above 3 percent per year since 1950. Higher growth rates since 1950 were also due to the shift of labor and other resources from agriculture to manufacturing and services. Turkey's rates of investment and growth have been close to long-term averages for the developing countries and the world as a whole. These proximate causes provide insights into the rise in productivity and the pattern of economic growth in Turkey in both absolute and relative terms. They do not tell us, however, why rates of investment in physical and human capital were not higher, why investment in technological innovation lagged behind, and why rates of growth in total factor productivity have remained low in Turkey since 1950. For answers to these questions, we must turn to the deeper determinants of economic growth and development.

Deeper Causes for Turkey since 1820

Although research on institutions and their role in long-term economic development in Turkey is in its early stages, a good deal of evidence does exist and this book will emphasize that in each period new institutions have facilitated some economic growth and at the same time created obstacles in the way of further growth and development. To understand the role of institutions in economic development in Turkey, it is necessary to understand how formal and informal institutions interacted and created pressures for institutional configurations that contributed to or prevented economic development. It is also necessary to examine how formal and informal institutions have interacted with economic development and social structure.

There was some popular support and also some support among the elites, but much of the formal institutional changes Turkey experienced during the last two centuries, especially those in the earlier period, have been top-down. In the Ottoman Empire before the nineteenth century, the economic elites, landowners, merchants, manufacturers, and money changers had enjoyed a good deal of local power and autonomy, but they were not represented in central government. Similarly, the nineteenth-century reform program called *Tanzimat*, literally re-ordering, enjoyed some support among the elites including the provincial notables, but it was designed and launched by the Ottoman central government. The reforms promised all Ottoman subjects, Muslim and non-Muslim, the same basic rights and equality before the law. The Tanzimat also promised to strengthen property rights and end the centuries-old practice of confiscating the wealth of government officials who had lost their positions. During the nineteenth century, the Ottoman government attempted to create a modern bureaucracy and a new educational system as well as reform the legal system and the tax collection system. There were also some changes in political institutions. The first constitution and a parliament with elected as well as appointed members that opened in 1876 could last only one year, but they both returned after the Young Turk Revolution of 1908.

Top-down institutional changes were continued after the end of the Ottoman Empire and the emergence of Turkey as a new nation-state following World War I. The radical modernizing reforms of the new republic built upon the secularization of state, law, and education begun one century earlier. With the adoption of the Swiss civil code and the Italian penal code in 1926, the linkages to Islamic law were abolished entirely. The public education system was completely separated from religion and the religious schools were closed in 1924. The public schools and some areas in civil service and the professions were opened in greater numbers to urban, middle-class women who embraced the new secularism of the republic. Following a few years with a pluralist parliament, however, the new regime in Ankara turned more authoritarian after 1925, eliminating the opposition in parliament and creating a one-party political system.

The political system was opened to greater participation with the transition to a multiparty system and regular elections after World War II. As urbanization began to gain momentum, the transition to a more open and competitive political system gave greater voice and power to the ordinary people, both rural and urban. At the same time, however, a series of military coups until the end of the century ensured that the military closely controlled the political system, guarding secularism and restricting political freedoms including the rights of the Kurdish minority.

Turkey's formal economic institutions and economic policies underwent extensive changes during the last two centuries. In each of the four periods I will define, the formal economic institutions as well as economic policies adopted by the governments have been influenced by the international or global rules such as free trade, the Bretton Woods system, and Washington Consensus principles which were enforced either by the leading global powers or more recently by international agencies. In fact, I will show that in each of these four periods, governments in Turkey adopted economic institutions and economic policies that were consistent with the most commonly adopted institutions and policies in the developing countries around the world at the time.

During the nineteenth century, in exchange for the support of the European states for the reforms, the Ottoman government agreed to pursue laissez-faire policies and keep the economy open to foreign trade and foreign investment. The economic institutions of this period were shaped to a large extent by the bargaining between the central government and the European states.

The open economy model of the nineteenth century ended during and after World War I. Interventionism, protectionism, and greater emphasis on national economies emerged as new principles guiding economic policy. With new political institutions and new leadership, the new nation-state strived to create a national economy within the new borders during the Interwar era. In response to the Great Depression, the government adopted protectionism and pursued a state-led industrialization strategy.

Protectionist and inward-looking policies continued after World War II. Along with the shift to multiparty politics, however, the private sector increasingly took control of the economy in the post–World War II decades. After 1980, economic policies and institutions of the inward-looking industrialization era were abandoned in favor of Washington Consensus principles, most important, greater emphasis on markets, trade, and financial liberalization and privatization. The customs union agreement signed with the European Union in 1994 helped foster the growth of exports of manufactures.

These extensive changes in formal political and economic institutions played important roles in bringing about significant increases in per capita income as well as major improvements in health and education since 1820. Changes in formal institutions have been only part of the story, however. In order to understand the role of institutions, this book will also explore how the formal and informal institutions interacted and how they interacted with economic change, social structure, the distribution of power and expectations, and whether the new institutional configurations that emerged were growth-enhancing or growth-inhibiting.

The diffusion of the new formal institutions was slow during the nineteenth century and the first half of the twentieth century. The privately organized arrangements built from within communities and rooted in informal social networks continued to coexist with and often substituted for formal institutions in both urban and rural areas. With urbanization and economic growth as well as improvements in health and education after World War II, the fiscal, administrative, and legal capacities of the state also increased. These broad developments did not mean the disappearance of informal institutions, however. On the contrary, with rapid rural to urban migration, patronage, regional solidarity, and religious networks developed further and flourished in the urban areas since 1950, interacting with formal institutions and creating new institutions.

I will argue that there were a number of important reasons why formal institutions did not crowd out informal institutions but continued to coexist with informal institutions since the nineteenth century. First, many of the reforms were rather costly and required effective implementation and enforcement. In contrast, the fiscal, administrative, and legal capacities of the state were limited, especially in the earlier periods. The rural areas remained especially insulated from the top-down, secularizing reforms of the government. Second, the new formal institutions were not modular constructions but often interacted with other institutions. Other formal as well as informal arrangements were often necessary for the workings of the new formal institutions. At least some of these institutions were shaped by values, beliefs, and social norms as well as interests and distribution of power. While political institutions and laws could change very quickly, sometimes literally overnight, values, beliefs, social norms, and related institutions changed more slowly. Third, the design and implementation of the formal institutions remained top-down and they were not fully embraced by the public at large. In many situations, powerful groups tried to prevent changes because they believed that the new institutions would damage their own interests. In the earlier periods, opposition to the reforms also came from those who had controlled and benefited from some of the Islamic-Ottoman institutions. The opposition used both formal and informal institutions as strategic resources in the conflicts over distributional benefits and tried to undermine the new institutions.

I will offer examples throughout this text of how the new formal institutions interacted with informal institutions in various areas, ranging from the spread of education in rural areas and efforts to secure housing and access to local government services by recent migrants in urban areas, to the organization of the private sector to relations between the private sector and the government and more generally the workings of state interventionism in the economy. These examples will illustrate not only that the informal institutions continued to play important roles in the economy but also that the new formal institutions functioned differently as they interacted with the informal institutions as well as with social structure and the distribution of power.

Cleavages

The preceding discussion emphasized the importance of the two-way interaction between formal and informal institutions as well as the two-way interaction between institutions and economic outcomes. It also pointed to the importance of another two-way interaction, that between institutions and social structure. Institutions shape social structure not only through their influence on economic outcomes but also directly through their influence on the behavior of various actors as well as the relations among these actors. For example, formal and informal institutions play key roles in enhancing the ability of different social groups to solve their collective-action problems and pursue their common interests. Formal and informal institutions thus may contribute to and may also impede the cohesion and strength of different social actors. In turn, the social structure made up of many groups with diverging interests, alliances, and cleavages will influence the institutions. Formal and informal institutions shaped by trust and cooperation and other norms or their absence influence how these differences are handled, whether they are resolved or intensified. When the differences are not handled well, the result will often be political and economic instability as well as uncertainty, which will have significant implications on long-term economic development.

In Turkey since the nineteenth century, class cleavages have always mattered although their intensity varied over time in both urban and rural areas. Equally important have been the identity cleavages between the social groups and also between their elites. Some of these cleavages date back to the beginnings of the secular modernization project in the nineteenth century. The rise of Kurdish nationalism in the twentieth century added another dimension to them. In fact, the intensities of the identity cleavages between Muslims and non-Muslims, between seculars and conservative Muslims, Sunnis and other Muslims, between Kurds and Turks have at times been more important than those of class cleavages. While the identity cleavages often appeared to be based on culture, they often overlapped with competing economic interests between the different groups and between their elites. Rulers, politicians, and other elites often used Islam and exaggerated the existing cleavages to gain support among the population.

The configurations between the state and the elites and the various other groups, their alliances, coalitions, and cleavages varied considerably during the last two centuries. In each period, the relations, coalitions, and cleavages were also influenced by the global institutions and the economic models and policies allowed by the global economic system. The identity cleavages have made it more difficult for alliances and coalitions to emerge between the different elites. The cleavages also had negative consequences for state capacity and the ability of the state to enforce the formal institutions. Reaching an understanding if not consensus between the elites including the state elites and harnessing their different powers and capacities, as well as dealing with various collective-action problems, have been critical for the successful enforcement of the new institutions not only at the macro level but also at the micro level. If the distribution of benefits from an existing institution or a new institution was not consistent with the existing distribution of power in society, the various elites could mobilize, bargain, and exert pressure on others as well as the state to try to bring formal and informal institutions back into line. In these conflicts the competing elites often made use of informal institutions, including identity-based networks and patron-client relations.

The cleavages between the various competing elites, between the Muslims and the non-Muslims, the private elites and the state elites, between the secular and conservative elites, and between Turks and Kurds not only undermined state capacity, but they have often made it difficult to maintain political stability. Political order, which depends on the degree of understanding and consensus between different groups in society regarding basic rights, how to resolve conflicts, and the behavior of the state about the rules and their enforcement, is a necessary condition for political and economic development. By changing expectations and beliefs, increasing political uncertainty and instability can cause political and economic actors to behave very differently. The frequent military coups that occurred during the decades after World War II and the recent slide to authoritarianism indicate that Turkey's political system has not been able to manage these cleavages well.

The recurring periods of political instability have had adverse consequences for economic development both in the short and the longer term. In the multiparty era since the end of World War II, periods of political instability have typically resulted in growing macroeconomic problems and lower rates of economic growth. Even more important, the persistence of cleavages between elites, the use of informal networks as well as the mixed outcomes associated with state interventionism made it more difficult to bring together the resources and skills of people from different backgrounds. Many individuals and firms thus found it more expedient to use their resources to stay close to and seek favors from the government rather than invest in education, skills, and technology and pursue long-term gains in value added and productivity.

Outline

The following two chapters will extend this introduction. Chapter 2 will establish in greater detail Turkey's record in economic growth and human development since 1820, and chapter 3 will examine the role of institutions in economic development and the evolution of Ottoman institutions before the nineteenth century. In the rest of the book I will examine Turkey's experience with economic growth and human development since the Industrial Revolution in four historical periods. In each of these periods, governments in Turkey adopted the dominant economic model for the developing countries.

1. Growing specialization in agriculture under open economy conditions during the Ottoman nineteenth century
2. Transition from empire to the nation-state and an inward-looking economy during a difficult period that included two world wars and the Great Depression

3. Post–World War II decades when the import-substituting industrialization was led by the private sector
4. The recent period since 1980 when Washington Consensus principles
   were embraced and the economy opened up once again to international trade and investment

I will devote three chapters to the nineteenth century and two chapters to
each of the following periods. For each period, I will examine the evolution of
economic policies as well as the political developments and institutional
changes. I will then establish and evaluate Turkey's record in economic growth
and human development both in absolute and relative terms. I will also evaluate both the proximate and deeper causes of economic growth and human
development.

2

Economic Growth and Human Development since 1820

UNTIL THE END OF THE eighteenth century, increases in per capita incomes had remained limited around the world, and when and where they occurred, they could not be sustained for long. Economic growth, defined as sustained increases in per capita production or income, began in Western Europe during the centuries before the Industrial Revolution and began to spread to the rest of the world during the nineteenth century. By the second half of the twentieth century, significant increases in per capita production and incomes had been recorded in most regions and countries of the world and economic growth became the most fundamental process determining the wealth or poverty of nations around the world (Kuznets 1966, pp. 69–110). In Britain, for example, the per capita income or per capita purchasing power in 1820 was approximately half that of India today. Since that date, per capita income in Britain has increased twelvefold (Maddison 2007, pp. 359–86). Similarly, per capita income in 1820 in the area within Turkey's current borders was less than half the income per capita in Africa today. Between 1820 and 2015, Turkey's per capita income increased approximately fourteen times. In other words, without ignoring the measurement issues that merit attention and that will be discussed later, one can say that the average purchasing power in Turkey today is fourteen times higher than it was two centuries ago. This long-term trend will be at the center of this chapter and also of this book.

Economists have learned a great deal about modern economic growth since the end of World War II. The large and growing literature has emphasized that increases in productivity, achieved through technological progress on the one hand, and increases in per capita physical capital and education levels, on the other, were the most important factors contributing to economic growth. In many countries today, tools that embody more advanced technology are available and are being used in greater numbers. In addition, the labor force is much better educated than in 1820. The greater productivity and the increase in incomes achieved over time undoubtedly owe a good deal to these developments. In short, technological change and higher rates of investment in both physical and human capital are seen today as the leading proximate causes of economic growth since the Industrial Revolution. In the more recent period since the end of World War II, economic growth spread across the world as investment gained momentum and the pace of technological change increased, and per capita production and incomes began to rise steadily in the developing countries as well. A long wave of urbanization that began after World War II supported the higher rates of growth. As population shifted from agriculture to the urban economy, increases in investment and production were extended more rapidly to the urban sector and especially to industry (Kuznets 1966, pp. 86–159; Abramovitz 1986, pp. 385–406).

A recent and still developing literature has argued that institutions play important roles in promoting economic growth. This literature refers to the contributions made by productivity increases derived from advances in technology as well as the increases in physical and human capital as proximate causes of economic growth. In contrast, the social, political, and economic environments that influence the rate at which inputs and productivity grow or the institutions are defined as the written and unwritten rules of a society are increasingly seen as more fundamental determinants of economic development and of long-term differences in per capita GDP between countries. The role of institutions and institutional change in long-term economic growth will be examined in the next chapter.

Economic growth or increases in per capita income cannot be the only measure used to evaluate economic performance. In any assessment of long-term economic performance, quality of life, income distribution, health, education, and changing environmental conditions need to be taken into account, as well as production and income. If increases in income are unevenly distributed, for example, or if people's health is steadily deteriorating, societal welfare may decline while per capita income increases. An approach that focuses solely on increases in production inevitably ignores the negative impact of growth on the environment, including climate change. For this reason, a growing number of people in government, as well as economists and social scientists, in recent years have abandoned the approach, focusing solely on increasing per capita income, and emphasized the need to produce multidimensional indicators. Economists who work on these issues argue that, aside from production and income, the new multidimensional indicators produced to assess long-term economic development must also cover dimensions such as health, education, living standards, the environment, employment, and political participation (Stiglitz, Sen, and Fitoussi 2010).

To define and start using an indicator that reflects all or most of these dimensions, and that is widely agreed upon, will not be easy, however. Until a new and more satisfactory indicator is adopted, multidimensional assessments of the long-term development of economies have to be made by examining other available indicators. In recent decades, the measure most widely used to evaluate the development of economies, aside from per capita income, has been the human development index, which gives equal weight to health and education, as well as income per capita, but does not attempt to include other dimensions. In this chapter and throughout the book, I will examine trends in economic growth and human development in Turkey during the last two centuries.

I will express a country's per capita income as gross domestic product (GDP) per capita in 1990 US dollars, adjusted for purchasing power parity. This adjustment tends to reduce the gap in per capita income between high- and low-income countries in comparison to the earlier method using the current exchange rates. This is because the general price level in dollar terms is usually lower and the purchasing power of the dollar is higher in lower income countries. The purchasing power parity (PPP) adjustment is now the more widely accepted method because it produces more realistic results about the differences in average standards of living between different countries. For example, when the current exchange rate is used to make the comparison, the difference in per capita income between Turkey and the United States is estimated at approximately 1:5 (one to five) for the year 2015. Because the general price level in Turkey expressed in US dollars was approximately two-thirds of the US price level in that year, calculations with the PPP adjustment estimate that the disparity in per capita income between the two countries was approximately 1:3 in 2015. There is general agreement among economists that the latter ratio more realistically reflects the difference in living standards between the two countries (Maddison 2003; Madison 2007, pp. 375–86; Deaton and Heston 2010, pp. 1–35).

A number of important arguments have been made against the use of GDP per capita for measuring long-term changes in standards of living. Some of these arguments emphasize that GDP per capita tends to understate the long-term increases in standards of living and they need to be considered when interpreting the results. First, numbers of hours worked per week or per year have declined over time in many countries. In other words, GDP per capita does not take into account the value of increasing leisure. Second, GDP per capita does not take into account the fact that there has been a large decline over time in the physical difficulty and discomfort of work as it shifted from the farm and the factory to the office. Similarly, activities inside the home such as washing clothes or taking a bath have become less difficult thanks to running water, electricity, and the many appliances that were not available two centuries ago. Third, because consumption baskets have undergone great changes over such long stretches of time, there are important technical and philosophical problems in comparing standards of living over long periods. For example, for products that were not part of consumer baskets one hundred years ago, such as electricity consumption, a refrigerator, or a computer, the question of which prices should be included in indexes is not easy to answer. Prices of new products declined sharply in their early years due to technological change and economies of scale, yet official indexes typically begin to include the new products many years after they become available for sale. Fourth, there is a "quality bias" in the existing price indexes. The quality of many goods and services such as the power or energy efficiency of household appliances or quality of housing with indoor plumbing, electricity, and central heating have improved steadily over time, but the official price indexes do not make sufficient allowance for these improvements (Nordhaus 1997, pp. 29–70; Gordon 2016, pp. 1–19 and 329–565).

Objections have also been raised about the PPP adjustment calculations for international comparisons of per capita income and these also need to be kept in mind when interpreting the results. First, it has been argued that calculations of PPP adjustment do not pay enough attention to differences in the quality of products between high-income and low-income countries. It has been stated that if quality improvements over time and differences today are fully taken into account, the existing estimates for long-term growth rates as well as the estimates for the differences in GDP per capita between today's higher- and lower-income countries would need to be adjusted upward. Second, relative prices may differ significantly between countries, especially between developed and developing countries. As a result, the estimates of the differences in GDP per capita between countries depend to some extent on the countries whose prices are used in the calculations. This index problem adds a certain degree of ambiguity to the results of the international comparisons.

Economic Growth around the World since 1820

As the process of modern economic growth has attracted more attention from economists and economic historians, the latter, most notably Angus Maddison but also others, have also been trying to develop long-term GDP and GDP per capita series for all regions and countries of the world, especially for the period since the Industrial Revolution. For a better assessment of long-term trends in per capita income and standards of living, these studies have offered GDP per capita series adjusted for PPP in constant 1990 US dollars for each country. While annual values are available for each year and each country for the period after 1950, for many developing countries, estimates have been made only for selected benchmark years that are acknowledged as major turning points for the world economy for the earlier period, namely 1820, 1870, 1913, as well as 1950 and 1973 (Maddison 2003, 2007). After Angus Maddison passed away, a team of scholars set up "the Maddison project" to extend the data set and update the methodology (Bolt and Van Zanden 2014, 627–51). In this book, I have adopted the same benchmark years, but I used 1980 instead of 1973 as the start of the most recent period, as it makes more sense from the point of view of the economic model and policies implemented in Turkey.

Table 2.1 summarizes the patterns of growth in per capita income in different regions and countries of the world from 1820 to the present. It shows that while economic growth began in the nineteenth century and picked up pace in most regions during the twentieth century, growth rates and cumulative increases in per capita GDP have been quite uneven across the regions and countries around the world during the last two centuries. On the eve of the Industrial Revolution, Western Europe was already more urbanized than the rest of the world and per capita incomes in 1820 in Western Europe were already close to three times subsistence levels, while incomes ranged between subsistence and twice the subsistence level in the rest of the world. The Industrial Revolution that began in Great Britain spread first to a limited number of countries in Western Europe and North America. The spread of new technology, industrialization, and rise in productivity was relatively slow during the nineteenth century and until 1950. In contrast, the spread of industrialization and productivity increases was very limited in the developing countries. The latter continued to specialize in agriculture and remained, for the most part, producers and exporters of agricultural products until 1950. As a result, the per capita income gap between Western Europe and the United States on the one hand, and the developing countries of Asia, Latin America, and Africa on the other, increased sharply from above 2:1 in 1820 to less than 5:1 in 1913 and to more than 5:1 by 1950.

Since the end of World War II, however, the spread of the new technology to developing countries has accelerated along with urbanization, higher rates of investment, and industrialization. The per capita income gap between Western Europe and the United States, on the one hand, and the developing countries, on the other, declined slightly, to less than 5:1. In other words, while the trend was for strong divergence until 1913 and even 1950, there has been minimal convergence for the developing countries as a whole since 1950. Between 1820 and 2010, the per capita income increased approximately eight

TABLE 2.1. GDP per Capita in the World, 1820–2015

	GDP per Capita			Annual Rate of Increase (percent)		
	1820	1950	2015	1820– 1950	1950– 2015	1820– 2015
Western Europe	1200	4570	22000	1.0	2.6	1.5
United States	1250	9550	30800	1.6	2.0	1.7
Developed Countries	1200	5550	24900	1.3	2.4	1.6
Eastern Europe excl. Russia	750	2100	8600	0.9	2.4	1.3
Italy	1120	3500	19500	0.9	2.7	1.5
Spain	1000	2200	16800	0.6	3.2	1.5
Asia	580	720	7100	0.2	3.7	1.3
Japan	670	1920	22350	0.8	4.2	1.9
China	600	530	9500	−0.2	4.9	1.3
India	530	620	3800	0.1	3.0	1.0
Africa	480	890	2050	0.6	1.2	0.8
Egypt	600	1000	4450	0.4	2.3	1.0
Iran	550	1720	6500	0.9	2.1	1.3
South America	690	2500	7150	1.0	1.8	1.2
Developing Countries	570	850	6100	0.3	3.1	1.2
World	**670**	**2100**	**8100**	**0.9**	**2.3**	**1.3**
Turkey	**720**	**1600**	**11200**	**0.7**	**2.8**	**1.3**

Sources: Maddison 2007, 375–86; Bolt and Van Zanden 2014; and Pamuk 2006 for Turkey until 1950.
Note: GDP per capita in purchasing power parity (PPP) adjusted 1990 US dollars. For details, see the text.

times. During this period, per capita GDP or income in Western Europe is estimated to have increased eighteenfold, in the United States, twenty-three-fold, and in Japan, thirty-three-fold. In contrast, per capita incomes in Asia, excluding Japan, and South America increased tenfold, whereas in Africa they increased only fourfold.

Behind the pattern of uneven economic growth around the world since the onset of the Industrial Revolution has been the uneven pattern in the range and use of the new technologies. Because urbanization and industrialization remained limited in the developing countries of Asia, Latin America, and Africa until the middle of the twentieth century, income disparities between them and the early industrializers of Europe and North America increased rapidly between 1820 and 1950. After 1950, as industrialization stretched across developing countries, the gap between developed and developing countries as a whole changed little. At the same time, the period since 1950 and especially since 1980 has witnessed growing differentiation within the developing countries as the gap between the more rapid industrializers and the rest began to widen. While Africa lagged behind and Latin America stayed below developing-country averages, East and more recently South Asia attained significantly higher rates per capita income growth. The Middle East as a whole remained close to the averages for developing countries during the nineteenth century. Differences within the Middle East between the small and medium-sized oil exporting countries and the rest increased sharply during the twentieth century, especially since the 1970s.

Since the end of World War II, a few countries in Europe such as Italy, Spain, and Ireland, and in East Asia such as Japan, Taiwan, and Korea, have achieved very rapid increases in per capita production and income and succeeded in closing most if not all of the gap that separated them from high-income countries. Aside from these examples of "economic miracles," however, the general trend at global level shows that the per capita income gap between high-income countries and developing countries which opened during the nineteenth century has not closed in the past sixty or one hundred years. Table 2.1 also shows that while per capita incomes have increased many times in most countries and for the world as a whole, average incomes today are more unequally distributed between countries and regions in comparison to two centuries ago. In 1820, the difference in per capita income between the richest and the poorest countries was at most 3:1. In contrast, the difference in average per capita income between the highest-income and the lowest-income countries today is around 60:1 (Maddison 2007, pp. 375–86; Prichett 1997, pp. 3–17).

Similarly, in spite of the achievements of the few rapidly growing developing countries in recent decades, the decline in per capita income differences between developed and developing countries as a whole has been limited. After growing rapidly from the end of World War II until the 1970s, developed countries have grown more slowly since. Moreover, the differences in GDP per capita between the developed countries has also declined since the end of World War II. In contrast, the differences in per capita growth rates and in per capita incomes between the developing countries has been increasing in recent decades. While some, most notably the two largest countries, China and India, have grown rapidly since 1980, many developing countries actually have lower per capita GDP in the 2010s than they did half a century earlier. Rapid growth in some of the developing countries has narrowed the gap between them and the developed countries, but the gap between many other developing countries and the developed countries is actually much larger today than it was in 1950. As a result, studies conducted on the global distribution of incomes show that income inequalities between countries are far greater today than inequalities within countries. The reverse was true and income inequalities within countries were much larger than inequalities between countries two centuries ago.

In recent decades, more evidence has become available on the evolution of the distribution of income within countries. The available studies indicate that the distribution of income within developed countries increased during the nineteenth century and until World War I but declined from the 1920s until the 1970s. The evidence on income distribution within developing countries is very scarce for this early period. Recent studies show that income distribution within many developed countries has become more unequal since the 1970s. Even though the problems with income data in developing countries are subject to a greater degree of uncertainty, there is evidence that inequalities in income distribution in China and India and in many other developing countries have also been rising (Piketty 2014, pp. 321–30; Bourguignon 2015, pp. 47–73; Milanovich 2016, pp. 46–117). In addition, new studies have been emerging in recent years that aim to estimate the evolution of income distribution at the global level without taking into account the national borders. These studies show that global income distribution has become steadily more unequal from the early nineteenth century until the 1970s. They also show that even though the distribution of incomes within most countries is becoming more unequal, the distribution of income between individuals in the world as a whole has become more equal in recent decades. This trend has been primarily due to the significant increases in average incomes in the two large developing countries, China and India (Bourguignon and Morrisson 2002, pp. 727–44; Van Zanden et al. 2014b, pp. 279–97; Milanovich 2005 and 2016, pp. 46–117; Deaton 2013, pp. 218–63).

GDP per Capita Series for Turkey

This book presents for the first time a GDP per capita series for Turkey since the year 1820. This series will be an important part of the evidence for evaluating Turkey's absolute and relative economic performance during the last two centuries. While GDP per capita series for the period since 1923 and a few estimates for the years immediately before World War I have been available, no estimates had existed for the nineteenth century. In recent years, I have developed estimates for GDP per capita for Turkey for benchmark years of the nineteenth century both by extrapolating the existing estimates for 1913 backward in time and also by linking them to the estimates for the period before the nineteenth century.

PPP adjusted GDP per capita series in 1990 US dollars for twentieth-century Turkey were already included in the Maddison (2007) series as well as in United Nations and World Bank series. For the period before 1923 and for the area within Turkey's current borders, these estimates needed to be extended backward in time. For this purpose, I and a colleague first linked the annual GDP per capita series prepared by Tuncer Bulutay, Yahya S. Tezel, and Nuri Yıldırım for 1923–1948 which have been adopted by the official Turkish Statistical Institute with Vedat Eldem's national income calculations for the late Ottoman period by taking into account the population, agriculture, industry, foreign trade, and price series. In this exercise, we established that in the area within Turkey's current borders, per capita income or per capita GDP showed a significant drop during World War I and, despite the rapid recovery in the 1920s, per capita income attained in 1913 was reached again only in 1929. I then extrapolated the GDP per capita estimates for 1913 back to the benchmark years of 1870 and 1820, again making use of the series on daily wages, per capita tax collections, and per capita foreign trade (Maddison, 2007, pp. 375–86; Bolt and Van Zanden 2014; Eldem 1970, pp. 275–309; Bulutay, Tezel, and Yıldırım 1974; Özel and Pamuk 1998; Pamuk 2006).

For the period since 1948, I continued with the series produced by Turk-Stat. A number of revisions have been made in these official series over the years. Most recently in 2008, TurkStat created a new GDP series in both current prices and in 1998 constant prices for the years since 1998 based on the European Union standards. As a result, some activities, which were not included in previous official series, were included for the first time in the calculation of national income. Agriculture, industry, and services were then all revised upward and GDP was estimated to be approximately 30 percent higher than that given in the earlier series (TurkStat 2008). The new series have also been accepted by international institutions and are being used in international comparisons for the period since 1998.

The new series has created some problems for the estimates for the period before 1998. One option was to extend the new series as far back as 1923, using the annual growth rates of the earlier series, as the State Planning Organization and the Ministry of Development has already done. Unfortunately, this method is not very helpful or realistic, especially for the earlier period, because it means revising Turkey's income upward by approximately 30 percent, not just for the recent past but also, for example, for 1950 and 1929, which significantly alters Turkey's standing in international comparisons in these earlier benchmark years. According to this method, for instance, Turkey's per capita income in 1950 would be at the same level as that of Spain. Based on a series of comparisons I undertook for 1950 and the earlier years, this did not appear likely. In fact, the PPP adjusted Maddison series for Turkey better reflect Turkey's place in international comparisons in 1950 and in the earlier years (Maddison 2007, pp. 375–86; Bolt and Van Zanden 2014).

The assumption behind extrapolating the new series as far back as 1923, using the annual growth rates of the earlier series, is that the activities that were included in the new estimates but were not in the earlier estimates grew at rates identical to those of activities already included in the series. It would be more realistic to assume that the activities newly introduced to the income accounts in fact grew at rates significantly higher in the recent period. This problem is not unique to Turkey. In several other countries, as well, efforts to revise national income series have resulted in the creation of higher estimates. These new series were then extrapolated backward after sector-based studies and comparisons were undertaken. Looking at the procedures used by other countries, I have concluded that the best method for harmonizing the earlier and the more recent series is to accept the old GDP per capita estimates in a specific year in the distant past, such as 1950, and to revise the GDP and GDP per capita estimates between 1950 and 1998 upward gradually. If the old and new series are harmonized in this fashion, the annual growth rate between 1950 and 1998 will have to be increased by approximately 0.5 percent every year. Table 2.1 presents my revised estimate for GDP per capita for the benchmark year 1980 under this method. However, in later chapters of this book where I discuss sectoral and overall growth rates, I have chosen to use the growth rates based on the official series. Yet another revision in the national income accounts was announced by TurkStat in late 2016. The new series uses 2009 prices and revises the GDP series for the period since 1998 upward by another 20 percent. The new national accounts also present a rather optimistic view of Turkey's economy in recent years. Because the methodology behind this latest round of revisions has not been adequately explained and evaluated, they have not been taken into account in my series and analysis in chapters 11 and 12. Similarly, for comparative analysis of Turkey's growth record since 1950, I rely on the Maddison series and the first version of the Maddison project. The more recent version produced in 2018 presents a misleading picture for both Turkey's growth rates and comparisons with other countries (Maddison 2007, pp. 375–86; Bolt and Van Zanden 2014; Bolt et al. 2018).

The margin of error for Turkey's GDP per capita series is clearly higher for the earlier period, especially for the nineteenth century. However, frequent revisions in Turkey's official national income accounts in recent years suggest that the national income accounts as well as the GDP per capita series not only for the recent decades but more generally for the period since the end of World War II should also be treated with caution and should not be accepted as the final word. The same applies to international databases that have been uncritically accepting and using Turkey's recent revisions of its official series.

Turkey's Economic Growth Record since 1820

The GDP per capita series for Turkey presented in figure 1.1 in chapter 1 and table 2.1 show that per capita income, expressed in 1990 US dollars adjusted for PPP, rose from $720 in 1820 to $1,600 in 1950 and $10,500 in 2010. In other words, the purchasing power of per capita income in Turkey increased about fifteen times between 1820 and 2015. During the same period, the population of the area within Turkey's current borders increased more than sevenfold, from 9.4 million in 1820 to 79 million in 2015. As a result, PPP adjusted GDP for Turkey increased more than 15 × 7 = 105 times between 1820 and 2015.

Turkey pursued very different economic models and policies during these two centuries. These will be discussed in four distinct periods in the rest of the book. During the century from 1820 to World War I, free trade treaties kept the economy open and agriculture was the source of economic growth. From 1913 to 1950, a period that included two world wars and the Great Depression, interventionist policies—most significantly protectionism—generated some economic growth based on industrialization, but these gains were mostly dwarfed by the adverse impact of the two world wars. Domestic market-oriented industrialization remained the basic source of economic growth and increases in GDP per capita during the decades after World War II. Market-oriented policies were embraced once again and exports of manufactures emerged as a leading source of economic growth after 1980.[1]

Figure 1.1 and table 2.1 also show that long-term growth rates of GDP per capita in Turkey increased significantly after 1950. In fact, this is the case for most developing countries and the developing countries as a whole. The average annual growth rate of GDP per capita remained well below 1 percent, at 0.6 percent during 1820–1950, but it was sharply higher, at 3.2 percent, during 1950–2010. In other words, in the era before 1950, it took more than one hundred years for income per capita to double, whereas it has taken about twenty-two years, on average, for income to double since 1950. Needless to say, these increases in income per capita also translated into different rates at which standards of living rose in the two eras.

The large differences in growth rates in Turkey and in most developing countries in the periods before and after 1950 can be attributed to the speed at which the new technologies were adopted and productivity increases could spread. The proximate causes of the spread of the new technologies were, in turn, urbanization, industrialization, and the sharply higher rates of capital formation. In the case of Turkey and as in many other developing countries,

---

1. Growth rates calculated separately for each of the periods will be provided in later chapters of the book.

rates of increase of productivity and income in agriculture remained significantly lower. The high rates of migration from the countryside to the urban areas enabled rates of productivity and growth in per capita income in the rural areas to keep up with those in the urban areas since 1950. In contrast, the pace of long-term economic growth in the developed countries was not very different in these two periods, before and after 1950, as can be ascertained from table 2.1.

Since per capita incomes have been rising in most if not all parts of the world for the past two centuries, Turkey's growth record must be examined comparatively and in greater detail. Figure 1.2 in chapter 1 presented long-term trends in GDP per capita in Turkey, in the world, and in developing countries (Asia, Africa, and South America) as percentages of the average GDP per capita in Western Europe and the United States. Figure 1.2 and table 2.1 show that, although per capita income was rising in Turkey during the nineteenth century, the gap with developed countries widened significantly because of the rapid industrialization in the latter. Per capita income in the area within Turkey's current borders declined from 60 percent of average per capita income in Western Europe and the United States in 1820 to 29 percent in 1913. GDP per capita in Turkey then rose in the interwar period to reach 36 percent of Western Europe and the United States in 1939 before declining once again during and after World War II, back to 26 percent in 1950. In contrast, Turkey has done some catching up since the end of World War II. From 1950 to 2015, per capita income increased more than sixfold and the average annual growth rate has been slightly higher than in developed countries. As a result, per capita incomes in Turkey rose from 26 percent of the per capita income in Western Europe and the United States in 1950 to 31 percent in 1980 and 45 percent in 2015.

Table 2.1 and figures 1.2 and 2.1 also show that per capita income in Turkey has increased at rates slightly higher than the population-weighted averages for developing countries of Asia, South America, and Africa during the nineteenth century and until 1980, but lagged behind those averages since 1980. During the nineteenth century and until 1950, Turkey's growth rates were lower than those in South America but higher than those in other regions of the developing world. Since 1950, Turkey's long-term growth rates have been higher than the averages for South America, Africa, and the Middle East, all of which have grown more slowly than the population-weighted averages for the developing countries as a whole. In the most recent period since 1980, East and Southeast Asia, and especially the two large countries China and India, have experienced significantly higher rates of growth and have raised the averages for the developing countries as a whole. As a result, the population-weighted growth rates in developing countries have exceeded that of Turkey

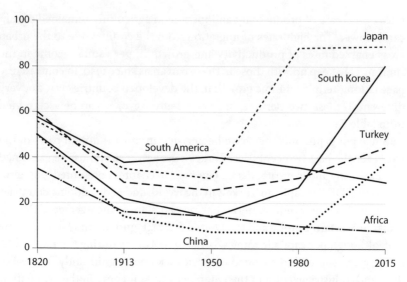

FIGURE 2.1. GDP per Capita in Turkey and the World, 1820–2015 (PPP adjusted and as percentage of Western Europe and the United States). Sources: Maddison 2007, pp. 375–86; Bolt and Van Zanden 2014; and Pamuk 2006 for Turkey until 1950.

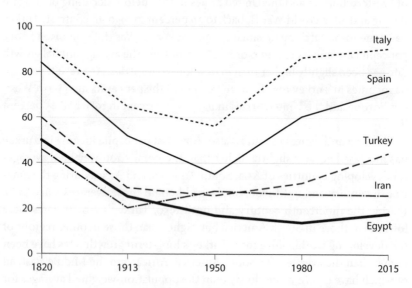

FIGURE 2.2. GDP per Capita in Four Other Countries and Turkey, 1820–2015 (PPP adjusted and as percentage of Western Europe and the United States). Sources: Maddison 2007, pp. 375–86; Bolt and Van Zanden 2014; and Pamuk 2006 for Turkey until 1950.

since 1980. However, per capita incomes in Turkey as well as long-term rates of growth of per capita income have been higher than for other large countries in Asia such as Pakistan, Philippines, and Indonesia since the end of World War II.

Comparisons with four countries with similar population, two in southern Europe and two in the Middle East, may provide additional insights into Turkey's long-term trajectory (figure 2.2). Early in the nineteenth century, Italy and Spain had higher levels of GDP per capita in comparison to Turkey. They began their industrialization during the nineteenth century and achieved higher rates of growth than Turkey during the nineteenth century and the Interwar period. Nonetheless, the gap between Italy and Spain, on the one hand, and the developed countries of Western Europe and the United States, on the other, continued to increase until 1950, as was the case for Turkey primarily because the rates of industrialization were lower in Italy and Spain than in the developed countries. Italy and Spain experienced very high rates of economic growth and were able to converge significantly to the level of the developed countries in the decades after World War II. Turkey's trajectory has moved in the same direction since the end of World War II but its convergence to the developed countries has been weaker than that of Italy and Spain.

Compared to Turkey, Egypt and Iran had slightly lower levels of GDP per capita early in the nineteenth century, and they experienced lower rates of economic growth during the nineteenth century. As a result, their GDP per capita levels were lower than that of Turkey in 1913 and the gap with the developed countries was even wider. The GDP per capita levels remained unchanged in Egypt during the Interwar period and the gap with the developed countries widened further until 1950. In contrast, Iran was able to raise its GDP per capita to Turkey's levels in 1950 thanks to large revenues from oil. From the end of World War II until 2015, GDP per capita levels in Egypt increased at the same rates as that of developed countries. As a result, the GDP per capita gap with Turkey continued to widen. GDP per capita levels in Iran increased at rates only slightly above those of the developed countries since the end of World War II. With the support of oil revenues, Iran's GDP per capita remained above that of Turkey until 1980 but has fallen behind since (figure 2.2).

A small number of countries in southern Europe, such as Italy and Spain, and others in East Asia, such as Japan and South Korea, as well as Hong Kong and Taiwan, have produced economic miracles and were able to close the gap significantly with developed countries since the end of World War II. During each of these catch-up or convergence episodes, annual rates of increase in per capita incomes in these countries remained above 5 percent for a period of at least 20–30 years. It is clear from the record summarized above that Turkey's economic growth performance did not come close to the catch-up performances exhibited by these more successful examples. In Turkey, increases in GDP per capita never reached 5 percent during any subperiod in the last two centuries. After falling significantly behind the developed countries during the nineteenth century and until 1950, Turkey's catch-up has been rather limited since. In short, Turkey's long-term growth performance has been close to but slightly above the averages for developing countries and close to the averages for the world during the last two centuries.

Human Development since 1820

In recent decades, the measure most widely used to evaluate the development of economies, aside from per capita income, has been the human development index (HDI). The human development index gives equal weight to health and education, as well as income per capita. The United Nations has been gathering data and publishing annually the national values for this alternative measure for assessing economic performance. The origins of the index go back to the work of Amartya Sen and others. Like other economists before him, Sen distinguished between economic growth and economic development, and he viewed increases in income as a means rather than the ultimate goal. He emphasized that the ultimate goal should be to enlarge the choices of individuals and the society, to enable them to live more freely and allow them to use their skills and talents in the way they wish. This new approach thus defines human development as freedom, the expansion of people's capabilities and choices, and the ability to live a longer, healthier, and fuller life; it aims to measure economic welfare through what people can do. For this reason, the human development index uses health and education indicators in addition to per capita income (Sen 2001; Srinivasan 1994, pp. 238–43).

The United Nations annual human development indexes use basic indicators for health and education because data for more complex indicators are not available for all countries. For instance, health is currently measured by life expectancy at birth. Knowledge and education are measured with two indicators: literacy rate and average school attendance of the population above the age of 15, expressed in years. Since the literacy rate has reached nearly 100 percent in many countries, the method of calculating the HDI was changed in 2010, and knowledge and education began to be measured using weighted mean years of schooling for the population above the age of 25 and the expected years of schooling of newborn babies. The fact that education-related indicators do not contain data about the quality of education or skills is an important drawback, but in many countries this kind of data has not been easy to collect.

Another indicator of human development frequently used by economic historians in recent decades is physical height. When the population is short in stature, that typically indicates that its members were nutritionally deprived in childhood or adolescence, either because they did not get enough to eat or because they lived in an unhealthy environment where disease, even if it did not kill them, left them permanently stunted. As a result, there is growing recognition that changes in heights over time are good indicators of variations in food availability and disease environment. Large numbers of studies in recent decades have attempted to establish the long-term trends in heights in different parts of the world going back not only centuries but millennia. However, there are large differences in average heights among regions of the world with similar levels of per capita income and food availability. Variations in diet and slow adjustment of heights spanning multiple generations to improvements in food availability and disease environment suggest that heights cannot be easily used in international comparisons of human development. Moreover, in the case of Turkey, data on heights during the last two centuries are very limited (Fogel 2004, pp. 1–65; Deaton 2013, pp. 156–64; Baten and Blum 2014, 117–37).

In what follows, I will review the broad trends in human development in the world and in Turkey since 1820. Since the HDI is a composite number that includes per capita income in addition to health and education measures, it is not easy to follow the different dimension of human development from the index number itself. For the sake of more concrete as well as international comparisons, I will focus on the basic indicators for health and education rather than the index itself.

Life expectancy at birth given in years is arguably the single most important measure of human development and the standards of living. It is derived from mortality rates of different age groups in a given year. These age-specific mortality rates are typically high in early years of life, they fall rapidly until teenage years, and then rise more or less steadily. Gains in life expectancy at birth around the world have been very uneven during the last two centuries. Broadly following the pattern of GDP per capita, life expectancy at birth diverged during the nineteenth century as it rose in Western Europe and the western offshoots while it rose very slowly if at all in the rest of the world. From the second half of the twentieth century onward, however, life expectancy in the developing countries (with the exception of Sub-Saharan Africa) began to rise rapidly. As the gains due to the declines in infant mortality in the developing countries were greater than the gains in life expectancy due to declines in adult mortality in developed countries, a global convergence in life expectancy emerged since the 1960s.

Another uneven pattern concerns the uneven declines in age-specific mortality rates and their contribution to the increases in life expectancy. Until recently, there were decreases in adult mortality rates but their contribution to the increases in life expectancy at birth was much less than the contribution of the decline in infant and child mortality. In fact, until the second half of the twentieth century in the developed countries and until very recently and even currently in many of the developing countries, mortality rates were high among all age groups, but as much as half or more of all deaths were among children under the age of five who died mostly of infectious diseases. The transition from high mortality rates due to infectious diseases among infants to lower mortality rates, with most deaths caused by non-communicable, chronic diseases such as cardiovascular disease and cancer in old age, began in the twentieth century in the developed countries and continues in the developing countries today (Fogel 2004, pp. 20–42; Deaton 2013, pp. 59–164).

Demographer Samuel Preston was the first to identify a positive relationship between GDP per capita and life expectancy at birth at the international level. Increases in food availability and nutrition and the increases in the capacity of the state to provide sanitation, health care, as well as education are the most important factors that explain this pattern. In addition, the curve has been shifting upward over time due to growing knowledge and the discovery of better ways of doing things. However, it is not easy to estimate the share of each of these broad causes in the total increases over time in life expectancy, and there is no doubt it varied from one country to another (Preston 1975, pp. 231–48; Riley 2001, pp. 1–31; Deaton 2013, pp. 59–164; Zijdeman and de Silva 2014, pp. 106–14).

For Turkey, life expectancy at birth as well as other measures of health, just like GDP per capita, increased slowly, and the disparities with the more developed countries rose during the nineteenth century. Measures of health began to record more rapid progress during the Interwar period and especially since the end of World War II. As is the case for most developing countries, the rapid increases in life expectancy at birth for Turkey point to a strong trend of convergence with the developed countries since 1950.

We have only one study for life expectancy at birth for Turkey for the period before World War I. Shorter and Macura offer an estimate of 32–33 years for the years before World War I (1983, pp. 66–101). Demographic data on the nineteenth century are not detailed enough to estimate life expectancy for earlier benchmark years. However, based on trends in comparable southern and eastern European countries, it is possible to offer a rough estimate for life expectancy at birth in Turkey of 26–27 years for 1820 (Zijdeman and de Silva

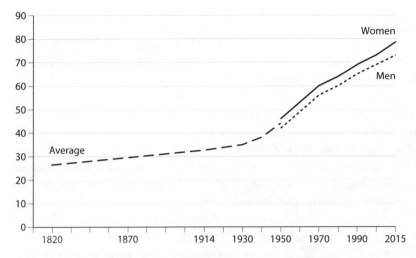

FIGURE 2.3. Life Expectancy at Birth in Turkey, 1820–2015 (years). Sources: Author's
estimates for the nineteenth century; Shorter and Macura 1983; and Zijdeman
and de Silva 2014 for the twentieth century.

2014, pp. 106–14). In other words, the limited evidence suggests that life expectancy at birth increased slowly and by a total of about six years during the
century until World War I. As will be discussed in the next section, the increases in the population of Turkey after the large flows of immigration are
taken into account also suggest that life expectancy was rising during the nineteenth century (figure 2.3).

The disappearance of the plague around the eastern Mediterranean during
the second quarter of the nineteenth century was an important reason for the
gradual increases in life expectancy. Public health measures in leading ports
such as the quarantine of ships probably played a role in the plague's disappearance. Improvements in nutrition also contributed to the decline in mortality rates and the rise in life expectancy. GDP per capita rose by about 60
percent during the century until World War I, and this total increase points to
an upturn in the amount of calories available to infants as well as adults, although these improvements were distributed unevenly. The more market-
oriented coastal regions and the west of the country participated more in
these increases than did the interior and the east. Nonetheless, because of
slowly rising agricultural production per capita, food availability also improved in the rural areas where more than three-fourths of the population
lived. Because of the absence of data, it is not clear how much of the limited
increase in life expectancy during the nineteenth century was due to the decline in infant mortality. Through its public health and other measures, the

government also played a role in the rise of life expectancy during the nineteenth century, although this role was yet limited.

Since most of the countries in the world have recorded significant progress in health, as well as per capita income, during the last two centuries, it would be useful to evaluate Turkey's experience comparatively. The available estimates summarized in figures 2.4 and 2.5 show that life expectancy at birth in Western Europe and western offshoots increased during the nineteenth century and reached 45–55 years on the eve of World War I. In contrast, the available evidence indicates that in the developing regions of the world, life expectancy at birth did not increase or increased very slowly during the nineteenth century. Argentina, which was a high-income country at the time, had life expectancy at birth of 45 years and Japan, 40 years on the eve of World War I. Elsewhere in Asia, Africa, and South America, life expectancy at birth ranged from 25 to 32 years. Life expectancy at birth in Russia in 1913 was 32 years. These estimates indicate that Turkey's life expectancy was close to averages for developing countries as a whole and perhaps slightly above them during the latter part of the nineteenth century for which estimates are available (Zijdeman and de Silva 2014, pp. 106–14).

Life expectancy at birth declined sharply in Turkey during World War I. Large numbers of military casualties and the massacres and deaths of large numbers of Armenians as well as the evidence for sharply higher mortality rates among the remaining civilian population all suggest that life expectancy must have decreased to less than 25 years. Life expectancy at birth in Turkey began to rise once again from the 1920s, reaching 35 years in the mid-1930s and 44 years (42 for men, 45 for women) in 1950. The role of the government in health care began to grow during the Interwar period. Efforts to eradicate infectious adult diseases such as malaria and tuberculosis as well as efforts at sanitation in the urban areas and better health-care practices in general, coupled with technological developments such as the discovery of antibiotics, contributed to the decline in mortality rates. Nonetheless, improvements remained limited mostly to urban areas. Rural areas where the great majority of the population lived received only a fraction of the state expenditures on health care.

In health, as in per capita income, Turkey experienced its fastest improvements since the end of World War II. Life expectancy at birth rose from 44 years in 1950 to 59 years in 1980 (57 for men, 61 for women) and to 76 years in 2015 (73 for men, 79 for women) (figure 2.3). In other words, life expectancy at birth rose by almost one full year in every two years since the end of World War II. Although declines in mortality rates in other age groups also contributed, the largest part of these increases in life expectancy since 1950 were due to the declines in infant mortality resulting from infectious diseases, from

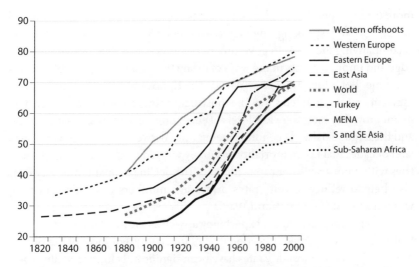

FIGURE 2.4. Life Expectancy at Birth in Turkey and the World, 1820–2010 (years).
Sources: Author's estimates for Turkey in the nineteenth century; Shorter and Macura 1983; and Zijdeman and de Silva 2014 for Turkey in the twentieth century and for the world.

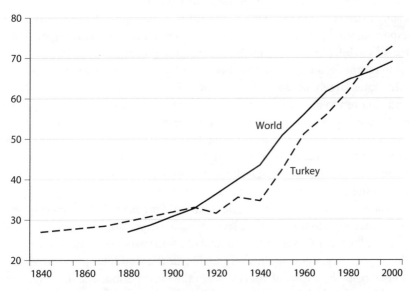

FIGURE 2.5. Life Expectancy at Birth in Turkey and the World, 1820–2010 (years).
Sources: Author's estimates for Turkey in the nineteenth century; Shorter and Macura 1983; and Zijdeman and de Silva 2014 for Turkey in the twentieth century and for the world.

more than 200 per thousand around 1950 to 125 in 1980, and to 12 per thousand in 2015. Broadly speaking, the increases in per capita incomes including the accompanying increases in government resources, as well as growing knowledge and improvements in the ways of doing things, were responsible for this outcome. For a long time after World War II, however, the decline in infant mortality rates remained slow. The most significant causes for continued high infant mortality rates were low levels of education for women in the rural areas and the large social and economic inequalities between regions. It was only in later decades that infant mortality in Turkey was reduced to the levels of countries with comparable per capita income. The decline in infant mortality rates also helped reduce fertility rates or average numbers of children born to women since the end of World War II.

The rapid increases in life expectancy as well as the declines in infant mortality were accompanied by a good deal of inequality. For most of the twentieth century, infant mortality rates have been significantly lower and life expectancy higher in urban areas where access to health care was much better and where rates of education for women were also higher. Substantial differences in both infant mortality and life expectancy persist to this day between the higher-income and more developed western regions and the east, especially the Kurdish areas. Rapid urbanization since the 1950s has contributed significantly to decreases in infant mortality and more broadly to the increases in life expectancy at birth. Urbanization has also tended to reduce the regional disparities in infant mortality and life expectancy at birth.

In recent decades, Turkey has been moving from a society with high mortality rates largely because of deaths from infectious diseases among infants and children to a society where most of the deaths are among older people and caused by chronic illnesses such as cardiovascular disease and cancer. Improvements in life expectancy are likely to be slower in the decades ahead, however, as the decline in infant mortality ceases to be the leading cause of the increases in life expectancy. Declines in adult mortality will be slower and will contribute less to increases in life expectancy at birth.

Turkey was not alone in experiencing rapid increases in life expectancy at birth since 1950. In the developed countries, life expectancy at birth continued to rise, albeit at a slower pace, by a total of 15–20 years since 1950. Increases in life expectancy were significantly higher in the developing countries as a whole, rising by a total of 25–35 years in the same period. The important exceptions are Sub-Saharan Africa and Russia, where total increases in life expectancy at birth since 1950 remained below 20 years. In other words, convergence was the broad trend in life expectancy for Turkey as well as the developing countries as a whole since 1950. Turkey's life expectancy at birth has been below those of Italy and Spain in southern Europe as well as those of

Western Europe since late in the nineteenth century. On the other hand, life expectancy in Turkey has been above those for South and Southeast Asia, Middle East, and Africa and close to those of China since the early decades of twentieth century (Zijdeman and de Silva 2014, pp. 106–14; figure 2.4).

The linkage between GDP per capita and life expectancy is useful in this context. In the case of Turkey, the causal link between GDP per capita and life expectancy as suggested by Preston has been strong. Moreover, this link can be followed from Turkey's position relative to world averages in both GDP per capita and life expectancy at birth. During most of the nineteenth century, when GDP per capita in Turkey was above world averages, Turkey's life expectancy at birth also remained above world averages. During the century between 1880 and 1980, Turkey's GDP per capita as well as its life expectancy at birth remained below world averages. Since 1980, both GDP per capita and life expectancy at birth in Turkey have risen and remained above world averages (compare figure 1.2 in chapter 1 and figure 2.5).

Turkey's experience with education shows a broadly similar pattern of slow improvement during the nineteenth century and more rapid improvement during the twentieth century, especially since the end of World War II. In spite of the education reforms in the nineteenth century, schools and schooling did not spread to rural areas where a major part of the population lived because of fiscal constraints and because the new schools were not easily accepted by the Muslim population. Based on data for student numbers and other sources, it would be safe to say that literacy rates for the population above the age of fifteen edged upward during the century to exceed 10 percent on the eve of World War I. Literacy rates were significantly higher in the urban areas, among non-Muslims and among men. In the Interwar period, the overall literacy rate rose faster but educational efforts remained limited mostly to the urban areas and did not reach the majority of the more than 80 percent of the population who lived in rural areas. The overall literacy rate stood at 33 percent in 1950, it reached 68 percent in 1980, and rose to 94 percent in 2010. Progress was even slower among women. In 1950, the literacy rate among women above the age of fifteen was only 19 percent, in 1980 it stood at 55 percent, and in 2010, it rose to 89 percent (figure 2.6).

Since literacy rates are not easily available for most developing countries in the early periods, for international comparisons we need to turn to another basic indicator, average years of schooling received by the adult population over the age of fifteen. This indicator for Turkey also edged upward very slowly during the nineteenth century and even during the Interwar period despite educational reforms dating back to the nineteenth century. Average years of schooling for the adult population remained well below 1 year in 1913 and stood at only 1.5 years in 1950. Along with urbanization and economic

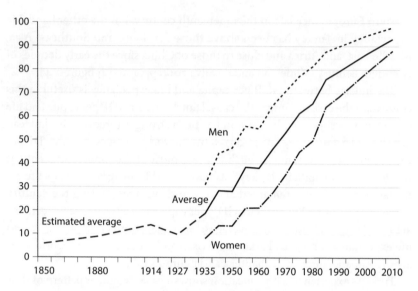

FIGURE 2.6. Literacy Rate in Turkey, 1850–2010 (percent). Sources: Author's estimates based on Fortna 2011, pp. 20–21 for the Ottoman era; official series based on Turkey, Turkish Statistical Institute 2014 for the period since 1927.

growth, they increased to 4.2 years in 1980 and 7 years in 2010 (Van Leeuwen and Van Leeuwen-Li 2014, pp. 89–96; figures 2.7 and 2.8).

Data from other regions of the world summarized in figure 2.7 indicate that in this basic education indicator Turkey has lagged behind not only the world averages but also the averages for the developing countries for most if not all of the last two centuries. Average years of schooling for the adult population in Turkey has been lower than Spain and Italy in southern Europe and also Russia and Eastern Europe as a whole, China, and Latin America, but above India, and Southeast Asia, the Middle East, and Sub-Saharan Africa since 1820. In other words, Turkey has remained below world averages in schooling rates and lagged behind countries with similar values of GDP per capita during the last two centuries (figure 2.8).

One important cause of this rather poor performance is the persistent gender inequalities. Gender differences in education remained very large while average literacy and schooling rates were increasing in Turkey during the nineteenth century and until the 1980s. These gender differences have been declining rapidly in recent decades, however, paralleling trends in most developing countries. The numbers of female students increased from 80 percent of male students toward parity among elementary school students between 1980 and 2010. More strikingly, numbers of female students increased from 32 percent to 85 percent of male students among high school students and from 32 per-

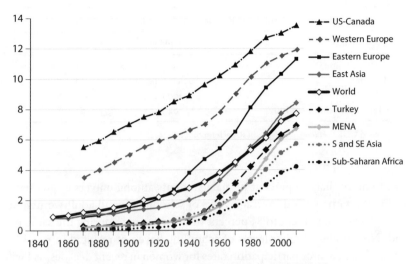

FIGURE 2.7. Years of Schooling of Adults in Turkey and the World, 1850–2010.
Sources: Author's estimates based on Ottoman education statistics for Turkey until 1913;
Van Leeuwen-Li 2014, pp. 89–96 for Turkey since 1923 and for the world.

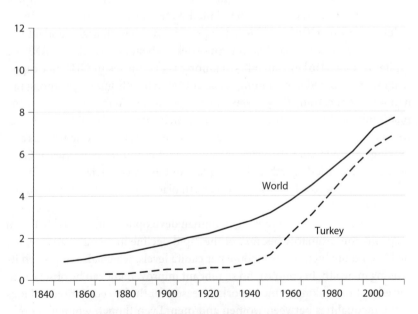

FIGURE 2.8. Years of Schooling of Adults in Turkey and the World, 1850–2010.
Sources: Author's estimates based on Ottoman education statistics for Turkey until 1913;
Van Leeuwen-Li 2014, pp. 89–96 for Turkey since 1923 and for the world.

TABLE 2.2. Turkey's International Rankings in Human Development, 1980–2010

Ranking in	1980	2010
GDP per capita	55 / 124	70 / 187
Health	129 / 187	80 / 187
Education	100 / 140	120 / 187
Human Development Index	64 / 107	94 / 187

Source: UNDP, Human Development Reports for 1982 and 2012.

cent to more than 90 percent of male students among university graduates during the same period. Average years of schooling for all adult women increased from 60 percent to 85 percent of those for men during the same period. Nonetheless, higher levels of schooling have not resulted in rapid increases in labor force participation rates for women in recent decades, as I will discuss in chapter 12.

For the recent decades, more detailed data on health and education are available and it is possible to make international comparisons of human development index (HDI) values. Table 2.2 presents Turkey's international rankings in HDI prepared by the United Nations for 1980 and 2010. These indexes show that Turkey achieved improvements in both health and education but continued to lag behind countries with similar levels of GDP per capita. In 1980, Turkey ranked 55th among 125 countries in GDP per capita rankings but ranked 129th among 187 countries in health and 100th among 140 nations in education. Turkey was in 64th place among 107 countries in the 1980 rankings for human development, which included GDP per capita as well as health and education. A similar pattern emerges in the calculations and rankings made in 2010. Turkey was ranked 70th out of 187 countries in GDP per capita but stood at 77th and 120th place out of 187 countries for health and education, respectively. Turkey was in 94th place among 187 countries in the HDI rankings for 2010.

Turkey's international ranking in human development improved between 1980 and 2010 primarily because of the rapid decline in infant deaths, which had been quite high for its income per capita levels, which also improved its ranking in health. In contrast, no significant improvement can be observed in the education rankings. One important reason for the low education rankings is the inequalities between women and men. Even though women's enrollment ratios have risen significantly toward parity with men at all levels of education in recent decades, gender differences for the educational levels of the adult population as a whole are still large. Another important reason for Turkey's low rankings in health and education are the large regional inequalities and the low levels of health and education as well as per capita income in the southeast region, where a majority Kurdish population lives.

There is no doubt that large gender and regional disparities have brought down Turkey's averages in health and education in the past. Below-average performance in health and education, in turn, has hurt Turkey's economic growth. The same inequalities and below-average human development present an even greater obstacle to economic development today by making it much more difficult to transition to a skill- and knowledge-based economy with a strong technology component. I will return to these issues later in the book when I take up human development and inequalities in each period.

Turkey's Population since 1820

This section will present evidence from Ottoman and Turkish and other sources and offer, for the first time, a two-century perspective on the population of the area within Turkey's current borders. I will show that Turkey's population increased by eightfold and slightly more rapidly than the world population during the last two centuries, from less than 10 million in 1820 to 16.5 million on the eve of World War I and to 79 million in 2015. As a result, Turkey's share of world population moved within a narrow range, around 1 percent, during these two centuries. In 2015 it was only a little higher than where it was in 1820 (table 2.3).

Turkey's population probably increased at a slower pace than the population of the world as a whole during the three centuries before 1820. While the population of the world as well as the population of both Europe and Asia

TABLE 2.3. Turkey's Share in World Population, 1820–2015

Years	Turkey's Population	World Population	Turkey's Share
	Millions	Millions	Percent
1820	9.4	1,055	0.89
1880	13.0	1,400	0.93
1913	16.5	1,800	0.92
1927	13.9	2,000	0.70
1950	20.8	2,520	0.83
1980	44.4	4,435	1.00
2015	79.0	7,300	1.08

Sources: Turkey, Türkiye İstatistik Kurumu (Turkish Statistical Institute) 2014 for Turkey since 1927; also see the text for Turkey in the earlier period; for world population: Livi-Bacci 2017.

roughly doubled from 1500 to 1820, Turkey's population increased by about 50 percent, from approximately 6 million to more than 9 million during the same period. In comparison to the earlier centuries, Turkey's population began to increase more rapidly during the nineteenth century, from about 9.4 million in 1820 to 16.5 million in 1914. Turkey's share of the world's population remained around 0.9 percent during this period. However, because Turkey's population declined by about 20 percent during and after the World War I, its share in world population retreated to 0.7 percent in the second half of the 1920s, its lowest point during the last two centuries. Turkey's population then increased to 20.9 million in 1950, 44.4 million in 1980, and to 79 million in 2015. Turkey's share in world population rose slowly but steadily since the 1920s and had reached 1.1 percent in the year 2015.

Immigration and Population Growth during the Nineteenth Century

While the many Ottoman censuses of the nineteenth century contain very useful information, because of their various limitations, it has not been possible to obtain from them reliable series for Turkey's population in the nineteenth century. For this reason, I will begin with an estimate of the population in 1914 and then move backward toward 1820 by taking into account information from a variety of sources, including the Ottoman censuses. Following Shorter, I begin with an estimate of 16.5 million for the area within Turkey's current borders in 1914, although there are estimates both higher and lower (Eldem 1970, pp. 49–65; Shaw 1978, pp. 325–38; Quataert 1994, pp. 777–97; McCarthy 1983, 2002; Behar 1996, pp. 21–66; Shorter and Macura 1983, pp. 21–66; Shorter 1985). As I extended the estimates back to 1820, I paid attention to three basic processes: immigration, emigration, and growth due to population's own internal dynamics. Throughout the nineteenth century, the Muslim population from regions that had seceded from or were neighboring the empire, from Crimea, the Caucasus, as well as the Balkans and the Aegean islands, migrated to areas within present-day borders of Turkey as well as present-day Romania, Bulgaria, Syria, Jordan, and Israel. These flows intensified during and in the aftermath of major wars, during 1856–1866, 1877–1890, and 1912–1913, but they continued in other periods as well. Most of these migrants came from rural areas and the Ottoman government gave them land and settled them in rural areas across the empire (Karpat 1985a, pp. 60–77). During the decades preceding World War I, there was some emigration mostly by Greeks and Armenians to Europe and especially to the Americas. Their numbers, however, remained small compared with those arriving from outside Turkey's present borders (Karpat 1985b).

In moving from the population estimate in 1914 to another in the year 1820, there is the risk that overestimating the migration inflows will lead to an un-

TABLE 2.4. Population within Present-Day Borders of Turkey, 1820–2015

Year	Total Population Millions	Annual Rate of Increase Percent
1820	9.4	—
1840	10.0	0.3
1860	10.8	0.4
1880	13.0	0.9
1900	14.8	0.7
1914	16.5	0.7
1927	13.9	−1.3
1940	17.8	1.9
1950	20.9	1.6
1960	27.8	2.9
1970	35.6	2.5
1980	44.4	2.2
1990	55.1	2.2
2000	64.3	1.6
2010	73.0	1.3
2015	79.0	1.5

Sources: Turkey, Türkiye İstatistik Kurumu (Turkish Statistical Institute), 2014 for 1927 and later years; see the text for earlier years.
Notes: Estimates above include the population in the Kars-Ardahan region that were not part of the Ottoman Empire late in the nineteenth century but are within present-day borders of Turkey, as well as the population of Hatay during the Interwar period. The margin of error is higher for the nineteenth-century estimates.

derestimation either of the total for the year 1820 or of the rate of internal growth of the total population. Balancing these concerns and taking into account the evidence from the Ottoman censuses, I estimated the total inflows into Turkey at around 4 million during the period 1820–1914 (Pamuk 1987, pp. 205–7). This means more than half of the total population growth of Turkey was a result of immigration during the century before World War I. Table 2.4 also presents some additional estimates for total population for some benchmark years, allowing for the fluctuations in the immigration.

Table 2.4 makes clear that the trend of strong population growth in the nineteenth century stands in sharp contrast to earlier periods. While the population of Turkey had increased by about 50 percent during the three centuries until 1820, it almost doubled during the century until World War I. Even if an important part of this increase was due to immigration, it still points to a critical transformation that occurred in the nineteenth century. The decline in epidemics as well as wars, and the greater political stability and security that emerged before and after the Tanzimat reforms, supported the economic recovery, the rise in incomes, and the population increase. Nonetheless, Turkey remained an underpopulated country during the nineteenth century. For example, population densities were much lower that those in most of Europe until World War I.

Population Losses during and after World War I

I have estimated that in 1914 some 20–22 percent of the population, or approximately 3.3–3.6 million people, were non-Muslim (Greeks, Armenians, other Christians, and Jews) in the area within Turkey's current borders. The Greek and Armenian communities each had around 1.5 million members, while the other ethnic or religious groups were smaller. The majority of Greeks lived in Western and Central Anatolia as well as the Eastern Black Sea, while the majority of Armenians lived in Eastern Anatolia, both mostly in rural areas where they were engaged in agriculture. Nonetheless, compared to the Muslim population, a higher ratio of both Greeks and Armenians lived in the urban areas during the nineteenth century. All of the Jewish population, estimated at close to 300,000, lived in the urban areas, mostly in the west (Eldem 1970, pp. 49–65; Behar 1996, pp. 21–66; McCarthy 1983, 2002).

Turkey's population underwent major changes between 1914 and 1925 because of the impact of wars and ethnic conflicts. Total population decline during this period is estimated at more than 3 million, or close to 20 percent. Within this total, the losses of the Muslim population in wartime, especially during the First World War, were closer to 1.5 million. The decline in the non-Muslim population is even more striking. Their share in the total declined sharply, from 20–22 percent in 1914 to around 3 percent at the time of the first census in Turkey in 1927. As a result of these major changes, Turkey's population o was significantly smaller and was ethnically as well as religiously more homogeneous in 1925 in comparison to 1914.

The Armenian population within Turkey's current borders declined from approximately 1.5 million in 1914 to less than 200,000 by 1927. This was due to the massacres and deaths that followed the government order of forced emigration of all Armenians outside Istanbul to the Syrian desert in 1915. Large numbers died from attacks or hunger and disease during this march. Others escaped to Armenia in the east or Syria and Lebanon in the south. After Russia occupied a large part of Anatolia beginning in 1915, more Armenians and many Muslims died in the clashes. In 1915 and later, many Armenian children who had lost their parents, especially female children, remained in Turkey and were raised by Kurdish and Turkish families.

The Greek population within Turkey's current borders also declined sharply during the wars and the transition from the empire to the nation-states. In 1913, after the Balkan Wars which led to the migration of large numbers of Muslims to Turkey, some Greeks were forced to leave Thrace and Western Anatolia under pressure from the Ottoman government. Larger numbers of Greeks left in 1922 and later, after the Greek occupation army was defeated and the Turkish army marched toward the port city of İzmir. During the Lausanne peace negotiations in 1923, the Turkish and Greek governments decided to exchange all of the Muslim population in Greece with all the Orthodox Greeks in Turkey, with the exception of the Muslims in Western Thrace in Greece and the Orthodox Greeks in Istanbul. Within a short period, more than 1 million Greeks in Turkey, including those who had left earlier, moved to Greece, while some 400,000 Muslims left Greece for Turkey as part of this agreement (Arı 1995; McCarthy 2002; Yıldırım 2006, pp. 87–188).

Population Growth and Urbanization in the Twentieth Century

Turkey's population increased at high rates during the rest of the twentieth century. The annual rate of population increase is estimated at 1.9 percent between the two world wars. Because of the decline in mortality rates, annual rates of growth increased further after World War II, to a peak of 2.9 percent in the 1950s and at the beginning of the 1960s. Due to the rapid decrease in the fertility rate, however, population growth rates have been declining since then. Annual rates of growth averaged 1.3 percent during the first decade of the twenty-first century.

In the century before World War I, close to half of the total population increase had been a result of immigration. The contribution of immigration has been more limited since the 1920s. After the population exchange of the 1920s, the Muslim population arriving from the Balkans, especially Bulgaria and Yugoslavia, is estimated at close to 2 million during the next century (Kirişci 2008, pp. 175–98). The other large wave of international migration took place only recently. Close to 3 million Syrians migrated to Turkey between 2011 and 2015 as a result of the civil war in that country. While most of them are likely to stay and live in Turkey in the longer term, Turkey's official population statistics do not yet include them as residents.

In the other direction, approximately 4 million people emigrated to Germany and other Western European countries as workers or workers' relatives between 1961 and 1973. The emigrants were not all skilled or better educated. Many came from rural areas. Turkey's population was growing rapidly and large numbers of people were migrating from rural to urban areas at the time. As a result, emigration to Europe did not create labor shortages for Turkey's economy. On the whole, it tended to reduce the impact of rapid urbanization

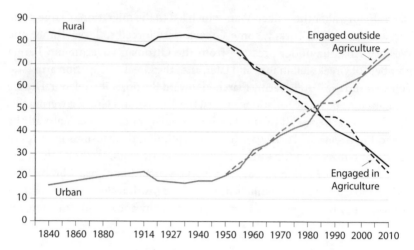

FIGURE 2.9. Urbanization and the Shift of the Labor Force from Agriculture, 1840–2010 (shares in total population and total labor force in percent). Sources: Author's estimates based on Ottoman population statistics summarized in Karpat 1985a and Issawi 1980, pp. 34–35 for the period until 1913; official series from Turkey, Turkish Statistical Institute 2014 for the period since 1927.

for a decade or so. After Western European countries stopped taking in workers because of the economic recession that began in 1973, emigration declined sharply (Turkey, Devlet İstatistik Enstitüsü [State Institute of Statistics] 1995; Hacettepe University Institute of Population Studies 2008, pp. 1–25).

One of the most important demographic developments in Turkey since the end of World War II has been urbanization. During the nineteenth century, the urbanization rate, defined here as the share in total population of centers with at least ten thousand residents, had edged upward from about 18 percent to 23 percent on the eve of World War I (figure 2.9).[2] The large decreases in the population during and after World War I, including the loss of most of the Armenian and Greek populations which were more urban than the average, led to a sharp decline in the share of urban population to about 17 percent, where it stood until the end of World War II. The powerful wave of rural to urban migration that began after World War II continues today. In 1950, Turkey's population continued to live mostly in rural areas with the share of population living in urban centers of 10,000 at no more than 18 percent. It is estimated that close to 10 million men, women, and children mostly under the age of thirty during the period 1950–1980, and an additional 12–15 million from

2. For the Ottoman period, my calculations are based on Issawi 1980, pp. 34–35; for the Republican era, see Turkey, Turkey, Türkiye İstatistik Kurumu (Turkish Statistical Institute), 2014.

1980 to 2015, migrated from the rural areas to urban areas. As a result, the numbers of people living in centers with more than ten thousand people increased more than fifteenfold, from less than 4 million in 1950 to 20 million in 1980 and to more than 60 million in 2015. Their share in total population or the urbanization rate rose to 45 percent in 1980 to about 80 percent in 2015.

Regional and rural to urban migration has been driven primarily by economic causes. Landlessness and unemployment ranked high among the causes of emigration from rural areas. However, migrants were also attracted to the cities by the prospect of higher incomes and better education and health services, for their children if not for themselves. The direction of migration was mostly from the rural areas of poorer, mostly agricultural regions in the east and the north along the Black Sea coast toward the urban areas of more developed regions in the west, in the Marmara and Aegean regions, and to a lesser extent in the south along the Mediterranean coast. The share in total population of the four sending regions in eastern, northern, and central parts of the country declined from 61 percent of the total population in 1950 to 54 percent in 1980 and 41 percent in 2015. In contrast, the share of total population of the receiving Marmara, Aegean, and Mediterranean regions in the west and the south increased from 39 percent in 1950 to 46 percent in 1980 and to 59 percent in 2015. The strong migration flows did not reverse the large regional differences in per capita income, but they ensured that eastern and southeast regions did not fall even further behind (Kırdar and Saraçoglu 2008, pp. 545–66).

The rapid shift of the population from the rural to the urban areas that began after the end of World War II thus corresponded to an equally dramatic shift of the labor force from lower productivity agriculture to industry and services and the transition to an era of higher economic growth rates. As a result, share of agriculture in the labor force and employment declined from more than 80 percent in 1950 to about 20 percent in 2015. Its share in GDP declined from more than 40 percent to less than 10 percent during the same period.

One important process that accompanied the rapid urbanization since the end of World War II has been the demographic transition from a regime characterized by high birthrates and high death rates to one with low birth- and death rates. While some decrease in death rates began to occur already in the Interwar era, one needs to point to the era after World War II for the demographic transition in Turkey. With the spread of medical facilities and new technology, increases in income, and better nutrition, mortality rates started declining after 1950. The decline in birthrates began somewhat later but has been equally dramatic. Total fertility rates, defined as the average numbers of live births per woman, have declined from more than 6 in the

1950s to less than 4 in the 1980s and 2.1 in 2010. As in the case of death rates, there have been significant differences in the birthrates and fertility rates across the country, between rural and urban areas and the west and the east, but these differences have been declining since 1980 (Shorter and Macura 1983, pp. 15–101; Turkey, Devlet İstatistik Enstitüsü [State Institute of Statistics] 1995; Hacettepe University Population Studies Institute 2008, pp. 26–35). It is clear that even if Turkey has not yet completed its demographic transition, it has left behind the decades with the most rapid declines in mortality and fertility rates.

One important consequence of the demographic transition has been the changes in the age structure of the population. After World War II, when the fertility rate was still high and the death rate had begun to decline, the share of young people in total population was high and rising. Because of the subsequent decline in the birthrates, however, the same share has been declining in recent decades. The median age has risen from 20 in 1950 and also in 1980 to 31 in 2015. The share in the total of working-age population, the 15–64 age group, has been rising and will continue to rise for the next several decades before it begins to decline. Along with the aging of the population, the share in total of people over age 65 has also risen in recent decades from 8.5 percent in 1980 to 11.6 percent in 2015 and is expected to rise further and more rapidly during the decades ahead (Behar 2006, pp. 17–31).

3

Institutions and the Ottoman Past

Institutions and Economic Development

How does one explain the long-run differences in economic development across different historical settings? Since the 1980s, a diverse and still developing literature has renewed the argument that institutions play important roles in promoting market exchange, trade, industrialization, and economic growth. North, Greif, Acemoglu, Robinson, and others have been emphasizing the importance of formal and informal institutions or written and unwritten rules of a society and their enforcement, which affect the incentives to invest and innovate. They have offered valuable empirical and theoretical insights into the development of institutions, their long-term consequences, and their relationship to state-building (North 1981, 1990; Hall and Soskice 2001; Greif 2006; Acemoglu, Johnson, and Robinson 2001, 2005a; Hillman 2013). The first half of the chapter will review this recent literature on the role of institutions in long-term economic development. The second half will examine institutional change and economic development in Ottoman Turkey in the centuries before the Industrial Revolution. I will argue that while institutions are not the only things that matter, it is essential to examine their role in order to understand Turkey's experience with economic growth and human development during the last two centuries.

The economics and economic history literature has also been making a related and important distinction between the proximate and deeper sources of economic growth. The proximate causes refer to the contributions made by the increases in inputs, land, labor, and capital and the productivity increases. The deeper causes refer to the social, political, and economic environment as well as the historical causes that influence the rate at which inputs and productivity grow. While research on institutions is still in early stages, there is growing consensus that institutions, construed broadly enough to include policies, are more fundamental determinants of economic development and of long-term differences in per capita GDP between countries than rates of physical and human capital accumulation or research and development themselves.

Institutions also matter for dimensions of human development, health, as well as education. While economic growth and development contribute to the levels of health and education in a society, one also observes significant differences in levels of health and especially education between countries with similar levels of per capita income. An important question, then, is why some countries invest much more resources in education and why they are more innovative than others. Recent studies suggest not only that rates of physical and human capital accumulation are higher and new technologies are developed in countries with better institutions, but also that the existing physical and human capital stock are used more efficiently in those countries with better institutions. In other words, differences in institutions are now seen as the main factor behind the intercountry differences in total factor productivity (Hall and Jones 1999, pp. 83–116; Helpman 2004, pp. 111–42; Platteau 2000, pp. xv–xx).

Written or formal rules or laws legislated from the top down that facilitate economic exchanges by enforcing contracts, protecting property rights, and monitoring all parties to ensure that they adhere to their commitments are formal institutions. States are typically expected to enforce these and other formal institutions. Institutions that matter for economic development are not limited to these formal institutions, however. Family, kinship, and ethnic ties, religious networks, patronage networks, coalitions, business partnerships, guilds, and foundations are all examples of arrangements that began as small-scale, bottom-up efforts in order to regulate and reduce uncertainty in economic life and to develop cooperation between different individuals and groups. Over time, many of these institutions began to be enforced at least partly by the state. Moreover, organizations are also subject to these rules, but many organizations such as firms or a governmental bureaucracy are institutions themselves because they have internal structure and can generate certain kinds of behavior among their members.

The developing literature emphasizes the key role played by political institutions. The distribution of de facto political power and interests as well as the formation of alliances and coalitions among the elite will influence the choice of political and economic institutions. Economic institutions and the political institutions that underpin them often were designed to secure privileged access to rights and resources for some elites while excluding other groups from their benefits. The ability of the elites to shape the institutions will depend on their ability to resolve conflicts between competing groups and cooperate; however, just as elites or coalitions of elites use their power to shape institutions, once they are shaped, the institutions, in turn, allow elites to maintain power. The resulting political equilibrium may persist for long periods of time.

Institutions are not limited to formal rules enforced by the state. There are also large numbers of informal institutions which are self-enforced or enforced by non-state actors. These privately organized arrangements, typically built from the bottom up within communities and rooted in social networks, usually do not work by themselves but interact or work together with constellations of other informal and formal institutions. In fact, informal institutions are often necessary for the workings of the formal arrangements. Informal institutions interact with other formal and informal institutions in a variety of ways. Some can only be substitutes while others are complimentary to the formal institutions. Informal institutions can coexist with formal institutions when, for example, individuals, groups, or organizations choose to follow or make use of informal rather than formal arrangements or when governments are either unable or unwilling to supply or enforce the formal institutions. Informal rules and norms shaped by values and preferences as well as conflicting interests and power relations will thus shape informal and formal institutions, and in turn, will be shaped by them as well as by the economic outcomes.

The ways that informal institutions will interact with formal institutions and how they will adjust to opportunities arising from economic development will vary. For example, because of the limitations of the rule of law and state enforcement, not all behavior norms will lead to the same market outcomes. Certain behavior norms regarding cooperation, trust, honesty, fairness, reciprocity, work ethic, distribution, and others are always necessary for ensuring favorable market outcomes. The strong correlations and complementarities between formal and informal institutions thus ensure that the emergence of formal institutions does not necessarily and inevitably crowd out informal institutions (Platteau 2000, pp. 241–324; Roland 2004).

While some institutions, especially formal institutions, can change very rapidly, many others, especially informal institutions, tend to change slowly. Political institutions and laws can change very quickly, sometimes literally overnight when revolutionary moments occur. In contrast, while some social norms and values change rapidly, in general, social norms, values, and related institutions change slowly. Legal systems tend to change faster than social norms, but the effectiveness of the legal system and the enforcement of the laws depend not only on state capacity but also on the acceptance of the laws as well as the expectations of different actors. A given law can be changed overnight, but legal systems are rarely changed as rapidly as political institutions, such as electoral rules. The effectiveness of the legal system and the enforcement of laws depend on their acceptance and legitimacy in society and on the expectations of many actors. For this reason, the legal system is very similar to social norms, except that the system of rewards and punishments is legally codified and can be changed more rapidly than social norms (Roland 2004, pp. 116–17).

Formal and informal institutions also play key roles in enhancing the ability of different social groups to solve their collective-action problems and pursue their common interests. Interests of different groups are central to the shaping of institutions. To what extent and how political institutions allow different social groups to pursue their interests is key to what extent and which interests can shape institutions. However, informal institutions that often emerge from the bottom up and are shaped by values, beliefs, and norms regarding cooperation, organization, and conflict resolution are also necessary for social actors to function effectively in the defense of their interests. Informal as well as formal institutions thus both contribute to and may also impede the cohesion and strength of different social actors.

In order to understand institutional change and the role of institutions in economic outcomes, it is necessary to understand how formal institutions, often designed and implemented in a centralized way or through a political process, and informal institutions, which often emerge in an uncoordinated or bottom-up fashion, interact. This interaction is not one-sided: formal institutions exercise causal pressures on informal institutions, and the latter, often built from the bottom up, can influence the path of formal institutions. How formal and informal institutions interact and adapt will often determine what kinds of new institutions will emerge and whether the latter will be growth-enhancing or growth-inhibiting. This complex interaction between the formal and informal institutions also suggests that a single set of institutions will not be suitable for all societies, and the institution constellation that will facilitate economic growth will vary from one society to another (Platteau 1994, 2000; Roland 2004; Kingston and Caballero 2009, pp. 151–80).

There is a good deal of evidence that informal institutions have made and continue to make important contributions to economic growth and human development. It is also true, however, that many informal institutions are typically based on social networks with clearly defined borders. These borders limit the geographic, social, and political reach of such institutions, and they often tend to serve primarily the narrow interests of an exclusive group. For economic exchanges to reach beyond the confines of close-knit groups, for the emergence of economic transactions, cooperation, and partnerships involving larger numbers of people and more complex organizations bringing together resources and skills on a larger scale, many of the private order institutions thus need to be replaced by more universalistic and formal arrangements (North 1990, pp. 107–40; Greif 2006, 153–301).

In other words, the existing institutions in a given society are not necessarily efficient or effective in promoting economic development. Institutions may have different effects on economic growth. Some may encourage accumulation of human and physical capital and innovation, while others may encourage seeking privileges for narrow groups. In fact, institutions often favor activities that restrict opportunities rather than expand them. It has been argued, for example, that the economic institutions of the early modern era such as guilds and merchant monopolies were not generalized institutions whose rules and entitlements applied uniformly to everyone in society. They existed not necessarily because they maximized the size of the economic pie, but because they enabled powerful groups to distribute larger slices of that pie to themselves (Ogilvie 2011, pp. 414–34).

Institutional economics and economic historians have also come to recognize that while institutions do change, they do not change quickly or easily. Recent studies have provided plenty of evidence that some institutions may be deeply rooted in the history of that society and may persist for long periods of time. One reason for the persistence of institutions may be the unwillingness to change long-standing beliefs, norms, or values. Another important reason for the persistence of institutions is that they serve the interests of social groups that have political power. These benefits may also enhance the capacity of such groups to prevent the adoption of new institutions (Acemoglu 2003, pp. 620–52).

External forces have also played important roles in shaping the institutions of a given society. In earlier periods, trade and other contacts have led to the transmission of institutions from one society to another and their adaptation. There are also many examples of institutions borrowed from other societies that did not survive. The cases of colonies or formal colonies where an outside power shapes the formal institutions are examples of more recent and more direct external influence. Even in the case of formal colonies, however, the formal institutions often emerged and evolved as the result of the interaction between domestic and global forms and forces. Equally important during the last two centuries has been the influence of international or global rules such as free trade, the gold standard, the Bretton Woods system of rules and organizations that were shaped after World War II, and more recently the Washington Consensus principles of reliance on markets, trade liberalization, and privatization, which are often enforced either by the leading global powers or international agencies and which interact with and strongly influence a country's formal economic institutions, including policies. Unfortunately, the recent literature on institutions has not addressed adequately the role of external or global forces in the shaping of a society's institutions.

While the new and growing literature has provided both a theoretical framework and empirical evidence that institutions matter for long-term economic development, it also has significant limitations. For one thing, how economic institutions are shaped and why they vary across countries is not well understood. The literature has so far not examined in detail the mechanisms through which they shape economic and political outcomes. Similarly, the recent literature has not addressed adequately how institutions may change in the longer term. Here, more attention must be given to the role of agency, the role of different groups in bringing about institutional change. In other words, while evidence is growing that institutions matter, we need to learn more about how they are shaped, how they work, how they persist, and how they change (Banerjee and Iyer 2005, pp. 1190–1213; Dell 2010, pp. 1863–1903; Nunn 2009, pp. 65–92).

Another important limitation concerns the possibility that at least some of the institutions are endogenous, that is, the interaction between institutions and economic change as well as as technology, politics, social structure, distribution of power, beliefs, ideologies, and expectations work both ways. Institutions influence the others but are also influenced by them. While it may be easier to isolate the effect of institutions on economic development if we believe that institutions evolve independently of the path of economic development, it will not be easy to do so if the other variables also influence the evolution of institutions. The case for attributing economic growth to institutions alone would be weaker if institutions are endogenous and are influenced by economic change as well as the other variables (Engerman and Sokoloff 2005, pp. 639–66). The emphasis on the role of institutions should not deny the role of broad political and social forces such as classes or groups and individual actors that shape the outcomes. Instead, they point to the ways in which institutions structure and mediate these struggles and in so doing influence their outcomes. To acknowledge that there is some endogeneity to institutions does not imply that institutions do not matter or that they have only a limited impact on long-term economic development.

Determinants of Institutions

How economic institutions are shaped and why they vary across countries is not well understood. The recent institutional economics and economic history literature proposes a number of causes or determinants of institutions. Most important among them are (i) geography or resource endowments; (ii) religion and, more generally, culture; and (iii) interests or political economy. These factors often interacted with each other in the shaping and evolution of institutions. Moreover, the importance of each of these broad determinants varied from one country to another. In what follows I will briefly discuss these determinants and the role each of them played in the Ottoman-Turkish context, and I will argue why some are more important than others.

Geography

One important determinant of institutions that has been discussed in the literature is resource endowments, location, and, more generally, geography. Two proponents of this thesis, Engerman and Sokoloff, have argued with respect to the Americas that variation in initial climate conditions had an enduring impact on variation in political institutions and the extent to which they fostered sustained economic growth. What mediated between geography and institutional development was the wealth distribution among elites and the ensuing degree of political participation (Sokoloff and Engerman 2000, pp. 217–32). There is no doubt that in some countries and societies, geography and natural resources have played an important role in shaping institutions, in their early history, for instance. In countries that accrue their income from large amounts of oil, valuable minerals, or other natural resources, for example, economic and political institutions were also influenced to a great extent by these revenues. The political struggle then revolves around the way these natural resources are shared, and this struggle also has a powerful influence on political and economic institutions. Similarly, whether a country is landlocked or is located close to large and dynamic markets plays an important role in shaping institutions and the trajectory of economic growth.

There is also no doubt that economic institutions in the Middle East have been influenced by geography or resource endowments. The most important example in this respect is Egypt, an important province of the Ottoman Empire where the land regime, fiscal institutions, and role of the central government have been shaped to a large degree by the needs of irrigated agriculture. A favorable location can be a substantial stimulus for economic development, and it is true that the shift of the intercontinental trade routes to the Atlantic Ocean had an impact on Turkey and more generally the Middle East. By that time, however, the region had already begun to lag behind northwestern Europe. Similarly, while institutions in Turkey certainly have been influenced by geography and resource endowments, the latter have not been very different from those of other temperate areas of the world. Oil or another resource has not played an important role in Turkey's economy. As a result, in this text I will consider Turkey's location, geography, and resource endowments as an important but not the leading determinant of institutions in Turkey or the primary cause of its relative economic standing.

Religion and Culture

Religion has long been offered as a primary cause of the differences in economic outcomes between Western Europe and the rest of the world. Since the early modern era, a long line of European authors have focused on Islam as the key to societies in the Middle East and the primary cause of economic stagnation in the region. Max Weber's analysis of Islamic societies emphasized the contrasts between them and those in Western Europe in a number of areas, including religion and law as well as the political system. Weber minimized the considerable differences that existed within Europe and within the Middle East and presented idealized versions of societies, institutions, and patterns of long-term economic change in these two regions. More recently, Timur Kuran has argued that even though Islamic law originally provided the Middle Eastern societies with effective legal regimes that encouraged trade and economic development, features of Islamic law such as the egalitarian inheritance system and absence of the concept of corporation prevented more complex, impersonal, and flexible organizational forms. By the nineteenth century the Middle East lagged so far behind that the region's only way forward was to accept European legal and organizational forms and seek ways to insert them into Islamic society (Weber 1978; Kuran 2011).

There are many examples where Islam appears to have played an important role in the shaping of institutions in the Middle East. However, the direction of causality and the role of religion in these examples are not always clear. Moreover, the role of Islam and Islamic law in particular in the shaping of institutions that matter in long-term economic development may have been less important or less consequential than it often has been claimed. Those who have argued for the central role of religion have tended to ignore social structure and the long-term configuration of power in Middle East societies. Islamic law was not an unchanging and autonomous sphere in the Ottoman Empire. The society, and especially the central government, occupied an important place and played a prominent role in shaping the law and its implementation in medieval Islamic states and the Ottoman Empire. Interpretation of Islamic law changed with changing needs and power relations. Recent research has shown that the central government was closely involved in the interpretation of law and day-to-day administration of justice in the early modern Ottoman Empire (Gerber 1994). With changing social structure, the interpretation of law and day-to-day administration of justice also changed. In the seventeenth and eighteenth centuries, for example, the provincial notables rose as a new social group thanks to their control of the local tax collection process. The rise of the urban notables and the power struggle between them and the central government were reflected in the interpretation of Ottoman law and its implementation, especially in the provinces.

There is a large body of evidence indicating that, when the need or demand was present and when power relations allowed, Islamic societies have often circumvented or adapted those religious rules that appear to prevent change, including economic change. For example, medieval Islamic societies of the region and later the Ottomans developed a variety of methods for circumventing the ban on interest and allowing credit relations to flourish, as I will discuss later in this chapter. From the fifteenth century, the Ottomans took these practices one step further and local communities developed in a bottom-up fashion a new institution called cash *vakıf* or pious foundation. The maintenance costs of many local mosques and other charitable works as well as some of the services in the urban areas were financed with the interest income of these foundations. Many cash vakıfs continued their operations until the nineteenth century.

Similarly, Ottoman institutions of tax collection and state borrowing experienced many changes along with changes in military organization as well as Ottoman social structure and the demands of the state from the sixteenth through the eighteenth centuries. As I will also discuss later in this chapter, agricultural taxes, the leading source of revenue for the central government, were collected under the prebendal *timar* system which also equipped the army with the cavalry and soldiers during times of war until the end of the sixteenth century. With the changes in military organization and the need to maintain larger permanent armies, the Ottomans shifted to tax farming in the eighteenth century, and with the growing need for long-term borrowing, they shifted to lifetime tax farming during the eighteenth century. Institutions for domestic borrowing also experienced a good deal of institutional change during this period despite the apparent ban on interest (Pamuk 2004). In other words, some institutional changes did in fact take place when demand for them was present and when the social structure and power relations allowed them. If Islamic law could be adapted to the changing circumstances and it could be interpreted in different ways according to changing needs and demands, it becomes difficult to argue that Islamic law was the primary obstacle to the evolution of institutions and economic development (Gerber 1994; Çizakça 1996, pp. 65–85).

In response to the arguments focusing on Islam and Islamic law, Jean-Philippe Platteau has recently emphasized that there is a systematic misconception about the true nature of the relationship between Islam and politics, and by extension, the economic outcomes. He has argued that it is not the unique aspects of Islam that are ultimately responsible for the unfavorable political and economic outcomes. It is in fact politics that tends to dominate and use Islam. Because of the lack of a centralized religious authority structure and the great variability of interpretations of Islam and Islamic law, rulers in Muslim countries have been able to choose from and manipulate the many interpretations of Islam. Both the rulers and their political opponents often try to outbid each other by using the religious idiom that raises the risk of an "obscurantist deadlock" (Platteau 2011, pp. 243–60; Platteau 2017).

In a similar vein, Jared Rubin has also emphasized the use of Islam by rulers who tried to acquire political support or religious legitimation by relying on religious authorities when those authorities had the capacity to legitimize or support their rule (Rubin 2017, pp. 27–72). When the rulers relied on the religious establishment for support and legitimation, they were less likely to adopt policies that threaten the religious establishment and more likely to pursue laws and policies against change. As a result, laws and policies did not change in response to changes in the outside world. Rubin argues further that obtaining religious legitimacy was important for the Ottoman rulers and they often aligned their policies with the religious elites rather than the economic elites during the early modern era, not because the rulers were inherently more conservative but because their interests pushed them in this direction.

Rubin points to the banning of the printing press in the Ottoman Empire as an important example of what happens when rulers seek support and legitimacy from the religious establishment. The movable-type press, the most important information technology of the early modern era, was invented in Germany around 1450. In 1485, the Ottoman sultan Bayezid II banned printing in the Ottoman Empire, and the ban remained in effect for more than two centuries, until 1727. It applied to Ottoman subjects printing in the Arabic script but not to the non-Muslim communities printing in other scripts. In other words, the Ottoman government was not against the printing press per se but against printing in the Arabic script. Demand for the printing press may have been low in the Ottoman Empire, but that was not the primary reason why it was banned. The printing press threatened the religious establishment's intellectual monopoly over the transmission of religious knowledge. The Ottoman sultan was in fact seeking legitimacy from the religious elites who believed that the press would lead to the loss of their monopoly over the transmission of religious knowledge which had been a largely oral process dominated by the religious authorities. The religious establishment was not threatened by printed works in other languages. As Rubin argues, without the ban, the printed works would have indeed undermined the monopoly of the religious establishment over intellectual life and may have allowed greater power to the merchants and producers in the formulation of laws and policies (Rubin 2017, pp. 99–118; also Coşgel, Miceli, and Rubin 2012, 357–71).

A related and more general determinant of institutions that has been emphasized in the literature is culture, which is often viewed as beliefs, values, and preferences based on experience accumulated over centuries and shared by some subset of society. Throughout history different societies have exhibited different attitudes toward work, thrift, and usury, toward respect of private property, creativity, education, and toward women's participation in different economic activities. Many authors have argued that these beliefs, values, and preferences, as well as social networks that support the circulation of reliable information and reputation mechanisms, all shape the choice of institutions and influence the specific trajectory of economic development. Those that argue for the importance of culture emphasize that while economic development will change cultural values, change will be slow. While political institutions and laws can change very quickly, values, beliefs, social norms, and related institutions change more slowly (Platteau 2000, pp. 241–338; Roland 2004, pp. 109–31).

There are many channels through which culture may affect economic development. Mokyr has argued that the Industrial Revolution in Britain and more generally modern economic growth was due to the changes in European culture and institutions during the early modern era. It was the creative ferment brought about by the Enlightenment and the associated set of radical changes in beliefs, values, and preferences that led to the growth of technological creativity and innovation across Europe (Mokyr 2009, 2017). There is growing evidence in recent years that culture as measured by indicators of individual values, beliefs, and preferences such as trust in others, willingness to cooperate, tolerance, beliefs in certain institutional taboos, respect for authority, ability or willingness to resolve conflicts and reach compromises—whether between elites or between different religious or ethnic groups—is important for long-term economic development (Greif 1994, pp. 912–50; Greif 2006, pp. 55–152, 269–304). Similarly, there is growing evidence that social networks that support the circulation of information and reputation mechanisms and their interaction with unequal power relations shape economic institutions and have a causal effect on long-term economic development.

There is also evidence that low levels of trust make it difficult for people to enter economic transactions or partnerships with people who are not close to them or who do not belong to their group. As a result, societies with low trust may make it more difficult for partnerships establishing a firm, thereby raising transaction costs. In international surveys of values, contemporary Turkey is characterized by relatively low levels of trust, low levels of civic participation, and higher levels of respect for authority, giving support to the arguments by those who emphasize that the role of culture is important (World Values

Survey, www.worldvaluessurvey.org). Similarly, the extent to which elites and larger groups were able to cooperate and resolve conflicts has been very important in Turkey's history and it is equally important today. Culture may also influence political institutions and political outcomes. There is evidence that the impact of culture may also operate through the functioning of state institutions. Moreover, cultural values do not necessarily influence institutions by themselves but may interact with other causes of institutions to shape political and economic institutions. The interaction work both ways. The institutions, in turn, influence culture (Guiso, Sapienza, and Zingales 2006; Tabellini 2010, pp. 677–716; Alesina and Giuliano 2015, pp. 898–944).

Culture matters for economic outcomes, and taking culture seriously not only helps enrich our understanding of economic phenomena but can also help us explain them better. However, one uncertainty, and debate, regarding the role of culture revolves around whether or not the culture of a society changes over time along with economic development. In other words, the causal interaction between culture and economic outcomes may work both ways. If culture changes over time with economic development, that is, if culture is influenced by the economic environment, then it is not possible to view culture as a fundamental and permanent determinant of economic development. There is in fact evidence that with economic development many norms and values do change in a generation or two. Similarly, there are many examples suggesting that deeper forces affect both culture and economic outcomes or that cultural values and preferences depend on other outcomes or variables. For example, as a cultural variable, trust has severe limitations because it is not only an inherited variable. People can develop trust, for example, because of the quality of the legal system. In other words, where the state fails to provide the public goods, generalized trust is likely to remain weak and emphasis on informal institutions remains strong. As a result, there are serious empirical problems in measuring the impact of culture.

Another criticism directed at the arguments for the role of religion and culture has pointed out that religion and culture can in fact be compatible with a wide spectrum of behaviors, and the effects of culture on institutions and economic performance are contingent on a range of factors. According to this view, culture should be viewed as an ensemble of resources that enhance behavior as well as rules that constrain behavior. There are different elements in every culture, including Islamic culture. Individuals do not necessarily adhere slavishly to a script that is written for them but may choose different elements from what is available depending on the context. In other words, culture should not be taken only as rigid constraint but may be compatible with a wide spectrum of actions and outcomes under different conditions. With economic growth and development, the possibilities offered by culture can thus be enhanced (Granovetter 1985, pp. 481–510; Di Maggio 1992, pp. 27–57). For many decades culture had been invoked as the root cause of economic stagnation in East and South Asia. Along with dramatic shifts in economic performance in these two regions, institutions that once seemed durable and persistent in the earlier period in fact proved highly vulnerable to transformations that brought about large gains in economic performance.

Conflicting Interests and Political Economy

Scholars in the recent institutional economics literature who adhere to a social conflict or political economy explanation of institutions argue that change is driven by social forces that favor it and is opposed by social forces that would lose because of it. The balance of power between those two groups determines the dynamics of change. Because different groups and individuals typically benefit from different institutions, there is generally a conflict over the choice of institutions. That conflict itself will be influenced by the existing institutions as they help or hinder different groups in solving their collective-action problem and determine how representative and participatory the political system is. The process of institutional change thus involves significant conflict between different groups and is ultimately resolved in favor of groups with greater economic and political power. For this reason, political economy and political institutions are considered as key determinants of economic institutions and the direction of institutional change (Acemoglu, Johnson, and Robinson 2005b, pp. 385–471; Rodrik, Subramanian, and Trebbi 2004, pp. 131–65; Ogilvie 2011, pp. 414–34).

The fact that institutions reflect to a large extent the interests and preferences of powerful groups gives them resilience and permanence, and it makes it more difficult to change them. The fact that institutions are shaped according to the interests of a strong group or a coalition of strong groups also suggests that institutions and institutional reforms do not necessarily evolve in a way that encourages economic development. Inefficient institutions may provide significant distributional advantages to powerful actors within a society. Those that may have already played an important role in the emergence of these institutions may try to prevent changes because they believe that institutional reforms needed for economic development will damage their own interests. For instance, in many societies, major landowners and guilds opposed demands for institutional reforms and for industrialization to be extended to broader groups. As a result, new institutions that promote economic development may emerge only after lengthy struggles.

Beliefs, norms, and culture as well as interests may play important roles in the shaping of institutions and in the efforts to prevent the emergence of new institutions. Institutions that will support economic development may lead to accommodating changes in cultures and values over time. However, if there are distributive conflicts between different groups, values and norms may not always evolve to support apparently beneficial institutions. Those that resist the institutional changes may then use both formal and informal institutions as strategic resources in the conflicts over distributional benefits and try to undermine the new institutions. In other words, although it is often difficult to distinguish between interests and culture as the ultimate cause of behavior, many of the patterns and outcomes that appear to be due to beliefs, norms, customs, and more generally culture may in fact be explained by interests and power (Knight 1992, pp. 123–214).

The State

The characteristics of a state and the role it should play in economic development are among the most basic and most frequently asked questions not only in economic history but more generally in social sciences. Historically, once trade expanded beyond local boundaries, the limits of local norms and social structures and communal networks began to emerge. At that point, economic development required generalized institutions that would replace particularized ones and an organization that has a comparative advantage in enforcement, and in most settings that organization was the state. The near-exclusive exercise of coercive power also put the state in an ideal position to act as an enforcer of public law and order, including the protection of property rights. However, there is growing consensus that the role of the state in economic development is not limited to providing external and internal security, protecting property rights, and enforcing contracts. The state also plays a key role as an important focal point for the conflict over institutions and institutional change.

Historically, the relations between competing elites and their relations to the state have been critical in the formation of the state and its policies. State elites, the bureaucracy, and the military have also played important roles in this process as they pursued their own interests by themselves or in cooperation with some of the other elites. Reaching an understanding if not consensus between elites and harnessing the different powers and capacities of the various elites was a key aspect of state formation and state policies. State-building in the early modern era entailed the building of formal institutions that govern the relationship between state elites and rising commercial and political elites, which were rarely monolithic blocks. Bargaining over political commitments, privileges, and resources became particularly important in the often conflict-ridden relationship between rulers and economic elites. The negotiations, the bargaining over, and institutions of tax collection as well as dealing with the various collective-action problems were key processes during state-building. In the absence of a durable arrangement between the state and the elites, however, the competition could escalate and become a serious threat to political stability and order (Acemoglu et al. 2005b, pp. 546–79; North, Wallis, and Weingast 2009, pp. 1–76).

The power balances as well as the coalitions between the state and the various elites were critical in shaping and protecting not only macro-level but also micro-level institutions. If the distribution of benefits from a new or existing institution was not consistent with the existing distribution of power in society, the various elites could mobilize, bargain, and put pressure on others as well as the state to try to bring formal and informal institutions back into line. The competing elites often made use of informal institutions, including identity-based networks and patron-client relations in these conflicts. In other words, the extent to which formal institutions can be enforced or rule of law prevails often depended on the relations and the degree of understanding if not consensus between the elites and the state (Olson 1965, pp. 5–65; Granovetter 1985, pp. 481–510; Knight 1992, pp. 123–214).

Fiscal, legal, and other capacities of the state emerged in this process as key issues regarding the effectiveness of the state not only for enforcing the existing laws but also for bringing about institutional change. The relations between the elites and the state and the degree to which elites supported or opposed the state played an important role in shaping state policies and also in state capacity. To the extent that state actions were consistent with the interests of the elites, the latter were willing to support increases in state capacity. However, divergences between the aims of the state and the interests of the elites as well as cleavages among the elites could reduce the willingness of the elites to support increases in state capacity. While weak states clearly were not helpful, any state strong enough to protect property rights was also strong enough to confiscate property. Douglass North and others have emphasized the role of negotiations and bargaining between the rulers and the elites in constraining the rulers. Strong states need to be constrained and their capacity needs to be directed toward economic development. Even if the state did not directly support private accumulation, it is essential that the state does not engage in behavior that would hurt the economy and the various actors in the private sector (Hillman 2013, pp. 261–64).

Others, however, saw the role of the state in the early modern era differently. For S. R. Epstein, the key issue in removing obstacles to growth in early modern economies was not about limiting the predatory tendencies of coercive rulers. He argued, instead, that what was often missing was the coordination and integration of markets precisely because access to economic rights was not universal but rather upheld selectively as privileges to particular corporate groups, such as merchant guilds or trade monopolies. Such privilege-driven markets were often aggravated by jurisdictional fragmentation and the absence of a centralized political authority that could enforce property rights universally against the barriers of local interests. In contrast, jurisdictional centralization led to market integration by reducing preexisting seigniorial dues, by overcoming coordination failures between rival feudal and urban monopolies, by systematizing legal codes, weights, and measures, and by increasing the ruler's responsiveness to political pressure. In other words, limitations to, rather than excesses of, state sovereignty was what restrained the rise of competitive markets in the early modern era, according to Epstein (Epstein 2000, 147–74; Besley and Persson 2010, 2011; Johnson and Koyama 2017).

The experience of Britain and the later industrializers in Europe during both the early modern era and the nineteenth century show that states played key roles in economic development not only by providing security and enforcing laws and contracts, but also by supporting markets and long-distance trade and in most cases protecting domestic production against foreign competition. While Britain is often viewed today as the home of laissez-faire economic policy, the British government in fact pursued a policy of active interventionism during the eighteenth century. It supported the industrialization process through a system of restrictions, privileges, and encouragements (Chang 2002, pp. 13–68; O'Brien 2011, pp. 408–46). During the nineteenth century, it was generally recognized that in the presence of industrializing Britain, countries in Continental Europe could not develop new industries without state intervention—not only tariff protection but also other forms of state support. Alexander Gerschenkron has shown how competing with British industry was beyond the capacity of the local entrepreneurs in Continental Europe and how the state had to go beyond providing a suitable environment for the private sector and become actively involved in organizing financial markets. The specific institutions varied from one country to another depending on the histories of the countries and their degree of relative backwardness (Gerschenkron 1962, pp. 5–71).

States in developing countries had limited capacity and played limited roles in economic development during the nineteenth century. The 1930s was an important turning point for many developing countries, however. As the Great Depression persisted, states in many developing countries, as well as some of the elites, realized that the model based on a specialization in agriculture was in trouble and they supported industrialization through protectionism and various other incentives. In the absence of a coherent theory, developing as well as developed countries experimented with various interventionist policies in response to the Great Depression. Studies by Carlos Diaz Alejandro and Angus Maddison show that the developing countries from Latin America to Southern Europe and Asia that shifted to greater interventionism and inward-oriented economic policies during the 1930s did better than those that continued with the earlier strategies based on the export of agricultural products (Diaz Alejandro 1984; Maddison 1985, pp. 13–44). In the 1960s and 1970s, interventionist government policies spread and many developing countries adopted a detailed set of policies called import-substituting industrialization. This new package included protectionism to support domestic industry against the competition from imports, overvalued exchange-rate policies, subsidies to private firms, intervention in the financial markets to suppress interest rates, and preferential access to credit. While the opportunities provided by a protected domestic market were exploited in the consumer goods and to some extent intermediate goods, export orientation of the manufacturing industry remained weak (Hirschman 1968, pp. 1–26).

The experience of developing countries in East Asia such as Taiwan, South Korea, and Hong Kong during the last half century with state interventionism and industrialization stands apart from other developing countries in many ways. In these powerful examples, in addition to the protection of domestic industry and strong promotion of exports, governments were involved in strategic targeting of sectors, promotion and coordination of industrial investment decisions, promotion of high-technology sectors, and close control of the banking sector. In each of these countries, one or a small number of pilot agencies within the central bureaucracy led the decision-making and brought about very high rates of investment in the selected sectors. While the state actively interacted with society, it also maintained a high degree of autonomy when confronted with the short-term interests of this or that group. The formal and informal institutions that facilitated the consultation and cooperation of the public and private sectors played key roles in the successful outcomes in these East Asian countries. State policies supported by these institutions not only changed the behavior of the private sector; they also enabled new institutions to emerge and made it easier for the new institutions promoting industrialization to become stronger over time. The institutional structure created during the industrialization process thus gained permanence over time and continued to influence behavior in later periods (Amsden 1989; Wade 1990; Evans 1995).

It has not been easy to replicate the success of East Asian countries with interventionism in other countries, even though the same formal institutions and similar strategies of support for export-oriented manufacturing have been adopted. The problem has not been just that state capacity or the capabilities of the formal agencies charged with enforcement duties was weak. Even more important, the East Asian state and its relationship with the private sector was the product of unique historical circumstances. The configuration of power between the state and the competing private elites which allowed high degree of bureaucratic autonomy and state capacity as well as close cooperation between them was a by-product of Japanese colonial rule and did not exist in the other developing countries. Without the strong and autonomous state and relatively weak elites, the interventionism in East Asia would not have had the same long-time horizons and high implementation capabilities. Other features of East Asian countries were also important, including internal and external pressures to adopt growth strategies. In contrast, states in other developing countries could not harness the different powers and capacities of the elites and deal with various collective-action problems. The distribution of benefits from the enforcement of the new institutions and policies of interventionism was not in line with the existing distribution of power in society. Powerful groups and organizations often chose to develop formal and informal institutions different from those defined by the state that would serve their interests better (Öniş 1991, pp. 109–16; Stiglitz and Lin 2013, pp. 1–13).

These historical examples show that state interventionism and a strong state played an important role, not only in supporting the industrialization process of the developing countries in the twentieth century, but also in earlier industrialization of Western Europe. The existence of such examples does not mean, however, that state interventionism will always produce results that favor economic development and industrialization. As the results of attempts to replicate the East Asian experience with industrialization show, even if the same formal institutions and the same economic policies are adopted, the outcomes can be different because new institutions interact with other existing institutions as well as the existing social structure and distribution of power.

Institutions before the Nineteenth Century

In Turkey as in most other countries, a wide range of institutions have been shaped by deeply historical processes involving many causes, resource endowments, and geography; Islam and culture;social structure and conflicting interests. Both the formal institutions enforced in varying degrees by the state and the informal institutions that were shaped from the bottom up by private networks, as well as their interaction, played important roles in shaping political and economic outcomes in the Ottoman era. In this section, I will argue that while geography, culture, and Islam did influence Ottoman institutions in the Balkans and Anatolia, the core areas of the empire, the most important determinant of institutions and the direction of institutional change before the nineteenth century, was the social structure and the changing balances of power between the state and the various competing elites, including the state elites. External influences on institutions remained limited as the empire maintained its independence during this period.

Until the end of the fifteenth century, politics in the emerging Ottoman state revolved around the power struggle between a provincial aristocracy of Turkish origin and a central administration composed mainly of conscripted non-Muslims (*devşirme*). In the second part of the fifteenth century, with Mehmed II's successful centralizing drive, the balance tipped in favor of the center. As the land-based aristocracy was defeated, the state seized land under private ownership and put it in the hands of the central government (Imber 2002, pp. 27–44, 318–25). The empire's institutions and the state's economic policies then began to reflect much more strongly the priorities of the central administration. Baki Tezcan has argued that the power of the sultan and the central administration began to be limited during the seventeenth century by the growing influence of the janissaries and the *ulema* (Tezcan 2010, pp. 227–44). Nonetheless, the central government always strived to maintain a traditional order and its position at the center of that order. As long as the activities of the economic elites, merchants, leading artisans, and moneylenders contributed to the perpetuation of this social order, the state encouraged and supported them but did not welcome their rapid enrichment (Genç 2000).

Institutions continued to be shaped during the following centuries according to the distribution of political power, cooperation, conflicts, and struggles between the state elites and the various other elites, especially those in the provinces. An important priority for the central administration was to thwart political threats and control social groups that could present a danger to the center. After the mostly Muslim urban notables began to control local tax collection and increased their power in the provinces during the seventeenth and eighteenth centuries, the central administration was forced to enter into negotiations with them and tried to prevent them from joining forces, resorting to the "divide and rule" method whenever necessary (Barkey 1994, pp. 229–42). For their part, the various elites including those in the capital rarely if ever acted together as a bloc. Cooperation and coordination among the provincial elites was also made more difficult by the fact that the empire covered a large geographical area and the different ethnic groups and elites did not always act together. Even in the eighteenth century, when the provincial notables were at their strongest, the creation of formal political institutions that reflected the new balances between the center and the provinces and that could secure political stability was not possible. The Charter of Alliance (*Sened-i Ittifak*), also known as the Ottoman Magna Carta and signed in 1807 precisely for this purpose, was not supported by either side and was never implemented (Yaycioglu 2016, pp. 203–38).

The State and Provincial Elites

Early modern states supported economic development not only by providing security against external and internal threats but also by issuing laws and enforcing them. A certain level of state capacity was crucial for these purposes. Equally important was the extent to which the state supported or hindered the development of the private sector. While the Ottoman central administration was strong enough to influence the direction of many of the institutional changes during the early modern era, its record in supporting economic development was mixed. It was relatively strong during the sixteenth century and was able to provide some security, law, and order, build infrastructure such as roads and irrigation, and protect the domestic trade routes. However, its capacity in these areas diminished considerably during the seventeenth and eighteenth centuries with the rise of the *ayan* or the urban notables in the provinces.

The rising power holders in the provinces came from two different groups: prominent notables whose families had been among the local elites, and centrally appointed officials who subsequently put down local roots. Either way, the rise of the ayan had important implications for market integration and long-distance trade. The ayan played important roles maintaining security and urban life in their districts and ensuring safety of the trade routes. They thus contributed to the development of trade especially during the first half of the eighteenth century (İnalcık 1980, pp. 283–337; Hourani 1966, 83–110; Yaycioglu 2016, pp. 65–116). The central government could play only a limited role in coordinating and integrating the distant markets inside the large empire during this period. The ayan also played an important role in the shaping of institutions. In the conflicts with other elites and in their relations with the state, they often made use of informal institutions including identity-based networks and patron-client relations. Local and more informal arrangements began to replace or substitute for the functions of the central administration in security, judiciary, law enforcement, and the regulation of local markets during the seventeenth and eighteenth centuries. Despite the increase in the ayan's power, however, the central administration did not lose control of the law and the judiciary and continued to oppose private ownership on agricultural land, for example. As tensions between the center and provinces rose in the second half of the century, trade, especially internal trade, may have declined. Among other direct causes of market fragmentation during this latter period were fiscally motivated internal and external tariffs as well as import and export prohibitions.

As the central administration's power began to diminish in the provinces, so did its capacity to collect taxes and bring the revenues to the center. The local notables together with various other groups at the center began to control the tax collection process and retained a large part of the revenues. While the pressures of warfare helped most states across Europe to increase significantly the revenues collected at the center, two central governments—the Ottomans, along with Poland—were unable to achieve virtually any increase in per capita tax collection during the seventeenth and eighteenth centuries. Annual per capita tax revenues that reached the treasury in Istanbul did not exceed three days' wages earned by an unskilled laborer until the end of the eighteenth century. The difficulties in fiscal centralization were in part due to the large size and great geographical diversity of the empire. The large geography also made it difficult for the local elites to coordinate their actions and challenge the central administration to change the political institutions (Karaman and Pamuk 2010; Pamuk 2012; Coşgel 2015).

Not surprisingly, declining fiscal capacity led to diminished military power. The Ottomans frequently lost territory in the wars they fought against Russia and Austria in the second half of the eighteenth century and early part of the nineteenth century. The central administration's inability to collect taxes also had a negative impact on institutions and the economy. Especially from the 1760s to the 1830s, when wars were frequent, seizing the assets of public officials and urban notables in the provinces in order to secure additional revenues became common practice. Also under fiscal pressure, local monopolies were created in domestic and international trade and put up for sale. These measures seriously undermined trade and shrank the economy even further. As a result, while the Industrial Revolution was taking place in Britain and later in the Continent, the Ottoman central administration struggled with frequent wars, as well as a severe and prolonged fiscal crisis. Economic conditions deteriorated sharply, leading to a significant divergence with Western Europe.

Relations with the Private Sector

Late medieval and early modern states all had to address a common range of economic problems. However, they had limited capacities and had to be selective in their goals. Due to their diminished fiscal capacity, this was especially true for the Ottomans. One important economic priority for the Ottoman central administration was the provisioning of the urban areas, which was considered necessary for political stability (Genç 1989, pp. 175–85; İnalcık 1994, pp. 179–217). The central government wanted to assure a steady supply of goods especially for the capital city and the army. With the territorial expansion of the empire during the sixteenth century, long-distance trade and some degree of control of the trade routes became increasingly important for these needs.

The emphasis on provisioning also necessitated an important distinction between imports and exports. Imports were encouraged as they added to the availability of goods. As a result, the Ottomans never used protectionism as economic policy. They did not attempt to protect domestic producers from the competition of Indian textiles during the seventeenth and eighteenth centuries, for example. In contrast, exports were allowed only after the requirements of the domestic economy were met. As soon as the possibility of shortages emerged, the government did not hesitate to restrict the activities of the merchants and prohibit the exportation of basic necessities, especially foodstuffs and raw materials (İnalcık 1970, pp. 207–18).

The relationship between the governments and the merchants was not a relationship between equals. On the one hand, governments tolerated and even encouraged the activities of the merchants who were considered indispensable for the functioning of the urban economy. When the merchants found opportunities to pursue their activities with less intervention from the government, they often flourished. Yet, the activities of merchants occasionally led to higher prices of raw materials, which put pressure on the guild system and more generally the urban economy. Moreover, the state elites opposed economic and institutional changes when they thought these changes would transform the existing order and make it more likely for them to lose political power. Thus, the central administration often considered as its main task the control of merchants, not their protection. The control of merchants was much more difficult than the control of guilds, however. While the guilds were fixed in location, the merchants were mobile. Needless to say, the official attitude toward financiers and money changers was similarly ambiguous (Inalcik 1969, pp. 97–140; Faroqhi 2009). For their part, the merchants could not achieve a sufficiently powerful identity of interests with their rulers which would have enabled them to influence the government to use its material and military resources to further their own commercial interests. They certainly could not declare "l'état c'est moi" but they could plausibly claim, during the best of times, "l'état n'est pas contre moi" (Udovitch 1988, pp. 53–72).

One of the more extreme examples of Ottoman state policies toward domestic merchants involved the meat supply of the capital city. By the second half of the sixteenth century, Istanbul had emerged, once again, as the largest city in Europe. The state strived to keep food prices at low levels in the capital city. For this purpose, it often tried to make use of the price ceiling (*narh*) system. When the announced price ceilings for meat were established below market prices, however, merchants refused to bring the livestock to the capital on foot or by sea. In response, the Ottoman central administration began to identify wealthy merchants and assign them the task of supplying meat to the capital city. Merchants who were given this assignment often ended up with large losses and faced sharp declines in their wealth. Not surprisingly, they tried to avoid this obligation. The state soon began to assign this task to merchants who were engaged in illegal activities or who offended the government. This example suggests that while the state needed the merchants for the provisioning of the cities and especially the capital city, in important issues, it could follow policies rather unfriendly to the merchants. These harsh practices were relaxed after the sixteenth century, however, and the capital city began to rely increasingly on markets for its meat supply and the relative prices of meat tended to rise (Greenwood 1988).

Ottoman merchants, especially those from the Arab provinces, had been able to develop trading networks and large presences in north Africa and south Asia. However, their inability to control a significant share of the trade with Europe hurt them in the longer term. While the governments of European countries often encouraged, backed, and supported merchants who were their subjects or citizens, Ottoman governments did not view the protection of their own merchants as a priority. Moreover, from the twelfth century onward, most European countries promulgated laws forbidding the lengthy sojourn, permanent settlement, or engagement in commerce by foreign nationals including Muslims. As a result, Muslim merchants who had been active in the trade with Europe began to lag behind non-Muslim Ottoman merchants, who were able to take advantage of their growing international networks and connections with European merchants (Gilbar 2003, pp. 1–36). The fact that the wealthiest Ottoman merchants were non-Muslims, mostly Greeks and Armenians, made it even more difficult for their economic power to be converted to political influence during the eighteenth and nineteenth centuries.

While the policies of the Ottoman government toward local merchants were characterized by a great deal of ambiguity, the government, like others in the Middle East since the twelfth century, was willing and ready to offer commercial and legal privileges to European merchants. These privileges were granted not because these governments were coerced by the more powerful European states. Through these privileges, the rulers sought to increase the circulation of goods, especially luxury goods in their local markets, and increase state revenues from trade. Another motive was to use the privileges as an instrument of foreign policy and gain influence and friendship in Europe. Among the privileges granted to European merchants living in Ottoman port cities, the most important were the right to trade and travel within the empire, to transfer products from one region to another, and to use vessels carrying the flag of their own countries. These privileges gradually expanded and ceased to be unilateral grants during the eighteenth century. They began to be referred to as the "capitulations" due to the many headings under which they were grouped in the original Latin texts in the medieval era. Some of the new privileges began to conflict with the sovereignty of the empire, such as the right for European traders to set up their own tribunals in the Ottoman

Empire, and to take trade disagreements to these courts. In addition, customs duties paid by European merchants were kept at the lowest levels, and in many cases, foreign traders paid less customs taxes than local traders (İnalcık 1971; Boogert 2005; Kuran 2011, pp. 209–27; Agir 2013, 571–98; Artunç 2015, pp. 720–48).

These practices clearly put Ottoman traders in a disadvantaged position compared to European traders in Ottoman markets and played an important role in the transfer of large segments of the Ottoman long-distance trade as well as coastal and long-distance shipping to European merchants. Early in the nineteenth century, the government tried to improve conditions for the Ottoman merchants in their competition against the Europeans by establishing consulates in major Mediterranean trading centers, but the Ottoman merchants could not compete against the by then much more powerful European merchants, and the former were not supported by a system of privileges like those provided to their European counterparts under the capitulations. Because the Ottoman merchants remained weak, it was difficult for them to have more influence and provide more input into their government's trade policies or change the commercial or economic institutions. In contrast, as European states and merchants increased their economic and political power, they began to influence the direction of institutional change in the Ottoman Empire.

Institutional Change

There was a good deal of institutional change in the Ottoman Empire during the early modern centuries. This section will briefly examine the evolution of formal institutions as they interacted with informal institutions shaped from the bottom up in land regime, private finance, tax collection, and state borrowing during the early modern era to argue that these changes were shaped less by geography or Islam and more by the distribution of power, struggles, negotiations, and bargains between the state and the various elites, especially the rising urban notables in the provinces (Pamuk 2004, pp. 225–47).

Land Regime

During the early stages of Ottoman territorial expansion, lands taken over from the neighboring states in the Balkans were registered as state lands. In contrast, private property on land continued in areas taken from the Islamic principalities in Anatolia. With the centralization drive in the second half of the fifteenth century, however, state ownership of agricultural lands was established as the basic form in the core regions of the empire, in both the Balkans and Anatolia. It has been estimated that as much as three-fourths or more of the agricultural lands in these core regions were under state ownership during the first half of the sixteenth century (Barkan 1953–54, pp. 251–329).

Hereditary usufruct of these state lands was given to peasant households which typically cultivated it with a pair of oxen and family labor. The peasant family farm thus emerged as the basic economic and fiscal unit in the rural areas in most of Anatolia (İnalcık 1994, pp. 103–79). These family farms were typically cultivated with family labor and a pair of oxen. The Ottoman state utilized the *timar* system to tax the rural population and support a large provincial army in these state lands. Under this system, *sipahis*, state employees often chosen for their wartime valor, lived in the rural areas, collected taxes from the agricultural producers, and spent the revenues locally on the training and equipment of a predetermined number of soldiers as well as their own maintenance. The Ottoman central administration did not attempt to impose the *timar* regime in all of the conquered territories, however. In many of the more distant areas such as Eastern Anatolia, the Ottomans were eager to collect taxes but altered the existing land regimes either to a limited extent or not at all. The most important reason for this preference was the desire to avoid economic disruption and possible popular unrest. It was also not clear whether the central government had the fiscal, administrative, and economic resources to establish a new regime in these areas.

Despite the decline in the power of the central government and the rise of urban notables (ayan) in the provinces during the seventeenth and especially the eighteenth centuries, the central administration refused to recognize the conversion of these state lands to private property, with the exception of orchards and vineyards. Most important, the rights to the cultivation of these lands passed from father to son but they usually could not be bought and sold in the market. Law and the judicial system, which remained mostly under the control of the central administration, played an important role in this struggle. Records of the Islamic courts provide details of some cases of land sales during the early modern era, but these are limited in number. In contrast, urban real estate as well as orchards and vineyards changed hands quite easily. The urban notables acquired economic power through their control of the tax collection process. Over time, many notables began to increase their control of agricultural land which was being cultivated by peasant families. However, records listing the assets of the provincial notables make clear that, in most cases, privately owned land was often a small part of their assets. In other words, the ayan were unable to translate their rising economic as well as administrative and political power into changes in law and to long-term control if not ownership of agricultural land (Keyder and Tabak 1991, pp. 1–16; Coşgel 2011, 158–77). Changes in formal institutions of land tenure thus remained limited until the nineteenth century.

Another important category on land was the vakıf, or pious foundation. Islamic law allowed individuals who had private property including land under private ownership to convert some or all of these assets to vakıf status and direct their income in perpetuity for a predetermined social service. Many of the urban services were supplied by vakıfs during the Ottoman era. Vakıf assets were considered sacred and were protected from confiscations by the state which were directed most often to the assets of state employees. At the time of the endowment, private ownership terminated. A board of trustees was then appointed to rent out or otherwise manage the property and direct the revenues toward the designated purpose. Control of the board of trustees over vakıf lands usually weakened over time and tenants began to enjoy greater autonomy and pay less rent. Despite occasional state expropriation, substantial amounts of agricultural land as well as urban real estate remained under vakıf status. However, the extent of both vakıf lands and legally recognized private property on land remained small in relation to land under state ownership until the nineteenth century (İnalcık 1994, pp. 103–53).

Private Finance

It has often been assumed that the prohibition of interest in Islam prevented the development of credit, or at best, imposed rigid obstacles in its way. Similarly, the apparent absence of deposit banking and lending by banks has led many observers to conclude that financial institutions and instruments were, by and large, absent in Islamic societies. While usury and interest are sharply denounced in a number of passages in the Qur'an and in all subsequent Islamic religious writings, already in the medieval era, Islamic law had provided several means by which the anti-usury prohibition could be circumvented just as the same prohibitions were circumvented in Europe in the late medieval period. Various legal fictions, based primarily on the model of the "double-sale" were, if not enthusiastically endorsed by jurists, at least not declared invalid. Jared Rubin has argued further that because the Middle East rulers continued to rely on the legitimacy provided by the religious authorities, they did not completely eliminate the ban on interest. It is clear, however, that neither the Islamic prohibitions against interest and usury nor the absence of formal banking institutions prevented the expansion of credit and trade in the medieval Middle East (Udovitch 1970; Rubin 2011, pp. 1310–39).

Similarly, neither the Islamic prohibitions against interest and usury nor the absence of formal banking institutions prevented the expansion of credit in Ottoman society. Utilizing the Islamic court records, the late Ronald Jennings has shown that dense networks of lenders and borrowers flourished in and around the Anatolian cities of Kayseri, Karaman, Amasya, and Trabzon during the sixteenth century. Most lending and borrowing was small scale and interest was regularly charged on credit, with the consent and approval of the courts and the ulema. In their dealings with the court the participants felt no need to conceal interest or resort to tricks in order to clear legal hurdles. Annual rates of interest ranged from 10 percent to 20 percent (Jennings 1973, pp. 168–216).

One important provider of loans in Istanbul and the Anatolian urban centers were the cash vakıfs, pious foundations established with the explicit purpose of lending their cash assets and using the interest income to fulfill their goals. The cash vakıfs were a bottom-up Ottoman innovation and began to be approved by the Ottoman courts in the early part of the fifteenth century. By the end of the sixteenth century, they had become popular all over Anatolia and the Balkan provinces. The cash vakıfs rarely lent to entrepreneurs, however; they provided mostly consumption credit. Despite the pragmatism, the cash vakıfs faced serious shortcomings. The interest they charged was fixed by the original founders and could not respond to later changes in market conditions. More important, their capital was limited primarily to the original endowment and whatever extra could be added by re-investing the profits and other marginal means. Moreover, in Bursa, during the eighteenth century, for example, the cash vakıfs began to allocate the available funds increasingly to their administrators, who then used the borrowed funds to lend at higher rates of interest to large-scale moneylenders at Istanbul. They then pooled the funds to finance larger ventures, most significantly, long-distance trade and tax farming. As the borrowing requirements of the central government rose sharply later in the same century, the cash vakıfs responded to the new and growing demand. Financiers began pooling the funds of large numbers of small cash vakıfs and lending these funds to the central government (Çizakça 1995, pp. 313–54; Mandaville 1979, pp. 289–308).

Even though an insurmountable barrier did not exist against the use of interest-bearing loans for commercial credit, this alternative was not pursued in the medieval Islamic world and in the Ottoman Empire. Instead, numerous other commercial techniques were developed initially by private networks which played the same role as interest-bearing loans and thus made the use of loans unnecessary. These included a variety of business partnership forms and credit arrangements, transfers of debt and letters of credit, all of which were sanctioned by religious theory. Ottoman merchants widely used these business partnerships, practiced in the Islamic world since the classical era (Udovitch 1970, pp. 170–217; Çizakça 1996, pp. 65–76). There were some innovations over the centuries; for example, some interesting combinations of the Islamic business partnership *mudaraba* and putting-out activities were developed. New forms of private ownership of productive assets within the guild system called *gedik* emerged in the Istanbul region during the eighteenth century. Ottoman institutions of private finance thus reflected a high degree of pragmatism and the willingness to circumvent the Islamic prohibition on interest. However, there was limited change in the institutions of lending and in partnership forms. Like the cash vakıfs, Ottoman business partnerships remained small in scale and of short duration (Çizakça 1995, pp. 313–54; Gedikli 1998, pp. 85–120; Agir 2018, pp. 133–56).

Historians and social scientists have explored the reasons why there was little change in the Islamic forms of private finance during the Ottoman era. One explanation focuses on the persistent simplicity and smallness of Islamic commercial partnerships and adds that the absence of an Islamic concept of corporation inhibited the emergence of indigenous business corporations as alternatives to partnerships. In other words, banking did not emerge both because financial partnerships remained small and simple, and because the corporate form of organization was not an available option (Kuran 2011, pp. 63–77, -117–66). Murat Çizakça has also focused on the continued dominance of small-scale firms or partnerships. He has argued, however, that because growth opportunities remained limited, the firms did not grow and demand for changes in institutions of private finance remained weak (Çizakça 1996, pp. 65–85). A comparison of these two approaches suggests that the causal relationship between institutions and economic development was not one-directional. Just as institutions influenced the degree and direction of economic development, economic development or its absence also influenced the institutions and their evolution. Another important reason for the limited nature of institutional changes in this area was that the economic elites were never in a position to influence the state elites and push for institutional changes that would favor the growth of the private sector. Because the state elites were able to retain their leading position in Ottoman society and politics, the influence of various social groups, not only of landowners but also of merchants, manufacturers, and money changers, over economic matters, and more generally over the policies of the central government, remained limited.

Tax Collection and State Borrowing

One important reason why the Ottomans were able to keep unified an empire that spread across three continents until the nineteenth century was their flexibility, pragmatism, and tradition of negotiation in the face of threats and dangers, both internal and external. The Ottomans displayed these characteristics from their early days. During the period of conquest and expansion, they did not refrain from learning from others or borrowing the institutions of others, and in places where they were not able to establish their sovereignty, they negotiated with the local elites and tried to secure the support of at least some of them. While the Ottomans prevented the Muslim population from using the printing press for centuries, closing their door to one of the most important pre–Industrial Revolution technologies as I discussed earlier in this chapter, they continued to closely follow and adopt the recent military technologies, not only in the fifteenth and sixteenth centuries, but also in the seventeenth and eighteenth centuries (Barkey 1994, pp. 229–42; Grant 1999, pp. 179–201; Agoston 2003, pp. 15–31).

This flexibility and pragmatism as well as the selective nature of institutional change in the Ottoman Empire during the early modern era can be seen most clearly in the evolution of Ottoman institutions of tax collection and domestic borrowing by the state. Until the end of the sixteenth century, wars and the Ottoman army were largely financed by taxes collected locally and returned to the army locally under the *timar* system. With the changes in military technology during the sixteenth century and the need to maintain larger, permanent armies at the center, however, pressures increased to collect a larger part of the rural taxes at the center. Deterioration of state finances and frequent wars also increased the pressures on the central government to take greater advantage of the tax-farming system for the purposes of domestic borrowing. Further steps were taken toward using future tax revenues for present borrowing with the introduction, at the end of the seventeenth century, of the *malikane* system in which the revenue source began to be farmed out on a lifetime basis in return for a large initial payment to be followed by annual payments. In comparison to the straightforward tax-farming system, the *malikane* represented an important shift toward longer term borrowing by the state (Özvar 2003, pp. 29–92).

With the extension of their term and the introduction of larger advance payments, the long-term financing of the *malikane* contracts assumed even greater importance. The option of borrowing in the European financial markets was not available to the Ottoman government until the middle of the nineteenth century. Consequently, the private financiers began to play an increasingly important role in the tax collection process. Over the course of the eighteenth century, some 1,000–2,000 Istanbul-based individuals, together with some 5,000–10,000 individuals based in the provinces, as well as innumerable contractors, agents, financiers, accountants, and managers, controlled an important share of the state's revenues. This grand coalition of Istanbul-based elites and the rising elites in the provinces constituted a semi-privatized but interdependent component of the regime. For both the well-connected individuals in the capital city and those in the provinces, getting a piece of government tax revenues became an activity more lucrative than investing in agriculture, trade, or manufacturing. The central government did not have the power to take control of the tax collection process. The various elites both in the capital and in the provinces were unable or unwilling to arrive at a different solution (Salzman 1993, pp. 393–423; Balla and Johnson 2009, pp. 809–45).

Nonetheless, the central government continued to experiment with other methods for tax collection and domestic borrowing during the eighteenth century. Rising military expenditures and increasing fiscal pressures during wartime were once again responsible for the institutional changes. After the end of the war of 1768–1774, which had dramatically exposed the military as well as financial weaknesses of the Ottoman system, the financial bureaucracy started a new and related system of long-term domestic borrowing called *esham*. In this system, the annual revenues of a tax source were divided into a large number of shares which sold to the public for the lifetime of the buyers while the revenues continued to be collected by tax farmers. As the linkage between the annual government payments to *esham* holders and the underlying revenues of the tax source weakened, the *esham* increasingly resembled a life-term annuity quite popular in many European countries of the period. Eager to ensure that the Islamic law prohibition against interest rates and usury did not apply to the new instrument, the government declared that an *esham* share was not structured as a loan since the government had the option to redeem it whenever it wished. The markets embraced the new instrument quickly (Genç 1995, pp. 376–80).

The evolution of Ottoman institutions of tax collection and state borrowing from short-term tax farming to lifetime tax farms to government borrowing with tax revenues as collateral and finally to government annuities and bonds in the early nineteenth century, despite the apparent prohibition of interest by Islamic law, illustrates the state's pragmatism as well as its ability and willingness to reorganize in response to changing circumstances, albeit slowly and often with considerable time lags. The central administration not only experimented with new fiscal and financial institutions, but it was also willing to come to terms with the limits of its power by entering into broad alliances with elites and financiers in the capital city as well as those in the provinces in order to finance its urgent needs, which escalated rapidly and dramatically during periods of war. However, there were limits to how much could be achieved with pragmatism and flexibility alone. At the end of the eighteenth century, the Ottoman central administration, along with Poland, collected the lowest level of taxes in Europe on a per capita basis. Low tax collections led to diminished military power. The Ottomans frequently lost territory in the wars they fought against Russia and Austria in the second half of the eighteenth century. At the end of the eighteenth century, the Ottoman Empire, like Poland, was in serious danger of dismemberment and disintegration (Pamuk 2000, pp. 77–87; Karaman and Pamuk 2010, pp. 593–618).

Local Tax Collection

Changes in the arrangements regarding the collection of various taxes at the local level provides another good example of how Ottoman fiscal institutions evolved during the early modern era, depending on the changing balances of power between the central administration and the rising urban notables in the provinces. Until the sixteenth century, the tax obligations of the local population were defined in detail in the law codes issued separately for each province. With the decline in the power of the central government and its local representatives, the provincial tax registers became increasingly dated. With the rise of urban provincial notables in the seventeenth century, new taxes and new methods of collection thus emerged. One of the most important changes was the expansion of lump-sum tax collection as a result of which officers, tax collectors, and tax farmers began to ask provincial communities to deliver aggregate amounts for tax obligations and left the collection and apportionment of the taxes to community leaders (Yaycioglu 2016, pp. 117–33).

Local courts and judges who were appointed by the central government and who served as a channel for the central government to communicate with the local communities played a key role in this process. They brought in the court Muslim notables who were often the tax farmers responsible for the collection of taxes together with the community leaders in order to decide on the amounts due and oversee the delivery of the collected revenues. Most notables worked with moneylenders to ensure timely delivery of tax revenues to the central government, especially during extraordinary times such as wars. Some of the local communities coincided with the religious communities, as in the collection of head tax on non-Muslims, but many other communities were made up of people from diverse backgrounds. While households within each community were expected to pay taxes in proportion to their income and wealth, the communities were expected to reach consensus through negotiation. As a result, it was the communities and their leaders and not the state that ultimately decided on payment amounts. Some of the taxes thus collected were then spent for local needs, including municipal services. The rest was taken by the local notables who then delivered the promised amount to the central government and kept the rest. The state's inability to supply or enforce the formal institutions of tax collection combined with the rise of new local elites thus led to a new arrangement in which the privately organized arrangements, typically built from within communities and rooted in informal social networks, coexisted and interacted with the formal institutions.

One striking conclusion that emerges from the review of these four sets of institutions is the sharp contrast between the extensive changes in the institutions of public finance and the limited changes in the institutions of private finance during the early modern era. For one thing, this contrast makes it difficult to explain the evolution of institutions and the pattern of long-term economic development in terms of the rigidities of Islam or Islamic law. Instead, such contrasts need to be explained either in terms of the different levels of demand for different kinds of institutional changes and/or in terms of political economy and the disparities between the powers of state elites in comparison to the powers of elites in the private sector. Second, while flexibility and pragmatism enabled the state elites to retain power and keep the empire together until the modern era, it needs to be recognized that most of this pragmatism and flexibility was utilized for the defense of the existing traditional order. Institutional changes that may threaten the leading position of the central bureaucracy position were resisted more forcefully than others. Institutional change thus remained selective and many of the key institutions of the Ottoman order such as state ownership of land, urban guilds, and restrictions on private capital accumulation remained intact until the nineteenth century.

On the Eve of the Industrial Revolution

Recent studies on wages and per capita incomes in Europe and Turkey during the early modern era have provided new insights into their trajectories before the Industrial Revolution. These studies show that wages in northwestern Europe were slightly higher than those in Turkey in the sixteenth century. While urban wages and per capita incomes in Turkey fluctuated, they rose in northwestern Europe, widening the gap before the nineteenth century. In contrast, the differences between Turkey and the rest of the continent were limited and they did not increase very much until the Industrial Revolution.

The purchasing power of the wages of skilled and unskilled construction workers in the leading cities of southern Europe (Italy and Spain) and northwestern Europe (Britain and Holland) were approximately 50 percent higher than those in Istanbul during the sixteenth century. These differences were primarily due to the differences in productivity in the agricultural sector where, on both sides, the largest share of the population was earning a living. While wages in Istanbul and other cities in Turkey fluctuated during the following centuries, urban wages in Britain and the Netherlands increased and

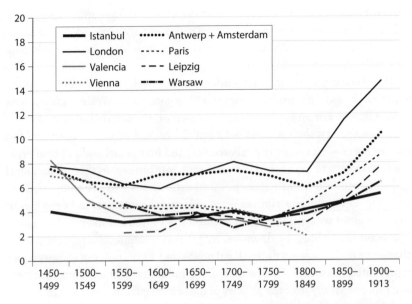

FIGURE 3.1. Real Wages of Unskilled Construction Workers in Istanbul and Other
European Cities, 1450–1913. Sources: Özmucur and Pamuk 2002; Allen 2001.

created a gap of 2:1 or even higher before the Industrial Revolution. In contrast, wages in southern Europe declined and urban wages in Turkey and central, eastern, and southern Europe remained close until the nineteenth century (figure 3.1).

For the period before 1820, aggregate-level production and even taxation
data are not available for constructing estimates of total GDP for the area
within the present-day borders of Turkey. Moreover, population series are not
sufficiently reliable. Under the circumstances, I began by estimating a simple
relationship, for six European countries, between changes in the GDP per
capita on the one hand, and changes in urban unskilled real wages and urbanization rates on the other. I then applied this relationship to Turkey by making use of urban unskilled wage series for Istanbul and estimates for urbanization rates for Turkey as a whole to arrive at estimates of GDP per capita.
During the three centuries from 1500 to 1820, per capita income in Turkey is
estimated to have fluctuated between one and half and two times' subsistence.
During the same period, in northwestern European countries, especially in
Britain and the Netherlands, per capita income was estimated to have increased a total of 60–80 percent, to three to four times subsistence. Similar
studies on southern European countries Spain and Italy and on other parts of
the continent indicate that per capita incomes did not show a strong upward

trend in those regions (Pamuk 2009; Broadberry et al. 2015, appendixes). The differences in both wages and per capita incomes between Turkey and all regions of Europe, especially northwestern Europe, would increase considerably during the century until World War I.

This chapter has argued that while many institutional changes took place in the early modern Ottoman Empire, a divergence with Western Europe was unmistakable. For an explanation, it focused on the internal organization of Ottoman society, the relations between the central administration and the various elites—especially the urban elites, and how social and political organization may have influenced the economic institutions. In the late medieval and early modern Middle East, political institutions and economic policies and practices of the government often reflected the interests and priorities of the state elites who ruled with or without the support of the religious elites. The economic elites, landowners, merchants, manufacturers, and money changers enjoyed a good deal of local power and autonomy, but they were not represented in central government. Their influence over economic matters, and more generally over the policies of the central government, remained limited. Institutional change thus remained selective and reflected, above all, the interests and priorities of the state and the state elites.

Differences in government policies and the institutional environment between Western Europe and the Middle East had remained limited until the early modern era. With the rise of the Atlantic trade, however, the merchants in northwestern European countries increased their economic and political power substantially. They were then able not only to bring about major institutional changes in their countries but also to induce their governments to defend and develop their commercial interests in the Middle East more forcefully. Merchants of the region thus found it even more difficult to compete against them after the sixteenth century. As they began to lag behind the European merchants even in their own region, it became even more difficult for them to provide input into their government's trade policies or change the commercial or economic institutions in the direction they preferred.

Many of the key institutions of the traditional order such as state ownership of land, urban guilds, and restrictions on private capital accumulation remained intact until the end of the eighteenth century. While the Industrial Revolution began to unfold in Europe, local manufacturing activity in the Middle East was still mostly intact but the region was not in a position to achieve its own Industrial Revolution. Beginning early in the nineteenth century, economic policies and institutional changes in the region also began to reflect the growing power of European states and companies. As a leading political scientist of the region recently observed, one of the most important historical legacies in the Middle East today is the large discrepancy between the economic and political power of the merchants and more generally of economic elites. As was the case in the past, merchants in most parts of the modern Middle East can become wealthy but they cannot expect to attain political power or influence (Özbudun 1996, pp. 135–37). This absence, on the part of the economic elites, of political power and capacity to influence economic institutions explains better than any other single factor, better than geography or resource endowments, Islam or culture, the growing economic divergence between Western Europe and the Ottoman Empire before the Industrial Revolution.

4

Reforms and Deficits: Ottoman Response to European Challenges

THE INDUSTRIAL REVOLUTION PLAYED A key role in the spread of economic growth, first in Western Europe and later and to a lesser extent in the rest of the world during the nineteenth century. Beginning in the late eighteenth century, the Industrial Revolution transformed first Britain and then other economies of Western Europe into mass producers of manufactured products. External markets played an important role in the development of the British cotton textile industry since the eighteenth century. After the end of the Napoleonic Wars, Britain and other western European countries turned their attention to the rest of the world as they sought markets for their manufactured products and cheap sources of food and raw materials. Trade between the European manufactured products and agricultural commodities of the rest of the world thus expanded at an unprecedented pace until World War I. Technological changes in maritime and overland transportation including steamships and the construction of railroads in Europe and elsewhere also contributed to the expansion of this trade (Findlay and O'Rourke 2007, pp. 311–428; Broadberry and O'Rourke 2010, vol. 1; Allen 2011; Berend 2013; Hobsbawm 1968; Osterhammel 2014).

The growing economic linkages between industrializing European economies and the rest of the world were not limited to trade. Export of capital from western European countries became increasingly important especially in the second half of the nineteenth century. Approximately 40 percent of the capital that was exported from Europe was lent to non-European states. European financiers also invested large amounts in infrastructure such as railways and ports in the rest of the world, aiming to expand international trade. In contrast, European capital invested directly in production activities such as agriculture or industry in the rest of the world remained limited until World War I. The spread of monetary institutions such as bimetallism and the gold standard facilitated the growth of both international trade and international investment (Eichengreen 2008, pp. 6–42).

The unprecedented expansion of foreign trade and foreign investment led to new specializations and production patterns in the countries of the periphery. While a higher share of agricultural production began to be directed toward markets, both domestic and global, traditional crafts began to decline in the face of growing competition from manufactured products originating in Europe. By reducing the cost of transportation to the hinterland, the railways built by European companies brought agricultural or mineral resources-rich regions closer to European ports like Manchester, Marseilles, or Hamburg, thus playing an important role in their integration into a new division of labor. In contrast, the spread of industrialization around the world was quite uneven. The extent to which industrialization proceeded in different parts of the world can help explain a large part of the variation in economic growth observed around the world during the century until World War I (Kemp 1983, 1993; Williamson 2006, pp. 7–86; Williamson 2011, pp. 65–86).

The Industrial Revolution thus led to sustained increases in per capita production and income both in Western Europe and to a lesser extent in the rest of the world. For the century from the end of the Napoleonic Wars until World War I, the annual rate of increase in GDP per capita in Western Europe and North America averaged above 1 percent, for a total increase of about 200 percent. In southern and eastern Europe, economic growth began later and proceeded more slowly. The gap between Western Europe and the rest of the continent thus widened in the course of the century. In comparison to Western Europe and North America, per capita incomes in the rest of the world increased more slowly or did not increase at all. As a result, the gap between Western Europe and the rest of the world also widened significantly until World War I (Maddison 2007, pp. 375–86).

For Ottoman society and economy, the nineteenth century was very different from earlier periods. Despite the frequent wars during the seventeenth and eighteenth centuries, the traditional structures of Ottoman society, economy, and state had remained mostly intact. During the century from the 1820s to World War I, in contrast, they were confronted with the growing military, political, and economic power of Western Europe. The economy began to open up to a new order originating in Western Europe.

The Ottoman government, faced with the challenges from provincial notables and independence movements that were gaining momentum in the Balkans, on the one hand, and the growing military and economic power of Western Europe, on the other, began to implement a series of reforms in the early decades of the nineteenth century. These reforms and the opening of the economy began to transform the political and economic institutions very rapidly. The social and economic roots of modern Turkey thus need to be sought, first and foremost, in the changes that took place during the nineteenth century. This chapter will examine the Ottoman reforms as well as the efforts to finance them. The next chapter will examine the economic consequences of the reforms and the opening of the economy to international trade and investment. Chapter 6 will then review the record in economic growth, income distribution, and human development for the areas within present-day borders of Turkey in both absolute and relative terms. It will also evaluate the role of institutions and institutional change in economic development during the century until World War I.

Ottoman Reforms and Centralization

From the beginning of the nineteenth century, the Ottoman government was confronted with important developments at home and abroad. As a result of the technological advances brought on by the Industrial Revolution, Western Europe had made significant strides in the economic and military fields. The Ottomans could not yet foresee the implications of the economic changes in Western Europe, but Napoleon's invasion of Egypt in 1798 illustrated clearly the consequences of European military advances. Another issue of concern for the Ottomans was the policy of southern expansion long pursued by Russia. From the late 1760s until the end of the 1820s, the Ottomans frequently went to war with Russia and they were defeated in many of these conflicts. Aside from the large territories ceded to Russia, the Treaty of Küçük Kaynarca, signed in 1774, had forced the Ottoman government to give up its monopoly on trade and shipping in the Black Sea and to accept the principle that Russia could defend the rights of the Orthodox Christian population in the Ottoman Empire.

Inside the empire, provincial notables and local lords were acting independently of the central government and effectively controlled large territories in many regions, retaining a major share of tax revenues. The power of provincial notables reached its pinnacle with the Charter of Alliance signed between them and the central government in 1808. Some of the provincial notables supported the central government, but many others opposed it. As long as the central government was unable to increase its tax revenues, it seemed impossible to increase its military power, both domestically and abroad. In Anatolia, foreign trade remained limited in the eighteenth century, but trade between the Balkan provinces of the empire and Western Europe was increasing steadily. The development of trade strengthened the position of non-Muslim merchants in the Balkans and, inspired by the currents of thought unleashed by the French Revolution, they began to take the lead in nationalist movements aiming to secede from the Ottoman Empire. As these movements secured the support of Western European countries, the fight for independence began first in Serbia, followed by Greece and later Romania.

The reformist sultan Selim III had tried to create a new army called *Nizam-ı Cedid*, or the New Order, to replace the Janissaries but was killed by them in 1808. His successor sultan Mahmud II and his aides were aware that the empire could break up. In response, they sought to increase the power of the central government against both external and domestic challenges. They knew that the government needed to build a powerful army for this purpose and increase its tax revenues at the expense of the local groups in the provinces. The reforms pursued by the governor of Egypt who was also fighting the central government in Istanbul provided Mahmud II with a powerful model.

Muhammad Ali Pasha, an officer of the Ottoman army in Egypt, had seized the governorship after Napoleon and the French armies were driven out, declared independence from Istanbul, and launched a reform program aimed at establishing a powerful state. Thanks to measures designed to improve the efficiency of tax collection and the creation of state monopolies in foreign trade, he had bolstered the state finances. With the financial resources he raised, Muhammad Ali established a number of state industrial enterprises and, above all, a strong army and navy. He successfully resisted the pressure from European countries and especially from Britain, whose commercial interests were harmed by the trade monopolies, inflicted heavy defeats on the Ottoman armies, and forced Istanbul to recognize his son as the governor of Syria in 1833 (Panza and Williamson 2015, pp. 79–100).

During his more than thirty-year reign, Mahmud II took major steps in pursuit of the reforms inspired by a Western model. His earliest initiatives also focused on the military. In 1826, Mahmud II dissolved the Janissary corps, which was resisting the introduction of Western methods in the army. Within a short time, a new army of 75,000 men was formed, trained by officers brought from Europe. Military schools were established to continue to train the army. To strengthen the central government, politically and financially, the power of local notables had to be curbed and the influence of Istanbul had to be extended to the provinces. From the end of the 1820s, Mahmud II thus focused on destroying the economic and financial bases of the opposition. The right to collect taxes in the name of the state was the main source of economic power for the provincial notables. Mahmud II began to withdraw the authority to collect taxes from the more powerful notable families and gave it to others, most often their local rivals. Across the Balkans and Anatolia, some of the vast tracts of land, which were effectively controlled by the notables, were seized and distributed to local peasants (Zürcher 2004, pp. 36–70; Davison 1963, pp. 36–52; Hourani 1966).

In addition to the notables in the provinces and the janissaries, the Otto-man centralization drive of the nineteenth century also moved against the religious hierarchy or ulema. With the abolition of the janissaries, the ulema, who had effectively opposed earlier attempts at reform, lost a powerful ally. To curb their power further, the assets, mostly land and buildings, of the vakıfs (or pious foundations), were brought under the control of the central govern-ment. A new ministry was created in 1831 to oversee these assets and channel at least some of their revenues to the central treasury.

After the top-down initiatives by sultans Selim III and Mahmud II, the Ot-toman reform efforts during the middle decades of the century were led by three grand viziers, Reşit, Ali, and Fuat Pashas and the bureaucracy. With the proclamation of the Tanzimat (literally re-organization) in 1839, the govern-ment promised to grant all Ottoman subjects the same basic rights and equal-ity before the law, irrespective of their religion. The Tanzimat also promised to strengthen the property rights of all subjects and formally ended the centuries-old custom of confiscating the wealth of government officials who had lost their positions and, at times, even the wealth of the provincial nota-bles. The government also promised to reform the tax-farming system and end the ongoing abuses in tax collection. In the context of equal rights, the *cizye* or head tax collected from non-Muslim citizens was also abolished. Because the central government did not want to draft non-Muslims into the army, however, a new tax, called the *bedelat-i askeriyye*, was soon imposed (Zürcher 2004, pp. 50–70; İnalcık and Seyitdanlıoğlu 2006). Building a modern and more powerful army required large resources that could be raised only with a more efficient and better functioning system of taxation, which in turn could be achieved only through a more modern and efficient central and provincial bureaucracy. The main aim in central administration reforms was rationaliza-tion and specialization of the government departments, including a complete set of ministries based on the European model. Reform efforts thus began to extend from the fields of military and central administration to taxation and provincial administration, to education, the judiciary, and communications (Davison 1963, pp. 36–52, 136–71; Berkes 1964, pp. 89–200; Shaw 1971, pp. 71–199; Zürcher 2004, pp. 39–42; Findley 1980, 69–220; Puryear 1935; Ortaylı 1983).

The Tanzimat Decree also abolished the forced labor and other obliga-tions that tenants and agricultural laborers owed to landowners. Forced labor practices were not common in Anatolia but were encountered more fre-quently in the Balkans. The abolition of forced labor created expectations among the peasantry that the state would also abolish some of the taxes it collected. When it became clear that Istanbul had no such intention, how-ever, peasants as well as the urban population engaged in many waves of rebellion and resistance during the 1840s and 1850s (İnalcık 1973, pp. 97–128; Uzun 2002, pp. 1–38).

Important changes were made in the judicial system, many of them related to the changing position of the non-Muslim communities. The empire had always been ruled under a dual system with sultanic decrees functioning side by side with Islamic law, *shariat*. In the new era, Islamic law was not abrogated but its scope was limited to family law. A new commercial code and a new maritime code were introduced along European lines. In addition, mixed tribunals were introduced for commercial cases involving foreigners. Not only the institutions of the state but also those of the Christian *millets* began to be secularized, most importantly those of the Armenian and Greek communities.

The reforms also led to changes in political institutions, but only briefly. A constitution was adopted, and a parliament with elected as well as appointed members opened in 1876, but these were suspended by sultan Abdulhamid II after only one year. Power then returned to the palace. Abdulhamid was well aware that many Muslims felt left behind the non-Muslims as the economy opened to foreign trade and commercialization of agriculture proceeded unevenly. In response, he tried to make use of Islam to mobilize political support both domestically and also in foreign policy realms. The Tanzimat reforms had already eroded the power of the ulema. Abdulhamid did not aim to obtain the support of the ulema. He recognized, instead, the growing discontent among the conservative Muslims and wanted to obtain their support. He tried to strengthen the Islamic character of the state and reach out to the Muslim peasants and the land-based Muslim elites across the empire. He supported the religious orders and networks. While he is known as a conservative and authoritarian sultan, Abdulhamid II continued the reforms on many fronts. The spread of education especially to the Muslim population was an important component of the reforms he directed until the Young Turk Revolution of 1908. He also tried to recruit the sons of provincial notables into the new elites by broadening the education system (Karpat 2001, pp. 208–52).

The diffusion of elementary schools and more generally Ottoman efforts at educational reform faced two major challenges, however: the creation of a new school system and new curriculum that would offer practical and natural scientific content, and the expansion of public schools in the provinces and rural areas. With regard to the first, primary schools traditionally had been considered within the religious realm and were controlled by pious foundations. Attempts to reform these Quran schools were not successful. The alternative was to establish new primary schools beginning in 1872. The challenge of expanding public schools in the provinces and especially in the rural areas was not overcome until the end of the empire (Somel 2001; Fortna 2010, pp. 15–26).

In addition to the schools for the Muslim population, each of the non-Muslim communities, Greeks, Armenians, and Jews, developed their separate modern school systems during the nineteenth century. Rates of schooling and literacy as well as the diffusion of the new schools into the provinces were higher in each of the non-Muslim communities than those of the Muslims. The teaching of Turkish, the official language, in these schools did not start until the 1890s, however. In addition, schools run by European and American missionaries directed at the non-Muslim population expanded. American missionary schools began to educate a significant share of the Armenian population, especially in Eastern Anatolia where the Armenians accounted for a significant share of the population.

The modern schools of higher education also began to turn out graduates to staff the bureaucracy and the military at different levels. Students in these military and other schools were taught subjects such as modern physics, medicine, and biology which inevitably induced a rationalist and positivist mentality in the students. In addition, schools of agriculture at different levels began to teach the more recent techniques of cultivation mostly to the children of more prosperous farmers. Questions have been raised about the contents of the new educational system as well as its products, however. It has been argued, for example, that the new system of public education was most successful in producing individuals believed to be in a patrimonial state and who could best serve in the civil service. The same system also educated many graduates with a progressivist worldview who believed in the role of the state to organize and transform society and who played key roles in the emergence of the new nation-state after World War I (Somel 2001).

It would be wrong to attribute these reform efforts to foreign pressure alone. Although obtaining European and especially British support in international affairs was an important motive, this reform program was also the result of genuine belief on the part of the high-level officials that the only way to save the empire was through European-style institutional change. The effectiveness of the reforms differed hugely from province to province and from period to period, with the main determinant appearing to be the abilities of the government official in charge. Some provincial administrators gained a reputation for efficiency and honesty wherever they went. Their administration could sometimes yield spectacular results in terms of public works programs, improved health and safety, and local institutions of banking as well as tax revenues for the state. But these were the exceptions rather than the rule (Zürcher 2004, pp. 60–61).

Ultimately, the reform efforts faced two major handicaps which persisted throughout the century. First, they were expensive but lacked a strong fiscal and economic basis. The existing resources of the government were insufficient for the task and, as a result, fiscal problems remained a permanent part of the scene. Second, the reforms were not the result of popular pressure and were ultimately the choice of the sultan and associates at the top who believed that the empire had to be saved by the adoption of European methods and institutions. The design and implementation of the reforms remained top-down and they were not fully embraced by the public at large. In fact, they were often resisted by the conservative elites in the provinces and the rural areas.

Changes in Economic Institutions

The most important change in Ottoman economic institutions during the reform era was the signing of the Baltalimanı Free Trade Treaty with Great Britain in 1838, just before the proclamation of the Tanzimat. It was followed by other free trade treaties containing similar provisions, signed with France and other European states. The Baltalimanı Treaty changed the Ottoman customs regime for the rest of the nineteenth century. Before 1838, the Ottoman state collected customs duties of 3 percent on both imports and exports. In addition, local and foreign merchants had to pay an 8 percent internal customs tax when transferring products from one region of the empire to another. The Baltalimanı Treaty increased the tax on exports to 12 percent while fixing the duty on imports at 5 percent. In addition, while local merchants continued to pay internal customs, foreign merchants were exempted from this practice. Foreign, especially European, merchants thus secured an important privilege. By lowering customs duties and abolishing extraordinary taxes, the treaty was making it easier for external trade to develop. Furthermore, the Ottoman state was losing an important source of revenues that it turned to especially during periods of financial crisis. In the next conflict, the Crimean War, the state was unable to collect taxes on foreign trade and these fiscal pressures made it easier to begin borrowing in the European financial markets (Pamuk 1987, pp. 18–21; Kurmuş 1983, pp. 411–17).

Another important change introduced by the Baltalimanı Treaty was the elimination of the *Yed-i Vahit system*, which had allowed the state to grant a private individual a monopoly for the trade of a given region. These monopolies began to be granted for fiscal reasons during the late eighteenth century. Moreover, in years when certain raw materials or food items were in short supply, the export of these products could be prohibited. In wartime, exceptional taxes could also be applied to both exports and imports in order to secure additional receipts for the treasury. With the Baltalimanı Treaty, this regime of monopolies on foreign trade was being abolished and the Ottoman government gave up the right to impose extraordinary taxes or limitations.

Because the treaty could not be terminated unilaterally, in 1838 the Ottoman government also gave up the option of following an independent foreign trade policy at a later date. After the treaty was signed, European states waited for an opportunity to lower customs duties further. During the financial crisis and the political turmoil in Lebanon in 1860–61, the Ottoman state agreed to lower the customs duties collected on exports to 1 percent, where it remained until World War I. When medium-sized manufacturing establishments and factories using the new technology began to emerge in Anatolia and in other regions of the empire toward the end of the nineteenth century, customs duties could not be raised to protect them. The ad valorem taxes collected on all imports increased from 5 percent to 8 percent in 1861, then to 11 percent in 1905 and 15 percent in 1908. Partly because of the low levels of tariffs, industrialization attempts progressed very slowly until World War I. During the peace negotiations at Lausanne in 1922–23, European states preferred to keep Turkey's markets open and were reluctant to give the new nation-state the right to set its own foreign trade policies. Turkey's government began to set its own tariffs only in 1929.

The motives of the Ottoman government in signing this treaty have long been debated. Did Grand Vizier Reşit Pasha and other high-level officials who would later launch the Tanzimat believe in the benefits of free trade, or were they coerced by Britain? It would be a mistake to argue that the Ottoman government signed the free trade treaty in a moment of confusion or with excessively optimistic expectations regarding its longer-term consequences. The Ottoman government faced a severe political and military crisis during the 1830s and needed the support of the British government to keep the empire together. In many ways, the free trade treaty was the price to be paid for that support.

Great Britain had emerged from the Napoleonic Wars with an unrivaled position in the world markets. British commercial and industrial capital had been looking for markets outside Europe. In the period from the 1820s to the 1840s, the British government signed a number of free trade treaties with countries ranging from South America to China, reaching agreements with local governments whenever possible and resorting to gunboat diplomacy if necessary. Trade between Great Britain and the Ottoman Empire had grown rapidly since the 1820s. Nonetheless, British merchants complained about the Ottoman government's interventionism and the obstacles it set in their way, and they wanted long-term legal framework for trade (Hobsbawm 1968; Bailey 1940; Puryear 1969).

The long-awaited opportunity for British diplomacy was provided by Muhammad Ali Pasha, the governor of Egypt, whose military power had become a serious threat to the Ottoman dynasty. After the defeats it suffered against Muhammad Ali earlier in the 1830s, the Ottoman government faced the risk of losing not only Egypt and Syria but also large parts Anatolia. There was even the possibility that he might replace the Ottoman dynasty in Istanbul. The political situation around the eastern Mediterranean had become a severe international crisis. Confronted by Muhammad Ali Pasha, on the one hand, and Russia's growing influence on the other, the Ottoman leadership found salvation in a rapprochement with Britain. It hoped that in exchange for opening the economy, it would obtain the support of Great Britain for the territorial integrity of the empire. The British government also wanted to abolish Muhammed Ali's state monopolies on foreign trade and state industries, as they were hurting British interests in Egypt. The 1838 treaty abolished the foreign trade monopolies, destroyed the fiscal foundations of Muhammed Ali's unusual experiment, and opened Egypt's economy to trade. It also facilitated the rapid expansion of Ottoman foreign trade with Western Europe until World War I (Zürcher 2004, pp. 46–49; Puryear 1969; Owen 1981, pp. 57–76).

In other areas, political, military, and fiscal priorities continued to guide the economy-related policies of the Ottoman central government during the nineteenth century. As part of the initial Tanzimat reforms, the government moved away from fixing prices in urban markets, which was used rather frequently in the late eighteenth and early nineteenth centuries, and reliance on state intervention for the provisioning of the urban areas, toward greater emphasis on markets. In later decades, efforts were also made to promote the agricultural sector and develop the basic infrastructure such as railways, roads, ports, and urban utilities. However, fiscal limitations placed serious constraints on how much could be achieved in these areas.

Until the early decades of the nineteenth century, trade with Europe had been limited and the Ottoman guilds remained intact. The Ottoman government supported the guilds during this period as it needed them to supply the army, the palace, and the urban areas. With the rapid expansion of external trade during the nineteenth century, branches of manufacturing and trade organized around guilds declined steadily, especially in fields that faced competition from imports. The central government was unable to protect the guilds from foreign competition, but it continued to support them politically, especially in the capital. At the end of the century, the most powerful guild in the capital city, for example, was that of the port workers and not of any branch of manufacturing or trade. In most branches, the guilds survived only in name until they were formally abolished just before World War I (Quataert 1983, pp. 95–120; Quataert 1994, pp. 890–98).

The industrialization drive launched by Mohammad Ali Pasha in Egypt and the military successes he enjoyed as a result against the Ottoman army had impressed the Ottoman government. As part of the initial reforms in the 1830s and 1840s, the government imported machines using the latest technology from Europe, set up a series of state-owned factories, essentially to meet the needs of the army, the navy, and the palace. Most of these enterprises were formed in Istanbul and its surroundings, and the cotton and wool weaving plants, the fez factory, the armory, the shipyards, and the foundries were among the most important. The silk weaving plants in Hereke and the paper factory in İzmir were part of the same drive. Highly paid engineers, technicians, and even laborers were brought in from Europe to work in these factories and lead the production. Tariffs remained low and the competition from imports continued, however. Although the goods produced were bought by the state as a protection against competition from imported products, many of these factories could not sustain their operations; within a short time, they were forced to stop production. By 1850, in the words of a European observer, not much was left of this industry that was producing textiles in Turkey with European machines, European raw materials, and European master workmen (Clark 1974, pp. 65–76; Owen 1981, pp. 57–64).

Gradual elimination of taxes on trade within the empire was another component of the economic reforms. Trade within the empire had been subject to tariffs and the duties were collected at ports and customs gates on land. In the second half of the eighteenth century, as the financial difficulties of the central government intensified, these taxes had been raised, reaching their highest level at the end of the 1830s. From the 1840s onward, taxes on internal trade collected on land began to be reduced, and they were eliminated by 1874. However, customs duties on coastal trade within the empire were lifted only at the beginning of the twentieth century (Quataert 1994, pp. 798–842).

Another priority for the central government was the development of basic infrastructure, most importantly railroads but also ports, roads, and others. The government did not have the resources to build the railroads, but it actively supported and often subsidized their construction by European companies. Ports, quays, and harbor facilities, steamship lines, postal and especially telegraph service which supported long-distance trade and economic development were built up to some extent with public funds and mostly by European companies. The new infrastructure for transportation and communication also increased the capacity of the central administration to collect taxes, conscript armies, and maintain law and order.

Toward the end of the nineteenth century, the Ottoman government began to take a more direct interest in economic development and focus on the modernization of agriculture as the leading sector. In 1888, the Agricultural Bank was established by the state to provide credit mostly to medium-sized and large, market-oriented agricultural producers. The new bank opened many branches across the empire. In addition, agricultural schools were opened to educate producers in recent techniques and introduce new crops and seeds. Due to the budget constraints, however, these programs remained rather modest (Quataert 1975, pp. 210–27).

Fiscal Centralization

In the seventeenth and eighteenth centuries, the central government's ability to collect taxes had been limited. Provincial notables and other groups kept a large part of the tax revenues. Only 3 percent, or an even smaller share, of the annual production or GDP of the empire reached the central treasury, the rest was kept by the various elites including the provincial notables (Karaman and Pamuk 2010, pp. 598–618; Pamuk 2012, 317–31). In other words, the frequent fiscal crises and recurring budget deficits of this earlier period were due less to the weakness of the economy than to the weakness of the central government.

While the central government could collect very little in taxes, the reforms of the nineteenth century were quite expensive. A larger and better equipped army as well as a larger bureaucracy required large resources. As a result, an important part of the reform efforts was directed at centralizing state finances and increasing the revenues that reached the central government. The Deed of Alliance signed in 1808 was viewed as an agreement between the central government and the mostly urban notables in the provinces. In the following decades, however, neither side was eager to pursue the same course. The central government sought to increase its tax revenues not by negotiating with the notables but by undermining their power and their hold on the tax collection process. Political centralization thus went hand in hand with fiscal centralization for the rest of the century.

With the Tanzimat Decree, the central government continued its efforts to boost state finances and to undermine the foundations of the notables in the provinces. It was aware that in order to collect more taxes, it needed to collect more information about the revenue sources. As a result, detailed censuses were undertaken in both rural and urban areas to assess the tax revenue potential during the 1830s. After the proclamation of the Tanzimat, the government announced in 1840 that it would reform the tax-farming system by appointing salaried collectors. Within a short time, however, it became evident

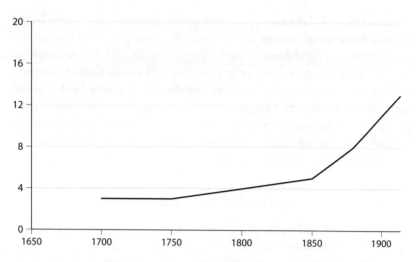

FIGURE 4.1. Fiscal Centralization in the Ottoman Empire, Revenues of the Central Government, 1700–1914 (as percentage of GDP). Source: Pamuk 2012.

that the new system was not working. The new *muhassıls* were helpless against local elements. The government was forced to resign and the new government returned to the tax-farming system and accepted the practice of sharing tax revenues with the tax farmers and various other groups.

Despite the failure of this attempt, the central government continued to try to undermine the power of provincial groups and to increase its revenues throughout the nineteenth century. Technological developments in the military, transportation, and communications such as the railways, steamships, and the telegraph, gradually shifted the balances in favor of the center. Tax farming remained in place, but the revenues retained by the tax farmers declined steadily as they were reduced from powerful regional families at the beginning of the century to modest entrepreneurs on the eve of World War I, at least in the areas within present-day borders of Turkey. In contrast, tax revenues of the central government rose slowly but steadily. My calculations suggest that after approximately one century of centralization, annual tax revenues of the central government had increased from about 3 percent early in the nineteenth century to about 12 percent of GDP on the eve of World War I (figure 4.1). The official rate of the tithe, which was the most important source of revenue for the central government, was kept constant at one-tenth throughout the nineteenth century, except in wartime. The significant rise in tax revenues was thus achieved not by raising the official rates but by steadily reducing the share of tax farmers and increasing the pressure on the mostly small and medium-sized producers. The response of the producers to increasing demands of the state varied across regions. In the coastal regions, which benefited from the commercialization of agriculture, these demands could be met more easily. On the other hand, in Eastern Anatolia, which was not near the leading ports of export, incomes increased little or stagnated. Rising demands on Armenian peasant producers by the state and by the mostly Kurdish tax farmers only contributed to the rise of ethnic tensions (Shaw 1975, pp. 421–59; Özbek 2012, 770–97; Özbek 2015, 37–91).

Budget Deficits, Money, and Debt

Even though the central government's revenues rose significantly, its expenditures also rose during the nineteenth century. Reforms were expensive and the military expenditures necessary for keeping the empire together were even more costly. As a result, financial difficulties as well as the efforts to reduce and finance the budget deficits continued until World War I. The methods used by the central government to finance its budget deficits had direct implications for the monetary system and price stability and more generally for macroeconomic stability. In response to the frequent wars late in the eighteenth century and during the first half of the nineteenth century, the central government tried to finance the deficits by domestic borrowing and by resorting frequently to debasements or reductions in the silver content of the currency. This strategy provided revenues in the short term, especially during the wars, but it also led to monetary instability and high rates of inflation. Debasements were abandoned in the 1840s with the adoption of the bimetallic system. In the face of continuing budget deficits, the Ottoman government soon began borrowing in the European financial markets. Two decades of rapid external borrowing resulted in a default in the 1870s. The subsequent negotiations led to the establishment of the Ottoman Public Debt Administration and the Ottoman government was forced to surrender part of its sources of revenues to this European creditor organization for the service of the debt. The persistent financial problems and foreign borrowing thus turned into an ever-deepening source of weakness not only for the economy but also for the Ottoman state in its international relations. The rest of this chapter will examine the changing methods used by the Ottoman government for financing the budget deficits as well as their implications for the evolution of monetary and financial institutions.

Debasements and Monetary Reform

Because of more frequent wars and growing military expenditures, the fiscal difficulties were especially severe from the late 1760s until the 1830s. To close its budget deficit, the central government was borrowing at high interest rates from the big moneylenders at the capital known as the Galata bankers, while also seeking to create additional revenues through the frequent debasement of silver coinage in circulation. The Ottoman economy experienced the highest rates of debasement and inflation in its history and the general price levels increased twelve- to fifteenfold during this period. The exchange rate of the Ottoman currency, the kurush or the piaster, also plummeted from 23 kuruş to one pound sterling in 1814, to 110 piaster to the pound by 1839 (Cezar 1986, pp. 235–80; Pamuk 2000, pp. 193–200; Kazgan 1980, pp. 115–30). By the 1830s, debasing metallic coins to obtain additional revenue had become a rather costly method. The frequent debasements and the waves of inflation that followed led to a good deal of social and political turmoil. Moreover, the debasements and inflation were reducing the tax receipts in real terms and the exchange rate fluctuations were inhibiting foreign trade. Merchants, both local and European, also demanded greater monetary stability.

Monetary reform thus joined the long list of initiatives in play during the reform era. Following the example of Muhammad Ali Pasha's Egypt and many other countries, the Ottomans shifted to the bimetallic system and started minting gold and silver coins with new standards and fixed values. One hundred silver piasters equaled one gold lira after the Monetary Reform Act (*Tashih-i Ayar* or *Tashih-i Sikke*) in 1844. The government put an end to debasements as a means of creating additional fiscal revenue after this date. The standards of Ottoman currency as well as its exchange rate against leading European currencies remained unchanged until World War I (Issawi 1980, p. 329–31). The adoption of the new bimetallic system and the introduction of new coinage did not mean that the fiscal difficulties had ended. Throughout the century, the government was forced to adopt a variety of methods to deal with the recurring budget deficits.

Another method used from the late 1830s onward to secure additional revenue was to issue paper money known as *kaime*. Amid rising military expenditures and reform initiatives, many state agencies started issuing debt certificates to sustain their expenditures after depleting their budgets. The kaime was relatively successful until 1852 because the amounts remained limited. When the kaime began to be issued in large volume during the Crimean War, however, its market value declined rapidly from par, or 100 to 400 to the lira. The first experiment with paper money in Ottoman history thus ended in a major wave of inflation more than twenty years after it began. Following widespread protests, the state withdrew the kaime from the market in 1862 with the short-term credit it had obtained from the Ottoman Bank (Akyıldız 1996, pp. 25–89). A similar episode of inconvertible paper money occurred during the Russian war of 1877–78. This time the new paper money was used throughout the empire as salaries of state employees were paid with the new kaime, villagers would sell their products against the kaime, and they would pay taxes with the kaime. Because of their large volume, however, the market value of the kaime declined to the 450 paper kurush = 1 gold lira within two years and they were drawn from circulation soon after the end of the war. Aside from these two episodes, however, prices were generally stable and rates of inflation were lower between 1844 when debasements were ended and World War I.

Domestic Borrowing

Financiers specializing in transactions in money markets including lending with interest were called *sarraf* in the Ottoman era. The mostly Greek and Armenian sarrafs of Istanbul had formed a guild and moved their workplaces to the other side of the Golden Horn, to Galata, in the late seventeenth century. The sarrafs were also active in the provinces, financing trade and the tax collection. The Ottoman state always relied on the sarrafs and encouraged their activities. From the 1760s, as the fiscal situation deteriorated, the sarrafs' role and power expanded considerably. They began to lend to the state in growing volume, and thanks to their ties to European financial networks, they began to secure short-term funds in European markets for the Ottoman state. The sarrafs were thus transformed from traditional moneylenders with mostly domestic operations into large-scale financiers with international ties. They were able to establish their first bank only in the 1840s, but even before that date the sarrafs of the capital city began to be known as the Galata bankers.

The Galata bankers' financial power reached its peak toward the middle of the nineteenth century. In the meantime, the state's budget deficits and its reliance on debt had increased rapidly. After the state began to borrow directly in the European financial markets in 1854, the Galata bankers faced greater competition from European banks and bankers, who began to open new banks and branches in the capital as well as the provinces. Although they lost their unrivaled position, the Galata bankers did not give up easily. Entering into partnerships with European financial capital groups and opening new banks, they pursued their activities. During this new period, the Ottoman state continued to make use of the Galata bankers for its short-term requirements, in between selling long-term bonds in European financial markets.

The state's persistent fiscal troubles soon pushed it to seek a more powerful European institution. In 1863, as a French group joined the British owners of the Ottoman Bank with a 50 percent stake, the Imperial Ottoman Bank was established. An important characteristic of the bank was its dual identity as a private Franco-British bank on the one hand, and as a state bank in Istanbul on the other. Daily activities were directed from London and Paris by a board of directors. In exchange for offering the state short-term debt and agreeing to help the state in removing the paper kaimes, the most important transactions of the Treasury including payments on the external debt were given to the bank. In addition, the state gave the bank the monopoly to introduce new, gold-backed paper money which was circulated only in limited quantities until World War I. The Imperial Ottoman Bank thus began to assume many of the functions of a central bank (Kazgan 1995; Eldem 1999, pp. 29–126; Clay 2000, 1–229; Al 2007).

After the Ottoman government was forced to default on its mostly external long-term debt in 1876 and a war with Russia erupted the following year, the Ottoman Bank refused to provide new loans. In response, the Ottoman government, turned once again to the Galata bankers. During this difficult period, the Galata bankers, most of whom were Ottoman citizens, embraced or made use of a series of patriotic slogans and resumed lending to their oldest and largest customer, which had played such an important role in their rise (Pamuk 2000, pp. 211–13; Clay 2000, pp. 279–380; Eldem 1999, pp. 127–80).

External Borrowing

Budget deficits typically increased during periods of military tension or conflict. After the monetary reform of 1844, European financiers and state representatives began to suggest that the Ottoman government turn to long-term foreign borrowing as a solution to its financial problems, but the government was hesitant. Tthe outbreak of the Crimean War sharply increased the need for new expenditures, and the Ottoman state started selling long-term bonds in London, Paris, Vienna, and Frankfurt in 1854. The first two issues during the Crimean War carried the guarantee of the British government, but bonds issued after the war did not. The bonds typically had a maturity date of one hundred years and carried an annual 4 percent coupon. The Ottoman state's persistent financial difficulties and the high interest rates it was willing to pay soon made the business of lending to the Ottoman state as well as the organization of new bond issues very profitable for the financiers, both local and international. The commissions the intermediaries received were very high, as much as 10 percent or even 12 percent, of the amount offered as debt. European banks and financial houses kept some of the bonds and sold most of them in the markets.

Ottoman long-term borrowing in the European financial markets until World War I is best examined in two periods. The first period extends from the first long-term bond issue in 1854 until the default of 1875–76. The second period began with the establishment of the Ottoman Public Debt Administration in 1881. During the first period, the Ottoman government borrowed large amounts of money under very unfavorable conditions and interest rates sig-

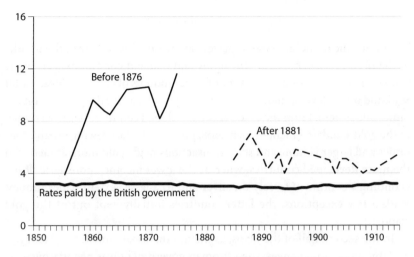

FIGURE 4.2. Interest Rates Paid by the Ottoman Government in External Borrowing, 1854–1914 (percent). Source: Pamuk 1987, pp. 72–75.

nificantly higher than those paid by other countries at the time. The receipts of the Ottoman government net of bankers' commissions typically remained below half of the face value of the debt. An important part of the borrowed funds was used to cover current expenditures, including military expenditures. Only a small fraction was directed to infrastructure investments that might increase future tax revenues (Kıray 1988).

By the second half of the 1860s, the Ottoman government had to secure new debt in order to continue its interest and principal payments. The high interest rates on the bonds and the high commissions paid to the bankers kept the process going, however (figure 4.2). As the impact of the financial crisis of 1873 began to be felt in the European financial markets, securing new funds did become much more difficult. The Ottoman state's long-term and mostly externally held debt had reached close to 200 million pounds sterling. Principal and interest payments were 11 million pounds a year. The annual revenues of the Ottoman treasury were approximately 18 million pounds during this period. In other words, to sustain payments on its long-term debt, the Ottoman government had to set aside more than half of its annual revenues. The Ottoman government announced in the autumn of 1875 that it would halve all its debt payments, and it stopped all debt repayments the following year. The Ottomans were not alone in default. In the crisis environment of the 1870s, some twenty countries in Latin America and the Middle East, including Egypt and Tunisia, were also forced to stop their debt payments (Owen 1981, pp. 100–21; Pamuk 1987, pp. 56–62).

The Limping Gold Standard

The bimetallic monetary system performed reasonably well until the middle of the nineteenth century, when supply and demand conditions worldwide were more stable. But the discovery of large amounts of silver in Nevada after 1850, and other developments in Europe, began to increase the pressure on the bimetallic system. From the 1870s, more developed countries began to switch to the gold standard (Eichengreen 2008, pp. 15–42). The growing urban economies and larger volume and scale transactions made gold more attractive in the more developed countries, whereas the lower income, more agricultural economies continued to rely on silver and to a lesser extent paper money. With a few exceptions, the latter countries initially kept out of the gold standard.

In the second half of the 1870s, as the international monetary system was undergoing major changes, the Ottoman government was negotiating a restructuring of its large external debt. The future of the Ottoman monetary system became an important issue in the debt negotiations. The European creditors as well as the Ottoman Bank demanded that the Ottoman government shift to the gold standard in order to keep the Ottoman economy strongly tied to the major European economies and currencies, and equally important, to facilitate future debt payments. The Ottoman government agreed to abandon the bimetallic system as part of the debt restructuring agreement of 1881. The link between silver and gold was severed and the Ottoman monetary unit started to be defined in terms of gold only. While the government decided to limit the amount of silver coinage in circulation, the silver coinage continued to be widely used in daily transactions across the empire. The resulting system, known as the limping gold standard, took its main support from gold, but in practice continued to rest on silver. This system was thus a de facto compromise between the interests and preferences of European merchants and creditors and the realities of a lower income agricultural economy (Pamuk 2000, pp. 214–16).

If the Ottoman government had somehow returned to silver in the 1880s, as some other developing countries did at the time, exporting and import competing sectors would have seen their competitiveness rise thanks the decline in the value of silver. However, the Ottoman government also had a large amount of external debt defined in gold. A shift or return to silver would have led to rising debt burden as silver depreciated against gold. A shift to silver may have also had a negative impact on inflows of foreign direct investment. More generally, staying out of the gold standard would have weakened relations between the Ottoman economy and the European economies until World War I.

In the decades until World War I, the Ottoman Bank played a very important role in the new system, seeking to stabilize the exchange rate between the
Ottoman lira and European currencies and create a stable environment for
international trade and capital movements. The Bank also tried to stabilize the
exchange rate between the gold lira and the silver *kurush*. It maintained its
monopoly position in the supply of gold-backed banknotes and expanded
their supply very slowly. This cautious stance and the relatively stable monetary environment kept the economy well anchored in the European trade and
capital networks and benefited, above all, the European merchants, creditors
and companies that had invested in the empire (Eldem 1999, pp. 145–275).

The Ottoman Public Debt Administration

The negotiations between the Ottoman government and representatives of
French, British, Austrian, German, and other creditors which were suspended
during the Ottoman-Russian War of 1877–78 finally resulted in an agreement
in December 1881. Known as the Decree of Muharrem, after the month in the
Islamic calendar when it was signed, the agreement reduced the amount of
outstanding Ottoman debt by half and restructured the payment schedule. In
exchange, the government agreed to the establishment of a new organization
that would act as the creditors' representative in the empire and would take .
over and develop some of the revenue sources of the Ottoman state, collect
their taxes, and transfer them to European creditors. The salt and tobacco monopolies, taxes collected from fishermen, and those imposed on alcoholic
drinks, the tithe collected from raw silk, and the annual taxes paid by the province of Eastern Rumelia in present-day Bulgaria were all surrendered to the
new institution known as the Ottoman Public Debt Administration (OPDA).
These sources accounted for about one-third of the total tax revenues of the
Ottoman state (Blaisdell 1929; Parvus 1977; Birdal 2010, pp. 63–180; Tunçer
2015, pp. 53–78; Keyder 1979, pp. 37–48). In addition, the Ottoman government agreed to grant monopoly privileges within the empire for the control
of tobacco production, the purchase and sale of tobacco, as well as the production of cigarettes to a Régie Company, which was established with European
capital in 1883. A share of the Régie's annual profits would be handed to the
OPDA and directed toward the debt payments (Quataert 1983, pp. 13–40;
Birdal 2010, pp. 129–66).

The OPDA was governed by a board consisting of the representatives of
the holders of Ottoman bonds. To develop the resources that had been placed
under its control and to collect taxes more effectively, it developed a large
organization with some five thousand employees in twenty cities of the empire. Close to two hundred Europeans occupied the higher echelons of this

organization, while the rest of the employees were Ottoman citizens. The OPDA focused on developing the production and export of agricultural commodities whose taxes had passed under its control, such as tobacco and silk. It was much more efficient than the Ottoman state revenue developer and tax collector. By its example and through its training of young personnel, the OPDA contributed to the growing efficiency of the Ottoman financial bureaucracy and later in Turkey.

The thirty-three years that extend from the foundation of the OPDA to World War I mark the second period in Ottoman external borrowing. The detailed and strict control imposed on Ottoman finances had reduced the risk attached to Ottoman bonds. As a result, the Ottoman government could again borrow long-term in European financial markets at more favorable terms and lower interest rates (figure 4.2). Furthermore, because military expenditures and the budget deficit remained limited for the early part of this period, the need for new borrowing declined. As a result, the Ottoman payments of principal and interest remained well above the new debt issues for the first two decades (Pamuk 1987, pp. 56–62; Akarlı 1976).

From the beginning of the twentieth century, however, the government turned once again to foreign debt frequently and in larger amounts. By 1914, total outstanding debt of the Ottoman government had reached 160 million pounds sterling or about 75 percent of the GDP of the empire. As military expenditures and fiscal pressures increased, the government was forced to find new loans. By this time, British investors had lost interest in Ottoman bonds. The government tried to take advantage of the competition between France and Germany in order to sell new issues in European financial markets, but with each new loan, it was forced to make new political and economic concessions to European states and companies.

At the end of the eighteenth century, the tax revenues the Ottoman government could bring to the central treasury in Istanbul remained very low, at no more than 3 percent of the GDP. The Ottoman Empire could not match the fiscal and military power of their neighbors to the west and were in serious danger of breaking up. Thanks to the centralizing reforms, the government was able to raise the tax revenues to more than 10 percent of GDP until World War I by reducing the share of the intermediaries and by raising the tax burden of the population. In the meantime, however, it became clear that reforms were expensive, and the military expenditures kept rising. As a result, the central government struggled throughout the century to balance its budget and finance its deficits. How the government handled the budget and how it chose to pay for the deficits had direct implications for the monetary and financial institutions.

In the longer term, a heavy price was paid for the persistence of the budget deficits. Early in the century, debasements were the preferred method for financing the deficits and the high rates of inflation were the main economic and political cost. In the second half of the century and until World War I, the government opted for monetary stability and external borrowing as the basic method for dealing with the deficits. Greater monetary stability undoubtedly helped external trade and attracted foreign investment. It also led to low rates of economic growth. However, the long-term costs of ceding a large part of the government revenues to the European creditors and increasing political dependence in foreign relations in the decades leading up to World War I were equally if not more costly. More broadly, both the reform efforts and continuing fiscal difficulties of the central government strongly influenced the patterns of economic change during the century until World War I, as will be examined in the following chapter.

5

Opening to Foreign Trade
and Investment

DURING THE CENTURY UNTIL WORLD War I, the economy of Turkey remained under the influence of two powerful and related processes, the reform
efforts of the government and greater integration with the world economy.
The latter was closely related to the former not only because the Ottoman
governments recognized that greater integration with world markets would
generate the additional tax revenues necessary for the reform efforts, but also
because the European governments demanded free trade and the opening of
the economy to foreign investment in exchange for their support of Ottoman
reform efforts. As a result, along with rising international trade and investment, production for market and specialization in agriculture increased while
the share of manufacturing in overall output declined. This chapter will begin
by examining the basic trends in international trade and European direct investment in Turkey and then focus on changing patterns of production, the
growing commercialization of agriculture, and the decline in crafts-based
manufacturing activities. In contrast, industrialization or industrial activity
making use of the new technologies remained limited until World War I.

Reforms and Opening of the Economy

The reform efforts of the Ottoman government had important implications
for the economy throughout the nineteenth century. For political support
against external and internal threats as well as support for the reform process
itself, the government often turned to western European states. The recurring
financial needs of the central government only added to this search for external support. For most of the century, the British as well as the other European
governments saw the reforms and reinforcement of the Ottoman state as an

important aspect of their policy in the Eastern Mediterranean. In exchange for the military, political, and financial support they offered, European states demanded the creation of a market economy specializing in agriculture and trade, which was open to the outside world and offered special privileges to European companies and citizens of European states. The reform initiatives, from the very beginning, were thus accompanied by economic concessions granted to European states, especially to Britain.

As a result, the major changes the Ottoman economic institutions went through during the nineteenth century were shaped by the interaction between the Ottoman government, European governments, and European capital. As the economy opened up to European trade and investment, the power of European states and businesses within the empire kept growing. The interaction between the reforms and the opening of the economy resulted in the emergence inside the empire of spheres of influence for competing European governments and European capital by the end of the century. The reformist initiatives launched to strengthen the central government thus led to contradictory results, with the central government getting stronger militarily and politically, on the one hand, but losing control over the economy, on the other.

This contradictory aspect of the reforms can be observed in most of the new institutional arrangements. The most important turning point in the opening of the economy was the free trade treaty signed with Great Britain in 1838 and with other European countries soon afterward. In the last chapter I emphasized that the Ottoman government was facing a severe political and military crisis at the time and they signed the free trade treaty for political reasons, in order to secure the political support and commitment of Great Britain toward the territorial integrity of the empire. The beginning of external borrowing during the Crimean War in 1854 and the concessions given to European companies from the 1850s onward for the construction of railroads were other important milestones in the opening of the Ottoman economy. The Reform Edict of 1856 allowed for direct foreign investment, and in 1867, foreigners were given permission to own agricultural land in the empire. One can include in this list the economic and legal privileges enjoyed by European citizens and companies inside the Ottoman Empire. These privileges were first offered by the Ottoman government from a position of strength during the sixteenth century, but they were expanded during the nineteenth century. At each one of these turning points, the Ottoman government faced serious military, political, and financial difficulties and agreed to these institutional changes in return for the support of the European governments. In each step taken toward further opening the economy, the Ottoman government placed much greater priority on the short-term political or financial support they would secure from European states, rather than the longer term economic consequences (Owen 1981, pp. 57–153; Issawi 1982, 1–43; Pamuk 1987, 1–17).

In other words, it was the concerns of the central government and those of European states and companies that shaped the institutional changes related to the opening of the economy. Unlike the experiences of some other countries during the nineteenth century, the opening of the economy did not proceed through alliances formed between landowners, merchants, and European businesses, but through bargaining, pressure, and step-by-step compromises between the central government and European states and companies. The influence of various domestic groups, landowners, guilds, merchants, and financiers over the opening of the economy remained very limited.

For the central government, the progressive opening of the economy increased the risks of losing control since the growing ties with the world economy would give greater power to merchants and big landowners as well as the European companies. These concerns, however, did not prevent the central government from continuing with the bargain. The military, financial, and political difficulties the central government frequently faced during the nineteenth century thus created many opportunities for European governments and European companies which were often in competition with each other. In most of these crises, a European state would offer political, military, or financial support and, in exchange, would extract economic concessions from the central government, for example, the permission to launch a major investment project. Within a short time, companies from other European countries would also enter through the same door, and the opening of the economy would proceed further.

Nonetheless, in comparison to colonies or countries where domestic groups were more powerful and more actively supported integration with the world economy, the opening of the Ottoman economy proceeded more slowly. Because the central government was concerned that it may lose political control as a result of greater integration with the world economy, it remained a reluctant partner, and there were limits to the concessions it could grant to European companies or financiers. In the next chapter, I will briefly compare the opening of the Ottoman economy with that of Egypt during nineteenth century. I will argue that compared to Egypt, where the political power was first in the hands of big landowners and was later transferred to the British colonial administration, the opening of the economy within Turkey's current borders, measured by the ratios of exports to GDP and direct foreign investment to GDP, remained more limited until World War I.

The Expansion of Foreign Trade

The Ottoman government faced a severe political and military crisis during the 1830s and needed the support of the British government. In many ways, the Baltalimanı Free Trade Treaty was the price paid for that support. The treaty also reflected the large political, economic, and military disparities between Great Britain, which had completed its Industrial Revolution, and the Ottoman economy, where textiles and other manufacturing activities in Anatolia and the Istanbul region were organized around traditional guilds, almost entirely in small or medium-sized workshops.

At the end of the eighteenth century and early in the nineteenth century, the volume of exports of the area within Turkey's current borders was very small in relation to total production or GDP. Trade with Iran and India to the east and trade with parts of eastern Europe accounted for a significant part of this external trade. Trade within the empire was far more important than external trade at that early stage. During the century from the end of the Napoleonic Wars to World War I, this picture changed significantly. The volume of trade between Turkey and the industrializing countries of western and later central Europe expanded very rapidly. The Ottoman economy, and that of Anatolia in particular, was transformed into an economy that was exporting large volumes of agricultural commodities and raw materials while importing in exchange manufactured products and some food items.

It is not easy to estimate the extent to which the volume of foreign trade in the area within Turkey's current borders increased during the nineteenth century. Turkey's trade with Europe was already increasing and more than doubled during the eighteenth century. During the century from 1820 to World War I, however, total foreign trade in the same area increased much more rapidly, by more than twentyfold. The share of exports in GDP increased from approximately 2 percent in 1820 to more than 11 percent by 1914 (Pamuk 1987, pp. 18–54; 148–71; figure 5.1).

Agricultural commodities such as tobacco, wheat, barley, raisins, figs, raw silk, mohair, hazelnuts, opium, cotton, and olive oil were Turkey's leading exports at the beginning of the twentieth century. An important characteristic of these exports was their diversity. In fact, no single commodity accounted for more than 12 percent of total exports in any year during the decades before World War I. Considering that the share of agriculture in total GDP was greater than 50 percent during this period, and taking into account production for domestic markets, these figures suggest that close to one-fourth of total agricultural production was being exported on the eve of World War I. This ratio was significantly higher in western Turkey and along the coastal regions.

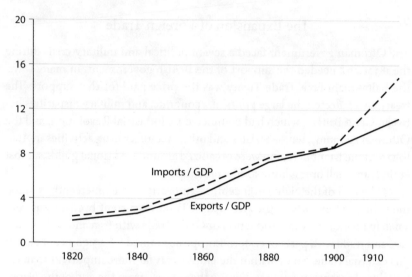

FIGURE 5.1. Opening to Foreign Trade, 1820–1914: Ratios of Imports and Exports to GDP in Turkey (percent). Sources: Based on Pamuk 1987 pp. 148–50, and Eldem 1970, pp. 302–6 for the Ottoman era; official trade and national income series from Turkey, Turkish Statistical Institute 2014 for the period since 1923.

The only manufactured item that occupied an important place among exports was hand-woven carpets and *kilims.*

In the decades before World War I, more than half of the imports of the area within the present-day borders of Turkey consisted of manufactured products, especially cotton, and to a lesser extent, woolen textiles. By the start of the twentieth century, most of the population, whether city dwellers or peasants, rich or poor, were consuming either imported cotton textiles or cotton fabrics locally woven with imported cotton yarn. Foodstuffs also featured prominently among imports, accounting for as much as one-third of the total. Imported foodstuffs included commodities like sugar, tea, and coffee, which were not produced locally. In addition, however, large quantities of wheat, flour, and rice were imported in the early twentieth century. Wheat imported by sea from the Balkan countries or from Russia, and even flour imported from Marseille, could be sold more cheaply in Istanbul than wheat produced in the interior of Anatolia. The weakness of the internal transport network was one reason why this mostly agricultural economy was not self-sufficient in cereals. Equally significant, the 1838 Treaty was an important cause behind the large imports of grain, as it prevented the adoption of protectionist customs duties. In contrast, many European states were able to adopt tariffs to protect their own cereals producers against foreign competition during the nineteenth century.

Foreign Direct Investment

From the 1850s, the opening of the economy took on an additional dimension. European companies began to establish enterprises within the borders of the Ottoman Empire. Those European companies who wanted to invest applied to the Ottoman government to obtain the necessary concessions. In the period leading up to World War I, around 75 million pounds sterling were invested directly in these enterprises. As the inflows of foreign capital increased, so did the power of foreign companies, which had considerable influence with laws and other institutional changes.

A high proportion, approximately two-thirds, of foreign direct investment, excluding the foreign debt of the Ottoman state, was invested in railway companies. In addition, significant amounts of European direct investment went into trade companies, banking, insurance, ports, and municipal services like water and utilities. Only 10 percent of foreign direct investment went into mining, agriculture, and industry. This sectoral distribution suggests that most direct foreign investment in the Ottoman Empire and in Turkey directly or indirectly supported foreign trade rather than production during the nineteenth century (Pamuk 1987, pp. 62–81).

The construction of railroads by European companies played a key role in the opening of the interior regions of the country into the global economy and the encouragement of additional direct European investment in the same regions. The Ottoman government expected various benefits from the construction of railways. Chief among them was ensuring internal security, enabling the power of the central government to reach the farthest corners of the empire, and the easy transport of soldiers and equipment in times of war. With the construction of the railroads, the central government also hoped to collect taxes more effectively and reduce the proportion of tax receipts that went to locally powerful groups.

Even more critical, by reducing the cost of transportation between regions with uncultivated but fertile land, such as Central Anatolia, and major domestic markets and ports of export such as Istanbul and İzmir, the railroads would allow new land to be opened up to agricultural production. Increasing agricultural production meant more tax receipts. The central government granted concessions for the construction of railroads to foreign capital companies and, when necessary, promised to make additional annual payments, known as kilometric guarantees, to the railway companies for each kilometer built.

In most cases, these commitments meant additional burdens on Ottoman finances, as the railroads did not generate the expected level of traffic and revenues.

From the point of view of the British, French, Austrian, Belgian, and German companies who undertook their construction and operation, the railroads represented profitable investment opportunities, particularly thanks to the kilometer guarantee paid by the Ottoman state. The railroads also played an important role in the emergence of European spheres of influence inside the Ottoman Empire. The construction of a railroad brought about significant reductions in costs of transportation and led to increases in agricultural production, especially export-oriented production, while craftsmen in the region began to face the competition of European manufactured products. In later stages, companies from the same European country would embark on other investments in the region. The regional power of merchants and bankers from the country that had built the railroads made it more difficult for merchants and investors from other European countries to compete in the same region (Quataert 1994, pp. 804–15).

This pattern could be observed in many regions of Turkey during the half century until World War I. At the end of the 1850s and the beginning of the 1860s, for example, the İzmir-Aydin railway, and later the construction of the İzmir-Kasaba line, strengthened British capital in Western Anatolia. After the construction of these railways, trade between this region and Britain grew rapidly, and British companies invested in other sectors like mining, industry, and municipal services (Kurmuş 1974, pp. 76–122; Kasaba 1988, pp. 87–112; Baskıcı 2005, pp. 31–158). From the end of the 1880s, the construction of the İzmir-Ankara and Eskişehir-Konya lines, as well as the construction of the Baghdad Railway, which eventually extended as far as Southeastern Anatolia, paved the way for investments by German companies in Central and Southern Anatolia. As the railroads expanded trade with Germany, the Ankara, Konya, and Adana regions were increasingly seen as being capable of meeting Germany's wheat and cotton needs. German investments in the region, as demonstrated by the Çumra irrigation project in Central Anatolia, were also directed at infrastructure and encouraged plans to settle German communities in this area. Germany's defeat at the end of World War I brought about the end of these plans, however (Özyüksel 2011, pp. 109–36; Özyüksel 2016, pp. 42–239; Quataert 1977, pp. 139–59).

An overview of the emerging formal banking sector during the nineteenth century will provide important insights not only about the changing economic institutions and structure but also the changing distribution of economic power in an increasingly open economy. While private financiers or moneylenders known as sarrafs had existed since the earliest times in the Ottoman Empire, formal banks began to emerge only in the 1840s. The earliest banks in Turkey were established by European capital and later by the domestic sarraf in alliance with British, French, and Austrian groups mostly to lend short-term to the Ottoman government and meet other financial needs of the Ottoman state. The Imperial Ottoman Bank was also founded during this early period in 1863 as a private Franco-British company as well as a state bank. The bank not only provided short-term loans to the Ottoman state in between long-term bond issues in European financial markets, but it soon assumed many of the functions of a central bank, including the introduction of limited amounts of gold-backed paper money (see chapter 4; also Pamuk 2000, pp. 211–13).

In the period after 1881, the Imperial Ottoman Bank, now more than 80 percent French owned, maintained a leading role in lending to the Ottoman government. It also developed an extensive network of branches across Turkey and the rest of the empire. The bank also supported and to some extent coordinated the activities of French capital groups not only in the floatation of Ottoman bond issues but also various direct investment projects, in railways, ports, utilities, mining, and insurance companies. As British capital and financial groups began to scale down their interests and investments in the Ottoman Empire after 1880, German groups spearheaded by the Deutsche Bank emerged as the main rival to French interests. An intense competition soon developed between European commercial banks, both large and small, as many of them rushed to open branches in the Ottoman Empire (Eldem 1999, pp. 145–304; Pamuk 2000, pp. 221–22; Thobie 1977).

In addition, domestic groups, mostly Greeks, established a small number of regional banks in this period, but most of these were outside the present-day borders of Turkey. Numbers of banks founded with domestic capital increased significantly after 1910 as a result of the policies of the Young Turk government that promoted the development of domestic capital and a Muslim-Turkish bourgeoisie. As a result, four banks in Istanbul and two in Anatolia were established with the initiative and capital of domestic groups until World War I (Toprak 1982, pp. 126–64). The most important domestic bank of the nineteenth century, however, was the Agricultural Bank established by the state in 1888 to support agricultural development through the extension of low-interest credit to medium-sized and large-scale cultivators. The bank established more than four hundred branches, more than any other financial institution. Although it could not meet the full needs of cultivators, it initiated an alternative to the high rates demanded by the traditional moneylenders. As the only major domestic bank in the empire, it was an important part of government-organized efforts to finance economic development from domestic savings (Quataert 1975, pp. 210–27).

The transition to modern banking was going to be a long, drawn-out process, however. The new banks, both foreign- and domestic-owned, operated mostly in the more commercialized regions, and they could meet only a small fraction of the demand for credit. The rest of the economy's demand for credit, especially in the rural areas and in less commercialized regions, and the demand for small-scale credit continued to be met by moneylenders. In addition, even though the volume of their activities declined, the cash vakıfs, an institutional legacy of the Ottoman era before the reforms, continued to provide small-scale credit.

Commercialization of Agriculture

During the century until World War I, the expansion of commodity exports and rising levels of foreign direct investment as well as the reform efforts of the government had far-reaching consequences for agriculture, which was the principal source of income for close to 80 percent of the population of Turkey. The population of Turkey increased by about 75 percent during the century until World War I from approximately 9.4 million to 16.5 million (see chapter 2 for details). Existing evidence suggests that agricultural production increased more rapidly and per capita agricultural production was rising perhaps at the rate of 0.5 percent per year during the nineteenth century (Pamuk 2008, pp. 376–78). Moreover, a rising share of the agricultural output was directed to urban and export markets and the rural population was drawn into market relations more strongly than in earlier periods. In comparison, changes in technology, in ownership patterns, and in tenancy relations proceeded more slowly and remained limited during the nineteenth century.

One basic cause of the increases in agricultural production was the improvements in security in the provinces during the first half of the nineteenth century after a very difficult and long period of wars. The reform initiatives and centralization contributed to the improving conditions in the rural areas and helped agricultural production, especially production for the market. Rural population began, albeit very gradually, to leave remote settlements away from roads and cities and to move to the valleys, where they started producing on more fertile land. More arable land was thus opened for production and establishing a stronger transport network between rural areas and cities became possible at the same time. It was under such circumstances that Çukurova and Söke plains and many other fertile valleys opened for production in the nineteenth century. Second, because Anatolia was underpopulated and additional land was available, the amount of land under cultivation could increase along with the rural population in many areas for most of the century. Of the 75 percent increase in total population, close to a half was due to natural growth and the rest was due to net immigration from seceding areas of the empire as well as Crimea and the Caucuses (Quataert 1994, pp. 843–87; Pamuk 2008, pp. 376–87).

The increasing market orientation of agricultural production was also supported by other long-term trends during the nineteenth century. Part of the increases in agricultural production was directed to urban markets. The urban population of Turkey more than doubled during the nineteenth century because of the increases in total population and also due to the gradual rise in the urban share of the total. Second, along with the expansion in foreign trade, agricultural exports to European markets increased steadily. Agricultural commodities like tobacco, wheat, barley, raisins, figs, raw silk, mohair, opium, hazelnuts, olive oil, and others made up more than 90 percent of all exports. Third, in the aftermath of the Industrial Revolution, the terms of trade between agriculture and industry shifted and remained in favor of agriculture for most of the century until World War I. Railroads and steamships reduced the costs of transportation for the bulkier agricultural commodities and helped this trend. The construction of railroads made it easier for agricultural commodities produced in the more remote regions to reach both domestic urban markets and ports of export, and it opened up new tracts of land in internal regions to production for distant markets. Supported by these trends, the rural population increased its specialization in agriculture. A large share of agricultural producers started buying some of the non-agricultural products that they previously made for their own consumption; chief among them were textile products such as yarn and cloth, and they began devoting a greater share of their time to agriculture. In other words, the rural population, with its women, men, young people, and children of working age, began spending more time in agriculture, especially market-oriented agriculture.

The share of exports in total agricultural production rose steadily during the nineteenth century and exceeded 20 percent in the years before World War I. When production for export is combined with production for urban markets, close to but less than half of the agricultural production was being produced for markets on the eve of World War I. This ratio was higher in the more urbanized and more export-oriented western and coastal regions and lower in the interior and the east (Pamuk 1987, pp. 18–26, 150–53; Pamuk 2008, pp. 375–88; and figure 5.1).

Small Producers, the State, and the Market

In spite of the growing power of notables in Anatolia in the eighteenth century, large agricultural holdings and especially large farms had remained limited. Small-scale production or family farms which cultivated around 4–6 hectares every year using family labor and a pair of oxen continued to account for a large share of production both for domestic and export markets in the nineteenth century as well. Large landholdings continued to exist, but their owners preferred to divide their holdings into small plots and have them cultivated by sharecropping families. Large farms using year-round wage laborers remained the exception (Güran 1998; Keyder and Tabak 1991, pp. 1–16; Gerber 1987, pp. 43–66).

One important reason why small and medium-sized family enterprises remained dominant during the nineteenth century is the state. From the early stages, Mahmud II's efforts to strengthen the central government were directed toward undermining the economic foundations of provincial notables and supporting the family farms. To better control rural regions and seize a greater share of the agricultural surplus, the central government sought to undermine large holdings on *miri or* state-owned lands. It started to expropriate many of the large-scale holdings under the control of provincial notables. More important still, the central government tried to withdraw the tax-collecting privileges of provincial notables, which was the most important source of their economic power. For example, in 1813, in order to break the Karaosmanoğlu family's monopoly on the collection of taxes in Western Anatolia, someone outside the family was appointed and put in charge of tax collection in the region. In addition to Western Anatolia and the Eastern Black Sea regions, even in regions where the power of the central government had always been more limited, such as in Eastern and Southeastern Anatolia, the lands under the control of some Kurdish tribal leaders were seized and these holdings were distributed to peasant families. These measures had only limited success, however, and large holdings persisted in most regions.

In contrast, small and medium-sized producers constituted the fiscal foundation of the Ottoman state. The tithe on agricultural production and the animal tax were the central government's most important sources of revenue. The Tanzimat Decree fixed the tithe, which had different rates in different regions of the empire, at 10 percent of gross output everywhere. But, in periods of severe financial crisis, the state could raise the tithe up to 12.5 percent, even up to 15 percent. The continuation of the tax-farming system increased the tax burden on small producers. The tax farmers could arbitrarily fix the amount paid by each producer on the harvest. Big landowners were better protected from the abuses of tax farmers and the small producers often ended up paying at higher rates (Özbek 2015, pp. 17–112). Throughout the nineteenth century, the central government, while trying to limit the power of local elements and big landowners, made it harder to confiscate the land of small producers for debt default or other reasons, while increasing the tax pressure on small and medium producers.

Another reason why small and medium-sized family enterprises remained the most important form of enterprise in agriculture was the relative scarcity of labor and the relative abundance of land. Although the population increased, scarcity of labor continued to make itself felt throughout the century. These relative proportions increased the small producers' bargaining power against the big landowners and supported family enterprises. Peasant households that did not own a pair of oxen were often forced to work as sharecroppers. Wages remained high in rural areas, especially during harvest time. Large enterprises that employed wage laborers did not become common, except in the cotton-growing Çukurova region in the south. Relative abundance of cultivable land was the other side of the coin. When transport opportunities were secured and foreign or urban demand increased, new lands were opened to cultivation. The increase in the amount of land cultivated and in agricultural production along with the growth of rural population suggests that additional land was available and could be brought under cultivation relatively easily (Pamuk 1987, pp. 82–107; Kasaba 1988, pp. 87–122; Baskıcı 2005, 121–58).

Another important support for family enterprises in agriculture came from millions of Muslims who migrated to Anatolia and other regions of the empire during the nineteenth century. Total number of immigrants arriving in Turkey during the century until World War I from the Crimea and the Caucasus and from areas in the Balkans that seceded from the empire, Bosnia, Serbia, Bulgaria, Greece, Macedonia, as well as the Aegean islands is estimated at around 4 million (Karpat 1985a, pp. 60–77). These inflows accounted for close to half of the total increase in population in the area within Turkey's current borders during the nineteenth century. Despite the population growth, Turkey remained an underpopulated country until World War I (for details, see chapter 2).

The Ottoman administration tried to encourage the incoming population to engage in agriculture by settling the newcomers in rural areas. A decree issued in 1857 provided a twelve-year tax exemption to immigrants who settled on state lands and began producing in Anatolia. Because they were forced to migrate under conditions of war, most immigrants did not bring large sums of money or belongings with them. The majority of immigrants who came to Turkey were settled in regions where empty lands suitable for cultivation were available. The Bursa and Balıkesir regions south of the Sea of Marmara, the Black Sea, and Aegean coasts, and the Eskişehir-Ankara-Konya triangle in the vicinity of the newly constructed railroad in Central Anatolia which was particularly suitable for grain production, were areas where immigrants settled in greater numbers (Clay 1998, pp. 1–32).

One important institutional change in agriculture during the nineteenth century was the Land Code of 1858, which recognized private ownership of agricultural land and freed the sale and purchase of agricultural land. Until that date, most of the agricultural land had *miri* status and belonged to the state. Peasant families had tenure rights on these lands, but they could not sell or transfer these rights. With this law, the Ottoman state hoped to strengthen property rights on land and increase agricultural production, thereby raising tax revenues as well. In 1867, the government introduced an amendment that extended the right to buy and sell agricultural land to foreigners. After this law, European investors and farmers started buying large amounts of land, especially in Western Anatolia. The European farmers had difficulty securing wage workers, however. Because the local peasants preferred to work on their own family plots and because the Ottoman government was reluctant to find a solution for the the Europeans, most of them were eventually sold the lands they had purchased. The consequences of the Land Code varied greatly from one region to another. The outcome depended, most importantly, on social structure and the distribution of power in each region. Family plots prevailed where land was abundant and the state was able to support the small farms. Large ownership prevailed where large landowners were powerful and where land was more scarce and valuable (Gerber 1987, pp. 84–90, 119–86; Keyder and Tabak 1991, pp. 1–16; İslamoğlu 2004; Aytekin 2009, pp. 935–51).

Regional Differences in Agriculture

One of the most important features of Turkey's agriculture in the nineteenth century was the large and slowly increasing differences between regions. These disparities can be linked to two causes. First, even though small and medium-sized holdings occupied an important place in all regions, climate and soil conditions, proximity to large domestic and export markets, ownership and tenancy patterns, and the composition of production showed major differences from region to region. Second and relatedly, commercialization of agriculture proceeded unevenly until World War I. Export-oriented production was concentrated in coastal areas, in Western Anatolia, the Marmara, Eastern Black Sea, and Adana regions. Central Anatolia began to turn toward domestic and foreign markets only after the construction of the railways in the 1890s. In contrast, the Eastern and Southeastern Anatolia regions remained largely excluded from domestic and foreign markets. These latter regions also received a very low fraction of the large numbers of immigrants that arrived from Crimea, Caucasus, and the Balkans. A brief review of these regional disparities will provide a better understanding not only of agricultural development during the nineteenth century but also the persistence of some patterns into the twentieth century.

Notables in Western Anatolia had a good deal of political and economic power in the eighteenth century, both because they were leading tax farmers and also as de facto owners of large tracts of land. As a result of the centralizing initiatives of the state at the beginning of the nineteenth century, however, their political power was curtailed and they lost their monopoly in collecting taxes for the state. Some of the lands under their control were taken away and distributed to small producers. For the rest of the century, large landowner-ship coexisted in Western Anatolia with small and medium-sized holdings. Because of suitable land and climate conditions as well as its proximity to main ports, Western Anatolia had been the region most oriented toward ex-ports in the eighteenth century. As exports increased rapidly, this trend be-came even stronger in the nineteenth century. Tobacco, raisins, figs, cotton, and olive oil constituted the main exports from Western Anatolia. European and local merchants based in the port cities, and their local partners, tried to encourage more agricultural producers to produce for the markets by offering loans and entering forward contracts with the producers (Kasaba 1988, pp. 87–112; Baskıcı 2005, pp. 121–58).

After the Ottoman government extended property rights on agricultural land to foreigners in 1867, British investors began buying large amounts of land in order to establish large-scale capitalist farms in the İzmir-Aydin region. Because of the relative scarcity of labor and availability of land, however, these investors could not easily secure the wage laborers they needed to run these large enterprises. They were unable to entice peasants, who were cultivating their own fields or who were sharecroppers away from their farms. As a result, the British capitalist farmers were soon forced to abandon their project and had to sell back these lands (Kurmuş 1974, pp. 76–122). Other projects de-signed to encourage the settlement of European populations in Anatolia dur-ing the nineteenth century also failed. In countries where European states had been able to establish colonial administrations, the latter were able to create wage laborers in rural areas by imposing taxes if needed or by destroying exist-ing production relationships by force. The Ottoman state, in contrast, retained its formal independence. Despite pressure from British investors and the Brit-ish government, the Ottoman state was reluctant to move against the small producers on whom it relied strongly for fiscal reasons and sever the ties to their own lands.

Two other regions where agricultural production for export also expanded were the coastal regions of the Eastern Black Sea and Çukurova in the south. Hazelnuts and tobacco were the leading export commodities in the Eastern Black Sea region and production was undertaken mostly by small producers. In the cotton-growing Çukurova, the fertile lands passed into the hands of powerful local groups after the plains were drained beginning in the 1830s and especially during the 1860s. As the cultivation of cotton began to expand, labor emerged as an important problem. Both the large landowners and the central government, which wanted to increase its tax receipts, supported the settlement of local nomadic Turkmen in the plain and the inflows of seasonal workers to the area. The extension of the Baghdad railway beyond Central Anatolia to the south as well as the purchase of the Mersin-Tarsus line from the British increased the influence of German capital in the region. The railway company played an important role in the development of market-oriented production by extending credit to landowners to enable them to use high-quality seeds and to import agricultural vehicles and machines from Germany. Close to 100,000 migrant workers who left distant regions in Eastern Anatolia such as Harput, Bitlis, and even Mosul arrived at the plain every year to pick cotton produced in large holdings. On the eve of World War I, the Çukurova area was the area in Anatolia where agriculture had become most commercialized and where wage labor and mechanization were most widespread (Kasaba 2009, pp. 99–122; Toksöz 2010; Toprak 2016, pp. 199–207).

In the Central Anatolia region, on the other hand, the production of commodities such as angora wool and opium poppies for distant markets remained limited because of the high costs of transport by camel caravans. After the construction of the Anatolian Railway linking Eskişehir, Konya, and Ankara to Istanbul as well as İzmir in the 1890s, the production of wheat and barley for domestic and foreign markets increased rapidly. The distribution of state-owned land to immigrant families further reinforced small and medium-sized holdings in the region. In the early twentieth century, Central Anatolia began to gain importance as a cereal-growing region for Germany. The Anatolian Railway Company owned by German capital contributed to the growing market orientation of agriculture in this region by distributing high-quality seeds, providing credit for the purchase of agricultural implements, and launching large-scale irrigation projects (Baskici 2005, pp. 121–214).

In contrast, market orientation of agricultural production proceeded more slowly in Eastern and Southeastern Anatolia, mostly because of the large distances from the major urban markets and ports of export and the absence of railways and other inexpensive means of transport. With the exception of wool, most market-oriented agricultural production in the region was directed to local urban demand. In the Southeast region, where an important part of the population consisted of nomadic Kurdish tribes, the central government had never been powerful. In spite of the government's centralizing initiatives during the nineteenth century, tribal leaders in the region retained their political, social, and economic power. As the tribes started to shift to settled agriculture, the tribal leaders were able to register large amounts of land to their name. The Ottoman agricultural censuses undertaken at the beginning of the twentieth century show that, after Çukurova in the south, Southeastern Anatolia had the most unequal distribution of land in Anatolia (Güran 1998). Elsewhere in Eastern Anatolia, production for distant markets remained limited, but the production of fruits and vegetables as well as cereals for local markets was increasing, especially in the rural areas where the Armenian population lived. The latter came under increasing pressure during the decades before World War I as ethnic tensions rose and tax collection and land ownership emerged as the focus of growing conflicts between Armenians and the mostly Kurdish Muslim population in the region.

Decline of Manufacturing

As Fernand Braudel and Ottoman historian Halil İnalcık have emphasized, Ottoman crafts and manufacturing were mostly intact until early in the nineteenth century because the volume of imports was limited, and they consisted mostly of English woolens and Indian cotton textiles for the higher income groups in urban areas (Braudel 1979, pp. 467–84; İnalcık 1992, pp. 254–306). The volume of manufactures imported from Britain and other European countries expanded rapidly during the nineteenth century. Faced with competition from the products of the Industrial Revolution, some branches of crafts-based production activities were able to resist, but many others declined. The most important crafts-based branch of production was textiles, both in rural and urban areas. With the increase in productivity achieved in Europe after the Industrial Revolution, prices of cotton textiles products declined by as much as 80 percent in the first half of the century. These decreases in prices made it very difficult for local production in Turkey to survive. Istanbul and the coastal regions were first to be affected by the imports, followed by internal regions. The construction of railroads facilitated the movement of imported cotton textiles into both the urban and rural areas in the interior.

On the eve of World War I, imports accounted for as much as 80 percent of the domestic consumption of cotton textiles. Recent research has also shown, however, that local producers put up strong resistance along the way. While spinning of cotton yarn was mostly discontinued in the second half of the century, local weavers, using imported yarn that was cheaper and more durable, were able to maintain their existence by producing varieties of textiles that were popular in the local markets. Local weaving activity was also supported by the

shifts in the international and domestic terms of trade in favor of manufacturing during the last quarter of the century. In what follows, I will begin with
textile production activities in rural areas mostly for personal consumption
before examining the crafts-based production in the urban areas.

Rural Manufacturing

At the beginning of the nineteenth century, a large proportion of the goods
required by people living in rural areas, such as items of clothing or agricultural tools, were produced and consumed within the village economy. Peasants would typically sell some small fraction of the agricultural commodities
they produced in local markets, and in exchange, they would buy some manufactured items. Wool obtained from the animals or the cotton produced locally would be cleaned and spun into yarn by women in periods when agricultural activity slowed down, and in most peasant homes these yarns would
later be used on handlooms to produce cloth for the household's consumption needs.

Since more than 80 percent of the population lived in rural areas, most
spinning and weaving activity took place in rural areas and was for own consumption during the first half of the nineteenth century (figure 5.2). In other
words, the crafts-based textiles production often cited by outside observers in
the urban areas represented only the "tip of the iceberg." In addition to production for personal consumption, merchants and workshop owners organized peasant women around a putting-out system, especially around towns
where craft production was more developed. They provided the wool, cotton,
and other raw materials and paid rural women on the basis of the yarn they
spun and simple cloth they wove during the off-season. As agricultural production for the market began to expand and imported cotton yarn and cloth
began to reach local markets, however, these rural manufacturing activities
began to decline. Linkages between rural areas and markets grew stronger,
peasants began to spend a greater proportion of their time on market-oriented
agricultural activities and bought imported products for a greater share of
their textile needs. By the last quarter of the century, cotton yarn spinning had
mostly disappeared in the coastal regions but survived to some extent in the
interior of Anatolia.

The decline if not disappearance of cotton yarn spinning did not mean that
the weaving of cotton cloth was also abandoned. While the Industrial Revolution had brought about large increases in productivity in the production of
cotton yarn, the increases in productivity at the weaving stage were more limited. Furthermore, in Anatolia and in other regions of the empire, local tastes

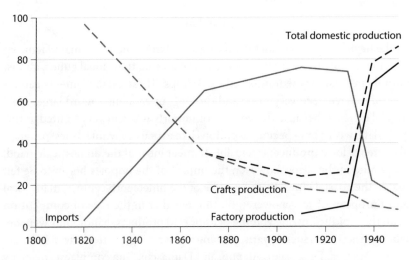

FIGURE 5.2. Shares of Domestic Production and Imports in Cotton Textiles
Consumption, 1820–1950 (percent). Sources: Pamuk and Williamson 2011;
Tekeli and İlkin 2004b.

continued to matter. The cotton cloth industry in Lancashire did not produce
a large variety of products in response to local tastes, which differed considerably from one region to another. Cloth weaving using imported yarns thus
survived in rural Anatolia for a longer period. Poor peasants and those of
moderate means continued to weave for themselves some of the cotton cloths
they wore. Those with higher incomes, on the other hand, would buy more of
the textiles they used at local markets (Pamuk 1987, pp. 108–129; Pamuk and
Williamson 2011, pp. 159–84).

Another important development in the nineteenth century was the rise of
export-oriented carpet weaving in the rural areas. For most of the century,
local and European merchants traveled through rural areas, collecting carpets
woven by peasant women and exporting them. As demand from Europe and
America grew, European investors began to organize production on a larger
scale. In 1908, they founded in Uşak in Western Anatolia, long-known for its
hand-woven carpets, the Oriental Carpet Manufacturers Company, and began
to produce and provide rural women machine-spun yarn and other materials
and equipment and pay them on a piece basis, particularly in those rural areas
where opportunities for agricultural production were limited. On the eve of
World War I, nearly fifteen thousand women worked for the company and
hand-woven carpets accounted for approximately 5 percent of Turkey's exports (Quataert 1993a, pp. 134–60; Quataert 1993b, pp. 225–70).

Urban Crafts

At the beginning of the nineteenth century, textiles and other manufacturing activities in the urban areas were organized around traditional guilds, almost entirely in small or medium-sized workshops. These establishments cannot be said to have been very lively and thriving, or evolving toward larger scale units. However, because the volume of imports was still very limited at this early date, with a few specific exceptions like expensive wool fabrics, paper, or glass items, local producers were able to meet most of the domestic demand. Beginning in the 1820s, however, the impact of the imports began to be felt first in the coastal cities. By the middle of the nineteenth century, many local and European observers were pointing out that in the face of competition from the rapidly growing volume of imported products, handlooms were declining in activities such as yarn spinning and weaving, particularly in Istanbul, Bursa, Amasya, Diyarbakir, Aleppo, and Damascus. The complaints made by owners of small workshops and guild workers about the competition of imported products lasted throughout the century (Issawi 1980, pp. 298–305; Issawi 1982, pp. 150–54; Quataert 1993a, pp. 49–104; Toprak 2016, pp. 251–62).

During the last quarter of the century, however, the pressure from imports subsided as relative prices began to shift in favor of manufactures (Pamuk and Williamson 2011, pp. 164–71; Quataert 1993a, pp. 80–104). Especially in regions where foreign trade links were weaker, such as Eastern and Southeastern Anatolia, the resistance of crafts against the competition from imported products was strengthened by these changes in relative prices. Using imported yarns and weaving fabrics according to local tastes as well as the tastes in Syria and even Egypt, and, equally important, by taking advantage of the low local wages, these small and medium-sized urban workshops were able to recover and survive until World War I.

The degree of resistance put up by the crafts should not be overstated, however. In evaluating the trends in domestic, crafts-based textile production and how well they fared against the imports, it would be more appropriate to look at the shares in total domestic consumption rather than absolute levels of production. From the end of the 1870s until World War I, Turkey's population increased approximately 40 percent thanks to the acceleration of immigration, especially from the Balkans. Our calculations summarized in figure 5.2 suggest that while crafts-based textiles production recorded absolute increases during these decades, their share in total domestic consumption continued to decline while the share of imports continued to rise. Domestic textiles production was able to increase its share of the domestic market, and very sharply, only after 1929 when the new nation-state was able to raise its tariffs. In other words, in the cotton textile sector as well as in many other branches of manufacturing, import-substitution industrialization began in 1929 and not earlier (Pamuk and Williamson 2011, pp. 159–84; Tekeli and Ilkin 2004b, pp. 409–64).

Large-scale Industrial Enterprises

In addition to rural household production and crafts-based urban workshops, the third form of manufacturing enterprises that emerged during the nineteenth century used imported steam engines and other machines developed during and after the Industrial Revolution and employed wage workers to produce textiles and other manufactured items in workshops and factories. These industrial enterprises were established first in the Istanbul area and later in parts of Western and Southern Anatolia in two different waves.

The first wave of factories was launched by the Ottoman state in the 1830s and 1840s as part of the initial reforms and essentially to meet the requirements of the army and the state. Many of these enterprises were forced to stop production within a short time, however, due to various problems and shortcomings. The second wave of capitalist enterprises using imported technology began to be established by local entrepreneurs in the 1890s. Because of the free trade treaties in existence, however, these enterprises could compete against imports only in sectors where transport costs were high, raw materials could be found locally and cheaply, and where low wages created an important advantage. The emerging industrialists were weak at the time and they could not obtain much support from the government for their enterprises (Clark 1974, pp. 65–76; Quataert 1992; Panza 2014, pp. 146–69).

The largest of the industrial enterprises established before World War I were textile factories producing cotton, woolen and silk yarn, and cloth. In addition, factories producing processed foods, oil and soap factories, as well as establishments producing construction materials such as cement and bricks, were established. The leading industrial center in the empire was Salonica, until it joined Greece at the end of the Balkan War in 1912. In the cotton textiles sector, for instance, more than half of the total factory production capacity in the empire was concentrated in the Salonica region. Factories in the area within Turkey's current borders were operating mainly in Istanbul and, to some extent, in İzmir and Adana. The Ottoman Industrial Census indicates that on the eve of World War I, the large-scale enterprises in these three areas employed an estimated five thousand workers (Panza 2014, pp. 146–69; Karakoç, Pamuk, and Panza 2017, pp. 145–49; Ökçün 1970).

The majority of workers in these manufacturing enterprises were employed in small-scale workshops employing at most five workers. However, large numbers of workers were also employed in large-scale enterprises, such as railways, ports, shipyards, mines, electricity, gas, as well as water companies or tobacco processing plants. A growing number of women worked for low wages in carpet-weaving workshops, raw silk spinning, tobacco processing, and cigarette factories as seasonal or permanent workers. After the 1908 Revolution, workers, especially those employed in large-scale enterprises, started organizing for better pay and better working conditions in Salonica, Istanbul, İzmir, and Adana, and they organized strikes through which they were able to secure significant increases in their wages. The Ottoman parliament voted in 1909 to curb strikes and even ban them completely in many sectors. Strikes were reduced to a large extent after this date, but they did not stop entirely (Quataert 1983, pp. 71–146; Karakışla 1995; Ökçün 1982, pp. 1–134, Toprak 2016, pp. 13–264).

The gradual rise of industrial enterprises in the decades before World War I also led to demands for protectionist policies even if the existing free trade treaties in force did not allow for that possibility. The government officials of the Tanzimat era had not given sufficient thought to the long-term economic consequences of free trade treaties. Their main concern had been to ensure the political and military support of Britain for the territorial integrity of the empire. The traditional approach to the economic issues persisted among government policy makers, and the central government's fiscal priorities continued to dominate their attitudes toward tariffs. After a century of expansion of foreign trade and export-oriented agricultural production, merchants and some large landowners argued in the early years of the twentieth century that since the empire's comparative advantage was in agriculture, the state's limited resources as well as private investments should be directed to the agricultural sector and to infrastructure such as railways, roads, and ports, which would enable the development of agricultural production and foreign trade.

Especially after the 1908 Revolution, however, arguments supporting industrialization and defending protectionist tariffs began to be heard as well. A growing number of pieces in newspapers and journals published in Istanbul and İzmir defended the need to adopt selective customs tariffs and support industrialization through mild protectionism. They argued that it was only thanks to such policies that the United States, as well as European countries like Germany or Italy, experienced economic development and that industrialization was the only way to overcome the European control over the Ottoman economy.

The liberal political and economic positions that were embraced after the 1908 Revolution with the aim of bringing together the various ethnic elements within the empire around the concept of an Ottoman nation began to be abandoned after the defeats suffered in the Balkan Wars of 1912–13. The leadership of the Committee of Union and Progress, which had seized power, was leaning toward Turkish nationalism. Together with ideas of Turkish national-ism that were beginning to gain strength, they began to question the existing economic policies and favored the establishment of national companies, na-tional banks, and the organization of Muslim craftsmen and merchants be-hind tariff walls. The Provisional Law for the Encouragement of Industry, legislated in 1913, was one of the first steps in that direction. It offered subsi-dies, tax exemptions, and other forms of state support to domestic industry. Aside from this exception, however, the existing policies in favor of an open economy were not abandoned until the outbreak of the world war (Toprak 1982, 168–81).

6

Economic Development and Institutional Change, 1820–1914

Economic Growth

The Industrial Revolution played a key role in the spread of economic growth, or sustained increases in per capita production and income, first in Western Europe and later and to a lesser extent in the rest of the world during the nineteenth century. After the end of the Napoleonic Wars, international trade started expanding at an unprecedented pace, first between Western European countries and later between them and the rest of the world. Technological changes in overland and maritime transportation further increased the pace of expansion of this trade. However, the spread of industrialization around the world was quite uneven during the nineteenth century. The extent to which industrialization proceeded in different parts of the world can help explain much of the variation in economic growth observed worldwide until World War I (Findlay and O'Rourke 2007, pp. 311–428; Kemp 1983, 1993; Allen 2011, pp. 27–130; Williamson 2011, pp. 25–86).

Thanks to the work of Angus Maddison and many others in recent decades, we are now able to estimate per capita GDP reasonably well for countries in Western Europe and North America during the nineteenth century, while the margin of error for other parts of the world is wider (Maddison 2007, pp. 375–86; Bolt and Van Zanden 2014, pp. 627–51). Sustained increases in per capita GDP during the centuries before the Industrial Revolution were limited and confined to northwestern Europe. In Britain in the eighteenth century, for example, the annual rate of increase of per capita income was only about 0.3 percent. In other European countries, per capita incomes increased more slowly or did not increase at all. In contrast, industrialization led to significantly higher increases in per capita income during the nineteenth century. For the century from the end of the Napoleonic Wars until World War I, the annual rate of increase of per capita income, in Western Europe and North

TABLE 6.1. GDP per Capita in the World and in Turkey, 1820–1913

	GDP per Capita		Annual Rate of Increase (percent)
	1820	1913	
Western Europe	1200	3460	1.2
United States	1250	5300	1.6
Industrializing Countries	1200	3960	1.3
Eastern Europe excl. Russia	750	1700	0.9
Italy	1120	2560	0.9
Spain	1000	2060	0.8
Asia	580	700	0.2
Africa	480	640	0.3
South America	690	1500	0.8
Egypt	600	950	0.5
Iran	550	800	0.4
Developing Countries	570	720	0.3
World	**670**	**1500**	**0.9**
Turkey	**720**	**1150**	**0.5**

Sources: Maddison 2007, pp. 375–86; Bolt and Van Zanden 2014; and Pamuk 2006, for Turkey.
Note: GDP per capita are given in purchasing power parity (PPP) adjusted 1990 US dollars. For details, see chapter 2.

America, averaged above 1 percent, for a total increase of about 200 percent. Economic growth in North America was even more rapid. Economic growth in Southern and Eastern European countries began later in the nineteenth century. Even though some countries recorded increases of more than 1 percent annually during the second half of the century, the gap between Western Europe and the rest of the continent widened until 1913 (table 6.1).

In comparison to Western Europe and North America, per capita incomes increased more slowly or did not increase at all in the rest of the world. The gap between the early industrializers and today's developing world thus increased significantly until World War I. In most parts of South America, although no significant industrialization took place, the abundance of empty land allowed growth rates close to that of Western Europe or North America, toward the end of the nineteenth century. As a result, the gap with the industrializing countries opened to a lesser extent. In Asia and Africa, however, increases in income per capita increased very slowly or did not increase at all. In China, the world's most populated country, per capita incomes declined during the nineteenth century. The significant exception in Asia was Japan, which was able to prevent the gap with Western Europe and the United States from expanding, thanks to rapid economic growth and development that began in the 1870s. Around 1820, the differences in per capita income between Western Europe and North America and the rest of the world are estimated, on average, at around 2:1. On the eve of World War I, the difference in per capita income between Western Europe and Southern and Eastern Europe had risen to 3:1. The gap between Western Europe and North America on the one hand, and Asia and Africa, on the other, had risen to 5:1 or even 6:1 (table 6.1 and figure 6.1).

Turkey's economy opened to foreign trade and foreign investment and specialization in agriculture increased during the nineteenth century. While the share of manufacturing activities declined, agricultural production for markets, both domestic and foreign, expanded, especially in the coastal regions. Was the growing specialization in agriculture accompanied by increases in per capita incomes? Vedat Eldem was the first to argue as early as 1970 that the Ottoman economy experienced some growth in the nineteenth century. The calculations he made, using population data and tax revenues of the central government from 1880 to World War I, led him to conclude that per capita production and income had risen at rates close to 1 percent per annum (Eldem 1970, pp. 275–309). Other series also suggest that per capita incomes rose during the nineteenth century. For example, data on urban wages provide evidence of rising incomes and standards of living. The purchasing power of the wages of construction workers in Istanbul and in Anatolian cities increased by more than 50 percent during the nineteenth century. However, calculations I made in recent years show that, because the state's ability to collect taxes had improved significantly and because the share taken by intermediaries in the provinces was declining steadily, rate of increase in tax receipts of the central government is not a good measure for the rate of growth of the underlying economic activity during the nineteenth century. Bringing together evidence from a variety of sources, real wage series, foreign trade series, as well as central government tax revenues, I have estimated that in the area within Turkey's current borders per capita income increased on average by 0.5 percent annually in the period between 1820 and 1913, a total increase of about 60 percent until World War I (Eldem 1970, pp. 275–309; Okyar 1987, pp. 7–49; Güran 2003; Özmucur and Pamuk 2002, pp. 292–321; Pamuk 2006, pp. 809–28). These estimates indicate that in terms of GDP per capita, Turkey did better than the developing countries as a whole, as well as Asia and Africa, but lagged behind Latin America during the nineteenth century (table 6.1).

A comparison with four countries with similar population, two in southern Europe and two in the Middle East, should provide additional insights into Turkey's trajectory. Italy and Spain began the nineteenth century with higher levels of GDP per capita in comparison to Turkey and experienced higher growth rates throughout the century. Around 1820, GDP per capita in Italy and Spain was about 50 percent higher than that in Turkey. After one century

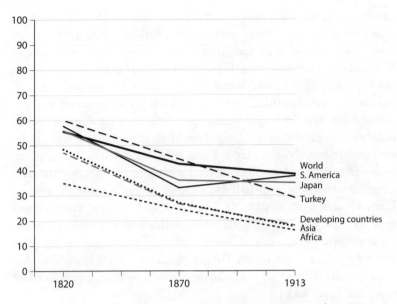

FIGURE 6.1. GDP per Capita in the World and in Turkey, 1820–1913 (PPP adjusted and as percentage of Western Europe and the United States). Sources: Maddison 2007, pp. 375–86; Bolt and Van Zanden 2014; and Pamuk 2006 for Turkey.

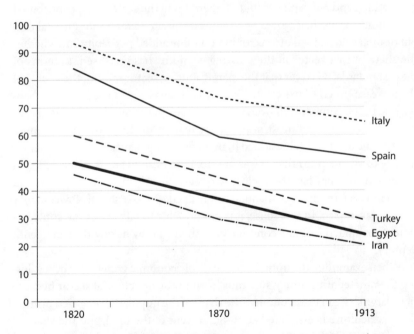

FIGURE 6.2. GDP per Capita in Four Other Countries and Turkey, 1820–1913 (PPP adjusted and as percentage of Western Europe and the United States). Sources: Maddison 2007, pp. 375–86; Bolt and Van Zanden 2014; and Pamuk 2006 for Turkey.

of higher growth rates, close to 1 percent per year compared to 0.5 percent per year for Turkey, the gap in per capita incomes between Turkey on the one hand and Italy and Spain on the other stood at roughly 2:1 on the eve of World War I. One key difference between these two countries and Turkey was the beginning of industrialization in both Italy and Spain and the acceleration of economic growth during the second half of the nineteenth century, while there was very little industrialization in Turkey until World War I. Nonetheless, the gap between Italy and Spain, on the one hand, and the developed countries of Western Europe and the United States, on the other, continued to increase, as was the case for Turkey primarily because the rates of industrialization were lower in Italy and Spain than in Western Europe and the United States. Compared to Turkey, Egypt and Iran had slightly lower levels of GDP per capita early in the nineteenth century. They experienced little industrialization and lower rates of economic growth during the nineteenth century. As a result, their GDP per capita levels were lower than that of Turkey in 1913 and the gap with the developed countries was even wider (table 6.1 and figure 6.2).

I now turn to the proximate causes of the rise in per capita income. Because the population of Turkey increased by about 75 percent during the nineteenth century, a distinction needs to be made, at the outset, between total output or value added and per capita output. In identifying the sectors that contributed to economic growth, it would be more appropriate to focus not on total output or total value added of a sector but on value added per capita and whether the share of that sector in the growing economy has increased. In terms of these standards, it is clear that the manufacturing sector was not the source of the increases in GDP per capita. In fact, as emphasized in the previous chapter, due to the competition from imports, many branches of crafts-based production activities and most importantly textiles declined during the nineteenth century. Total value added in manufacturing may have been higher on the eve of World War I than it was in 1820. In per capita terms, value added in manufacturing may have been close to or even slightly higher than its levels in 1820. However, the share of manufacturing in GDP was distinctly lower in 1914 than it was in 1820. In this sense, it is not possible to talk about the contribution of manufacturing to economic growth in Turkey during the nineteenth century.

When examining the immediate causes of economic growth in Turkey during the nineteenth century, one must turn to the agricultural sector because of its large share in the economy. The share of the population engaged primarily in agriculture is estimated at 75–80 percent of the total, and the share of agriculture in GDP is estimated at 50–60 percent in the decades before World War I. Rates of aggregate investment were probably not higher than 5–6 per-

TABLE 6.2. Basic Economic and Social Indicators for Turkey, 1820–1913

	1820	1913
Population (millions)	9.4	16.0
Urbanization Rate (%)		
Centers above 10,000 / Total Population	17	23
Life Expectancy at Birth (years)	26–27?	32–33?
Literacy Rate (%)	less than 5	14?
Share of Agriculture in Labor Force (%)	75–80?	75–80?
Share of Agriculture in GDP (%)	?	50
Exports / GDP (%)	2	11
Imports / GDP (%)	2	14
Investment / GDP (%)	5?	8
Revenues of Central Government / GDP (%)	4	13

Sources: Eldem 1970; Pamuk 1987; and see the text.

cent of GDP for most of the century, but rose to as much as 8–9 percent during the decades before World War I (Eldem 1970, pp. 275–309; table 6.2). As much as one-third of the investments in fixed capital after 1880 were undertaken by European companies that concentrated in railroad construction, infrastructure for foreign trade, and urban utilities. Low rates of investment, slow spread of the new technologies, and slow increases in productivity mostly in agriculture and to a lesser extent in trade were the leading proximate causes of the low but positive rates of economic growth before World War I. The Ottoman state borrowed large sums in European capital markets from mid-century until World War I, but only a small fraction of these funds was invested in infrastructure. However, as the composition of agricultural production shifted from subsistence crops to cash crops such as cotton, tobacco, grapes, figs, hazelnuts, and others, the producers may have spent more labor throughout the year, but incomes per person or household as well as the value of output per unit of land increased.

One important trend supporting growing market orientation of agriculture was the favorable movements in terms of trade for most of the century. As relative prices of imported manufactured goods declined and those of agricultural commodities increased, the rural population began to spend more time on agricultural activities and less on others (Pamuk and Williamson 2011, pp. 159–84). As imported and inexpensive cotton yarns began to reach even the most remote towns and villages, agricultural producers, especially women, gave up yarn spinning to a large degree and devoted more of their time to market-oriented agricultural activities.

Another and related source of the increase in per capita incomes was the opening of new land to cultivation and the rise in land cultivated per producer along with the increasing market orientation of agricultural production. In rural areas, plenty of empty land that could be used for production was available during the nineteenth century. With the expansion of market opportunities and improvements in the terms of trade for agriculture, producers began to expand the land under cultivation. Especially in regions where production was oriented toward domestic and foreign markets, such as the Aegean, Çukurova in the south, and Central Anatolia, opening new land for cultivation contributed to the increases in total and per capita production. The construction of railroads as well as ports and other infrastructure lowered transportation costs and brought some distant areas, especially Central Anatolia, within reach of long-distance markets, both domestic and export (Issawi 1980, pp. 183–93). Part of the increases in land under cultivation especially in these rural areas was due to the settlement by the government of immigrant families, but the partial evidence we have suggests that in areas where land was available and markets were close, lands cultivated per family tended to increase during the course of the century (Güran 1998, 2003).

There were also some organizational and technological changes in agriculture during the nineteenth century, but these and their contribution to economic growth remained limited. Some technological change took place during the decades before World War I, mostly in the more commercialized coastal regions of the country. While evidence on changes in agricultural techniques or implements is scarce, the shift in the crop mix toward cash crops and the introduction of new crops by the immigrating farmers is more readily observable. Similarly, the growing market orientation of agriculture expanded the market and foreign trade related services, especially in the urban areas, but the contribution of the latter to employment and economic growth was limited in comparison to the contribution of agriculture (Quataert 1992; Quataert 1994, pp. 843–87).

While the average growth rate of 0.5 percent per year and 60 percent total increase in per capita income for the century as a whole was certainly significant and unprecedented, the proximate reasons why growth rates were not higher need to be explored as well. One reason the growth rate remained low was because the market orientation of agriculture remained limited mostly to the coastal regions. A second and related reason was that because of the limited capacity of the central government and the agricultural sector, rates of investment in infrastructure and in agriculture remained low. The third and more general reason why Turkey's growth rate remained low in the nineteenth century was the difficulty in achieving increases in productivity and incomes with an agriculture-based model. Growth remained limited in the majority of countries that sought to specialize further in agriculture during the nineteenth century. For this reason, with the exception of a few countries in South America, which had large amounts of empty land, the gap between the countries that were industrializing and those that continued to specialize in agriculture widened steadily (Maddison 2007, pp. 375–86; Bolt and Van Zanden 2014, pp. 627–51). This pattern applied to Turkey as well. Differences in per capita income between Turkey and the industrializing countries of Western and Southern Europe increased from about 2:1 at the beginning of the century, to 3:1 before World War I (table 6.1 and figure 6.1).

Rapid economic growth could be achieved primarily through industrialization in the nineteenth century. Late industrializing countries around the world including those in Europe and North America could succeed only by adopting protectionist policies (Allen 2011, pp. 114–30). The private sector was rather weak in Turkey during the nineteenth century. Equally important, the Ottoman government was not ready to adopt protectionist policies. Ottoman governments did not embrace a strategy of economic growth through industrialization until after the Young Turk Revolution of 1908. Moreover, while the Ottoman state was officially independent, there were limits to its independence. After the free trade treaty of 1838, it did not have the power to unilaterally raise customs duties and adopt other protectionist measures to support domestic industry (Toprak 1982, pp. 99–118).

Income Distribution

Institutions and institutional changes played key roles in the evolution of the distribution of income during the nineteenth century. The institutional change with the strongest impact on the distribution of income was the embrace of free trade by the Ottoman government. Growing integration into the world economy under conditions of free trade led to increasing specialization in agriculture and the decline in urban crafts-based manufacturing activities due to the competition from imports. Another set of institutional changes that was important, especially for top incomes, was the reforms associated with the centralization and the rise in the power of the government at Istanbul, which raised the share of its tax revenues and led to the decline in the share of tax revenues retained by the provincial groups.

To examine the long-term changes in income distribution during the century uuntil World War I, I begin with the rural areas and the agricultural sector, which employed the largest share of the population. Quantitative evidence on the distribution of land and land use and how they evolved over time is limited. We do know, however, that rural areas in Anatolia were underpopulated and there was a good deal of uncultivated land. Evidence on land rents is also scarce, but the relative proportions of labor and land favored labor and the small family enterprises rather than the owners of large plots. Small and medium-sized family farms either cultivating their own land or sharecropping for owners of large plots thus remained the most common form of enterprise in agriculture. The arrival of close to a million immigrant families from the Caucasus, Crimea, and the Balkans, and their settlement by the government in rural areas throughout the century, further reinforced the small and medium-sized family farms (Karpat 1985a, pp. 60–77). The significant exceptions were the fertile plains newly opened for production, such as Çukurova in the south, where large landownership and large enterprises using wage labor spread.

With growing external trade and the decline in transportation costs, relative prices of agricultural cash crops increased and the relative prices of imported manufactures declined for most of the century. These price movements tended to benefit the market-oriented producers in Western Anatolia and in other coastal regions. By contrast, peasants who could not produce significant amounts for the markets either because they cultivated small amounts of land or because they were away from markets did not join this trend. For example, in Eastern Anatolia, where market-oriented production was more limited, increases in agriculture and agricultural incomes remained limited. As a result, regional disparities in income tended to increase along with the uneven pattern of agricultural commercialization. While Western Anatolia, and more generally, the coastal regions benefited, Eastern and Southeastern Anatolia, where railroad construction and production for long-distance markets remained limited, lagged behind. By the beginning of the twentieth century, some of the largest inequalities were likely to be found within the agricultural sector and were associated, above all, with patterns of land ownership. The most prosperous people in the rural areas were the larger landowners in the west, and the poorest groups were the peasants with small amounts of land or sharecroppers in regions with lower levels of commercialization, such as Eastern Anatolia (Pamuk 1987, pp. 82–107).

The evidence on urban-rural differences in per capita income is limited but the decline in urban manufacturing activities as well as the long-term trends in relative prices in favor of agriculture suggest that these differences did not tend to rise. The limited increases in the urbanization rate also suggest that the urban-rural differences in average incomes remained limited. The most rapidly growing cities during the nineteenth century were not industrializing cities, but port cities like İzmir, Samsun, and Mersin, whose trade with Western Europe was expanding rapidly. Moreover, wages in the urban areas tended to rise more or less proportionally to the increase in per capita income, suggesting that limited growth in urban areas did not lead to increases in inequalities (Boratav, Ökçün, and Pamuk 1985, pp. 379–406; Özmucur and Pamuk 2002, pp. 292–321). In short, during the nineteenth century when industrialization had not yet begun and economic growth was limited, inequalities between rural and urban areas remained limited because prices evolved in favor of agriculture.

Changes among the top income groups in the urban areas also provide insights into the dynamics of long-term change in income distribution. Until the middle of the nineteenth century, most of the highest income groups in the urban areas were connected to the networks of tax collection for the state. It has been estimated that some 1,000–2,000 Istanbul-based individuals, together with some 5,000–10,000 individuals in the provinces, as well as innumerable contractors, agents, financiers, accountants, and managers, controlled an important share of the state's tax revenues during the eighteenth century and until the second quarter of the nineteenth century. These individuals and their households were in the top 1 percent of the income and wealth distribution across the empire. In the capital city, high-level, mostly Muslim bureaucrats were able to accumulate large wealth by purchasing tax farms in partnership with non-Muslim financiers and then selling them off to subcontractors. Non-Muslims were often prohibited from holding tax-farming contracts, but Greeks, Armenians, and Jews were very much part of this elite as financiers, brokers, and accountants. Behind the individual, often a Muslim, who joined the bidding in the tax-farming auctions, there often existed a partnership that included financiers as well as the agents who intended to organize the tax collection process itself, often by dividing the large initial contract into smaller pieces and finding subcontractors. Assets of the prominent government employees were often expropriated after they lost their office or died, however. In the provinces, the richest people in the urban areas belonged to the notable families who were politically powerful, controlled tax collection, and retained a large fraction of the tax revenues. Some of the notables were also engaged in long-distance trade and owned land, but their economic power was tied, above all, to tax collection. They lived in the interior rather than in the port cities (Salzman 1993, pp. 393–423; Keyder, Özveren, and Quataert 1993, pp. 519–58).

As a result of the increasing political and fiscal centralization during the nineteenth century, the mostly Muslim notables in the provinces began to be squeezed out of tax collection and a larger fraction of the tax revenues began to flow to the central treasury. While tax collection declined as the leading source of private wealth, long-distance trade, especially trade with European countries, emerged as the leading source of large income and wealth. Most of the large merchants were Greeks and Armenians who sometimes partnered with European merchants or merchant houses. In contrast, accumulation of large wealth in the hands of artisans and large-scale manufacturers was rare in Turkey both before and during the nineteenth century.

It is thus clear that the institutional changes and the opening of the economy during the century until World War I did not have the same impact on the incomes of Muslims and non-Muslims. The average incomes of both groups increased, but the evidence points to higher increases for the non-Muslims. The significant rise in trade with Europe as well as direct European investment benefited the mostly the non-Muslim merchants who were part of the growing commercial networks between the port cities and their agricultural hinterlands. In the countryside, the non-Muslim agricultural producers were more strongly connected to the markets and benefited more from the increases in the market orientation of agriculture, in comparison to the Muslims. At the same time, the Muslim ayan or urban notables and other Muslim elites in the provinces who had gained power by controlling the tax collection system and keeping a large share of the tax revenues in earlier centuries experienced decline in their wealth and political power as a result of the political and fiscal centralization that accompanied the reforms. The differences in the economic trajectory of the two groups help explain why the reforms were met with resentment and opposition by at least some of the Muslims in the agricultural towns as well as the countryside in the interior (Keyder, Özveren, and Quataert 1993, pp. 519–58; Karpat 2001, pp. 89–116).

Top-down Institutional Change and Its Limits

While discussing the proximate causes of the low rates of economic growth experienced during the nineteenth century earlier in this chapter, I emphasized that the low rates of economic growth were a result of the increasing market orientation of agriculture supported by favorable movements in relative prices rather than productivity increases arising from technological change in agriculture or industrialization. This explanation was incomplete as it did not include the deeper causes of economic growth, most importantly, institutions and institutional change. This section reviews the contribution and limitations of the institutional changes that most directly affected the economy.

For the Ottoman Empire, the nineteenth century was a period very different from those that preceded it. Europe's growing military and economic power on the one hand, and the growing independence movements in the Balkans as well as the challenges by the notables in the provinces, on the other, had brought the empire to the brink of disintegration. In response, the Ottoman government launched a series of centralizing initiatives and institutional changes inspired by European examples. Top-down reform efforts in military, provincial administration, state finances, law, the judiciary, education, and other fields continued over the course of the century. The introduction of these new formal institutions did not guarantee that they would bring about higher rates of economic growth and development, however. For one thing, for the reforms to succeed, the Ottoman government needed the support of European states against both external and internal challenges. In return, European states and companies demanded the creation of a market economy specializing in agriculture and trade, which was open to the outside world and offered special privileges to European companies. The reforms and the opening of the economy thus progressed under the growing influence of European states and companies. The free trade agreement signed in 1838, the foreign borrowing process that began in 1854, and the construction of the railways that started in the 1850s were major turning points in the process of opening the economy. At each of these important watersheds for the economy, the central government faced military, political, or financial difficulties. In the negotiations, the Ottoman government was thinking more about the short-term political or financial support they would receive from European states than about the long-term economic consequences. European states and European capital thus continued to have a good deal of power in the shaping of the institutions, especially formal institutions that influenced the direction of the economy.

The free trade treaty of 1838 turned out to be irreversible. The Ottoman government was unable to make significant changes in the treaty until World War I. By supporting the specialization in agriculture and delaying the beginnings of protectionism and industrialization, as southern European countries were able to achieve, for example, the free trade treaty prevented higher rates of growth for the Ottoman economy. Moreover, not all institutional changes demanded and obtained by the European states and companies can be said to have supported economic growth in the context of an open economy model. For example, the capitulations, or economic and legal privileges of European citizens and companies which had their origins in the concessions offered to European merchants by the Ottoman government in the sixteenth century, expanded considerably during the nineteenth century as the power of European states rose and the involvement of European merchants and investors increased. Since Ottoman citizens were prevented from competing under equal conditions with the Europeans, these privileges had negative consequences for the activities and development of Ottoman entrepreneurs. The issue was debated and discussed many times, but the European governments were unwilling to consider any changes in the capitulations (Boogert 2005; İnalcık 1971, pp. 1179–89; Artunç 2015, pp. 720–48).

The central government was also aware that as the economy opened up to foreign trade and investment, its control weakened and the division of the empire into spheres of influence among European countries proceeded further. In response, the central government tried to slow down the opening of the economy. Even though it signed the free trade agreements and at times reluctantly provided various concessions to European companies, it also tried to protect small producers and the related institutions, especially the family enterprises in agriculture which, with their taxes, formed the fiscal foundations of the Ottoman state. For example, Ottoman courts were often unwilling to expropriate the lands of small producers who were unable to pay their debts. Under such circumstances, the opening of the economy to foreign trade and foreign investment proceeded more slowly in Ottoman Turkey in comparison with colonies of European powers or, for instance, in Egypt, as I will discuss later in this chapter.

In addition, the introduction of the new formal institutions did not guarantee that they would be implemented successfully and comprehensively. In fact, the Ottoman reforms faced a number of major obstacles. First, many of the reforms were quite expensive and required effective implementation and enforcement. In contrast, the fiscal, administrative, and legal capacities of the state were limited and the state could not effectively enforce the new laws and policies. While laws could be changed and new policies could be announced overnight, fiscal, administrative, and legal capacities of the state improved slowly. The state's capacity to penetrate the rural areas where the great majority of the population lived and implement the reforms as well as deliver infrastructure, health services, and education remained low. Even the urban areas in the more distant provinces remained insulated from the government's reforms.

Second, the design and implementation of the reforms remained top-down and they were not fully embraced by the public at large. In many situations, powerful groups, including the central bureaucracy, resisted institutional changes or exerted pressure to ensure that an institution operated in a way that was different from the intended aim. Moreover, the distribution of benefits from the enforcement of these institutions was not always in line with the existing distribution of power in society. In response, powerful groups and organizations could develop institutions different from those defined by the state that will better serve their interests.

Third, the new formal institutions were not modular constructions but often interacted with others. They did not necessarily and inevitably crowd out the existing institutions. There were always large numbers of other institutions that mattered in the implementation of a new institution. Informal arrangements often built from the bottom up within communities and rooted in social networks were frequently necessary for the workings of the new formal arrangements. How and to what extent the new formal institutions functioned depended on how they interacted with the existing or new informal arrangements as well as the new outcomes. Political institutions, laws, and legal systems tended to change faster than social norms, but the effectiveness of the legal system and the enforcement of the laws also depended on their acceptance and legitimacy. Those that resisted the reforms could always make use of some of the informal institutions as well as other formal institutions as strategic resources (Roland 2004, pp. 109–31; Starr 1979; Starr and Pool 1974, pp. 533–60).

In other words, the reforms of the nineteenth century were accompanied by the two-way interaction between formal and informal institutions as well as the two-way interaction between institutions and economic outcomes. The preceding discussion suggests that the two-way interaction between institutions and social structure was equally important. The new formal institutions began to influence the various social groups not only through their influence on economic outcomes but also directly through their influence on the behavior of various actors as well the relations among these actors. The new institutions also began to create new economic and social cleavages. The various social groups with diverging interests responded by attempting to influence the institutions.

The reforms and the opening of the economy to foreign trade and investment were accompanied by some economic growth, especially in the more commercialized regions. However, the Muslims whose numbers increased by the immigration of literally millions of Muslims from Crimea, the Caucasus, and the Balkans during the second half of the century also noticed that the non-Muslims gained more and they were lagging behind. The Muslims, mostly farmers, small-scale merchants, and artisans thus began to unite in opposition to the secular reforms and the growing economic cleavages. In other words, the opening of the economy to globalization was accompanied by the rise of identity cleavages. The emphasis Sultan Abdulhamid II placed on Islam as he continued with many of the reforms after 1880 was based at least in part on the recognition of the growing discontent among the conservative Muslim elites and their communities. He made use not only of new technologies such as the railroads and the telegraph but also of religious orders and networks as well as patronage networks to reach the Muslim communities. Abdulhamid also supported the introduction of new schools to the Muslims and Muslim notables began to gain greater power as a result of the provincial administrative reforms and the rise of locally elected councils during his reign (Karpat 2001, pp. 89–116).

The Muslim elites often made use of informal institutions including identity-based networks and patron-client relations in these conflicts. The extent to which formal institutions could be enforced or rule of law prevailed often depended on the relations and the degree of understanding if not consensus between the elites and the state. As a result, the new formal institutions did not crowd out informal institutions but continued to interact and coexist with them. The opposition to the reforms and the emerging secular center-conservative periphery duality in the nineteenth century was not a purely cultural phenomenon and had deep economic roots (Mardin 1973, pp. 169–90).

Many of the new institutions were thus slow to spread, especially in the provinces. For example, the reach of the new courts remained limited. This was in part due to the limitations on state capacity, but there were obstacles on the demand side as well. Some of the local elites opposed the new courts and tried to limit their use by their communities, particularly in the Kurdish region in Eastern Anatolia where the centralizing reforms and the growing presence of the central government were resisted by many of the Kurdish tribal leaders. A similar pattern emerged in education. The spread of the new schools to the provinces and to the rural areas could gain momentum only toward the end of the century. One important reason was the limited fiscal resources of the state. Attempts were made late in the century to also mobilize local resources by encouraging the cooperation of provincial notables, but these efforts were not sufficient either. Equally important, the new schools were not easily accepted by the Muslim population and the conservative Muslim elites who did not embrace the ongoing reforms.

Opposition to the reforms also came from those who controlled and benefited from some of the Islamic-Ottoman institutions in the era before the reforms. The share of vakıfs or Islamic endowments is often exaggerated, but it is estimated that they accounted for as much as 20 percent of the agricultural lands early in the nineteenth century. Vakıf assets including the assets of cash vakıfs also accounted for a significant share of the productive assets in the urban areas. Some of the vakıf assets were confiscated by the state and the vakıfs began to be regulated by a new ministry after 1826. Many of the large vakıfs began to be managed directly by the central government and others, including the cash vakıfs, continued to operate but with greater controls. During the rest of the century, tens of thousands of immigrant families were settled in and given ownership of some of the largest agricultural vakıfs which were controlled by the ministry (Öztürk 1995, pp. 109–67). Those who had controlled the vakıf lands and the other vakıf assets and those who benefited from the incomes generated and the services provided by these institutions, families, and religious orders, as well as those who used and embraced the vakıfs for social and cultural reasons, remained opposed to many of the reforms and were reluctant to embrace many of the new institutions.

One very important institutional change, which had a long-term impact on the agricultural sector, was the 1858 Land Code. Until that date, a very large proportion of agricultural land had *miri* status or was owned by the state. Peasant families had tenure rights on these lands. Under the new code, agricultural lands began to transfer to private ownership. How the code interacted with existing institutions and existing power distribution especially in the rural areas is beginning to be studied but is still not well understood. It is clear, however, that the implementation and impact of the Land Code varied significantly between regions, depending upon the capacity of the state to enforce it and the distribution of political and economic power in the rural areas. In most cases, the new Land Code produced outcomes consistent with the existing distribution of power. Large ownership emerged in areas where powerful individuals already controlled large tracts of land and where land was more scarce and valuable. Family plots prevailed where land was more abundant and the state was able to support the small farms (Gerber 1987, pp. 84-90; İslamoğlu 2004; Aytekin 2009, pp. 935-51).

A Comparison with Egypt

In addition to their surface areas and populations, Egypt and Turkey showed important similarities as well as differences in patterns of foreign trade and foreign investment in the nineteenth century. Both Turkey and Egypt followed or had to follow economic policies that kept the economy open to foreign trade and foreign investment until World War I. As a result, Egypt, like Turkey, experienced increasing specialization in agriculture rather than industrialization during the nineteenth century and offers a useful comparison with Turkey. It is estimated that annual rates of increase of per capita GDP in Egypt, as in Turkey, averaged 0.5 percent per year during the century until World War I. (Pamuk 2006, pp. 809-28; Bolt and Van Zanden 2014, pp. 627-51; also table 6.1 and figure 6.1).

There were significant differences in the patterns of foreign trade and foreign investment of the two countries. These differences offer an opportunity to better understand the case of Turkey. First, the amount of foreign trade and foreign direct investment (FDI) in relation to GDP and more generally the degree of openness of the economy was much higher in Egypt. Second, while Anatolia exported a variety of crops none of which had more than 12 percent share in total exports, Egypt presents one of the strongest cases of monoculture during the nineteenth century. Share of cotton in Egypt's total exports exceeded 95 percent on the eve of World War I (table 6.3).

Geography is the first factor to consider in explaining these differences. Most of Egypt's population and agricultural land were located along the Nile Valley and especially in the Nile Delta. Linking this fertile and homogeneous region to export ports and world markets was relatively easy. On the other

TABLE 6.3. Foreign Trade and Investment in Turkey, Egypt, and Iran, 1914

	Exports per Capita	FDI Stock per Capita	GDP per Capita
Turkey	1.00	3	11
Egypt	2.65	9	9.5
Iran	0.40	< 1	7.5

Sources: Pamuk 1987, 2006; Owen,1969; Issawi 1981.
Note: Figures provided in current British pounds.

hand, in Anatolia, arable land was distributed across very different regions. In addition, building a transport network that linked the different regions to ports of export and urban markets was a much more difficult and expensive process. As a result, the market orientation of agriculture in Turkey proceeded unevenly and more slowly. While coastal regions linked to markets very quickly, the cereal-growing areas of Central Anatolia were excluded from world markets until the construction of railways at the end of the century. The eastern part of Anatolia, where almost a quarter of the population lived, was much less affected by the expansion of trade with Europe until the First World War.

In terms of social structure and distribution of power, too, there were important differences between the two countries. The differences in political and economic institutions between the two countries reflected these differences in social structure and distribution of power as well as geography. The distribution of land was very unequal in Egypt, and the family of Muhammed Ali Pasha and the elites around them had a great deal of economic and political power. As a result, the state strongly supported the development and growing export orientation of agriculture. State policies in support of agricultural development such as irrigation, distribution of seeds, and investment in transportation that began with Muhammad Ali Pasha in the early part of the century were continued later on. A rising share of state resources was directed to promoting cotton and the monoculture model in later decades. These investments were continued with funds borrowed in European financial markets in the 1860s (Owen 1969; Owen 1981, pp. 122–52).

After Egypt was occupied by Britain in 1882, the colonial administration continued the focus and policies on cotton production and exports with large-scale irrigation projects, financed mostly by local funds and to some extent by European investments. The emphasis on a single export-oriented crop developed further during the British era and agricultural productivity and revenues increased until early in the twentieth century. The main beneficiaries of these

policies were the local landowners and the British economy, which had secured steady supplies of an important and much needed raw material. In
other words, the social structure as well as political and economic institutions, including economic policies, were strongly behind export-oriented
agriculture and brought about a sweeping transformation during the nineteenth century.

In Turkey, in contrast, mostly small-scale agricultural producers and merchants had much less power and the government had a great deal of autonomy
from these groups. The Ottoman government also supported market-oriented
agriculture because it would increase production and broaden its tax base.
Rather than the big landowners or large-scale European farmers, however, it
preferred to support small and medium-sized producers in agriculture, because it could more easily collect taxes from them and they did not represent
a political threat (Keyder and Tabak 1991, pp. 1–16; Kasaba 1988, pp. 49–85;
Özbek 2015, pp. 39–112). Moreover, aside from its support for the construction
of railways, the Ottoman government could direct only a small proportion of
its resources toward infrastructure investment in agriculture.

One important difference between Turkey and Egypt during the nineteenth century involved political institutions. While a colonial administration ruled in Egypt after 1882, none of the European states was able to exert
its influence single-handedly on the Ottoman Empire. The rivalry between
major European states created some room for maneuver for the Ottoman
state, which could play one European power against the other and resist external pressures to some extent, at least on some issues. The Ottoman government recognized that the economy opened up to foreign trade and investment, spheres of influence began to emerge inside the empire, and the
central government could lose control of the tax revenues at least in some
regions. For this reason, the Ottoman government was not as enthusiastic as
the government in Egypt in supporting integration with world markets. The
opening of the economy to international trade and investment thus proceeded more slowly, in part because of the struggles, bargaining, and compromises between the European states and financiers and the Ottoman central government.

In comparison to Egypt, the market orientation of Anatolian agriculture
proceeded more slowly under these conditions. Most of the production was
undertaken by small family farms. These enterprises were slow to embrace
investments or technological changes that would increase productivity. After
a relatively easy early period when exports expanded rapidly until the 1870s,
the rate of export growth from Anatolia slowed down. For example, in Western Anatolia, which began developing its exports earlier than other regions,

total value of exports from İzmir, the leading port of the region and the country, showed limited increases in the decades before World War I (Pamuk 1987, pp. 18–40; Kasaba 1988, pp. 87–112).

At the beginning of the twentieth century, Turkey had a mostly agricultural economy open to foreign trade and investment. European companies had a good deal of power, especially in the urban economy, and controlled part of state finances and external trade, most of the railways, and banking, but were not active in agricultural or manufacturing production. These features, which were broadly similar to many countries in the developing world during the nineteenth century and until World War I, were going to change significantly during the Interwar period with the decline of external trade and withdrawal of European investments.

Two other characteristics of Turkey's economy during the nineteenth century were going to persist during the twentieth century, however. In many ways, these characteristics set Ottoman society and economy apart from many developing regions and they constituted important parts of the Ottoman legacy. One of these was the power of the central government vis-à-vis other social groups or local elements. The central government benefited from the reforms and new technologies and strengthened its position during the nineteenth century. In contrast, the political power of elements in the provinces, landowners, and merchants remained limited. Moreover, although European states competed with one another in the nineteenth century, no single European state was able to exert its influence single-handedly on the Ottoman Empire.

The fact that the central bureaucracy was able to sustain its power, against both domestic elements and colonial interventions, brings us to the second characteristic that persisted in the twentieth century. Supported by the relative abundance of land and the relative scarcity of labor as well as state policies, small and medium-sized family enterprises were the most common form in agriculture. Small producers were also very common in the urban economy. The central government taxed small producers but also supported them against big landowners, both to strengthen its fiscal base and to prevent local elements in the provinces from getting stronger (Keyder 1987, pp. 25–48; Kasaba 1988, pp. 49–85; Özbek 2015, pp. 39–112).

Human Development

There is very limited quantitative evidence regarding health and education, the two basic dimensions of human development beside income, for nineteenth-century Turkey. We have only one study for life expectancy at birth for Turkey for the nineteenth century. Shorter and Macura offer an estimate of 32–33 years for the years before World War I (Shorter and Macura

1983, pp. 66–101). Demographic data on the nineteenth century is not detailed enough to estimate life expectancy for earlier benchmark years. However, based on trends in southern and eastern European countries, I have estimated that life expectancy at birth at 26–27 years for 1820. Such an estimate would also be in line with the existing estimates of life expectancy at birth in the developing countries during the nineteenth century (Zijdeman and de Silva 2014, pp. 101–16). This estimate would suggest that life expectancy at birth increased slowly and by a total of about six years during the century until World War I (figure 2.3 and table 6.2). One of the most important reasons why life expectancy at birth remained so low was the high rates of infant and child mortality, especially in rural areas where approximately three-quarters of the population lived. In fact, it is estimated that as much as half or more of all deaths were among children under the age of five who died mostly of infectious diseases during the nineteenth century and until the second half of the twentieth century. Part of the slow increases in life expectancy was probably due to the decline in infant mortality (Deaton 2013, pp. 59–100).

The frequent recurrences of the plague as well as of cholera had been important obstacles to population growth around the eastern Mediterranean in previous centuries. The disappearance of the plague after the 1830s contributed to rising life expectancy. While public health measures such as the quarantine of ships probably played a role in the disappearance of the plague during the second quarter of the nineteenth century, cholera outbreaks did continue. Even though wars became less frequent in the second half of the nineteenth century, they were short-lived. Moreover, armies were small and loss of life during wars had been limited. For this reason, decline in the frequency of wars probably did not change overall mortality rates by a significant amount.

Gradual improvements in nutrition were another cause of the decline in mortality. GDP per capita rose by about 60 percent during the century until World War I. The more market-oriented coastal regions and the west of the country benefited more from these increases than the interior and the east. Nonetheless, with slowly rising agricultural production per capita, food availability also improved in all rural areas where more than three-fourths of the population lived. Famines were not frequent occurrences before the nineteenth century in Anatolia. They declined further during the nineteenth century thanks to the gradual improvement in food availability and the improvements in transportation, including the construction of railroads.

Because of the limited availability of evidence, it is difficult to say very much about rural-urban differences in mortality during the nineteenth century. In the industrializing countries of Western Europe, urban areas had higher rates of mortality than the rural areas and they could not maintain their

populations without significant immigration from rural areas during the nineteenth century. It is not clear how urban and rural mortality rates compared
and whether urban rates were higher in the case of Turkey, however. Investment in sanitary infrastructure was restricted only to parts of large port cities.
While the urban areas were more significantly affected by the cholera outbreaks as well as the earlier occurrences of the plague, industrialization in
urban areas was late to start and remained limited. Moreover, urban growth
and population densities in the nineteenth-century Ottoman Empire did not
reach the levels experienced in Western Europe. On the other hand, per capita
incomes were lower in the rural areas and there were fluctuations in food
availability but not recurring famines. The information about the breakdown
of life expectancy at birth between different groups is also very limited. However, it is likely that non-Muslims had higher life expectancy because they had
higher per capita incomes and were somewhat better educated (Akder 2010,
pp. 210–20; Courbage and Fargues 1997, pp. 91–129).

Since many countries in the world recorded progress in health, as well as
per capita income, during the nineteenth century, it would be useful to evaluate Turkey's experience comparatively. The available estimates indicate that
life expectancy in Western Europe and western offshoots increased during the
nineteenth century and reached 45–55 years on the eve of World War I. In
contrast, the available evidence indicates that in the developing regions of the
world, life expectancy at birth did not increase or increased very slowly. Argentina had a life expectancy of 45 years and Japan 40 years on the eve of
World War I. Elsewhere in Asia, Africa, and South America, life expectancy at
birth ranged from 25 to 32 years. These estimates suggest that Turkey's life
expectancy was close to averages for developing countries as a whole and perhaps slightly higher during the latter part of the nineteenth century for which
estimates are available (Zijdeman and de Silva 2014, pp. 109–12; figures 2.4 and
2.5 in chapter 2).

Education was an important component of the nineteenth-century reforms initiated by the Ottoman state. A three-tiered education system was
established early, but the spread of the new schools to the provinces could
gain momentum only toward the end of the century. However, the numbers
of the new schools increased slowly over time and they did not replace the
Quran schools. One important reason was the limited fiscal resources of the
state. Attempts were made late in the century to also mobilize local resources
by encouraging the cooperation of provincial notables, but these efforts were
not sufficient either. Even more important, the new schools were not easily
accepted by the Muslim population and the conservative Muslim elites, who
did not embrace the ongoing reforms. The local Muslim population was often
encouraged to send their children to the Quran schools instead. As a result,

the challenge of expanding public schools in the provinces and in rural areas was not overcome until the end of the empire (Somel 2001; Fortna 2010, pp. 15-26). The modern schools of higher education also began to turn out graduates to staff the bureaucracy and the military at different levels. Students in these military and other schools were taught subjects such as modern physics, medicine, and biology. In addition, schools of agriculture began to teach the more recent techniques of cultivation mostly to the children of more prosperous farmers. In addition, the non-Muslim communities and the foreign missionaries who were able to take mostly non-Muslim students ran their own schools.

Numbers of students at all levels across the empire more than doubled from the 1860s until the end of the century. Within the area inside the present-day borders of Turkey, close to 20 percent of the school-age population was enrolled in the various schools by the end of the century. It is estimated that the overall literacy rate within the same area remained close to or was a little higher than 10 percent on the eve of World War I (Somel 2001; Tekeli and İlkin 1993; Alkan 2000; Fortna 2011, pp. 20-21). Even though quantitative evidence is limited, it would be safe to say there were large disparities in the schooling and literacy rates between urban and rural areas, between men and women, and between non-Muslims and Muslims. The vast majority of those who were literate at the beginning of the twentieth century were urban dwellers and male. Rates of schooling and literacy, as well as the diffusion of the new schools into the provinces, were higher in each of the non-Muslim communities than those of the Muslims. Literacy rates were probably higher in both the urban and rural areas in the west, but the extent of the regional differences in schooling and literacy rates is not clear. While the Ottoman government built more schools in the west and along the coastal areas, American and other missionaries were more active in the east where the majority of the Armenians lived. Estimates suggest that average formal schooling received by adults over fifteen years of age in the area within present-day borders of Turkey increased very slowly to about 0.5 years, while world averages increased to about 2 years on the eve of World War I. This level of average schooling placed Turkey well behind not only the developed countries of Western Europe and the United States but also Russia, Latin America, and China, and slightly ahead of Egypt, South and Southeast Asia, and Sub-Saharan Africa (van Leeuwen and van Leeuwen-Li 2014, pp. 93-97).

7

From Empire to Nation-State

SPANNING TWO WORLD WARS AND the Great Depression, 1914 to 1950 was a difficult period for the world economy. As the open economy model of the nineteenth century disintegrated under the pressure of these major events, interventionism, protectionism, and greater emphasis on national economies emerged as new principles guiding economic policy. The decline of the nineteenth-century liberal model began during World War I. The disruption of international trade and capital flows forced governments to seek their own solutions and reinforced tendencies toward self-sufficiency. The world economy was expected to recover after the war, but the underlying weaknesses persisted. The beginning of the Great Depression in 1929 led to sharp declines in economic activity first in the developed economies, and it then transmitted to the developing economies. The continuing political tensions and the absence of a country that would play a leading role in the world economy made it difficult for developed countries to coordinate their policies during the 1930s (Findlay and O'Rourke 2007, pp. 429–73; Broadberry and Harrison 2005; Eichengreen 2008, pp. 43–90; Kindleberger 1986, pp. 95–229; Rothermund 1996; Berend 2006, pp. 42–132).

The Great Depression had important long-term consequences for both the developed and developing economies. In the absence of a coherent theory, governments in developed countries experimented with various interventionist policies in response to the Great Depression. Most important among these were exchange-rate policies, various restrictions on imports, and expansionary monetary and fiscal policies. Many developing countries, especially those that were politically more independent of European powers, also adopted new policies of interventionism, protectionism, and industrialization in varying degrees. In addition, many governments undertook infrastructure investments, attempted to keep wages low, and defaulted on their debt. As a result of these measures, share of foreign trade in total production did decline and significant increases were achieved in manufacturing activities in many developing countries, from Latin America to Southern Europe and Asia. Studies by Carlos Diaz Alejandro and Angus Maddison show that countries that shifted to greater interventionism and inward-oriented economic policies during the 1930s did better in terms of economic growth than countries that continued with the earlier strategies based on the export of agricultural products (Diaz Alejandro 1984; Maddison 1985, pp. 13–44; Williamson 2006, pp. 109–43). Not all developing countries pursued interventionism during the 1930s, however. In many developing economies, especially those that belonged to overseas empires of European powers, the open economy model and the specialization in agriculture continued.

For almost a century since the end of the Napoleonic Wars, the Ottoman economy had remained open and foreign trade and foreign investment had expanded steadily. Economic policy did not change significantly after the Young Turk Revolution of 1908. Nor did it change even after the secular and increasingly nationalist Committee of Union and Progress seized power with a military coup in 1913 because the existing free trade treaties and the privileges or capitulations given to European states and citizens as well as the large outstanding debt seriously restricted the possibilities open to Ottoman governments. Beginning in 1914, however, major economic changes went hand in hand with major political changes. With the outbreak of World War I, the Ottoman economy turned sharply inward due to the disruption of foreign trade. The end of World War I led to the end of the Ottoman Empire and the establishment of a series of new states. After a war of independence, Turkey was established as a new republic in 1923. Thanks to the very different political and economic environment during the Interwar era, the new nation-state managed to acquire a good deal of autonomy to shape its own political and economic institutions and pursue its own economic policies. The new government at Ankara thus adopted policies of protectionism and industrialization during the Great Depression and until World War II.

Both world wars as well as the Great Depression had a significant negative impact on the economy. In addition, the transition from the empire to a new nation-state within new borders had long-lasting economic consequences. As a result, both total and per capita GDP fluctuated sharply during these decades. The first subperiod identified in table 7.1 includes World War I and the War of Independence until 1922. Population of the area within the present-day borders of Turkey declined by as much as 20 percent and total GDP by more than 50 percent during this decade. Along with peace and the establishment of the new nation-state, the economy recovered strongly until 1929, when levels of per capita GDP but not population and total GDP returned to pre–World War I levels. The decade of the Great Depression from 1929 to 1939 was characterized by protectionism, industrialization led by the state, and

TABLE 7.1. A Periodization of Economic Trends, 1913–1950

| Subperiod | Average Annual Growth Rates | | | | | Level of GDP per Capita at the End of Subperiod |
	Population	GDP	Agriculture	Manufacturing	GDP per capita	1913 = 100
1913–1922	−2.3	−6.4	?	?	−4.2	68
1923–1929	2.0	8.8	11.1	6.9	6.8	105
1930–1939	2.0	5.2	4.4	7.2	3.2	158
1940–1945	1.1	−5.8	−8.4	−6.7	−6.9	99
1946–1950	2.2	8.4	12.1	8.3	6.1	141
1913–1950	0.7	1.6	?	?	0.9	141

Sources: Author's calculations based on Eldem 1970, pp. 275–309; Bulutay et al. 1974; Özel and Pamuk 2006, pp. 83–90; the official national income series for 1923–1950 in Turkey, Türkiye İstatistik Kurumu (Turkish Statistical Institute) 2014.

moderately high rates of growth. Manufacturing output rose strongly and it was supported by increases in agricultural output. The per capita GDP during the Interwar period reached its peak in 1939. Even though Turkey did not participate in World War II, the disruption of foreign trade and the military mobilization had serious consequences for the economy until 1945. Nonetheless, the economic impact of World War II was not as severe as that of World War I. Another period of recovery followed the end of the war, but the 1939 levels of per capita GDP were not attained until after 1950.

This chapter will begin with global and national political developments and examine how they led to changes in economic policies and institutions as well as the consequences of these changes. The next chapter will review Turkey's record in economic growth, income distribution, and human development in both absolute and relative terms. It will also evaluate the role of institutions and institutional change in economic development during 1913–1950.

World War I

Nationalism, including economic nationalism, had been on the rise in the Ottoman Empire in the aftermath of the military defeats in the Balkan Wars of 1912–13. Nonetheless, the sharp changes in economic policies after 1914 were mostly due to the circumstances created by World War I. The almost complete disruption of foreign trade forced the wartime government of the Committee of Union and Progress to adopt very different policies in order to maintain the war effort. The closing of the economy and the shift to interventionism during

World War I turned out to be the beginning of a long-term change in the economic model. After the Great Depression began in 1929 and another world war soon appeared on the horizon, economic nationalism and concerns for self-sufficiency began to dominate economic policy. Protectionism and an inward-looking industrialization model continued after World War II and until 1980. A closer examination of the World War I era will provide insights into the origins of the basic model that dominated Turkey's economy for the greater part of the twentieth century.

The Ottoman Empire entered World War I with an underdeveloped, mostly agricultural economy, weak industry, a poor transportation network, and a state with limited capacity. It was less prepared than most of the other combatants to face the economic consequences of a general war of long duration. Neither the economy nor the state was able to respond effectively to the extraordinary pressures created by the war. Wartime government interventionism in the economy did not always yield good results. Despite all the shortcomings and having to fight on several fronts, however, it is remarkable that the Ottomans were able to remain in the war until the very end in 1918 (Erickson 2001, pp. 51–73).

Changes in Economic Policy and Institutions

Even before the war, in the aftermath of the Young Turk Revolution of 1908, an interesting debate regarding economic strategy had emerged among the two wings of these urban intellectuals, activist bureaucrats and military officers. On the one side were the defenders of a Western type of decentralization and economic liberalism who defended the open economy model based on trade and agricultural development. Finance Minister Cavid Bey of the Committee of Union and Progress, for example, defended liberal economic policies and emphasized the role of agriculture in economic development. Arguing against them were the proponents of Listian-style protectionism and a more self-reliant strategy based on industrialization. Equally interesting was the growing recognition by both sides that the traditional and overriding concern of the Ottoman state for fiscal revenue had to be abandoned in favor of policies that promoted economic development. The Ottoman government, however, had already committed itself to the free trade treaties and a regime of privileges for foreign companies and citizens in economic and legal affairs. As a result, these debates had little impact on policy until the war. One notable exception was legislation passed in 1913 to encourage domestic industry. Without increases in tariffs on the imports of manufactures, however, the impact of the law was likely to remain limited (Toprak 1982, pp. 168–81).

With the start of the war, Ottoman ports were blockaded and Ottoman trade with Europe came to a virtual halt. It appeared that the Ottoman war effort had to rely mostly if not entirely on domestic resources. Under these circumstances, the rupture in political relations with the leading European states like Britain and France gave the Union and Progress government the opportunity to make important changes in economic policy. First, the capitulations, privileges in law, judiciary, trade, and other fields given to Europeans were unilaterally abolished at the end of 1914, thus subjecting foreign companies and individuals to Ottoman laws. The most important impact of this decision on economic matters was that it enabled Ottoman citizens to compete with Europeans on an equal footing. In addition, various concessions granted to foreign companies were also abolished. Companies operating in the Ottoman Empire were asked to register under Ottoman law and be subject to Ottoman laws and regulations (Toprak 1982, pp. 69–98; Elmacı 2005, pp. 60–165).

Second, in 1915 the government adopted a new and selective tariff structure with different rates on different goods in place of the ad valorem tariffs which applied the same rate to all. The government would be able to adjust customs duties as it wished and protect specific sectors. At the same time, the coverage of the law to support domestic industry adopted in 1913 was broadened. Third, the Ottoman government suspended all payments on its large external debt, which was held mostly by French, German, and to a lesser extent by English investors, as well as the activities of the Ottoman Public Debt Administration. The Lausanne Peace Conference that paved the way for the emergence of the new nation-state in 1923 returned to these three issues, and each of them was negotiated extensively between Turkey and the representatives of the leading European governments.

Disruption of Foreign Trade and Production

The Ottoman economy was dependent on imports not only for manufactures and military materials but also for its food needs in some of the coastal cities, particularly in the capital city. The earliest and most immediate impact of the war was the disruption in external trade which was compounded by the commercial embargo of the Allies around the Mediterranean. As a result, Ottoman external trade was quickly reduced to the movement of goods obtained by rail from Bulgaria. Direct trade with Germany and Austria resumed overland only after the German occupation of Serbia at the end of 1915. By 1916, the volume of external trade had declined to approximately one-fifth of its prewar levels, and more than 90 percent of this trade was being conducted with Germany and Austria-Hungary. As a result, shortages quickly appeared in foodstuffs such as grains and sugar and also in various kinds of manufactures (Eldem 1994, pp. 47–82).

Ottoman manufacturing in military-related areas also remained very limited. On the eve of the war, production of pig iron and steel was insignificant. There was very little chemical production and petroleum refining. There was only one cannon and small arms foundry, one shell and bullet factory, and one gunpowder factory. Another key shortage to emerge during the war was in energy. Even though the empire had been self-sufficient in coal before the war, after the Russian bombardment of the Eregli coal mines on the Black Sea coast and the sinking of transport ships, coal had to be imported from Germany. As a result, wood was used in railroads in Southern Anatolia and Syria for most of the war. Until the restoration of railway lines and other overland communication lines with central Europe after the defeat of Serbia in late 1915, the empire suffered crippling shortages of war supplies and raw materials. The army remained dependent on imported arms and military equipment until the end of the war.

The first impact of the war on domestic industry was positive, as some import substitution occurred. Soon afterward, however, raw materials shortages began to emerge. In addition, the decline in coal production unfavorably affected whatever existed of industrial production. Equally important, urban areas had faced moderate levels of labor shortages, especially of skilled workers, even before the war. The mobilization of large numbers of males thus exacerbated the labor shortages in industry. The mobilization and employment of large numbers of women in urban areas did not resolve these shortages until the end of the war. Coal and other mining output also registered sharp declines, by 50–80 percent compared to their prewar levels. In cotton textiles, output was lower by 50 percent in 1918 compared to 1913 levels. The overall decline in industrial output during the war was likely in the 30–50 percent range.

Wartime conditions created difficulties for agricultural production as well. Since mechanization had remained limited, agricultural production did not depend on imported inputs or machinery. Nonetheless, it was unfavorably impacted by the special requirements of the military during wartime. In an economy that was experiencing labor shortages in both the agricultural and urban sectors even during peacetime, the conscription of large numbers of males created serious difficulties. In addition, requisitioning of draft animals by the military reached crippling levels in many parts of the country. Since agricultural techniques of production were rather primitive, machinery could not be easily substituted for labor or draft animals. Even though women assumed a greater burden in agriculture, acreage under cultivation and levels of output declined sharply. As a result of these pressures, both land under cultivation and yields began to decline starting with the first year of the war. By 1916, total wheat production had decreased close to 30 percent. Declines in the output of most of the exportable cash crops were even greater. By 1918, the decline in production in comparison to the 1913–1914 levels was close to 40 percent in wheat, more than 50 percent in tobacco, raisins, hazelnuts, olive oil, raw silk, and cotton. It is possible, however, that these official estimates overstate the extent of decreases in production because the peasant producers hid or understated their production levels so they could avoid wartime taxes or forced deliveries to the military (Eldem 1994, pp. 33–116; Pamuk 2005, pp. 121–31; Toprak 1982, pp. 267–312).

There were other causes of the decline in agricultural production. In Eastern Anatolia, the Ottoman government forced more than one million Armenians to march off to the desert in Syria in 1915. Many of them died during the march due to armed attacks by civilians and government-linked forces as well as from hunger and disease, while many others fled to neighboring regions. A large part of Eastern Anatolia was then occupied by Russia, which led to the return of some Armenians and the flight of Muslim peasants. These dramatic developments in turn led to the collapse of agricultural production in the region and further loss of life among both Armenians and Muslims.

More generally, there was a good deal of regional variation in the impact of the war. Typically, rural areas fared better since most of the rural population cultivated some amount of land and had direct access to food unless the harvest collapsed altogether. It also made a big difference whether a region was a net food exporter or importer. Most of the difficulties occurred in large urban areas located in food deficit regions. Military operations or the presence of large numbers of troops in a region added to the struggles. The prohibition of internal trade in grains and the confiscation of the surplus grain by local commanders exacerbated the shortages. Most severe shortages of foodstuffs occurred in Eastern Anatolia, northern Syria, and Lebanon (Pamuk 2005, pp. 118–31; Boratav 1982, pp. 61–75; Ögün 1999).

Food Supply Problems in Urban Areas

Wartime conditions created major difficulties for the Ottoman food supply. While imports and production declined sharply, demand for food actually increased because of the need to feed a larger army. In addition, the Ottoman transportation network, which was so essential for linking the areas with food surpluses to the areas with food deficit, could not respond satisfactorily to the pressures of wartime. Until the outbreak of the war, most of the external and a large part of the internal trade of the empire had been seaborne. After the Allied powers intercepted sea transport in the Mediterranean, the war effort had to rely almost entirely on land transport. The existing roads were quite poor and a good deal of the transport was undertaken by draft animals. The empire was also lacking in means of communication. The existing network of telegraph lines remained rather limited.

Shortages of food and hunger experienced during World War I were not always a result of a decrease in food availability, however. As Amartya Sen has argued, even though total availability of food may remain unchanged or decline only slightly, hunger and famine will result if some groups in society lose the ability to command food, or what he calls food entitlements. For example, wartime conditions may drive food prices beyond the reach of some segments of the population such as the urban poor. Food shortages and hunger thus depended not only on the total food availability but also on the distribution of the available food among different groups (Sen 1981, pp. 39–51). Both the decline in the availability of food and the inequalities in its distribution and consumption could seriously affect the morale and hamper the war effort. For this reason, securing the food supply of the urban population and the military and distributing the available food in an equitable manner was deemed one of the most important economic policy issues for the Ottoman government during World War I.

It became apparent to the government very early in the war that markets by themselves were not going to provide an adequate solution to this problem and various forms of intervention were necessary. The government's wartime food supply policies covered a large number of areas ranging from intervention in agricultural production to transportation and distribution and finally to consumption. At one end, the government attempted to reduce the consumption of the limited food supplies and ensure a more equitable distribution of the available supplies by implementing a system of rationing in the capital city. At the other end, the government attempted to intervene in and increase food production directly. The Ottoman parliament passed new legislation in September 1916, commonly referred to as the Agricultural Obligations Law, which held large corporations in the urban areas responsible for securing the necessary equipment and labor and cultivating specified amounts of land. Moreover, all farmers were required to cultivate a minimum amount of land per pair of oxen they had. The law also empowered the government to demand from all men and women not under arms to engage in agriculture. The government could ask families or individuals to work in farms that were experiencing labor shortages due to wartime mobilization. In extreme cases, battalions of women were organized by the army and were sent to fields to help with the cotton harvest in Southern Anatolia. In short, the legislation for a system of war agriculture was in place by the end of 1916. However, the results of this dramatic piece of legislation and the related measures remained limited in actual implementation (Yalman 1934, pp. 119–34; Toprak 1982, pp. 81–98; Ahmad 1988, pp. 265–86; Ökçün 1983).

Another area of intervention was the transport of cereal supplies from Anatolia to Istanbul. The capital city relied heavily on grains and flour imported by sea until 1914 despite the availability of the Anatolian Railway. With the outbreak of the war, these imports were disrupted and Istanbul was forced to turn primarily to the grain-producing plains of Central Anatolia. Under more normal conditions, Anatolian agriculture was capable of producing for Istanbul. But the wartime decline in production combined with the difficulties of transportation to create severe problems for the capital city's food supply.

For most of World War I, the bottleneck in the provisioning of Istanbul was shortage of space on the railroad connecting Central Anatolia to Istanbul and in ships arriving from the Black Sea. There was an intense struggle regarding their allocation. The environment of shortages raised by the provisioning needs of Istanbul gave the Union and Progress leadership the opportunity to select a small group of merchants close to the party and allow them to supply the city. The railroad car space and shipping permits were allocated to Muslim merchants linked to the party. This system enabled Union and Progress to share in the wartime profits as some of them were plowed back to the party. Equally important, it provided an opportunity to create a new group of Muslim-Turkish entrepreneurs with close links to the party. Monopolies were created for the importation and distribution of many of the scarce commodities and these were then awarded to the Turkish supporters of the party in Istanbul and the provinces. Attempts were made to transfer these profits to other areas, creating new companies involving other Istanbul merchants and merchants from areas close to the railway in Central Anatolia, as well as big landowners. The founders, as well as the capital for the National Economy Bank, established at the beginning of 1918, were drawn from the same groups. This strategy, of course, was well in line with the embrace, during World War I, if not somewhat earlier, of Turkish nationalism as the leading ideology by the Union and Progress (Toprak 1982, pp. 22–35; Yalman 1934, pp. 135–43; Tekeli and İlkin 2004a, pp. 1–44).

War Finance and Inflation

In the years before World War I, the Ottoman government had borrowed abroad to finance its budget deficits. After the war began, military expenditures increased sharply while the possibility of borrowing in European financial markets disappeared. One way of financing the war was to increase taxes. Direct and indirect taxes collected from consumers and enterprises were raised early in the war. In spite of all efforts, however, tax receipts did not in-

TABLE 7.2. Money and Prices during World War I

At the end of the year	1915	1916	1917	1918
Paper Money in Circulation (in millions of Ottoman liras)	8	46	124	161
Exchange Rate of Paper Money vs. Gold Lira (parity = 100)	105	188	470	438
Consumer Price Index for Istanbul; 1914 = 100	130	212	1,465	2,205

Sources: Yalman 1934, pp. 144–54; Eldem 1970, pp. 47–56; Toprak 1982, pp. 330–34.
Note: 1.1 Ottoman gold lira = 1 British pound in 1914.

crease; on the contrary, they declined. One of the causes was the significant decrease in agricultural and industrial production after the war began. In addition, as inflation picked up after 1915, many nominally fixed taxes could not be adjusted upward. The third and perhaps most important reason is that as shortages emerged, and production and income declined, the state's capacity to collect taxes weakened significantly and tax evasion became stronger in both the urban and rural areas.

While budget receipts in Ottoman liras remained below their prewar levels, increasing expenditures led to steadily widening deficits. The government tried hard to keep the deficits under control by cutting salary payments, for example. The amount of loans the government was able to obtain from the allied states, most importantly Germany, also remained limited. Faced with this worsening financial picture, the government decided to issue paper money called *kaime*. After 1915, printing paper money became the leading means for war finance. As the volume of paper money in circulation increased, the exchange value of the gold lira started to decline and silver coins disappeared from circulation. In Istanbul, the exchange rate of the kaime against the gold lira dropped from 105 kuruş at the end of 1915, to 188 kuruş at the end of 1916, 470 kuruş at the end of 1917, and 500 kuruş at the end of the war (table 7.2).

Prices increased very rapidly, especially in the last two years of the war, partly because of the monetary expansion and partly because of the food and other shortages in urban areas. According to the consumer price index prepared for Istanbul by the Ottoman Public Debt Administration, prices rose more than twentyfold during the four years. Because the capital city faced more severe shortages of food, increases in consumer prices in Istanbul were probably higher than those in other cities. Nonetheless, wartime inflation in Turkey was much higher than in other countries that participated in the war and comparable only to Russia before the 1917 Revolution (Gatrell 2005,

p. 270). While prices rose sharply, wages and salaries lagged far behind. The purchasing power of wages and salaries declined by as much as 80 percent or more during the war, with most of the decline occurring during the last two years. The decline in the purchasing power of public sector wages and salaries was greater than that in the private sector (Eldem 1994, pp. 55 and 133).

Long-Term Legacies of the Wars

The Ottoman Empire and Turkey were engaged in a series of wars from 1912 to 1922, first the 1912–13 Balkan Wars, followed by World War I and the War of Independence during 1920–22. This decade of wars had far-reaching political, demographic, and economic consequences. Most important, of course, World War I led to the end of the Ottoman Empire and the establishment of a number of individual states. In Anatolia, after the War of Independence led by a new parliament and government located at Ankara, Turkey was established as a new republic in 1923 (Zürcher 2004, pp. 133–75).

Major demographic changes were another important consequence of this decade of wars. The population of Turkey at the time the world war began in 1914 was around 16.5 million. The losses suffered by the Muslim population as a result of the wars is estimated at 1.5 million and most of these were residents of Turkey. In addition, Turkey's Armenian population dropped from about 1.5 million to less than 200 thousand as a result of their forced deportation by the government in 1915 and the related massacres, famine, disease, and flight of the Armenians to neighboring areas. After 1923, in accordance with the population exchange agreement signed between the Turkish and Greek states, approximately 1.2 million Orthodox Greeks left Anatolia and about a half million Muslim Turks from Greece and the Balkans came to Turkey. These figures also include the Greeks who were forced to leave Western Anatolia when the Greek occupation came to an end in 1922 (Arı 1995; Yıldırım 2006, pp. 87–188). As a result of these massive changes, the population of Turkey stood at around 13 million at the end of 1924, a decrease of about 20 percent from a decade before (see chapter 2 for details).

Ethnically speaking, the population of Turkey became much more homogeneous after a decade of wars. In 1913, the share of non-Muslims in the population of the area within Turkey's present-day borders was more than 20 percent. By 1925, the proportion of non-Muslims in the total population within the same area had dropped to about 3 percent. Most of the remaining non-Muslims, Greeks, Armenians, and Jews now lived in the Istanbul area. Muslim Turks and Kurds made up the rest.

The dramatic decline in Greek and Armenian populations had long-term economic as well as political, social, and cultural consequences. Many of the commercialized, export-oriented farmers across Anatolia as well as the artisans, leading merchants, and moneylenders who linked the rural areas to the port cities and the European trading houses in the long century before the war were lost. The private sector of modern Turkey would now be led by a Muslim-Turkish bourgeoisie that had benefited from the wartime nationalist policies of the Young Turk government. Many of them had also acquired the lands and other assets of the departing Greeks and Armenians. Yet, the power of this private sector consisting mostly of small and medium-sized enterprises would remain limited until the second half of the twentieth century (Keyder 1987, pp. 71–90).

After ten years of wars, the new nation-state had a less urbanized and poorer economy. The population of Istanbul declined from 900,000 to 700,000, and that of İzmir from 300,000 to 150,000 during this period. More generally, the share of population in centers of more than 10,000 had declined from 23 percent to 17 percent from 1914 to 1927. Because of the high numbers of men killed during the wars, widows and orphans constituted an important part of the population. In addition, agriculture, industry, and mining were all adversely affected by the deterioration and destruction of equipment, draft animals, and plants during this decade. It is not easy to make reliable estimates on per capita production and income levels due to the limitations of the available data. The existing evidence suggests that after a sharp decline until 1918, the economy recovered somewhat until the early 1920s when more detailed statistics become available. Nonetheless, per capita GDP and income was about 30 percent lower in 1923 than its levels in 1914 (Özel and Pamuk 1998, pp. 83–90).

Finally, another important and enduring legacy of this decade of wars was the rise of economic nationalism and government interventionism, both of which would be strongly supported by the international environment during the Interwar period. The leadership of the new Turkish Republic, military officers, bureaucrats, and intellectuals was strongly influenced by the wartime experience. They had strong political and social ties to the Young Turk movement that governed the Ottoman Empire until 1918. As the economy turned inward and self-sufficiency and preparedness for a new war became basic priorities in economic policy during the Interwar period, experiences with interventionism accumulated between 1912 and 1922 began to shape the economic policies of the new state. Starting in 1929, the economic policies of the new nation-state would turn increasingly protectionist, and the share of foreign trade in the economy would decline rapidly. In 1930, after the Great Depression began, industrialization led by the state was adopted as the basic development strategy. The origins of this model were to be found, to some extent, in the experiment with state interventionism during World War I.

The New Nation-State

The War of Independence against the occupation and partitioning of Turkey by the Entente powers lasted from 1920 to 1922. It was supported by a broad coalition of the provincial notables, merchants, landowners, and religious leaders. The parliament that opened in Ankara in 1920 was quite pluralistic and various views were represented openly. Many conservatives wanted to retain the sultanate and the caliphate and establish a constitutional monarchy after the war was won. Mustafa Kemal and his close associates had other ideas, however. After the abolition of the sultanate in 1922, the proclamation of the Republic in 1923 and the abolition of the caliphate in 1924, they adopted a strongly secular line and moved to eliminate the opposition. In response to a Kurdish uprising in the Diyarbakir region in the east in 1925, the parliament passed the Law for the Maintenance of Order which gave extraordinary powers to the government. The opposition Progressive Republican Party was soon dissolved and its members in the parliament were not re-elected.

The radical secularizing and modernizing reforms and institutional changes of the new republic were all undertaken by the one-party regime led by Mustafa Kemal and his close associates. The new leadership had been educated with notions of enlightenment and rational thought of the French Revolution in the schools established as part of the reforms during the nineteenth century. They viewed the building of a new nation-state and modernization through Westernization as two closely related goals. The first wave of reforms during the 1920s built upon the secularization of state, law, and education which had begun one century earlier and continued under the Union and Progress government from 1913 to 1918. The jurisdiction of Islamic law began to be limited primarily to family law during the nineteenth century. With the adoption of the Swiss civil code and the Italian penal code in 1926, the linkages to Islamic law were further weakened. Similarly, the educational system was brought under the control of the ministry of education. Primary education was made compulsory for girls even if this was not enforced, and higher education was opened to women by the Union and Progress government during World War I. The education system including the schools for the non-Muslims was unified and the religious schools were closed down by the Ankara government in 1924. The *medreses* or religious colleges were also closed and new schools were opened for preachers. In the following years, the public schools and some areas in civil service and the professions were opened in greater numbers to urban, middle-class women who embraced the new secularism of the republic.

The adoption of the Western clock and calendar in 1926, of Western numerals in 1928, and Western weights and measures in 1931 not only gave Turkey a

European image but also made communication and trade with the European countries much easier. The most radical measure in the same direction was the adoption of the Latin alphabet. In August 1928, president Mustafa Kemal announced for the first time that the new Turkish script using the Latin alphabet would replace the Ottoman alphabet. An alphabet mobilization was proclaimed and the president toured the country in the following months to explain and teach the new letters. In November, a new law made the new alphabet compulsory in public communications beginning on the first day of 1929. The government then launched literacy campaigns across the country to teach the new alphabet to adults who knew the Arabic alphabet and to the great majority who were illiterate. The results were mixed, however, with most of the progress recorded in the urban areas and among men rather than women until after World War II (Zürcher 2004, pp. 175–95; Çagaptay 2006, pp. 82–139).

Changes in Economic Institutions

The division of the Ottoman Empire into nation-states and the drawing of new borders had important economic consequences. Over the centuries, trade had developed across a large geography inside the empire and these were disrupted by the new borders. Most essential for Turkey, crafts in Southeastern Anatolia had thrived by producing for long-distance markets in Syria and even Egypt. With the emergence of a border and the rise of tariff barriers in southeastern Turkey, trade declined quickly. There were similar disruptions of trade in Thrace between European Turkey, including Istanbul and western Thrace and Bulgaria. The breakup of trade as well as social networks seriously hurt these regions and the impact of the new borders lasted for decades. Another important cost of the new borders was related to the transportation infrastructure. The railroad and roads network had to be redesigned in response to the border changes. From the onset the new leadership thus strived to create a national economy within the new borders. Construction of new railroads was seen as an important step toward political and economic unification of the new nation-state.

The Kemalist leadership was also keenly aware that Ottoman financial and economic dependence on European powers had created serious political problems. In the Lausanne Peace Conference in 1922–23, the new state had to fight hard for the right to determine the new institutions governing the economy's linkages to the rest of the world, especially to European powers. After lengthy negotiations, important changes were made on three fundamental issues, each of which had been first addressed by the Union and Progress government in the early part of World War I. First, the commercial and legal privileges of European citizens and companies were abolished. Second, the free trade agreements that the Ottoman state had signed and was unable to change unilaterally during the nineteenth century were cancelled. The new state obtained the right to decide on its own customs tariffs after a transition period that would end in 1929. The nominal tariffs established by the Union of Progress government in 1916 had declined substantially due to wartime inflation and they were to be kept at those levels until that date. Third, after rounds of negotiations that lasted until 1928, the Ottoman external debt was restructured and divided between the successor states. According to the agreement, Turkey would take over 67 percent of the total Ottoman debt and debt repayments would begin in 1929 (Hershlag 1968, pp. 16–27; Tezel 1986, pp. 163–96).

It has often been stated that the İzmir Economic Congress which convened in February 1923, at a time when the Lausanne Conference was suspended, gave important clues about the content of the economic policies that would be followed by the new state. At the İzmir Congress, farmers, merchants, industrialists, and workers were all represented. Although voices of big landowners and merchants were heard more than others, all groups expressed their views and demands for a national economy led by the private sector. Foreign capital was also welcome under certain conditions. Due to its delicate timing, many of the messages delivered for audiences at home and abroad were undoubtedly symbolic rather than concrete. Nonetheless, the Congress can still be viewed as reflecting the basic directions in economic policy until the Great Depression in 1929 (Ökçün 1968, pp. 387–437; Kuruç 2011, pp. 243–63).

One of the earliest initiatives of the new regime was to abolish in 1924 the tithe and the animal tax, and to introduce in their stead indirect taxes on commodities consumed by the rural population like sugar and kerosene, as well as some land taxes. The 10 percent tithe on agricultural production was collected for the state by local tax farmers and together with the animal tax they had been the Ottoman state's leading source of revenue for centuries. At the beginning of the twentieth century, these two items provided almost half of all the revenues of the Ottoman state. However, because of the difficulties encountered in the collection of these taxes during World War I and the War of Independence, their share in the receipts collected by the new state was not as high as in the past. The abolition of the tithe and the animal tax meant an important departure from the traditional policies that placed the largest tax burden on the agricultural producers. From the 1930s onward, the urban economy rather than agriculture began to provide a growing share of the state revenues.

The abolition of the tithe has been interpreted as a concession to big landowners who had supported the War of Independence. The new legislation did, of course, reduce the big landowners' tax burden. However, in taking this step, the new state's main concern was to provide a break for the small and medium-sized family producers, who constituted a very large share of the population and who had faced almost constant warfare for a decade. The government hoped that by easing their tax burden, agricultural production would recover sooner and more strongly. Agricultural production did in fact recover strongly until 1939 despite the sharp decline in agricultural prices due to the Great Depression.

The abolition of the tithe also had important consequences on power relations in the rural areas. In the nineteenth century, collecting the tithe and other taxes in the name of the state was an important source of profits and economic power for the leading families in rural areas. The tax collectors, often large landowners or merchants, also extended credit when needed to small producers facing difficulties, creating a dependence and a network of influence in rural areas. With the abolition of the tithe, these groups lost an important pillar of their power over small and medium-sized family producers (Keyder 1981, pp. 11–45; Birtek and Keyder 1975, pp. 407–38).

In the 1920s, the new regime envisaged an urban economy led by the private sector. Industrialization and the creation of a Muslim-Turkish private sector were viewed as key ingredients of national economic development. However, that private sector was weak and consisted mostly of small and medium-sized enterprises. While tariffs on imports remained low until 1929, the basic approach of economic policy was limited interventionism aimed at strengthening the private sector. The Law for the Encouragement of Industry adopted by the parliament in 1927 provided assistance and various incentives to industrial enterprises in food processing, textiles, construction materials, and elsewhere. The government was also concerned that the world could be dragged into another war. To avoid once more experiencing the severe shortages of World War I, the aim was to create a more self-sufficient economy. The three "whites"—flour, sugar, and cloth—became the focus of economic policies. The Ankara government was not against foreign capital. However, European investors had little appetite for investments outside Europe during this period. On the contrary, they were prepared to sell their enterprises in Turkey and leave if suitable buyers emerged (Boratav 1981, pp. 165–90).

İşbank (literally Business Bank), a semi-public company, is one of the leading examples of the private sector–oriented economic model and a good symbol of the policies followed in the 1920s. Founded in 1924 by prominent figures of the regime including Mustafa Kemal, the bank was directed by Celal Bayar who would later become a minister and prime minister in Republican People's Party governments in the 1930s. The bank's mission can be summarized as supporting and developing Turkey's private sector. The granting of privileges, transfer of resources by the bank to people close to the party became public very early. Because of the various cases of corruption, the various insiders benefiting from the bank's activities came to be known as *affairistes*, alluding to the bank's name. In addition to providing credit at low rates, the transfer of existing or newly formed state monopolies to people or companies close to the party were the most preferred methods for the creation of a Muslim-Turkish private sector during this period (Kocabaşoğlu 2001, pp. 1–298).

A national economy within the new borders needed a more developed network of railroads. Railways thus took up the largest share in public investments during the Interwar period. During the nineteenth century, railways built and operated mostly by European companies had supported foreign trade by linking fertile agricultural areas to the leading ports of export. The new economic model aimed at building a domestic market instead by developing the linkages between the new center in Ankara and the country's less developed central and eastern regions (Schoenberg 1977, pp. 359–72; Tekeli and İlkin 2004c, pp. 286–321). To the 4,000 kilometers of railways built by European companies during the half century before World War I, the new regime added 3,000 kilometers until 1939, financed mostly from the national budget.

Constructing railways was costly using the existing technology. For this reason, the resources allocated to the railways built during the Interwar period were quite large, in fact larger as a share of the annual budget and of GDP than the Southeast Anatolia dam and irrigation project, which became Turkey's largest construction project in the decades after World War II. As a result, the railway policy of the İnönü governments was much criticized within and outside of parliament. However, the railways played an important role in building a country within the new borders, not only economically but also politically. Thanks to the railway network, old and new, the major urban areas in the western regions of the country were supplied with wheat produced in Central and Eastern Anatolia from the 1930s, and especially during World War II (Tekeli and İlkin 2004c, pp. 286–321). In addition to the construction of new railroads, the government was busy nationalizing the railroads built during the Ottoman era. Because operating Turkey's railways was not a profitable business, and in fact most of those made were incurring losses, European companies were ready to hand over the lines they controlled. As a result, nationalization faced few obstacles.

The 1920s was a period of rapid recovery for Turkey's economy. After the wars ended, land under cultivation expanded and agricultural production started to increase. With the increase in agricultural incomes, the urban economy began to recover as well. New investments started to replace the physical capital destroyed during the wars. As demand in world markets rose, exports also expanded. Wages remained relatively high due to the recent losses in

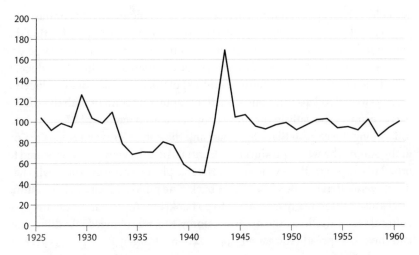

FIGURE 7.1. Domestic Terms of Trade, 1925–1960, Agricultural Prices/Prices of
Manufactures (index =100 in 1960). Source: Based on the implicit GDP deflators
from the national income accounts in Turkey, Turkish Statistical Institute 2014.

population and widespread scarcities of labor. All segments of the population
thus shared in the increases in production and income during this period
(Hansen 1991, pp. 312–18). Our calculations using data series on agricultural
production and exports suggest that per capita incomes returned to their 1914
levels in 1929. The population in the area within Turkey's current borders had
declined by close to 20 percent during and after World War I. For this reason,
prewar levels in total population and total production were not reached until
the mid-1930s (Pamuk and Özel 1998, pp. 83–90). Before that, however, the
onset of the Great Depression in 1929 would be a major turning point, both
for the world and for Turkey.

The Great Depression

As was the case in many developing countries, the Great Depression was first
felt in Turkey with the sharp decline in the prices of agricultural commodities.
Prices of wheat and other cereals declined by more than 60 percent from
1928–29 to 1932–33 and remained at those lower levels until the end of the
decade. Prices of the leading export crops—tobacco, raisins, hazelnuts, and
cotton—also declined, by an average of around 50 percent, although they recovered somewhat later in the decade. Since these decreases were greater than
the decline in the prices of manufactures, the external terms of trade deteriorated by more than 25 percent and the domestic terms of trade shifted against

agriculture by 30 percent from 1928–29 to 1932–33 (figure 7.1). In contrast, the physical volume of exports continued to rise after 1929, perhaps reflecting the continued recovery in output levels. Nonetheless, the result was large decreases in the real incomes of most market-oriented agricultural producers. The difficulties of the agricultural and export-oriented sectors produced a sharp sense of collapse and quickly led to popular discontent with the single-party regime, especially in the more commercialized regions of Western Anatolia, along the eastern Black Sea coast and the cotton-growing Adana region in the south. The wheat producers of Central Anatolia who were connected to urban markets by rail were also hit by the sharply lower prices. Those who had debts were often unable to pay them back. The rapid decrease in agricultural prices also caused many merchants to go bankrupt. As demand from the agricultural sector declined, the urban economy, too, was plunged into difficulties and the crisis spread (Kazgan 1977, pp. 240–65; Kazgan 2005, pp. 43–92; Emrence 2006).

The year 1929 had already been a difficult one for the economy. The expectations that tariffs on imports would be raised and payments on the external debt would start had already caused a minor crisis by increasing the demand for foreign exchange. In response, the government moved quickly toward protectionism and greater control over foreign trade and foreign exchange. While the leading importers of Istanbul were advocating more modest increases, the government adopted a new and much higher tariff structure in October 1929 as soon as the restrictions of the Lausanne Peace Treaty on commercial policy ended. Average tariffs on imports are estimated to have increased from 13 percent to 46 percent in 1929 and to more than 60 percent by the second half of the 1930s. Equally significant, tariffs on imports of foodstuffs and manufactured consumer goods were raised substantially but kept lower for agricultural and industrial machinery and raw materials. For this reason, the effective rates of protection on many of the final goods selected for protection were substantially higher. For example, tariffs on imported textiles exceeded 80 percent, while those on sugar exceeded 200 percent in the 1930s. In addition, quantity restrictions were introduced on the imports of a long list of goods in November 1931. The lists were updated frequently and some of the tariffs were raised further during the 1930s as import substitution spread to new sectors (Yücel 1996, pp. 74–84, 105–113; Tekeli and İlkin 1977, pp. 75–197).

In addition to the strong measures of protectionism, the increasing shift of the trade regime toward bilateral agreements and clearing-bartering types of regulations also reinforced the tendency to turn inward and curb imports. Even though the export volumes continued to rise, combined with growth in domestic production, these trends meant sharp decreases in the share of imports in GDP from 12.8 percent in 1928–29 to 6.9 percent in 1938–39, and the

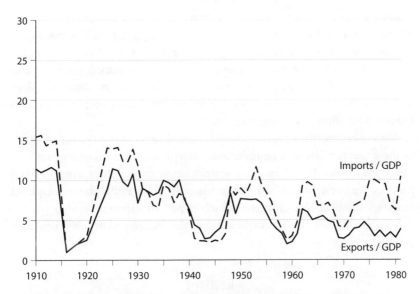

FIGURE 7.2. Closing of the Economy in Turkey, 1910–1980: Ratios of Exports and
Imports to GDP (percent). Source: Based on Pamuk 1987 pp. 148–50, and Eldem 1970,
pp. 302–6 for the Ottoman era; official trade and national income series from Turkey,
Turkish Statistical Institute 2014 for the period since 1923.

share of exports in GDP declined from 9.0 percent in 1929–29 to 7.0 percent
in 1938–39. The economy thus closed very rapidly and dramatically during the
Great Depression. This inward turn was to last for some time. The imports to
GDP and exports to GDP ratios, which had risen above 10 percent for the first
time in the decade before World War I, both remained below 10 percent after
World War II and until the end of the 1970s, a half century later (figure 7.2).

The onset of the global crisis had led many debtor countries to demand
restructuring of debt repayments or suspending them altogether. Creditors in
developed countries could not press their demands too adamantly under
these conditions. After making the first of the repayments agreed upon under
the Lausanne Treaty in 1929, Turkey also requested that the debts it had inherited from the Ottoman era be restructured. The negotiations led to decreases
of more than half in the annual payments for the rest of the decade. The government sought external funds for its industrial projects for the remainder of
the decade. Because of the world economic crisis, however, inflows of foreign
capital remained quite low (Tezel 1986, pp. 165–89).

In response to the declining agricultural prices, the state established the
Soil Products Office and began support purchases of wheat and tobacco from
1932. These purchases remained limited, however. Until the end of the 1930s,

wheat purchases averaged 3 percent of total production and about 15 percent of the amount sold on the market (Özbek 2003, pp. 219–38). Support purchases may have prevented wheat prices from falling further, but prices of agricultural crops did not recover and relative prices remained against agriculture until 1939. In fact, the price movements in favor of manufacturing, along with protectionism, were seen by the government as an opportunity for more rapid industrialization (figure 7.1).

Manufacturing thus began to meet a rising share of domestic consumption. In the absence of large-scale industrial enterprises, the immediate beneficiaries were the small and medium-scale manufacturing enterprises in many parts of the country consisting of textile mills, flour mills, glassworks, brick factories, tanneries, and others which began to experience high rates of growth. Industrialization through import substitution had begun (Yücel 1996, pp. 74–113).[1]

Etatism

As the unfavorable conditions continued in the world economy, the government decided to step up its commitment to industrialization by announcing a new strategy called *etatism*, or state-led import-substituting industrialization. In his speech on the occasion of the extension of the railway to Sivas in 1930, Prime Minister İsmet İnönü declared that "when it comes to the economy, we are moderately statist. The needs of this nation and its intellectual leanings encourage us in this direction." İnönü was thus trying to position himself in the middle of the political spectrum of the time, somewhere between liberalism and from socialism (Tekeli and İlkin 1977, pp. 124–215, and 1982; Kuruç 2011, pp. 351–417; Türegün 2016, pp. 666–90). In the 1930s, the role of the state in the economy was expanding not only in the Soviet Union but also in Europe in response to the Great Depression. While the model embraced by the Ankara government did not advocate socialism, it envisaged a more important role for the state sector than the examples across Europe. If one basic reason for this strong version of etatism in Turkey was the considerable autonomy of the central government from the private sector, the other related reason was the weaknesses of the private sector and the dominance of small and medium-sized enterprises with simple technology in the manufacturing, banking, mining, and other key sectors of the urban economy.

Etatism promoted the state as a leading producer and investor in the urban sector. A first five-year industrial plan was adopted in 1934 with the assistance of Soviet advisers. This document provided a detailed list of investment proj-

---

1. For the rapidly rising share of domestic production in the domestic market of cotton textiles, the most important branch of manufacturing after 1929, see chapter 5, figure 5.2.

ects to be undertaken by the state enterprises rather than an elaborate text of planning in the technical sense of the term. A second five-year plan was initiated in 1938, but its implementation was interrupted by the war. By the end of the decade, state economic enterprises such as Sümerbank and Etibank had emerged as important, and even leading, producers in a number of key sectors such as iron and steel, textiles, sugar, glassworks, cement, utilities, and mining. Etatism also involved the extension of state-sector activities and control to other parts of the urban economy as well. Railways, which were nationalized from European ownership, as well as the newly constructed lines, were transformed into state monopolies. Most of the state monopolies that had been handed over to private firms in the 1920s were taken back. In transportation, banking, and finance, state ownership of key enterprises was accompanied by increasing control over markets and prices (Tekeli and İlkin 1982, pp. 134–220; Tezel 1986, pp. 197–285; Boratav 1981, pp. 172–89; Hansen 1991, pp. 324–33).

As production and employment in manufacturing increased thanks to protectionism, shortages of labor developed in some urban areas. Because the great majority of the population lived in rural areas and cultivated some land, securing workers was not easy for manufacturers. Especially in the medium-sized cities where the large-scale state enterprises had been established, many of the workers originated in the countryside and worked in factories without severing their ties to the rural areas, returning to their villages for harvest. At the same time, the single-party regime maintained tight restrictions on labor organization and labor union activity. After the introduction of the Law for the Maintenance of Order, adopted in 1925, workers' rights to organize were curbed. Unions were not allowed and strikes were prohibited, but in later years some strikes, albeit limited in numbers, did take place. These measures paralleled the generally restrictive social policies of the government in other areas. Despite the considerable growth in the urban sector during the 1930s, real wages did not exceed their pre–World War I levels until the 1950s (Yavuz 1995, pp. 155–96; Ahmad 1995, pp. 75–94; Makal 1999).[2]

Even though the state sector expanded during the 1930s, it would be difficult to argue that the private sector was hurt. The largest private enterprises were in the foreign trade sector, and these were adversely affected by the contraction of foreign trade. This was, however, owing more to the disintegration of international trade than etatism itself. Elsewhere in the urban economy, most of the private enterprises remained small in size. By investing in large, expensive projects in intermediate goods and providing them as inputs, the state enterprises actually helped the growth of private enterprises in the manufacturing of final goods for the consumer. Private investments continued to be supported and subsidized during the 1930s. Nonetheless, the

2. For long-term trends in real wages, see chapter 9, figure 9.3.

private sector remained concerned that the state sector might expand at its own expense. Tensions between the two sides continued.

There is some admittedly crude evidence on the rates of investment by the state and private sectors which sheds additional light on their respective roles. These estimates show that total gross investment in Turkey averaged more than 12 percent of GDP during 1927–29. Private investment accounted for about 9 percent, and the rest came from the state sector, primarily in the form of railroad construction. With the onset of the Depression, private investment dropped sharply, to 5 percent of GDP, and stayed at that level for the rest of the decade. State investments, on the other hand, rose modestly, to an average of 5 percent of GDP by the end of the decade (Bulutay et al. 1974; Tezel 1986, pp. 362–88). These estimates suggest that the state sector made up for some of the decline in private investment during the Depression but was not able to raise the overall rate of capital formation. One can also argue that the investment rates of the late 1920s were unusually high because of postwar reconstruction and recovery. If so, one may then conclude that even though the aggregate rates of investment declined after 1929, they recovered in the second half of the 1930s.

The sectoral breakdown of public sector investment also provides important insights into policies of etatism. Close to half of all fixed investments by the public sector during the 1930s went to railway construction and other forms of transportation. This substantial commitment reflects the overriding desire of the single-party regime to create a politically and economically cohesive entity within the new boundaries. In comparison, industry received limited resources, attracting no more than a quarter of all public investment, or slightly higher than 1 percent of GDP during the second half of the 1930s. This low figure supports my earlier argument that the contribution of etatism to the industrialization process remained modest in the 1930s.

Etatism undoubtedly had a long-lasting impact in Turkey for decades after World War II. This experiment also proved to be a powerful example for other state-led industrialization attempts in the Middle East after World War II (Richards and Waterbury 2008, pp. 179–210). From a macroeconomic perspective, however, the contribution of the state sector to the industrialization process in Turkey remained modest until World War II. For one thing, state enterprises in manufacturing and many other areas did not begin operations until after 1933. In a country with 17 million people on the eve of World War II, the total number of active state enterprises in industry and mining did not exceed twenty. Official figures indicate that in 1938, total employment in manufacturing, utilities, and mining remained below 600,000, or about 10 percent of the labor force. State enterprises accounted for only 11 percent of this amount, or about 1 percent of total employment in the country. Approximately 75 percent of employment in manufacturing continued to be provided by small-scale private enterprises (Tezel 1986, pp. 233–37).

Macroeconomic Policies during the 1930s

In response to the Great Depression and rising unemployment, many developed and developing countries adopted state interventionism. Many of these countries also adopted expansionary fiscal and monetary policies to stimulate their economies, basically running budget deficits and printing money to finance them. In 1936, John Maynard Keynes would publish his General Theory, which provided theoretical justification for these practices. At the beginning of the 1930s, however, these practices were not based on any theory and represented a search in the dark, more than anything else.

While state interventionism expanded rapidly in Turkey as well after 1929, the government behaved very cautiously in macroeconomic policies and stayed away from expansionary fiscal and monetary policies until the end of the decade. In fact, the basic principle guiding macroeconomic policy during this period was "balanced budget-strong money." As the ratio of government revenues and expenditures to GDP rose from 12–15 percent in the late 1920s toward 20 percent by the end of the 1930s, the national budget was kept balanced (figure 7.3). The amount of banknotes in circulation also remained stable until 1938, while the real money supply increased significantly because

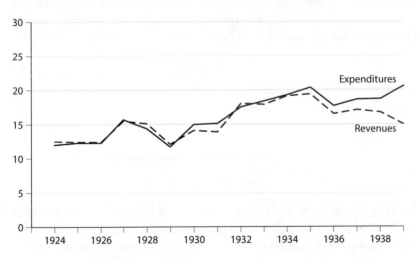

FIGURE 7.3. Fiscal Policy during the Interwar Period, 1924–1939 (Expenditures and Revenues as Percentage of GDP). Source: Based on official series from Turkey, Turkish Statistical Institute 2014.

of the rapid drop of overall price level after 1929. Furthermore, unlike the policies in many other countries, the government did not use exchange-rate depreciation to support domestic production. In fact, while many other countries were resorting to devaluation to reduce unemployment, the Turkish lira maintained its parity against gold. As a result, the lira gained 40 percent against the pound and the dollar until 1939 ((Tezel 1986, pp. 144–48, 368–88; Coşar 1995, pp. 259–92; Yücel 1996, pp. 55–73; Bulutay et al. 1974).

It is worth exploring the causes of this cautious and even conservative policy stance at a time when many countries were following expansionary policies in response to the Great Depression. Perhaps most noteworthy, the very strong measures of protectionism adopted in 1929 and the following years were doing most of the work and led to significant increases in manufacturing output. In other words, thanks to the strongly protectionist policies, some amount of industrialization and growth was being achieved without resorting to the measures later known as Keynesian. In fact, as I will discuss in the next chapter, not only industry but agriculture and the economy as a whole did reasonably well and achieved moderately high rates of growth during the 1930s. Moreover, İsmet İnönü, who was prime minister between 1924 and 1937, and many of his associates in government had closely observed the financial and monetary policies during the Ottoman era. Financing large budget deficits by external borrowing had created strong problems not just for the economy but also in foreign policy. In addition, the large volumes of paper money printed during World War I had led to record levels of inflation. The government was thus reluctant to repeat those experiences. For this reason, too, the policy makers did not feel the pressure to shift to more expansionary fiscal and monetary policies, or to devalue the currency. Finally, the Republican People's Party in power during the 1930s had eliminated all political opposition and did not face any competition during the 1930s. The party leadership and the government did not feel strong popular pressure to pursue more aggressive macroeconomic policies. The Republican People's Party governments were thus able to adopt and maintain a balanced budget-strong money stance during the 1930s.

World War II

Turkey pursued a policy of armed neutrality and full-scale mobilization during World War II. Although this policy protected the country from the devastation of the conflict, it did not make its economy immune to the war. The economic difficulties experienced during World War II were reminiscent of the troubles that arose during World War I. This time Turkey did not enter the war, however, and in the intervening quarter of a century, it had also boosted its infrastructure, thus limiting the negative consequences. Nonetheless, the sharp decline in imports and the diversion of large resources for the maintenance of an army of more than one million placed enormous strains on both industry and agriculture. Prices of foodstuffs climbed rapidly, and the provisioning of the urban areas emerged as a major problem for the government. As a result, the priorities and concerns of etatist industrialization were pushed aside. The five-year industrialization plans were discontinued and the struggle with wartime scarcities, shortages, and profiteering accentuated by economic policy mishaps became the order of the day. The available estimates indicate that GDP declined by about 35 percent from 1939 to 1945 (Bulutay et al. 1974; Turkey, Turkish Statistical Institute, 2014; Tekeli and İlkin 2014, pp. 17–207).

Turkey's economy had already experienced a substantial decrease in the relative size of the foreign trade sector during the 1930s. As a result of the difficulties in wartime maritime and shortages created in Europe by the mobilization, imports declined further during the war, to less than 3 percent of GDP (figure 7.2). As a result, the availability of many of the critical raw materials, intermediate goods, and manufactures diminished considerably, creating bottlenecks in all sectors of the economy. At the same time, Germany and the Allies competed for whatever minerals and agricultural commodities Turkey could export, particularly wheat early in the war, and chrome. Trade surpluses that had first emerged in the 1930s increased substantially, and gold and currency reserves continued to accumulate until the end of the war.

The agricultural sector, which had benefited from the demographic expansion of the interwar years, was hit hard by the wartime mobilization. Even though women assumed a greater share of the burden, the conscription of males and the requisitioning of draft animals by the military adversely affected both the area under cultivation and the yields, especially of cereals. The official statistics suggest that decreases in cereal production were quite dramatic, with wheat output declining by as much as 40 percent between 1939 and 1945. Food prices began to increase sharply after 1940, and the government attempted to use forced deliveries at below-market prices as well as taxation to secure the food supply of the urban areas and the military. In response, agricultural producers of all strata tried to resist by hiding, bribing, and more generally evading. As shortages in the large urban centers became more severe in 1942, the government was forced to reverse its policies. It began to rely more on the price mechanism and allowed the market sale of wheat by those producing above some threshold. The new policy benefited the middle farmers and large landowners, and those who could evade government demands in particular benefited from the sharply higher prices. In contrast, small, subsistence-oriented producers who could not take advantage of higher market prices assumed the heaviest burden of government policies. The rural poor who needed additional income traveled to the urban areas for temporary, seasonal work. For the rural poor, conditions in the urban areas were even more difficult, however. Access to food was easier in rural areas, for the great majority of the rural population that was able to cultivate some land (Pamuk 1991, pp. 131–37).

The shortages created by the decline in imports placed enormous strains on the industrial sector as well. Without the importation of raw materials, intermediate goods, and machinery, earlier levels of production could not be sustained. Manufacturing industry output is estimated to have declined by more than 35 percent between 1939 and 1945. With the increase in bottlenecks and shortages, black markets thrived, stockpiling and profiteering spread. Under these circumstances, the government was forced to abandon the earlier plans for new investments in manufacturing industry. Another reason for the abandonment of etatism was financial. Wartime expenditures could not be met with the existing revenues, and the budget deficits began to be financed by printing money. The result was the spiraling of inflation which accelerated the decline in the standards of living of a great majority of the urban population (Tekeli and İlkin 2014, pp. 17–207; Tezel 1986, pp. 156–60; Metinsoy 2007, pp. 132–272).

Both as a partial solution to its fiscal difficulties and as a response to wartime profiteering, in 1942, the government formulated a major initiative called *Varlık Vergisi*, or a one-time Wealth Levy, on leading merchants, industrialists, and other businessmen in the large urban centers. Although the text of the law did not discriminate, in practice, the Muslim businessmen were treated lightly and the levy was assessed mostly on the non-Muslim businessmen in Istanbul and other leading cities. Seventy percent of the revenues were collected in Istanbul and 65 percent of these collections came from non-Muslims, many of whom were forced to sell their real estate and businesses in order to raise cash. About 1,400 non-Muslim taxpayers who were unable to pay were sent to a camp, before being exiled to Aşkale in the east for hard labor. The government receipts from these emergency sales were not large enough to eliminate the budget deficits, but the sales themselves proved to be an important mechanism in the rise of many prominent Muslim-Turkish businessmen of the post–World War II era. After causing the government a great deal of embarrassment, the levy was discontinued in 1944 (Ökte 1951; Aktar 2000, pp. 135–243).

Declining production and sharply lower standards of living combined with increasing inequalities to turn large segments of the urban and rural populations against the single-party regime. At the same time, the merchants and industrialists as well as the larger, market-oriented producers in the countryside, many of whom benefited from the wartime opportunities, were searching for alternatives to etatism and government interventionism. The war years, and not so much the Great Depression and etatism, thus appear as the critical period in the political demise of the single-party regime. After the transition to a multiparty electoral system, the Republican People's Party was defeated in the first openly contested elections of 1950 (Pamuk 1991, pp. 137–39).

8

Economic Development and Institutional Change, 1914–1950

Economic Growth

Spanning two world wars and the Great Depression, the years from 1914 to 1950 were a difficult period for the world economy. The open economy model of the nineteenth century disintegrated under the pressure of two world wars and the Great Depression. Interventionism and protectionism emerged as new principles guiding economic policy during the Interwar years. These major events led to large fluctuations in the growth rates for the individual economies as well as the world economy. As a result of the differences in the impact of the two world wars and other causes, the per capita gap between North America and Western Europe widened significantly between 1913 and 1950. Extending a strong trend that began in the nineteenth century, the per capita income gap between developed and developing countries as a whole also continued to increase between 1913 and 1950.

How well different developing countries did during this difficult period also depended on the impact of the two world wars and the Great Depression. Countries that adopted greater interventionism and inward-oriented economic policies during the 1930s did better in terms of economic growth than countries that continued with the earlier strategies based on the export of agricultural products. However, in many developing economies, especially those that belonged to overseas empires of European powers, the open economy model and the specialization in agriculture continued. While per capita incomes rose in South America, Africa and especially Asia lagged behind. Among Asian countries, only Japan showed strong economic growth between the two wars, but it was severely impacted by World War II (table 8.1).

The period 1913 to 1950 was exceptionally difficult for Turkey. In addition to the two world wars and the Great Depression, the country had to deal with the difficulties of the transition from being part of a larger empire to becoming

TABLE 8.1. GDP per Capita in the World and in Turkey, 1913–1950

	GDP per Capita		Annual Rate of Increase (percent)
	1913	1950	
Western Europe	3460	4570	0.8
United States	5300	9550	1.6
Developed Countries	3960	6250	1.2
Eastern Europe excl. Soviet Union	1700	2100	0.6
Italy	2560	3500	0.9
Spain	2060	2200	0.2
Asia	700	720	0.1
Africa	640	890	0.9
Egypt	950	1050	0.3
Iran	800	1720	2.1
South America	1500	2500	1.4
Developing Countries	720	850	0.5
World	**1500**	**2100**	**0.9**
Turkey	**1150**	**1600**	**0.8**

Sources: Maddison 2007, pp. 375–86; Bolt and Van Zanden 2014, pp. 627–51; Pamuk 2006, pp. 809–28 for Turkey.
Note: GDP per capita are given in purchasing power parity (PPP) adjusted 1990 US dollars. For details, see chapter 2.

a nation-state within new borders. Available data suggest income per capita declined by as much as 40 percent during World War I and remained depressed until the end of the War of Independence in 1922. Per capita incomes then increased rapidly in the 1920s and caught up with their pre–World War I levels and may have even slightly exceeded them by 1929 (figure 8.1). Per capita incomes continued to rise at an average annual rate of 3.5 percent, or a total of 50 percent, until 1939. They then fell sharply, by more than 30 percent during World War II. The pre-war levels of per capita income were attained again only in the 1950s. In other words, 1939 was the year when per capita incomes reached their peak in the first half of the twentieth century. Given these very large fluctuations in per capita income as well as total population and total GDP, it makes a big difference which end years are used in calculating the average growth rates for this period.

Because finding data for the Ottoman era has been difficult, 1923, the year when the republic was established and the first year for which many data series as well as detailed national income accounts are available, has usually been used to assess Turkey's economic performance during the first half of the twentieth century. Calculations that accept 1923 as the base year show that

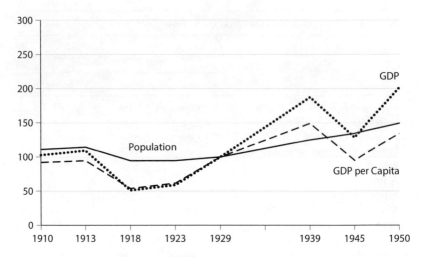

FIGURE 8.1. From Empire to the Nation-State, Basic Indicators for Turkey's Economy, 1910–1950 (all indexes = 100 in 1929). Sources: Author's calculations based on the GDP per capita and population series discussed in chapter 2.

GDP per capita increased at an average annual rate of 2.5 percent and income per capita more than doubled until 1950. It was an important achievement for the young republic to attain positive rates of economic growth despite the major adverse shocks. However, taking 1923 as the base year leads to an overly optimistic assessment, as that year came at the end of a decade of wars during which per capita incomes declined by more than 30 percent from their 1913 levels. The rapid increases in income per capita from 1923 until 1929 were in fact due to the recovery to pre–World War I levels. For this reason, I have used 1913 as the base year when calculating the average growth rates until 1950. Using 1913 as the base year also makes it easier to compare Turkey with other countries during the first half of the twentieth century since most international series, including those of Maddison, also use 1913 as the base year. I have estimated total increase in per capita income for the entire period 1913–1950 at close to 40 percent and the average growth rate of GDP per capita at 0.8 percent per year.

Comparisons with other countries and regions as well as countries with similar population in southern Europe and the Middle East should provide additional insights into Turkey's trajectory during this difficult period (figures 8.2 and 8.3). These figures show that the way each country or region fared in the two world wars made a big difference with regard to long-term economic performance. In both absolute and relative terms, Turkey was strongly affected by World War I but recovered during the 1920s and did well during the

1930s, reaching a peak for the first half of the century in 1939. Turkey's economy was once again hit hard by World War II, but the impact of that war was much more severe on the countries that participated in the military conflict. Italy and Spain continued to have higher levels of GDP per capita in comparison to Turkey during this period. GDP per capita levels rose in these two countries from 1913 to 1950 despite the two world wars and the Great Depression as well as the civil war in Spain. However, the gap between Italy and Spain, on the one hand, and the developed countries of Western Europe and the United States, on the other, continued to widen until 1950, as was the case for Turkey. The GDP per capita levels remained unchanged in Egypt, and the gap with the developed countries as well as with Turkey widened from 1913 to 1950. In comparison to Turkey, the impact of the two world wars on Egypt was more limited. However, while Turkey responded to the Great Depression with protectionism and industrialization, the same response was weaker in Egypt. Iran had lower GDP per capita levels than Turkey in 1913 but was able to raise them to Turkey's levels by 1950 thanks to large revenues from oil. In comparison to Turkey, the impact of the two world wars, especially of World War I, was also more limited on Iran.

The proximate causes of the considerable increase in per capita incomes in Turkey during the 1930s deserve additional attention since this was a time of significant changes in economic policy. At the outset, it is easy to eliminate some of the possible causes of the increases in incomes. The macroeconomic policies the governments followed after 1929 did not fit the standard expansionary package later known as Keynesian. Budgets remained balanced and nominal money supply did not increase until the end of the 1930s. Exchange-rate policy also was not used as an instrument against the recession; the lira in fact gained against leading currencies during the 1930s as the latter were devalued. Moreover, exports did not play a leading role in the increases in income either. The limited demand for raw materials from the world markets, especially when combined with GDP increases in the second half of the 1930s, led to a decline in the share of exports in GDP from more than 11 percent in 1928–29 to less than 7 percent in 1938–39. Finally, it proved impossible to obtain additional resources through foreign borrowing, and foreign direct investment also remained low during the 1930s.

In the absence of fiscal, monetary, and exchange-rate policies, the protectionist policies implemented after 1929 emerged as the most important policy behind the revival of the urban economy. With the increases in tariffs and quotas imposed on the imports of manufactured goods, especially final goods, and a system of bilateral agreements in foreign trade, the ratio of imports to GDP declined rapidly from 13 percent in 1928–29, to less than 9 percent in 1932–33, and below 7 percent in 1938–39. With the decline of

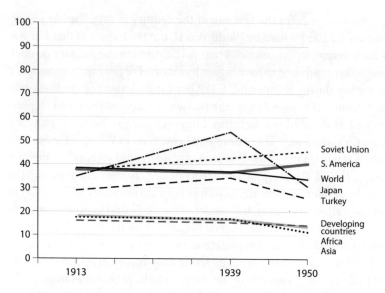

FIGURE 8.2. GDP per Capita in the World and in Turkey, 1913–1950 (PPP adjusted and as percentage of Western Europe and the United States). Sources: Maddison 2007, pp. 375–86; Bolt and Van Zanden 2014, pp. 627–51; Pamuk 2006 for Turkey.

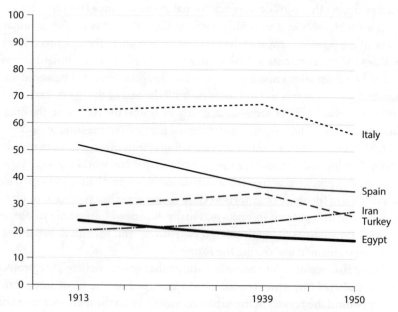

FIGURE 8.3. GDP per Capita in Four Other Countries and Turkey, 1913–1950 (PPP adjusted and as percentage of Western Europe and the United States). Sources: Maddison 2007, pp. 375–86; Bolt and Van Zanden 2014, pp. 627–51; Pamuk 2006 for Turkey.

imports, domestic manufacturing received a strong boost. Severe import repression thus created very attractive conditions for the domestic manufacturers after 1929. These mostly small and medium-sized producers achieved relatively high rates of output growth for the entire decade until World War II. Manufacturing output increased at annual rates above 8 percent or more than doubled during 1929–39 (Yücel 1996, pp. 89–130; Tezel 1986, pp. 102–3).

The sharp turn inward and import-substituting industrialization were not in conflict with global conditions during the 1930s. In fact, instead of trying to reverse or slow down the decline in agricultural prices, the government chose to let the urban economy and especially the manufacturing sector benefit from it. Lower raw material and food prices as well as lower wages created an opportunity for the manufacturing industry to generate higher profits and higher rates of investment. Public sector investments were also directed at the urban economy. In contrast, expenditures in rural areas, where more than 80 percent of the population continued to live and work, remained limited. This model was suited to the political preferences of the regime, because through protectionism and etatism, it created an economic structure that was more centralized and self-sufficient.

Another source of economic growth for Turkey's economy in the 1930s was the strong performance of the agricultural sector. Despite the adverse movements in price, agricultural output rose by about 60 percent during the 1930s. By the end of the decade, Turkey was in a position to export not only the traditional cash crops but also significant quantities of wheat (Hirsch and Hirsch 1963, pp. 372–94, and 1966, pp. 440–57). A number of not mutually exclusive explanations may be offered for rising agricultural production in the face of declining prices. Some of these concern government policies. The abolition of the tithe in 1924 supported the small and medium-sized family enterprises and paved the way for agricultural recovery. Moreover, the construction of railways by the state helped increase production, especially in Central and Eastern Anatolia, by linking them to major urban markets (Tekeli and İlkin 2004c, pp. 286–321). A second explanation focuses on the demographic recovery and how family enterprises reacted to the decline in agricultural prices. The decline of the total population by about 20 percent during World War I and the War of Independence, as well as the loss of millions of draft animals, had struck a major blow to agricultural production. After the wars ended, Turkey's population started rising rapidly, by approximately 2 percent annually. By the early 1930s, children born after World War I were beginning to contribute to the labor force in agriculture, and land under cultivation began to increase. Numbers of draft animals also increased by 40 percent during the same period.

In other words, thanks to the demographic and to some extent the economic recovery of peasant households, the amount of cultivated land registered an important increase during the 1930s. Agricultural production during this decade was supported not only by the rise in the numbers of family farms but also by an increase in the average amount of land cultivated per farm. It thus appears that the small and medium-sized family enterprises responded to lower agricultural prices by using more family labor and cultivating more land to obtain a certain income or consumption level (Kuruç 2011, pp. 451–86; Shorter 1985, pp. 417–41).

By continuing to provide inexpensive foodstuffs and raw materials, the agricultural sector supported the growth in the urban economy, especially in the manufacturing sector. Without the strong performance from the agricultural sector, the gains in the urban economy could not be sustained during the 1930s. The peak in per capita incomes as well as per capita agricultural production, industrial production, and the share of investments in GDP was reached in 1939 (figure 8.1). The strong gains of the 1930s were reversed during World War II, however. Even though Turkey stayed out of the war, both agricultural and manufacturing output declined sharply due to the adverse conditions created by the war.

Industrialization and economic growth were reasonably robust during the 1930s. Yet one also needs to point to the limitations of structural change and economic transformation during the Interwar period as a whole. The urbanization rate and the share of the urban economy in the labor force remained below 20 percent in both 1939 and 1950, as can be seen in table 8.2. Moreover, the ratio of investments to GDP was also low and could not yet sustain higher levels of economic growth. Arthur Lewis, who has provided important insights into the early stages of industrialization in developing countries, has suggested that for sustainable industrialization and growth, the ratio of investment to GDP needs to reach at least 12 percent (Lewis 1954, pp. 139–91). Turkey did not reach this threshold before World War I as the ratio of investments to GDP was around 9 percent in 1913. The ratio of investments to GDP fluctuated between 9 percent and 11 percent during the 1930s (table 8.2). However, the same ratio declined to less than 10 percent during World War II and its immediate aftermath (Bulutay et al. 1974). The ratio of investments to GDP would rise permanently above 12 percent only in the 1950s (see table 10.2 in chapter 10). These basic indicators suggest that the transition from the empire to the nation-state, coming on top of two world wars and the global depression, had created tough and adverse conditions. The peasant economy remained mostly intact and the economic transformations of the 1930s, including industrialization, remained limited.

TABLE 8.2. Basic Economic and Social Indicators for Turkey, 1913–1950

	1913	1950
Population (millions)	16.5	20.9
Urbanization Rate (%)		
Centers above 10,000 / Total Population	23	18
Life Expectancy at Birth (years)	32–33?	44 (M: 42; W: 46)
Literacy Rate (%)	14?	33 (M: 46; W: 19)
Average Years of Schooling of Adult Population over age 15		0.6
Share of Agriculture in Labor Force (%)	75–80?	75–80?
Share of Agriculture in GDP (%)	50	42
Exports / GDP (%)	11	8
Imports / GDP (%)	14	8
Investment / GDP (%)	8	11
Revenues of Central Government / GDP (%)	13	15

Sources: Eldem 1970; Pamuk 1987, Bulutay et al. 1974; Tezel 1986 and Turkey, Türkiye İstatistik Kurumu (Turkish Statistical Institute) 2014.

It may be useful here to extend to the Interwar period the comparison with Egypt that I began for the nineteenth century in chapter 6. Even though Egypt's involvement in the two world wars and their impact on the economy was much more limited, GDP per capita did not increase in Egypt between 1913 and 1950, while it increased by about 40 percent in Turkey (table 8.1 and figure 8.1). As a result, the gap in GDP per capita between the two countries widened considerably during this period. One basic reason for this difference is directly related to political economy and changes in economic institutions, including economic policies. In Egypt, landowners were much more powerful, and their power combined with the continued influence of Britain made it much more difficult to abandon the strategy based on agriculture and shift to protectionism and industrialization, even though the collapse of cotton prices had severe consequences for Egypt's agriculture. In other words, both Egypt and Turkey experienced increases in tariffs and manufacturing activity. However, while protectionist measures including non-tariff barriers were much stronger in Turkey, both the rise in tariffs and the increases in industrial production remained more limited and imports continued to account for a larger share of domestic consumption in key sectors such as textiles in Egypt. Also important was the contrast in land availability. While additional agricultural land was available in Turkey, limits to cultivable land had been reached in Egypt before World War I. As a result, agricultural output could increase together with the demographic recovery and create additional demand for manufactures in Turkey, but the same was not true in Egypt (Hansen 1991, pp. 64–109; Karakoç, Pamuk, and Panza 2017, pp. 149–54).

Income Distribution

The two world wars, recovery from each of them, and industrialization during the Great Depression led to large fluctuations not only in average incomes but also in the distribution of income. The extensive changes in political and economic institutions also shaped the distribution of income. Even if available data are not very detailed, the direction of changes in the distribution of income during the two world wars is reasonably well known. As average incomes declined by 30 percent or more in both world wars, income distribution became much more unequal. Because relative prices moved in favor of foodstuffs in both wars, those who had enough food to sell in the markets, large landowners, and merchants in the cities who were able to stockpile food were the main beneficiaries (Toprak 1982, pp. 313–44; Tekeli and İlkin 2004a, pp. 1–44). The urban poor, wage earners, and more generally urban population with low incomes faced the greatest difficulties in obtaining food.

During both wars, the government placed various demands on the small and medium-sized agricultural producers that made up the great majority of the population. How well they fared depended on how severe the government demands were and to what extent they were able to evade them. These demands changed from region to region during World War I and the government was not always successful in collecting taxes. It is also likely that the forced deportation and deaths of large numbers of Armenians in Eastern Anatolia as well as their flight to the neighboring regions during World War I had a strong negative impact on the income level in this region and increased inter-regional inequalities in the long term. World War II also had a significant effect on the economy as well as the distribution of income, but the impact was less severe in comparison to that of World War I as Turkey did not join the hostilities.

There were two other trends related to the ownership of physical assets during the world wars with important long-term consequences for the distribution of wealth and income. The first was the decline and destruction of physical assets such as buildings, plant and equipment and to a lesser extent agricultural land during both world wars and especially during World War I. Since higher income groups were the owners of these assets, their decline and destruction tended to make the subsequent distribution of wealth and income more equal. The second trend during both wars and their aftermath was the shift in the ownership of the assets of non-Muslims to Muslims. The massacres and deaths of many Armenians and the flight from Turkey of most of the rest during World War I as well as the exchange of population, Orthodox Greeks for Muslims, arranged between the governments of Turkey and Greece in 1923 led to the transfers of the urban and rural properties of both Armenians and Greeks to Muslim Turks and Kurds. The Wealth Levy imposed ostensibly on wartime profiteers but demanded mostly from non-Muslims during World War II produced a similar if more limited result by shifting the ownership of some of the assets of the remaining non-Muslims residing in urban areas to Muslims.

The 1920s as well as the second half of the 1940s were periods of rapid recovery after many years of war. The pattern of increases in agricultural incomes as well as wages after both wars suggests that the gains from the economic recovery were distributed across most groups in both rural and urban areas. Another important event regarding income distribution during the Interwar period was the Great Depression. The large movements in international and domestic prices against agriculture and the government's response in the form of protectionism and support for industrialization expanded the existing differences between the urban and rural areas in favor of the former (Tekeli and İlkin 1977, pp. 78–90; Tekeli and İlkin 1982). The abolition of the tithe in 1924 had eased the tax burden of agricultural producers, and the government did not attempt to reverse the decline in agricultural prices after 1929. As a result, agricultural incomes lagged behind those in urban areas that benefited from industrialization. Despite the considerable increase in agricultural output during both the 1920s and the 1930s, the share of agriculture and rural areas in total income was thus lower in 1939 in comparison to both 1929 and 1913. In fact, the existing national income accounts suggest that the gap between average incomes in the urban or non-agricultural sector and the average incomes in the agricultural sector rose to their highest levels of the past two centuries during the 1930s.

A comparison at the two end points of this period, 1913 and 1950, should provide important insights into the longer-term changes in the income distribution. Average incomes are estimated to have increased by about 40 percent from 1913 to 1950 within the area comprising Turkey today. It would be safe to say that a large share of this increase went to those in the urban areas, especially to those engaged in activities other than foreign trade. In contrast, the agricultural sector where the great majority of the population earned their living experienced limited gains during the same period. These broad trends probably apply to both more urbanized Western Anatolia and more rural Eastern Anatolia. Within the rural areas, the more commercialized regions and the more market-oriented producers tended to do better than the others, but they also lost more during the 1930s. Despite the rhetoric of the Republican People's Party to the effect that the peasant was the true master of the country, the rural areas did not receive significant amounts of compensating support from the government after 1929. In contrast, the urban economy benefited from favorable price movements, the severe repression of imports, the beginnings of import-substituting industrialization, as well as the policies of etatism.

As for the distribution within the urban economy, a simple measure, namely the ratio of wages to per capita incomes, can provide important insights in the absence of detailed data. As noted earlier, while average incomes were rising especially in the urban areas by as much as 40 percent or more from 1913 to 1950, real wages did not increase or increased very little during the same period. This simple measure thus suggests that during this period of protectionism and early industrialization, inequalities within the urban economy, as well as inequalities between urban and rural areas, were rising (for trends in real wages, see figure 9.3 in chapter 9; also Yavuz 1995, pp. 155–96).

Finally, the construction of new railroads in Central, Eastern, and Southeastern Anatolia during the Interwar period strengthened considerably the transport infrastructure in these less developed regions and their links to the rest of the country. However, because of the loss of most if not all of the Armenian population during World War I and because of the impact of the Kurdish rebellions during the Interwar period, these two regions were probably poorer in 1939 than in 1913. It is thus likely that the west-east differences in average incomes were higher in 1939 and 1950 than in 1913.

Role of Institutions and Institutional Change

After recovering from the impact of World War I until 1929, GDP per capita in Turkey increased at an average rate of 3 percent per annum during 1929 to 1939 thanks to high rates of protectionism and industrialization supported by demographic recovery and rising agricultural production. In what follows, I will focus on the Interwar period and especially the 1930s to assess the contributions and the limitations of the institutions and institutional changes associated with the new economic model during the transition from empire to the nation-state. I will argue that major changes in the international environment as well as far-reaching domestic changes in political institutions were responsible for the transformation of the formal economic institutions from those of an open economy in the nineteenth century to those of an inward-looking national economy during the Interwar period.

The far-reaching changes in Turkey's political and economic institutions during the Interwar era came from two main sources. The end of the Ottoman Empire and the formation of a nation-state in Turkey under new leadership led to important changes in political institutions. In addition, the institutions of the global economy and the institutions related to Turkey's relations with the world economy changed dramatically after World War I. As a result, the new leadership at Ankara could establish new economic institutions and pursue policies of protectionism and industrialization shaped by economic nationalism and the goal to create new economic elites, a Muslim-Turkish bourgeoisie. These major changes in formal institutions played important roles in bringing about significant increases in per capita income during the Interwar period. However, they did not crowd out informal institutions but continued to interact with them. In fact, informal institutions continued to play key roles in both politics and economic development during these decades, in both rural and urban areas as well as state interventionism. For a more nuanced assessment of the role of institutions during this period, it is thus necessary to also examine both the formal and informal institutions as well as their interaction, how new institutions emerged as a result, and how they contributed to or hindered long-term economic development.

The institutions of the global economy and the institutions related to Turkey's relations with the world economy changed dramatically between the nineteenth century and the Interwar period. The Ottoman government was bound by free trade treaties and had followed open economy policies during the nineteenth century. The economic institutions were shaped by the interaction between the central government and European governments and European companies until World War I. The interruption of external trade, the adoption of the principles of self-sufficiency, protectionism, and industrialization, and the shift to interventionism during World War I turned out to be the beginning of a long-term change in the economic model and the formal economic institutions. After the Great Depression began in 1929 and another world war soon appeared on the horizon, economic nationalism and concerns for self-sufficiency began to dominate economic policy. One basic reason for these radical economic changes was the new global circumstances. However, the dismantling of the Ottoman Empire and the formation of a nation-state in Turkey under new leadership also played a key role in the adoption of the new economic model.

As a result, the power of European states and European companies to influence the institutions and policies of the new nation-state was significantly less during the Interwar period in comparison to the nineteenth century. In the Lausanne Peace negotiations that concluded in 1923, the European governments reluctantly agreed to the end of the legal and economic privileges of the European citizens and companies. The new nation-state also gained the right to decide unilaterally on its own tariffs beginning in 1929. While some European companies continued their operations in Turkey during the Interwar period, many others, including banks and merchant houses, left during the

Great Depression and others, most prominently the railway companies, were bought out and nationalized by the government.

The end of the Ottoman Empire and the formation of a new nation-state in Turkey under new leadership led to important changes in political institutions. The War of Independence that lasted from 1920 to 1922 was supported by a broad coalition of the provincial notables, merchants, landowners, and religious leaders. After abolition of the sultanate and the caliphate and the proclamation of the Republic in 1923, however, Mustafa Kemal and his close associates moved to eliminate the opposition and began to adopt a narrower secular line (Zürcher 2004, pp. 166–95). In the nineteenth century, the central government had played a much more important role in shaping the formal economic institutions and policies than the various domestic groups including landowners and merchants. While the influence of European states and companies declined sharply during the Interwar period, the key role of the government and new state elites continued. The economic policies of the new leadership were shaped by economic nationalism and the goal to create a Muslim-Turkish bourgeoisie. The Muslim-Turkish private sector was weak and consisted mostly of small and medium-sized enterprises, however. As a result, industrialization led by the state was adopted as the basic development strategy in response to the Great Depression. A small number of large-scale state enterprises were established during the 1930s in key sectors such as manufacturing, banking, mining, and transportation.

As the new regime began to shape the new economic institutions and policies in the 1920s, however, consolidation of its power in the rural areas was an important priority. One important institutional change in the early years was the abolition of the tithe and tax farming in agriculture. Easing the tax burden of mostly small and medium-sized agricultural producers was an important goal. However, the abolition of the tithe also undermined what had remained of the power of the tax farmers and a key source of potential opposition to the new regime. Similarly, the prohibition of the activities of religious orders and networks did not entirely eliminate their activities but undermined their influence, especially in the provinces. Nonetheless, the cultural disconnect between the conservative peasantry and the secularizing policies of the new persisted. Despite the far-reaching changes in formal institutions and consolidating its power, the government was unable to increase its influence in the rural areas (Mardin 1973, pp. 169–90; Adaman, Akarçay, and Karaman 2015, pp. 166–85).

The role of the state in the economy as well as the aims and institutions of state interventionism also underwent important changes during the transition from the empire to the nation-state. In the nineteenth century, Ottoman leaders did not view the creation of a strong private sector in the urban economy as a leading goal. The government's initiatives for industrialization were oriented, for the most part, toward meeting the state's own needs, for example. In contrast, economic development and the creation of a stronger Muslim-Turkish private sector by the state were adopted as major goals by the new nation-state. In the 1920s, the government in Ankara began developing new methods for developing a private sector selected from among Muslim-Turkish groups close to the new regime by using its small and large purchases, construction projects, and the tenders it launched for that purpose, as well as the credits extended by the new public sector banks. The adoption of state-led industrialization as the basic economic strategy during the 1930s undoubtedly complicated the picture and relegated the private sector to a secondary role. Nonetheless, the private sector remained in the big picture and state support for it continued through these mechanisms. The single-party regime thus remained narrowly based on urban groups close to the party. Instead of opening the political and economic institutions economy to broader groups, the regime reproduced the existing inequalities and also created new inequalities. These emerging institutions, in other words, the formal as well as informal rules of state interventionism, would develop, diversify, and gain permanence in the decades after World War II as the state continued to distribute privileges within the private sector and play key roles in the selection of the winners in the economy (Keyder 1987, pp. 71–115; Boratav 1981, pp. 165–90; Buğra 1994, pp. 35–95).

Changes in the banking sector reflected these far-reaching changes in power relations and in institutions. European banks had dominated the emerging formal banking sector during the nineteenth century. The Imperial Ottoman Bank, owned by French and British shareholders, fulfilled some of the functions of a central bank and also functioned as a commercial bank across the empire. Many European banks departed or were sold to local owners during the Interwar period, however. The central banking functions of the Imperial Ottoman Bank were eliminated with a government decree and later handed to the new Central Bank founded in 1930. The Ottoman Bank continued as a commercial bank owned mostly by French shareholders. Turkey's banking system in the Interwar period thus consisted mostly of a small number of private and public sector banks.

İşbank, a semi-public bank committed to the development of the private sector, is a prominent example and indeed the symbol of the new economic model adopted by the Ankara government in the 1920s. From its early years, Işbank became an important instrument in the creation by the state of a new private sector led by Muslim businessmen. İşbank continued its prominent role in the economy during the second half of the twentieth century. After the Republican People's Party left the government in 1950, the mostly symbiotic relations between İşbank and the state changed. Nonetheless, the bank continued to pursue its activities, which extended beyond finance into areas like industrialization and development, with a status that was different from both a public bank and a private bank (Kocabaşoğlu 2001, pp. 1–298).

Sümerbank established in 1933 and and Etibank established in 1935 were new institutions that reflect the change in strategy in the early 1930s and the leading role of the state in industrialization. Sümerbank was founded to operate both as a bank and also as a leading manufacturer in textiles, the most important sector in import substitution. Its first large manufacturing facility was set up in Kayseri in 1935 with credits obtained from the Soviet Union, but its contribution to industrial production in the 1930s remained limited. After World War II, as control of the economy was transferred to the private sector, Sümerbank maintained its position among leading industrial enterprises. After Washington Consensus principles were embraced in 1980, the government decided to privatize Sümerbank. The privatization process, subject to many political and legal challenges, was also embroiled in corruption scandals and it could not be completed until 2001. In addition to banking, Etibank focused mostly on mining during the 1930s and after World War II. Its privatization after 1980 was also subject to corruption scandals and court cases that also continued into the twenty-first century (Tekeli and İlkin 1982, pp. 134–220).

The strategy based on strong protectionism and industrialization combined with the creation of a Muslim-Turkish private sector thus created moderately strong rates of economic growth in the urban areas. Another priority for the new regime was the expansion of the new institutions and the consolidation of its power in the rural areas where the great majority of the population lived. The results in this respect were mixed, however. The abolition of the tithe not only provided relief to family farms, it also undermined what had remained of the power of the tax farmers, a key source of potential opposition to the new regime. The government also tried to suppress the activities of religious orders and networks and develop new patronage networks linking the rural areas to the capital (Sayarı 2014, pp. 658–59). Despite the far-reaching changes in formal institutions, however, the capacity of the state to penetrate the provinces and especially rural areas remained limited. While the changes in formal institutions played important roles in bringing about significant economic growth until World War II, for a more nuanced assessment, it is thus necessary to examine the interaction between formal and informal institutions.

Limitations of the fiscal, administrative, and legal capacities of the state were not the only reason the new formal institutions did not crowd out informal institutions but continued to coexist with them. In addition, large numbers of other institutions were also involved in the implementation of a new institution. Many of these institutions were shaped by values, beliefs, and social norms as well as interests and power relations. While political institutions and laws could change very quickly, values, beliefs, social norms, and related institutions changed more slowly. Of equal importance, the distribution of benefits from the enforcement of the new institutions was not always in line with the existing distribution of power. Powerful groups resisted institutional changes or exerted pressure to ensure that an institution operated in a way that was different from the intended aim. The conservative Muslim elites often made use of informal institutions including identity-based networks and patron-client relations in these conflicts. The establishment and then the closure of the Village Institutes is a good example of how powerful interests could oppose and reverse government policies and formal institutional change (Roland 2004, pp. 109–31; Starr 1979; Starr and Pool 1974, pp. 533–60; Mardin 1973, pp. 169–90).

In other words, the formal institutions by the new nation-state were accompanied by the two-way interaction between formal and informal institutions as well as the two-way interaction between institutions and economic outcomes. The preceding discussion suggests that the two-way interaction between institutions and social structure was equally important. One of the areas where the limitations of the reforms can be seen most starkly is the spread of education to the provinces and the rural areas. The new nation-state also placed a good deal of emphasis on secular education. Some progress was made at all levels of education, but the diffusion of education to rural areas where close to 80 percent of the population lived remained slow. In addition, education levels of women remained well behind those of men. In basic indicators of education, Turkey continued to lag behind other developing countries with similar GDP per capita levels, as I will discuss in the next section.

Opposition to the reforms and the new regime also came from those who controlled and benefited from some of the Islamic-Ottoman institutions. With the reforms of the nineteenth century, the vakıfs were brought under the control of the central government and their share in both agricultural lands and urban assets had declined. The new government in Ankara began to sell to private owners or transfer to the various public entities the remaining vakıf assets under government control (Öztürk 1995, pp. 109–471). Even though the importance of the vakıfs and their assets had declined, those who had controlled the vakıf lands and the other vakıf assets, and those who benefited from the incomes generated and the services they provided—families and religious orders as well as those who used and embraced the vakıfs for social and cultural reasons, thus remained opposed to many of the reforms.

By the end of the 1930s, the vast majority of the population continued to live in rural areas and engaged in low-productivity agriculture. Even if the level of production was able to recover from the hard blows of two world wars and the Great Depression, small and medium-sized family farms using traditional technologies experienced very little transformation. With the decline in world market demand and prices, the countryside actually turned further inward during the Interwar period in comparison to the decades before World War I. The inequalities between the rural and urban areas increased significantly. It was very difficult to secure substantial increases in per capita incomes without the shift of the rural population from agriculture to the urban sector, where they could access more advanced technologies and achieve greater productivity.

Along with economic cleavages, religion and cultural values thus emerged as another axis of opposition in the countryside. The embrace of Islam and the spread of informal networks in response to the centralizing reforms of the secularist elites that began in the nineteenth century continued in the Interwar era. Although many of the provincial notables were integrated into the ranks of the Republican People's Party, the cultural as well as economic disconnect between the conservative peasantry and the secularizing policies of the new regime at Ankara persisted.

Human Development

In Turkey as well as most other developing countries during the first half of the twentieth century, life expectancy at birth was low due to high mortality rates among all age groups, but especially among infants and children. As much as half or more of all deaths were among children under the age of five who died mostly of infectious diseases. Thanks to declines in both infant and adult mortality rates across the country, life expectancy at birth rose from 32–33 years in 1913 to more than 35 years in the 1930s and to 44 years (42 for men, 45 for women) in 1950 (table 8.2).

There were large fluctuations along the way, however. Life expectancy at birth declined sharply during World War I. Large numbers of military and civilian casualties during World War I suggest that life expectancy must have decreased to less than twenty-five years during the war. For large segments of the civilian population, hunger and disease remained a constant threat until the end of the war. Moreover, the decline in mortality after the war proceeded very unevenly. Large differences persisted in infant as well as adult mortality rates between urban and rural areas. In rural areas in the east, more than a third of all infants did not reach their first birthday. Life expectancy at birth declined during World War II as well, but the decreases were much more limited in comparison to World War I. Even though there was some decline in food availability and nutrition, and mortality rates among infants, children, and the elderly rose particularly among the urban and rural poor, hunger and disease were not widespread during World War II in large part because Turkey did not participate in the war, but also due to a stronger economy and infrastructure. Nonetheless, infant mortality levels were still around 25 percent in 1950.

The new republic recognized the importance of health care. Resources allocated to health care increased, but public spending on health in rural areas where close to 80 percent of the population lived remained limited. Numbers of doctors, nurses, midwives, and other health-care personnel increased modestly from 1.9 per 10,000 population in 1928 to 2.5 in 1939 and more strongly to 4.4 in 1950. Equally important, growing knowledge and better health-care practices and more generally the discovery of better ways of doing things began to play an important role in these increases. Some improvements were achieved in the basic health services offered especially in the urban areas, and significant advances were achieved in the struggle against infectious diseases. An important part of the credit for the decline in child mortality in the urban areas must go to the control of disease through public health measures. With the increased presence of medical facilities, the fight against tuberculosis, malaria, and other contagious diseases, the discovery of antibiotics, some increases in income, and better nutrition, mortality rates started declining in Turkey in the 1930s (Akder 2010, pp. 220–24; Evered and Evered 2011, pp. 470–82). However, along with the gap in per capita income, the gap in life expectancy at birth between developed countries and developing countries including Turkey continued to increase during this period (Zijdeman and de Silva 2014, pp. 101–16; Deaton 2013, pp. 59–100).

The new nation-state also placed a good deal of emphasis on secular education. The educational system was completely secularized in 1924 and the religious schools were closed. The adoption of the Latin alphabet in 1928 was followed by literacy campaigns directed at adults across the country as well as efforts to expand the reach of schools. Some progress was made at all levels of education but the diffusion of education to rural areas where close to 80 percent of the population lived remained slow. Turkey continued to lag behind other developing countries with similar GDP per capita levels in basic indicators of education. Enrollment in elementary schools increased from about 30 percent of school-age children in 1930 to about 60 percent in 1950. However, fewer than half of the villages had elementary schools, and most schools had only one teacher for all students. Fewer than half of the students who attended elementary school stayed long enough to graduate. Similarly, only 4 percent of the age group graduated from the various secondary schools, and less than 1 percent of the age group graduated from four-year universities in 1950.

One important reason for the slow improvement in outcomes was the limited fiscal resources of the state. Only a small fraction of the budget and the GDP was allocated to education. Similarly, incomes of the population were low and their opportunities were limited. They often preferred their children to work in the fields rather than attend school. There was political opposition as well. Especially in the provinces and in rural areas, the new schools were not easily accepted by the Muslim population and the conservative Muslim elites and the religious networks who did not embrace the ongoing reforms. The challenge of expanding public schools in the provinces and in rural areas and ensuring that girls attended the schools thus remained a major problem.

Large disparities persisted in enrollment rates between urban and rural areas, between men and women, and between the west and the east until 1950. In the Kurdish areas in the east, literacy and schooling rates remained the lowest in the country. Women's literacy level rose from less than 5 percent in 1913 to 19 percent in 1950, while men's literacy level increased from about 15 percent to 46 percent (Turkey, Turkish Statistical Institute, 2014). While Turkey was one of the earliest countries to extend suffrage to women in 1934, and while the daughters of the urban middle class who embraced the new secularism of the republic did benefit from the availability of education, and some areas of civil service and the professions were opened to them, progress on women's education was very slow in the rural areas. Male-female differences remained high at all levels of schooling. In 1950, numbers of female students were about 60 percent of those of male students among elementary students and only 25 percent of those of male students amongst high school and university students. These gender differences were lower in urban areas and amongst middle- and higher-income groups but higher in rural areas, in less developed regions of the country, in the east and southeast, and in lower income groups (Arat 2008, pp. 391–96; Turkey, Turkish Statistical Institute, 2014).

There were attempts to extend the reforms to the villages, to spread modern techniques in agriculture, and to instill a secular and positivist attitude among the rural population. One important project of the early republic was the creation in 1940 of a limited number of Village Institutes in rural areas across the country. These new schools began to train young villagers in each region as primary school teachers as well as teachers of modern technical and agricultural skills to the rural population. The village institutes were very successful while they lasted, but with the transition to political pluralism after World War II, they began to be opposed fiercely by the conservative rural elites. As a result, the village institutes were reduced to ordinary teacher training schools before 1950 by the Republican People's Party itself and abolished altogether by the Democrat Party government in 1954 (Karaömerlioğlu 1998).

Average formal schooling received by adults over fifteen years of age increased slowly from about 0.5 years before World War I to about 1.2 years in 1950, while world averages increased from 2.0 to 3.2 years during the same period. These comparisons confirm that Ankara government's efforts on education remained focused on the urban areas and did not reach the rural areas, where the great majority of the population lived until after World War II. In terms of schooling for adults, Turkey lagged behind not only the developed countries of Western Europe and the United States but also the averages for Latin America and China, about the same level as Egypt, and South and Southeast Asia, and above Sub-Saharan Africa (van Leeuwen and van Leeuwen-Li 2014, pp. 88–97).

9

Inward-Oriented Development
after World War II

THE POST–WORLD WAR II INTERNATIONAL economic order designed at Bretton Woods by the United States and its Western allies was greatly influenced by the lessons drawn from the Interwar period, most notably the problems created by war debts, reparation payments, and beggar-thy-neighbor policies which had led to the breakdown of the international economy after 1929. The new order supported international trade but controlled international movements of capital and provided more room for national economies to follow their own policies. The United States and western European countries were thus able to expand the role of the state and implemented Keynesian macroeconomic policies. Welfare state policies and state expenditure on education, health care, and other social areas increased significantly. Centrally planned economies in Eastern Europe also experienced high rates of growth during the decades after World War II (Findlay and O'Rourke 2007, pp. 473–526; Berend 2006, pp. 133–262; Eichengreen 2008, pp. 91–133; Rodrik 2011, pp. 67–88).

Thanks to the Bretton Woods order, most developing economies also adopted government interventionism during these decades. Inward-looking policies and more specifically import-substituting industrialization (ISI) became the most frequently adopted strategy for economic development, especially in the medium-sized and larger developing countries (Kemp 1993, pp. 148–236; Hirschman 1968, pp. 1–26). These policies were not in conflict with the international monetary and trade arrangements of the Bretton Woods era and the Keynesian policies pursued in the developed economies. Rates of growth in the developing countries were also exceptionally high during the post–World War II decades.

This chapter will begin with global and national political developments and examine how they led to changes in economic policies and institutions as well

TABLE 9.1. A Periodization of Economic Trends, 1950–1980

| Subperiod | Average Annual Growth Rates | | | | | Level of GDP per Capita at the End of Subperiod |
	Population	GDP	Agriculture	Manufacturing	GDP per Capita	1950 = 100
1950–1962	2.8	5.9	4.5	7.1	3.0	142
1963–1980	2.4	5.8	1.9	9.1	3.3	248
1950–1980	2.6	5.9	2.9	8.4	3.2	248

Source: Author's calculations based on the official national income series in Turkey, Türkiye İstatistik Kurumu (Turkish Statistical Institute). 2014.

as the consequences of these changes. The next chapter will review Turkey's record in economic growth, income distribution, and human development in both absolute and relative terms. It will also evaluate the role of institutions and institutional change in economic development during these three decades.

The decades after World War II in Turkey are best examined in two distinct subperiods as summarized in table 9.1. After World War II, Turkey moved closer to the West and toward a multiparty political system. The shift to a more competitive political system brought about a shift toward an economic strategy based on agriculture as favored by the great majority of the population who earned their living from agriculture. While the state-led industrialization of the 1930s began to be abandoned as early as 1947, the new strategy was fully adopted by the Democrat Party government that came to power after the elections in 1950 (Zürcher 2004, pp. 206–40; Ahmad 1977). After some success, the new model ran into difficulties, however, due to macroeconomic mismanagement. After the IMF-led devaluation of 1958 and the military coup of 1960, a new economic model favoring import-substituting industrialization, this time led by the private sector, was formally adopted in 1963 with the launch of the first five-year development plan. ISI remained the basic economic strategy until 1980, when a severe political and economic crisis led to economic liberalization and the adoption of market-oriented policies.

Political and Economic Changes

After the end of World War II, international and domestic forces combined to bring about major political and economic changes in Turkey, which now had a population close to 20 million. The United States emerged as the dominant world power after the war, but it was also the Soviet territorial demands over the Turkish Straits after the war that pushed the government toward closer cooperation with the United States and membership in NATO. The Marshall Plan was extended to Turkey for military and economic purposes beginning in 1948 as the country began to be drawn increasingly into the American sphere of influence. Numerous foreign experts and official missions visited the country during this period to express their preference for a more liberal and more open economic system. Perhaps the most influential was the report prepared for the World Bank by a commission of American experts that called for the dismantling of a large part of the etatist manufacturing establishments, including the country's only iron and steel complex, greater emphasis on private enterprise, encouragement of foreign capital, a more liberal foreign exchange and trade regime, and greater reliance on agricultural development. These changes, the report stated, were necessary if Turkey was to benefit from US aid and inflow of private American capital in the postwar era (Thornburg 1949; Tören 2007, pp. 143–298).

Domestically, many social groups had become dissatisfied with the single-party regime by 1946. The poorer segments of the peasantry had been hit hard by wartime taxation and government demands for cereals for the provisioning of the urban areas. The gendarme and the tax collector had returned to the rural areas as symbols of government presence. After the war, however, the government tried to mend its relations with small producers in rural areas and passed a Land Reform bill through parliament which gave it the power to redistribute holdings above 50 *dönüms* or 5 hectares. The debate was heated and the bill was strongly criticized, especially by members who had links to medium and large landowners. The group that would later form the Democrat Party began to take shape during these debates.

In the urban areas, the Wealth Levy of 1942 had caused unrest and suspicion among the Muslim bourgeoisie even though the measures had been used to discriminate against the non-Muslims. After more than two decades of the single-party regime, the Turkish economic elites wanted to change their privileged but dependent status even though many of them had benefited from the wartime conditions and policies. They now preferred less government interventionism. Workers who constituted a small minority and other wage and salary workers including the civil servants had also been hit quite hard by the wartime inflation, shortages, and profiteering (Keyder 1987, pp. 112–14; Boratav 2011, pp. 63–67).

The opposition to the regime thus began to demand greater emphasis on private enterprise, the agricultural sector, and a more open economy. In response, the single-party regime led by President Inönü decided to open the political system to contestation and began to move toward a multiparty electoral system. The opposition, including the representatives of large landowners and merchants, founded the Democrat Party in 1946. The new party promised to promote the private sector, reduce the role of the state in the economy, and place greater emphasis on agriculture. In later years, party leaders would summarize the government's development philosophy with the slogan "creating a millionaire in each neighborhood."

In response, the single-party regime began to adopt some of the positions of the opposition. In 1947, the Republican People's Party decided to set aside the Third Five-Year Plan and began to move in the direction of greater reliance on private capital and greater emphasis on agriculture. It also offered a new definition of etatism which still reserved for the state such activities as public works, mining, heavy and military industry, and energy, but assumed the transfer of all other enterprises to private capital (Boratav 2011, pp. 73–81).

The Democrat Party also hoped that foreign capital would occupy an important place in its economic program. In spite of legislation that made it easier to transfer profits and the principal, however, direct foreign investments remained very low in the 1950s. Of the total foreign direct investments, which averaged less than $10 million annually, companies from the United States accounted for approximately 40 percent. Bilateral funds provided mostly by the United States under the Marshall Plan, NATO assistance, some multilateral loans and other programs, and reflecting Turkey's geopolitical importance in the Cold War environment, were larger. These public capital inflows averaged more than $100 million per year, or more than one-third of the country's annual export earnings during the 1950s.

Agriculture-Led Growth

The Democrat Party led by President Celal Bayar and Prime Minister Adnan Menderes won the elections and came to power in 1950. At the center of its economic policies was the agricultural sector, where more than three-fourths of the electorate earned their livelihood. After sharply lower prices during the Great Depression and difficult times during the war, the agricultural sector recovered and expanded after the war. By 1960, the volume of agricultural output had risen 60 percent above its 1948 level and it was close to double its pre–World War II level. One important reason was the expansion in cultivated area. Thanks to the availability of marginal land, total area under cultivation increased by 55 percent until 1953 (figure 9.1). Rapid expansion of the agricultural frontier was supported by two complementary government policies, one for the small peasants and the other for larger farmers. First, even though the Land Reform Law of 1946 included a clause for the redistribution of large holdings, it was used instead to distribute state-owned lands and open up communal pastures to peasants with little or no land. This policy served to strengthen small ownership across Anatolia, except in the southeast where the Kurdish landlords and tribal leaders dominated.

Second, the Democrat government used the Marshall Plan aid to finance the importation of agricultural machinery, and especially tractors, whose numbers jumped from less than 10,000 in 1946 to 42,000 at the end of the 1950s. Most of these were purchased by the more prosperous farmers, who were given favorable credit terms through the Agricultural Bank and used to expand the area under cultivation. According to a rule of thumb of the period, a pair of oxen could cultivate 5–10 hectares in a given year; a tractor raised that figure to 75 hectares. The tractors were also rented by smallholders who paid for their use by crop sharing (figure 9.2).

Agricultural producers also benefited from favorable weather conditions, increasing demand, and improving terms of trade during this period. Domestic prices began to move in favor of agriculture in the late 1940s, and the country's external terms of trade improved by more than 40 percent as world market demand for wheat, chrome, and other export commodities rose thanks to American stockpiling programs during the Korean War (Hirsch and Hirsch 1963, pp. 372–94, and 1966, pp. 440–57; Hershlag 1968, pp. 157–68).

The agriculture-led boom of the early 1950s meant good times and rising incomes for all sectors of the economy. It seemed in 1953 that all would go well and the promises of the liberal model of economic development would be fulfilled rather quickly. The GNP increased by an average annual rate above 8 percent from 1947 through 1953. Urban groups shared in this growth as evidenced by the increases of wages and salaries. Most important, however, were the gains of the agricultural sector, especially the market-oriented agricultural producers. The Democrat Party entered the 1954 elections under these favorable circumstances and won again, by an even wider margin (Keyder 1987, pp. 117–35; Hansen 1991, pp. 338–51; Yenal 2003, pp. 77–84).

The Democrat Party also pursued an ambitious policy of infrastructure-building, especially highways and secondary roads. In the Interwar period, the Republican People's Party had emphasized railroad construction. Railroads aimed especially to link the eastern part of the country with the center and other regions had been the most important investment item in the national budget. The railroads were not supported with highways and paved roads, however. The Democrat Party, with the backing of the Marshall Plan, decided to concentrate on highway transportation. A new government agency for highway construction began to develop the highway and road network, taking advantage of recent developments in road construction techniques and machinery. One important aim was to link villages to the cities and the cities with each other in order to support the agriculture-based development strategy. Railroads had been the monopoly of the state sector. With the shift to

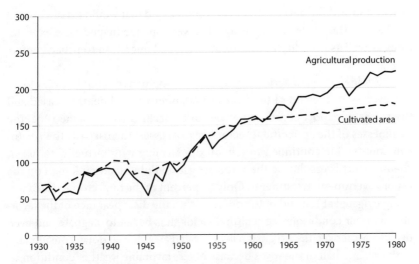

FIGURE 9.1. Total Cultivated Area and Agricultural Production, 1930–1980 (indexes = 100 in 1948). Source: Official series from Turkey, Turkish Statistical Institute 2014.

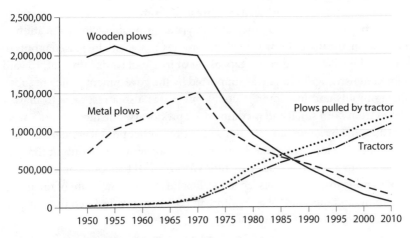

FIGURE 9.2. Changes in Agricultural Technology after World War II (numbers of agricultural equipment). Source: Official series from Turkey, Turkish Statistical Institute 2014.

the highways, the leadership in the transport sector was being transferred to the private sector and local enterprises (Tekeli and Ilkin 2004d, pp. 399–429). In addition, the foundations were laid for big infrastructure projects such as dams. In 1950, less than one-fifth of Turkey's population were able to use electricity in their homes. The government began to invest in electricity production and the development of a national grid that would extend toward rural areas. The roads and highways that were opened helped raise expectations as well as mobility in the countryside and migration to urban centers increased.

The golden years of agriculture-based development did not last very long, however. With the end of the Korean War, international demand eased and the prices of export commodities began to decline. At the same time, the weaknesses of the agricultural sector began to assert themselves. The Anatolian countryside continued to rely on dry farming with virtually no use of chemical fertilizers during the 1950s. Irrigation did not yet rank high on the list of government investments. Only 5.5 percent of the total cropped area was being irrigated at the end of the decade. With the disappearance of the favorable weather conditions, agricultural yields thus began to stagnate and even decline. Moreover, the expansion in cultivated area slowed down considerably in the second half of the 1950s because of less favorable weather conditions.

The agricultural sector was able to increase output relatively easily by bringing new land under cultivation. As the frontier was reached in land available for cultivation toward the end of the 1960s, however, increases in output became more difficult and costly (figure 9.1). From that point on, increases in output began to depend on increases in yields through the intensification of cultivation, the use of improved plant varieties along with increased inputs of chemical fertilizers and some expansion of irrigated lands. The shift toward more intensive agriculture was supported by the government policy of subsidizing inputs and low-interest credit but it was also a response to market forces from both small and medium-sized producers. The new varieties were first adopted by larger farmers, but after a time, other producers started using them too. The long-term trend rate of growth of agricultural output thus declined, from 4–5 percent per year after World War II to about 3 percent in the 1960s and 1970s. These rates lagged well behind the growth rate of the urban economy, and the share of agriculture in the economy declined from 38 percent in 1960 to 25 percent in 1980.

Populism

Rather than accept lower incomes for the agricultural producers in response to the decline in international and domestic prices, the Democrat Party government decided in 1954 to shield them from the adverse price movements by launching a large price support program for wheat. Price supports thus became the most important government program to affect agricultural incomes until the 1980s. The purchases of wheat were not financed directly out of the budget but by Central Bank credits to the Soil Products Office, the state agency responsible for the purchases as well as the distribution of low-priced

wheat to urban areas. These subsidies were the leading cause of the inflationary wave that began in the mid-1950s. The outstanding Central Bank credits to
the Soil Products Office account for most of the increase in the money supply
during this period. Another culprit was the credit extended from deposit
banks to the private sector, including the cooperatives (Hershlag 1968, pp.
143–56; Hansen 1991, pp. 344–46).

Despite the stagnation in agricultural output and the decline in international prices after 1954, the domestic terms of trade remained in favor of
agriculture and the rural producers managed to hold on to their gains until
1957 thanks to the price support policies of the government. The countryside thus emerged as the real beneficiary of the Democrat Party era. In the
meantime, however, exports declined even further due to the overvaluation
of the currency, and the foreign exchange reserves were quickly exhausted.
As imports began to be curtailed, the economy moved, from the relative
abundance of the early 1950s into a severe balance-of-payments crisis characterized by the shortages of many of the basic consumption items. From
coffee to sugar and cheese, many goods were in short supply and long
queues became part of daily life. Moreover, the inflationary wave squeezed
out wages and salaries in the urban areas (Boratav 2011, pp. 90–93). The
decline of the standards of living and social status of the military personnel
as well as civil servants during this wave of inflation played an important
role in the military coup of 1960.

One casualty of the crisis was the political as well as economic liberalism
of the Democrat Party. Just as it responded to the political opposition with the
escalation of political tensions and restrictions of democratic freedoms, in
most economic issues, the government was forced to change its earlier stand
and adopt a more interventionist approach. Quantity restrictions on imports
were generalized and controls on the use of foreign exchange were tightened.
In the domestic market, price and profit controls were initiated and credit
began to be allocated through non-price mechanisms. The government redis-
covered the state economic enterprises as useful instruments for coping with
their difficulties, for relieving some of the bottlenecks, and for capital formation in manufacturing, infrastructure, and mining.

With the balance-of-payments crisis of the mid-1950s, the experiment for
a more open, more market-oriented economy thus came to an end. Amidst
the shortages and bottlenecks induced by the severe restrictions on imports,
domestic industry began to produce some of the goods that were imported in
large volume only a few years earlier. In other words, a return to import-
substituting industrialization began, not yet as explicit government policy but
as a de facto shift out of necessity.

From 1956 until 1958, the government negotiated with the IMF and OECD
for loans and foreign exchange relief but refused to undertake the major

devaluation they demanded until after the elections of 1957. As a result, the crisis lasted for several years. The magnitude of the devaluation of 1958 from 2.80 to 9.00 to the dollar reflected the extent of the overvaluation of the lira. The stabilization program also included most of the elements of what was later referred to as the IMF package: import liberalization, changes in the export regime, removal of price controls, increases in the prices of state economic enterprises, and consolidation and rescheduling of the external debt. While the balance-of-payments picture improved and the rate of inflation declined as a result of these measures, the economy plunged into a recession which was then prolonged by the military coup until 1961 (Hansen 1991, pp. 344–48; Boratav 2011, pp. 73–81; Kazgan 2005, pp. 93–128).

In comparison to the Interwar period, the Democrat Party pursued a development strategy that was more open to the outside world and more focused on agriculture. After achieving good results early on, however, the government rushed to promise much more than it could deliver. In contrast to the cautious stance and the balanced budget-strong currency policies of the one-party era during the 1930s, the macroeconomic policies of the Democrat Party in the mid-1950s represented Turkey's first experiment with macroeconomic populism in the twentieth century. The government targeted a large constituency and attempted to redistribute income toward them with short-term expansionist policies with the predictable longer-term consequences. The increasing economic difficulties during the second half of the decade also suggested that a strategy based solely or mostly on agriculture was difficult to sustain.

Nonetheless, the Democrat Party era brought a good deal of mobility to agriculture. Tractors were introduced in large numbers, new land was brought under cultivation, and incomes rose. The construction of highways and roads increased mobility across the country. These market-oriented populist policies were welcomed by the small and medium-sized agricultural producers who constituted the majority of the country's population. That is an important major reason why the era of the Democrat Party and Prime Minister Adnan Menderes, a large landowner, is remembered as "the golden years," not just among the rural population and agricultural producers but also among their children and grandchildren, most of whom live in the urban areas today (Sunar 1990, pp. 745–57).

Migration and Urbanization

The 1950s also witnessed the dramatic acceleration of rural-urban migration in Turkey. The urbanization rate, defined as the share in total population of centers with at least ten thousand people, rose from around 17 percent in 1950 to 44 percent in 1980 and to about 80 percent in 2015. Landlessness and un-employment ranked high among the causes of the emigration from rural areas. However, migrants were also attracted to the cities by the prospect of higher incomes and better education and health services, for their children if not for themselves. The direction of migration was mostly from the rural areas of poorer, largely agricultural regions in the east and the north along the Black Sea coast toward the urban areas of more developed regions in the west, in the Marmara and Aegean regions, and to a lesser extent in the south along the Mediterranean coast. The strong migration flows did not reverse the large re-gional differences in per capita income, but they ensured that eastern and southeast regions did not fall even further behind.

The rapid shift of the population from the rural to the urban areas corre-sponded to an equally dramatic shift of the labor force from lower productiv-ity agriculture to industry and service. Share of agriculture in the labor force and employment declined from more than 80 percent in 1950 to 50 percent in 1980 and about 20 percent in 2015. Share of agriculture in GDP declined from close to 50 percent in 1950 to less than 10 percent in 2015. The share of the urban economy, or industry plus services, in the total labor force rose rapidly with urbanization from around 20 percent in 1950 to 50 percent in 1980 and to more than 80 percent in 2015. Its share in GDP increased from more than 50 percent in 1950 to more than 90 percent in 2015 (see chapter 2 and figure 2.9 for details).

As Arthur Lewis and Simon Kuznets pointed out some time ago, this shift of labor from rural to urban areas or structural change had far-reaching impli-cations for patterns of productivity and economic growth in the long term (Kuznets 1966, pp. 86–159; Lewis 1954, pp. 139–91). For one thing, the transi-tion from agriculture to the urban economy was possible only because of the increase in the productivity of the agricultural sector. Even if the decline in the agricultural labor force was not yet absolute, it showed that a smaller share of the country's total population could feed the entire population. Second, be-cause people who moved from the agricultural sector to the urban economy became, on average, more productive and received higher incomes, they con-tributed to raising productivity and per capita incomes at the national level. In fact, it has been estimated that at least a third and perhaps a greater share of Turkey's rapidly rising rate of economic growth after World War II was due to the shift of labor from the agricultural sector to the urban economy (Altuğ, Filiztekin, and Pamuk 2008, pp. 393–430).

Patterns of rural to urban migration were strongly influenced by the domi-nant pattern of independent peasant ownership. The average migrant contin-ued to have claims to some land in his village which was typically rented out or left to family members. More often than not, he came to the urban area with sufficient resources to build a squatter house (*gecekondu*—literally, landed at night) on land often owned by the state in a neighborhood already settled by the migrants from his own province if not village. The migrants were soon able to acquire the ownership title for their gecekondus as political parties competed for their votes and local governments provided roads, water, and electricity. After the initial move, the migrant and his family did not easily lose contact with the village. They returned during the annual leave and regularly received supplies in kind, often as compensation for their claims to the land in the village. The rural pattern of small and medium-sized land ownership whose origins go back to the Ottoman era was thus transferred to the urban areas within a few generations by way of the gecekondu and surrounding institutions (Keyder 1987, pp. 135–40; Karpat 1976; Tekeli and İlkin 2004d, pp. 390–429; Yıldırmaz 2017, pp. 51–200).

Only a minority of the migrants found employment in the new industries, however. Instead, they faced a hierarchy of jobs as they arrived at the urban areas. The unionized blue-collar jobs were at the top of that hierarchy and thus out of the reach of a recent migrant. At the lower echelons were a variety of jobs in the informal sector with low pay such as short-term wage work or street vendoring. In time and depending on their skills and connections, some of the migrants began to move up the urban ladder toward higher paying and more stable forms of employment (Keyder 1987, pp. 156–63).

The Age of Import-Substituting Industrialization

The agriculture-based strategy brought dynamism to the Turkish economy, but the populist economic policies contributed to their demise. One criticism frequently directed at the Democrats was the absence of any coordination and long-term perspective in the management of the economy. One of the first projects by the military regime was thus to establish the State Planning Organization (SPO) in 1960. The idea of development planning was supported by a broad coalition: the Republican People's Party with their etatist heritage, the bureaucracy, the large industrialists, and even the international agencies, most notably the OECD. Planning methodology and target setting were strongly influenced by Jan Tinbergen, who was invited as the chief consultant to the SPO to coordinate the preparation of the First Five-Year Plan.

The five-year development plans aimed, above all, at the protection of the domestic market and industrialization through import substitution by coordinating investment decisions. The planning techniques made heavy use of a restrictive trade regime, investments by state economic enterprises, and subsidized credit as key tools in achieving the ISI objectives. The plans were based on medium-term models and did not give much weight to short-term policy issues, most notably fiscal and monetary policy. They were binding for the public sector but only indicative for the private sector. In practice, the SPO played an important role in private sector decisions as well. Its stamp of approval was required for all private sector investment projects which sought to benefit from subsidized credit, tax exemptions, and import privileges, and have access to scarce foreign exchange. The agricultural sector dominated by family enterprises was left mostly outside the planning process (Milor 1990, pp. 1–30; Hansen 1991, pp. 352–53).

There were different views on the content of the plans and their role in industrialization. The center-right Justice Party, which succeeded the Democrat Party after the military coup of 1960, was initially opposed to planning. On the other hand, the military leadership and part of the Ankara bureaucracy, as well as the academics they had commissioned, were in favor of even stricter planning. They argued that the plans should guide not just the public sector, but also the private sector, and the SPO rather than the markets, should determine which sectors would be supported in the industrialization process. The private sector in Istanbul argued that the public sector should not compete with the private sector, and while the SPO was directing public sector decisions, it needed to support the private sector with tariffs, subsidies, and incentives. Within the Republican People's Party, opinions differed on the content and role of planning. The priorities of the plan would ultimately be determined by politics. However, the new institution gave technocrats and bureaucrats in Ankara new influence.

With the end of military rule and the return to multiparty politics, the power and influence of strict planning, which had received a good deal of support from the military, began to decline. When Prime Minister Inönü refused to adopt the recommendation to tax the agricultural sector in order to achieve higher rates of industrialization, a leading group of planners resigned. After the Justice Party came to power following the 1965 elections, Prime Minister Süleyman Demirel opted to live with the SPO rather than dismantle it. During his government, however, the SPO would not direct the private sector, but support it. He appointed Turgut Özal as undersecretary for the SPO. From then on, the planning and import-substitution industrialization process would be guided by the preferences of the private sector in Istanbul.

When the SPO was being established, some had viewed it as an autonomous institution which would direct the industrialization process as its counterparts did in East Asian countries. Within a short time, however, the SPO abandoned this role and became a body that responded to the needs of the private sector, open to daily politics and political pressure. The transition from an emphasis on the longer term and heavy industry, to a private sector–led model producing durable consumer goods for the domestic market, took place in these circumstances (Milor 1990, pp. 1–30; Türkcan 2010).

During the 1930s, when the private sector was weak, industrialization was led by the state enterprises and the state was able to control many sectors of the economy. In the postwar period, in contrast, the big family holding companies, large conglomerates which included numerous manufacturing and distribution companies as well as banks and other services firms, emerged as the leaders. Some of these, such as the Koç group, emerged in the 1920s but entered industry in the postwar years either independently or in joint ventures with foreign capital. The Sabancı group began their rise with textiles in the cotton-growing Adana region during the 1950s. There eventually emerged a crude division of labor between the two sectors. The state enterprises were directed to invest in large-scale intermediate goods industries. They accounted for more than 20 percent of the value added and about half of fixed investments in the manufacturing industry. In contrast, the private firms took advantage of the opportunities in the heavily protected and more profitable consumer goods. From food processing and textiles in the 1950s, the emphasis shifted increasingly to radios, refrigerators, television sets, cars, and other consumer durables. Foreign direct investment in the ISI industries remained modest. A large part of the technology was obtained through patent and licensing agreements rather than direct investment.

With the total population exceeding 30 million in the mid-1960s, the large and growing domestic market in Turkey stimulated manufacturing output. Despite the inequalities in income, large segments of the population including the civil servants, workers, and to a lesser extent, agricultural producers were incorporated to the domestic market for consumer durables. Behind the large and growing domestic market, political and institutional changes as well as market forces were occurring. Perhaps most important, real wages almost doubled during the 1960s and 1970s. While industrial growth increased the demand for labor, the emigration of several million workers to Western Europe kept the conditions relatively tight in the urban labor markets. In addition, the institutional rights obtained under the 1961 Constitution supported the labor unions at the bargaining table (Berik and Bilginsoy 1996, pp. 37–64). For their part, the large industrial firms not under pressure to compete in the export markets reasoned that they could afford these wage increases as they also served to broaden the demand for their own products. By the middle of the 1970s, however, the industrialists had begun to complain about the high level of wages and an emerging labor aristocracy (figure 9.3).

FIGURE 9.3. Purchasing Power of Wages in Manufacturing Industry, 1900–2015
(index = 100 in 1914). Sources: Özmucur and Pamuk 2002, Bulutay 1995 and
official series from Turkey, Turkish Statistical Institute 2014.

The political power of the agricultural producers had remained limited during the Interwar period. With the shift to a multiparty electoral system after
World War II, however, the large numbers of agricultural producers who made
up as much as three-fourths of the electorate obtained significant political
influence if not power. As millions of the more commercialized agricultural
producers began to vote for their pocketbook, a large populist bias began to
dominate national politics. Governments developed large-scale, multi-crop
programs to keep agricultural prices high and input prices low. These programs may not have contributed much to improving long-term productivity,
but they accelerated the incorporation of the rural population into the national market. The remittances sent from the family members in Europe added
to rural incomes during the 1970s. The villages thus became important markets not only for textiles and clothing but also for consumer durables, radios,
TV sets, and refrigerators. For example, share of households with refrigerators
rose from less than 3 percent to more than 70 percent between 1950 and 1980.
Many agricultural producers also purchased tractors and other agricultural
machinery and equipment with credit from public sector banks. Numbers of
tractors in the country rose rapidly, from 42,000 in 1960 to 100,000 in 1970 and
to 430,000 in 1980 (figures 9.3 and 9.4; Keyder 1987, pp. 165–96; Hansen 1991,
pp. 360–78).

These programs tended to support the small and medium-sized family
farms, a legacy of the Ottoman era. Large-scale farms using year-round labor

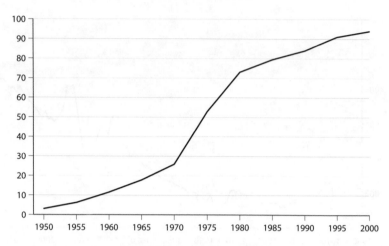

FIGURE 9.4. Share of Households with a Refrigerator, 1950–2000 (percent).
Sources: Based on Turkey, Turkish Statistical Institute 2014
and data from domestic manufacturers.

remained the exception, although more of them emerged in the Kurdish southeast as the tribal leaders registered tribal lands under their own name and began to evict the tenants. As family farms remained dominant in the countryside, agriculture continued to provide employment for more than 50 percent of the labor force at the end of the 1970s. Labor as well as land productivity in agriculture lagged well behind those of other southern European countries such as Spain, Italy, Portugal, and Greece (Pamuk 2008, pp. 382–86; Imrohoroglu, Imrohoroglu, and Üngör 2014).

Another important contribution toward the expansion of the home market came from remittances sent by the workers in Europe. Several million workers from both urban and rural areas emigrated to western European countries from 1961 until the recession in 1973 in response to the strong demand for labor during the golden age. Their remittances remained modest during the 1960s, but they jumped to 5 percent of GDP after the devaluation of 1970 and began to exceed total earnings from exports. The balance sheet for the remittances was mixed, nonetheless. While they supported the balance of payments and growth in the short term, they also contributed to the overvaluation of the domestic currency, thereby reducing the competitiveness of the tradable sectors. The aggregate demand they generated was met by the importation of intermediate goods which ended up hurting the import-substitution process. Remittances began to decline in the second half of the 1970s, however, as immigration restrictions in Europe led the workers to send less to Turkey (Paine 1974).

While industry and government policy remained focused on a large and attractive domestic market, exports of manufactures were all but ignored and this proved to be the Achilles' heel of Turkey's ISI. The share of manufactures in total exports edged up from less than 20 percent in the 1960s toward 35 percent in the 1970s, but that figure may be misleading because the share of exports in GDP remained below 6 percent throughout this period. Share of manufacturing exports in GDP thus remained well below 2 percent until 1980 (Turkey, Turkish Statistical Institute, 2014). A shift toward exports would have helped Turkish industry in a number of critical ways. It would have increased the efficiency and competitiveness of the existing industrial structure, acquired the foreign exchange necessary for an expanding economy, and even supported the import-substitution process itself in establishing the backward linkages toward the technologically more complicated and more expensive intermediate and capital goods industries.

For that major shift to occur, however, a new orientation in government policy and the institutional environment was necessary. Not only the overvaluation of the lira but many other biases against exports needed to be eliminated. Instead, the successes obtained within a protected environment created the vested interests for the continuation of the same model. Most of the industrialists as well as organized labor, which feared that export orientation may put downward pressure on wages favored the domestic market–oriented model. Moreover, the political conditions became increasingly unstable during the 1970s. The country was governed by a series of fragile coalitions with short time horizons. As a result, no attempt was made to shift toward export-oriented policies or even adjust the macroeconomic balances after the first oil shock of 1973 (Keyder 1987, pp. 165–96).

The years 1963 to 1977 thus represent for Turkey what Albert Hirschman has called "the easy stage of ISI" (Hirschman 1968, pp. 1–26). Annual rates of growth of manufacturing value added averaged above 9 percent during 1963 to 1980. Annual rates of increase of GDP averaged 5.8 percent and GDP per capita, 3.3 percent during the same period. Moreover, manufacturing industry and more generally the urban sector was able to provide employment to millions who migrated to the urban areas, especially in the northwestern region of the country. While manufacturing value added increased in both final and intermediate goods, value added in the technologically more difficult stage of capital goods lagged behind. Both the relatively low education of the labor force and the related reluctance of the private sector to move into higher technology sectors contributed to this outcome. Turkey lagged behind countries with similar levels of GDP per capita in Latin America and East Asia during these decades when it came to education and human capital, making it harder for manufacturing in both countries to transition toward higher technology, higher value-added goods, and sectors requiring higher skills (van Leeuwen and van Leeuwen-Li, 2014, pp. 87–100).

Moreover, manufacturing exports were also ignored until 1980, largely because of the sizable domestic market. Even though the share of manufacturing in total exports reached 35 percent in the 1970s, the low share of exports in GDP meant that the share of manufacturing exports in GDP remained less than 2 percent. Boosting exports required a new government policy and institutional environment, but protection strengthened vested interests in favor of the old policies. Equally important, political conditions became increasingly unstable during the 1970s. As a result, no attempt was made to adjust even after the oil shock of 1973. Coalition governments chose to borrow abroad under unfavorable terms and encouraged the private sector to do the same, leading to a major balance-of-payments crisis at the end of the decade (Tekin 2006, pp. 133–63; Hansen 1991, pp. 352–53).

Crisis

Long-lasting political instability played the leading role in Turkey's economic crisis at the end of the 1970s. When oil prices rose in 1973, the total oil bill was still small and the balance of payments awash with workers' remittances. With their short-term horizon, the fragile coalition governments chose to continue with the expansionist policies instead of adjusting. With the support of the foreign exchange reserves and an accommodating monetary policy, the governments directed the public sector toward an investment binge, eventually pulling along private sector investment. As the share of investment rose from 18.1 percent of GDP in 1973 to 25.0 percent in 1977, the growth rate of the economy reached its zenith at 8.9 percent in 1975 and 1976. Industrialists enjoyed the easy profits as they continued to produce for the protected domestic market. Unionized workers bargained for and received higher wages. It is estimated that real wages in manufacturing industry increased about 75 percent between 1970 and 1978 (figure 9.3). In its later stages, this drive was maintained by a costly external borrowing scheme. Just as the foreign exchange reserves were being depleted in 1975, the conservative coalition government of Süleyman Demirel, eager to stay in power, launched a scheme that provided private firms exchange-rate guarantees for all the external loans they could secure. Under inflationary conditions where the domestic exchange rate was already perceived to be overvalued, this was a signal to the private sector to borrow abroad and finance its day-to-day operations at the cost of the treasury. By the end of 1977, it became clear that the government was not in a position to honor the outstanding short-term external debt, which had risen from 9 percent to 24 percent of GDP. Equally striking as the behavior of the government was the willingness of the international banks, overflowing at the time with petro-dollars, to play along. As foreign lenders started getting jittery early in 1977, the stage was set for a debt crisis (Celasun and Rodrik 1989, pp. 615–808; Kazgan 2005, pp. 135–94).

At the end of the decade, Turkey found itself in its most severe balance-of-payments crisis of the postwar period. In return for the rescheduling of the outstanding debt and green light for new credits, the IMF demanded the implementation of a full-scale stabilization program including a major devaluation, extensive cutbacks in government subsidies, and elimination of controls on imports and exports. The new coalition government led by social democrat prime minister Bülent Ecevit was reluctant to accept a program of austerity. At the same time, it was too divided to pursue an alternative. As rising budget deficits were met with monetary expansion, inflation, which had been averaging 20–30 percent annually earlier in the decade, jumped to 90 percent in 1979, and the purchasing power of wages and salaries declined sharply. The government responded with various foreign exchange and price controls. Both investment and exports collapsed. The second round of oil price increase from 15 to 30 dollars a barrel only compounded the difficulties. As oil became increasingly scarce, frequent power cuts hurt industrial output as well as daily life. Shortages of even the most basic items arising from both the declining capacity to import and the price controls became widespread. The economic crisis coupled with the continuing political turmoil brought the country to the brink of civil war (Keyder 1987, pp. 165–96).

Perhaps the basic lesson to be drawn from the Turkish experience is that an ISI regime becomes difficult to dislodge owing to the power of vested interest groups who continue to benefit from the existing system of protection and subsidies. To shift toward export promotion in a country with a large domestic market required a strong government with a long-term horizon and considerable autonomy. These were exactly the features lacking in the Turkish political scene characterized by weak and unstable coalitions during the 1970s. As a result, the economic imbalances and the costs, both political and economic, of adjustment accumulated. It then took a crisis of major proportions to move the economy toward greater external orientation in the 1980s (Öniş and Şenses 2007, pp. 263–90).

10

Economic Development and Institutional Change, 1950–1980

Economic Growth

The decades after World War II were a period of unprecedented growth and prosperity for the world economy. In part because of the new international economic order designed at Bretton Woods, the world economy achieved the most powerful wave of growth and income increase in its history from the end of the World War II until the oil crisis in 1973. In the developed countries, GDP increased at rates higher than 4.5 percent and increases in per capita GDP exceeded 3 percent per annum during this period. Another important development with long-lasting significance was the rapid recovery of Japan which established itself as a world economic power by the 1970s. The socialist economies of the Soviet Union and Eastern Europe also experienced high rates of growth until the 1970s (table 10.1 and Crafts 1996, pp. 429–47; Eichengreen 2008, pp. 91–133).

In part thanks to the Bretton Woods order, most developing economies also adopted government interventionism during these decades. Inward-looking policies and more specifically import-substituting industrialization became the most frequently adopted strategy for economic development especially in the medium-sized and larger developing countries (Kemp 1993, pp. 198–236; Hirschman 1968, pp. 1–26). These policies were not in conflict with the international monetary and trade arrangements of the Bretton Woods era and the Keynesian policies pursued in the developed economies. Rates of growth in the developing countries were also exceptionally high during the post–World War II decades. As urbanization and industrialization spread, average rates of GDP growth in the developing countries as a whole rose to about 5.5 percent annually during these decades, but due to the higher rates of population growth, per capita GDP increased at close to 3 percent annually, which was quite similar to the rates in developed countries. The socialist econ-

TABLE 10.1. GDP per Capita in the World and in Turkey, 1950–1980

	GDP per Capita		Annual Rate of Increase (percent)
	1950	1980	
Western Europe	4570	13150	3.6
United States	9550	18600	2.2
Japan	1920	13400	6.7
Developed Countries	5550	14900	3.4
Eastern Europe, excl. Soviet Union	2100	5800	3.4
Italy	3500	13150	4.5
Spain	2200	9200	4.9
China	480	1050	2.8
India	620	940	1.4
South Korea	850	4100	5.4
Asia excl. Japan	640	1500	2.9
Africa	890	1500	1.8
Egypt	1050	2100	2.3
Iran	1720	4000	2.9
South America	2500	5450	2.6
Developing Countries	850	1920	2.7
World	**2100**	**4500**	**2.6**
Turkey	**1600**	**4750**	**3.1**

Sources: Maddison 2007, pp. 375–86, Bolt and Van Zanden 2014, pp. 627–51 and Pamuk 2006 for Turkey.
Note: GDP per capita are given in purchasing power parity (PPP) adjusted 1990 US dollars. For details, see chapter 2.

omies of Eastern Europe, too, expanded at a rate of more than 3 percent per year. In Japan and in some of the other economies in East Asia, the annual rate of economic growth exceeded 5 percent. The growth rates in China and India, by contrast, remained low. South American countries, which had expanded faster than the average for developing countries between 1870 and 1950, also remained below average (table 10.1 and figure 10.1).

The Bretton Woods system, which had facilitated the post–World War II expansion, came under considerable pressure in the 1970s. After the link between the dollar and gold was severed in 1971, the developed economies began to move gradually toward floating rates. The already vulnerable international monetary and trading system received another major shock with the OPEC-led increase in oil prices in 1973. Governments of the industrialized countries chose to respond by contracting domestic demand. Rates of inflation rose and economic stagnation spread. The global recession that followed brought about not only the end of a long period of expansion of the world economy but also the end of Keynesian-style macroeconomic management and welfare state policies in the developed countries and a shift toward policies that placed greater reliance on markets. With the end of the fixed exchange-rate regimes and Keynesian economic policies in the developed economies, the inward-looking industrialization strategy became more difficult to sustain in the developing countries. In the aftermath of the oil price increases, the large trade surpluses of the oil exporting countries created new liquidity and lower interest rates in the international markets. Rather than slow down their economies in response to the increase in oil prices, many developing countries attempted to take advantage of the new liquidity and borrowed large amounts in order to extend the ISI-related boom.

The decades after World War II were a period of rapid growth for Turkey as well. Despite the crises in the mid-1950s and in the second half of the 1970s, GDP per capita increased at an average annual rate above 3 percent and more than doubled during the period 1950–1980. These rates of growth were unprecedented for Turkey. During the nineteenth century and in the first half of the twentieth century, the long-term rate of growth of GDP per capita had remained below 1 percent per year. The only exception was in the aftermath of the Great Depression, when GDP per capita had increased at annual rates above 3 percent thanks to high levels of protection and the beginnings of industrialization. The long-term rates of growth achieved in Turkey after World War II were roughly comparable to the averages for both the developed countries and developing countries as a whole. As a result, the per capita GDP gap between Turkey and the developed countries remained little changed during this period. Table 10.1 and figure 10.1 also show that Turkey's rates of economic growth stayed well below those of the more successful countries such as Italy and Spain in southern Europe, and Japan, Korea, and Taiwan in East Asia during these decades.

Two very different economic strategies were pursued in Turkey during the decades after World War II. Agriculture was the main source of economic growth until the early 1960s. As summarized in table 9.1 in chapter 9, agricultural value added increased by 4.5 percent and GDP per capita increased by 3.0 percent per year during 1950 to 1962. Most of the increase in agricultural output was due to the expansion of agricultural land. After a shift in economic strategy, manufacturing industry, and more generally the urban economy, became the source of growth in the next two decades. Annual rates of growth of manufacturing industry averaged 9 percent and the urban economy expanded at rates above 8 percent annually during 1963 to 1979. Increases in GDP per capita and rising tax revenue enabled the government to undertake infrastructure investments in transportation, utilities, irrigation, as well as health and education. Rising incomes and standards of living in both the urban and rural areas can be followed in many series, including urban wages and the spread of

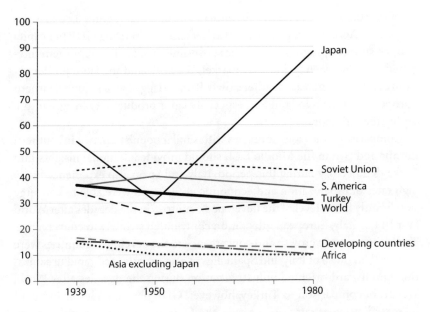

FIGURE 10.1. GDP per Capita in the World and in Turkey, 1950–1980 (PPP adjusted and as percentage of Western Europe and the United States). Sources: Maddison 2007, pp. 375–86, Bolt and Van Zanden 2014, pp. 627–51 and Pamuk 2006 for Turkey.

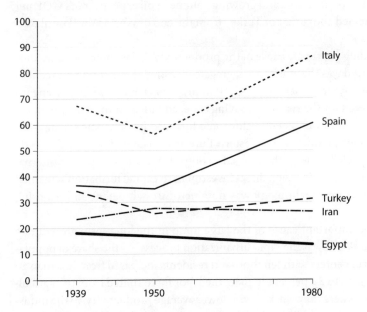

FIGURE 10.2. GDP per Capita in Four Other Countries and Turkey, 1950–1980 (PPP adjusted and as percentage of Western Europe and the United States). Sources: Maddison 2007, pp. 375–86, Bolt and Van Zanden 2014, pp. 627–51 and Pamuk 2006 for Turkey.

consumer durables in households, both urban and rural (figures 9.3 and 9.4 in chapter 9). Agricultural producers also benefited from rising GDP per capita as price support programs and other government subsidies kept them integrated with the growing domestic market. Yet, both land and labor productivity in agriculture increased rather slowly. Turkey lagged well behind southern European countries in land and especially labor productivity in agriculture during these decades.

Comparisons with four countries with similar population, two in southern Europe and two in the Middle East, should provide additional insights into Turkey's trajectory during this period. Italy and Spain also experienced very high rates of urbanization and economic growth and were able to converge significantly to the level of the developed countries in the decades after World War II. For Italy, European integration contributed strongly to convergence. Turkey's economic growth and convergence to the developed countries were weaker than those of Italy and Spain. Egypt also experienced rapid urbanization and inward-oriented industrialization during the decades after World War II. In comparison to Turkey, however, GDP per capita levels in Egypt increased at lower rates. As a result, the GDP per capita gap with Turkey continued to widen and Egypt was not able to reduce any of the GDP per capita gap with the developed countries. GDP per capita levels in Iran increased at rates higher than those of the developed countries and of Turkey until 1980 thanks to a large and growing volume of oil exports. Iran's GDP per capita remained above that of Turkey from the end of World War II until 1980 (figure 10. 2).

The leading proximate cause of the productivity and income increases during this period was the rise in the aggregate investment rate from 11 percent of GDP in 1950–52 to 22 percent of GDP in 1977–79 (table 10.2). Increasing incomes allowed for the rise in the savings rate, and most of the investments in physical capital as well as education were financed by domestic savings. Remittances sent by workers in Western Europe also contributed to domestic savings, especially during the 1970s. In contrast, the contribution of international borrowing and foreign direct investment to capital formation remained limited. Most new technology was obtained through patent and licensing agreements.

Another important cause of the large jump in the long-term growth rate after World War II was the rapid urbanization process. As the share of population in urban centers with ten thousand residents increased from less than 20 percent in 1950 to 44 percent in 1980, the labor force shifted from the agricultural sector, where they worked with lower average productivity, to the industrial sector, and more generally the urban economy, where they worked with higher levels of physical capital and were more productive. Thanks to this shift

TABLE 10.2. Basic Economic and Social Indicators for Turkey, 1950–1980

	1950	1980
Population (millions)	20.8	44.7
Urbanization Rate (%)		
Centers above 10,000 / Total Population	18	44
Life Expectancy at Birth (years)	44 (M: 42; W: 46)	59 (M: 57; W: 61)
Literacy Rate (%)	33 (M: 46; W: 19)	68 (M: 80; W: 55)
Average Years of Schooling		
of Adult Population over age 15	1.2	4.2
Share of Agriculture in Labor Force (%)	75–80?	50
Share of Agriculture in GDP (%)	42	25
Share of Manufacturing Industry in GDP (%)	13	17
Exports / GDP (%)	8	4
Imports / GDP (%)	9	11
Investment / GDP (%)	11	22
Revenues of Central Government / GDP (%)	15	13

Source: Turkey, Türkiye İstatistik Kurumu (Turkish Statistical Institute), 2014.

of the labor force, GDP per capita for Turkey as a whole grew faster than per capita productivity in both agriculture and the non-agricultural sector. Calculations show that more than a third of the total increases in labor productivity and per capita income achieved in Turkey during the period 1950–1980 were due to the shift of labor from the low-productivity agricultural sector to the more productive urban economy. The continuing rural to urban migration would make it easier for higher rates of growth to be sustained in later decades as well (Saygılı, Cihan, and Yurtoğlu 2005; Ismihan and Kıvılcım 2006, pp. 74–86; Altuğ, Filiztekin, and Pamuk 2008, pp. 393–430).

Another potential cause for the increases in productivity in both agriculture and the urban economy was the more efficient use of the existing resources including labor and capital, in other words, achieving increases in total factor productivity. As was the case in most developing countries during this period, however, total factor productivity increases in Turkey remained well below 1 percent per year during these decades. Moreover, most of these increases were caused by the shift of labor from the low-productivity agriculture to the higher-productivity urban sector. In other words, with the exception of the shift of labor from agriculture to the urban sector, most of the total and per capita increases in production were obtained not through increases in total productivity but through increases in total inputs. For this reason, it would not be wrong to characterize the production increases obtained in Turkey, as in the majority of developing countries during this period, as extensive growth.

One important reason for the low rates of increase in total productivity was the low levels of education and skills of the labor force. In fact, Turkey lagged behind not only the developed countries, but also the developing countries with similar levels of per capita income, making it also more difficult to move up to the production of goods with higher technology content and more generally to higher technology sectors with higher value added. The low levels and low rates of increase in total factor productivity were also due to the poor quality of institutions, which I will discuss later in this chapter.

Income Distribution

Institutional changes at both the global and national levels played important roles in the evolution of the distribution of income during the decades after World War II. The rules of the global economy decided at Bretton Woods in 1944 shaped the possibilities open to the developing countries during the following decades. Domestically, the institutional changes associated with agriculture-based growth during the 1950s followed by the strategy of import-substitution industrialization at a time of rapid urbanization shaped the changes in the distribution of income until 1980. Particularly important were changes in the political and economic institutions that gave greater voice to the agricultural producers and urban workers which raised their share of the national income.

Quantitative evidence about the distribution of income and its evolution during these three decades is limited, but it is possible to follow the general direction of the changes on the basis of some key indicators. I will examine the distribution of income at the national level in three stages: first, the distribution within the agricultural sector; then, the inequalities between agriculture and the non-agricultural sector or the urban economy; and finally, the distribution within the urban economy. The share of agriculture was declining and share of the urban economy was rising rapidly during these three decades. At the beginning of the period more than 80 percent of the population lived in rural areas and a similar proportion of the labor force engaged in agriculture. By 1980, the share of the rural population in total population had declined to 56 percent and the share of the labor force in agriculture had declined to about 50 percent. Similarly, share of agriculture in GDP declined from about 50 percent in 1950 to 25 percent by 1980. In other words, while the distribution within agriculture dominated the distribution of income at the national level during the earlier period, the disparities between agriculture and the urban economy and the distribution within the urban economy mattered more with each passing decade.

Regarding the distribution of income within the agricultural sector, evidence is limited on the key indicator, namely, the distribution of land ownership and land use during this period. The available data suggest that despite the considerable opening up to the markets and all the technological advances, the distribution of land ownership did not change very much. It is clear, however, that the gains from growing commercialization and production for the markets were distributed unequally. The more market-oriented western regions, as well as medium and large producers, benefited more from these opportunities in the decades after World War II.

The evolution of prices against agriculture under the impact of the Great Depression, and the emergence of large income disparities between the urban and rural areas, had been an important feature of the 1930s. In comparison, the domestic terms of trade between agriculture and the urban economy remained more in favor of agriculture during the decades after World War II. This was not due only to worldwide trends; it also reflected the political weight of the agricultural producers after the transition to the multiparty political regime. The Democrat Party during the 1950s, and its heir, the Justice Party in the 1960s, developed government programs to support crop prices and subsidize some of the input prices such as fertilizers. These programs and more generally the price movements in support of agriculture benefited the market-oriented medium- and large-scale producers more than the others and they may have increased the inequalities within the agricultural sector as a result (Keyder 1987, pp. 156–63).

High rates of rural to urban migration from the poorer agricultural regions toward the industrializing urban areas created far-reaching consequences for the distribution of income during these decades. Because the tendency to migrate was stronger among the young of poorer households, rural to urban migration tended to limit the inequalities within the agricultural sector as well as the regional differences between rural areas. Even though increases in total agricultural output did not match the growth of the urban economy, the movements in relative prices in favor of agriculture and emigration from rural areas tended to reduce the differences in per capita income between the agricultural sector and the urban economy (Derviş and Robinson 1980, pp. 83–122; Boratav 2011, pp. 135–44).

Evidence on the distribution of income and its evolution within the urban economy is also limited. In the absence of other evidence, one key indicator economic historians follow regarding the distribution of income within the urban economy is the ratio of urban GDP per capita to urban wages. An increase in this ratio suggests declining share of labor in income or an increase in the inequality of income in the urban economy. My estimates suggest that urban wages lagged behind increases in GDP per capita in the urban economy between 1820 and 2015. While GDP per capita in the urban economy rose by more than twelvefold, urban wages increased about sixfold during this period. As a result, the ratio of urban GDP per capita to urban wages rose during the

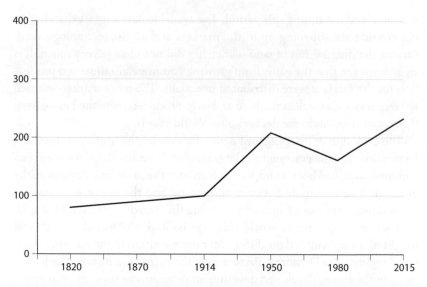

FIGURE 10.3. Long-term Trends in Inequality in the Urban Economy, 1820–2015
(Urban GDP per Capita / Urban Wages; index = 100 in 1914). Sources: Based on
the wage series in Boratav, Ökçün, and Pamuk 1985; Özmucur and Pamuk 2002;
figure 9.3 in chapter 9, and the GDP per capita series discussed in chapter 2.

last two centuries (figure 10.3). One important reason was that Turkey was an
underpopulated country until the second half of the twentieth century and
growth in population tended to reduce the share of wages in national income.
However, one period in which this long-term trend was reversed was the decades after World War II. With the support of laws that gave workers greater
rights to organize and strike, urban wages rose by more than 200 percent between 1950 and 1980. In fact, my calculations using the national income accounts as well as the urban wage series suggest that urban wages rose faster
than average income in the urban economy, and inequalities in income distribution in the urban economy tended to decline during these decades. Together with the earlier observations on more rapid economic growth and the
distribution of income in agriculture, these trends suggest that agricultural
producers and labor in the urban economy increased their share in total income during the decades following World War II.

It is also not easy to determine how inter-regional differences in per capita
income evolved during this period. There is strong evidence, however, that in
terms of both growing market integration of agriculture and the spread of industrialization, western and southern regions of the country did better than
the eastern and northern regions. The regional pattern of industrialization is
especially striking. Most of the industrial growth during the decades after

World War II occurred in western and especially northwestern parts of the country, while the northern and eastern regions experienced little increase in industrial activity. The poorest people in the country during these three decades were peasants who had small amounts of land or no land to cultivate in the poor agricultural regions such as Eastern or Southeastern Anatolia, which did not integrate with the markets to the same extent as other regions. Not surprisingly, rural to urban migration during this period also had a strong regional dimension. People moved from rural areas in the east and the north to urban areas in the west and, to a lesser extent, the south. These migration flows tended to reduce but probably did not reverse the widening regional differences in per capita incomes arising from differences in the market orientation of agriculture as well as industrialization. Migration thus appears to be the key reason why east and southeast regions did not fall even further behind in terms of per capita income in the decades after World War II.

Overall, growing commercialization of agriculture, rural to urban migration, and industrialization was accompanied by rates of increase in average incomes of approximately 3 percent per year. Per capita incomes more than doubled during these three decades. The available evidence suggests that market-oriented agricultural producers and labor in urban areas, especially in the faster growing western regions, shared these gains. The shift to a multiparty regime after World War II was an important development that gave the agricultural producers some power to ensure that politicians and governments would pay attention to their concerns. Also important were political changes ushered in with the constitution of 1961 which gave the workers and labor unions more rights to organize. In comparison to the historical periods both before and after, the more equal distribution of income and of the gains from economic growth during the decades after World War II cannot be explained by reference to domestic political changes alone, however. One also needs to point to the Bretton Woods international economic order of this era, which insulated the national economies, provided national governments with greater autonomy, and adopted an economic model that made such an outcome possible (Rodrik 2011, pp. 67–101; Boratav 1986, pp. 117–39).

Role of Institutions and Institutional Change

Turkey's formal political and economic institutions as well as the global economic institutions underwent major changes after World War II. The single-party regime gave way to a competitive multiparty system in 1950. After an experiment with agriculture-led growth, economic strategy settled in the early 1960s on import-substituting industrialization led by the rising private sector. The formal economic institutions associated with the latter strategy interacted with the institutions of the Bretton Woods system at the global level. These extensive changes in formal institutions played important roles in bringing about significant increases in per capita income. However, they did not crowd out informal institutions but continued to interact and coexist with them. In fact, informal institutions continued to play key roles in both politics and economic development during these decades, in rural and urban areas as well as via state interventionism. For a more nuanced assessment of the role of institutions in economic development, it is thus necessary to also examine both the formal and informal institutions as well as their interaction, how new institutions emerged as a result, and how they contributed to or hindered long-term economic development.

Significant changes took place in Turkey's political institutions after World War II. With the transition to a multiparty parliamentary system and competitive elections every four years, it became possible not only for big landowners, merchants, and industrialists, but also for the large numbers of small and medium-sized agricultural producers, to make their preferences heard. Thanks to the legal opportunities granted by the 1961 Constitution, workers also started to organize more efficiently. Labor unions wielded more power in the process of determining wages and working conditions. Changes in political institutions thus led to concrete economic outcomes. The limits of the changes in political institutions need to be emphasized as well, however. The military coups in 1960 and in 1971 gave the armed forces strong powers over the regime. In fact, the military became a leading partner in the ruling coalition with veto powers on many key issues, a position they maintained for almost a half century (Ahmad 2010, pp. 92–116). In the early 1970s, new restrictions on freedom of expression and organization were introduced, and it became harder for socialist movements, religious groups, and Kurds to organize or be represented in parliament, even if they were not entirely prevented from doing so. Continuing problems in the judiciary reflected the limits of political institutions and the unequal power relations in society.

Along with the changes in political institutions, the economic model evolved from etatism toward a mixed economy increasingly controlled by the private sector. One leading goal of economic policies during the Interwar period was the creation of Muslim-Turkish economic elites that would eventually lead the economy. The private sector was weak and dependent on the state during the Interwar period, but the new elites began to gain more power after World War II. The agriculture-based strategy adopted during the Democrat Party period reflected the preferences of the vast majority of the population. It was not realistic, however, to expect the agricultural sector to deliver long-term economic growth by itself. For this reason, and because of the short-term focus of the Democrat Party's policies, the 1950s strategy that focused heavily on agriculture was neither successful nor permanent. Import-substituting industrialization led by the private sector thus emerged as the basic economic strategy in the early 1960s. The large domestic market remained strongly protected from international competition. While the public sector continued to play an important role in economic development and especially industrialization, the control of the economy, particularly the urban economy, shifted to the large holdings companies of the private sector in Istanbul and the Marmara region. Economic institutions were also to a large extent shaped within the framework of this model. The State Planning Organization and the large holding companies were the key economic organizations of this period.

The SPO was established after the 1960 coup at a time when political power was shared between the military regime and the bureaucracy. The military leadership and part of the Ankara bureaucracy viewed the SPO as a strong, cohesive, and autonomous institution that would direct the industrialization process. In its early years the SPO was an elite organization inside the bureaucracy which was able to recruit some of the most qualified young graduates and provide them with good training. SPO developed a strategy of industrialization emphasizing intermediate goods, higher technology content, and a longer-term perspective. This model contained some elements that resembled the practices that were being adopted in East Asia at the time. The private sector in Istanbul, on the other hand, argued that the public sector should not compete with the private sector, and while the SPO may direct the urban public sector, it should only support the private sector with tariffs, subsidies, and incentives. It would be fair to say distrust between the public and private sectors and reluctance to cooperate was mutual. The private sector did not want to be led by and did not want to interact and cooperate with a strong public agency. Instead, it worked with the politicians to weaken the planning agency and its autonomy.

As political power shifted to the parliament and the civilian government in later years, the early model was abandoned and the priorities and goals of the SPO began to be determined increasingly by the private sector, and especially by the large holding companies. Rather than heavy industry and higher technology, the latter wanted to focus on durable consumer goods and automotive production for the domestic market, forming partnerships with multinational companies wherever necessary. Özal's appointment by Prime Minister Demirel as SPO undersecretary in 1967 reflects this transformation very well. Instead of directing an industrialization model that used higher skills and technology to produce more complex products and eventually direct them toward exports, the SPO evolved into a body that gave priority to the short-term goals of the private sector and distributed various subsidies, tax exemptions, foreign exchange allocations, and other privileges to the well-connected segments of the private sector. There was very little monitoring or public accounting of the benefits provided to the private sector. The transition of the ISI strategy from an emphasis on the longer-term, heavy industry and technology to a private sector–led model producing durable consumer goods for the domestic market, took place under these circumstances (Milor 1970, pp. 1–30; Türkcan 2010).

The holding companies or conglomerates best reflect the organizations that dominated the import-substituting industrialization process in the decades after World War II. From the early 1950s, leading firms and family groups in the urban economy had started to organize into holdings. Companies from sectors such as food processing, textiles, consumer durables, automotives, and tourism which were producing primarily for the domestic market were included in the holdings. To meet the credit needs of the companies within the group, the larger groups usually included a bank among their subsidiaries. If better cooperation among companies of the same group was one advantage of the holdings, another was the various tax exemptions, advantages, and subsidies granted to the holdings by law. All holdings paid special attention to nurturing good relations with the government and the bureaucracy in Ankara. OYAK, which was established for members of the armed forces, had an even more privileged position than other holdings.

After political instability increased in the 1970s, economic policies of short-lived governments focused increasingly on short-term goals. The import-substituting industrialization process moved even further away from long-term goals and measures such as efficiency, competition, and exports. In fact, the goal of directing the more competitive branches of manufacturing toward exports was essentially abandoned. For success in manufacturing, it became more important to stand close to the state and obtain its support. Decisions on which sectors should be included within the scope of protections, and in which branches local production would be promoted, were taken not according to long-term calculations of costs and competitiveness, but according to the demands of the holdings and their influence on the government.

Interaction between Formal and Informal Institutions

The diffusion of formal institutions had been slow during the nineteenth century and the first half of the twentieth century. The privately organized arrangements rooted in informal social networks continued to coexist with and often substituted for formal institutions in urban and especially rural areas. After World War II, urbanization and economic growth as well as improvements in health and education began to gain momentum. The fiscal, adminis-

trative, and legal capacities of the state began to increase as well. These important changes did not mean the disappearance of the informal institutions,
however. On the contrary, with rapid rural to urban migration, many of the
informal networks as well as power relations were carried from the rural to the
urban areas. Patronage, religious, and regional solidarity networks as well as
many other informal institutions that already existed in the urban areas developed further and flourished since 1950, interacting with formal institutions
and creating new ones. These informal relations played key roles for the recent
migrants in securing housing, urban services, and employment. The same informal networks or informal institutions also played prominent roles in the
business decisions of a large part of the rapidly growing private sector in the
urban areas (Erder 1999, pp. 161–72).

Some of the earliest organizations in the urban areas were based on localism. Relying on loyalty and solidarity allegedly reflecting a shared sense of
provincial origin, these new organizations became the building blocks of social, political, and economic networks. Overlapping to some extent with the
networks based on localism were the networks formed by religious communities, both Sunni and Alevi, and Kurdish communities. Another large set of
informal institutions that spread after World War II were patronage relationships. Without changing the fundamentals of the unequal power relations,
patronage networks responded to the demands of these groups. The roots of
patronage relations went back to the unequal relations between the big landowners and other powerful people and the poor peasants in the Ottoman era.
With urbanization and growing ties between the countryside and the urban
areas, patronage relationships spread in both rural and urban areas. Political
patronage in the multiparty era often involved the politicians and their local
allies obtaining the voters' political support by using their connections to local
and national government to find employment for people, solving their problems in dealing with local governments, ensuring that governments provided
infrastructure investments such as roads, running water, and electricity, and
other urban services to local communities. Making use of the growing volume
of low-interest credit expanded by public sector banks to small and medium-
sized agricultural producers as well as small businesses in urban areas was
another area where patronage relations mattered. Organizations such as the
Democrat Party and its successor the Justice Party, and not just individual
politicians, successfully benefited from the skillful use of patronage networks
and the influence of powerful people in rural areas, and they carried these
relationships to the urban areas (Sayarı 1977, pp. 103–13).

The demands of the broad segments of the rural and urban populations
within the context of a more open and more competitive political regime thus
led to the rise of clusters of other informal and formal institutions during the

decades after World War II. The spread of price support programs of the government from wheat and later tobacco to many other crops and the expansion of their coverage and annual budgets especially during election years was one such example. The gecekondu system involving the building of private housing by recent migrants on state-owned lands and eventually acquiring from the government the formal property rights to such lands, as well as obtaining from the local governments the infrastructure and other services to the rapidly growing districts, was another such example. The cluster of informal and formal institutions related to the gecekondu thus provided lower cost housing to the recent migrants when large amounts of unused urban land still existed (Öncü 1988, pp. 38–64).

Different formal and informal institutions may have different effects on economic growth, some positive and others negative. It would be safe to say the spread of these informal institutions and their interaction with formal institutions in the decades after World War II, on the whole, contributed to economic growth. Thanks to these informal institutions and their interaction with formal institutions, large segments of the population, both rural and urban, were also able to claim a larger share of the growing economic pie. The emergence of these institutions meant that urbanization and industrialization proceeded not through the dispossession of the recent migrants to the urban areas, but by transferring the small property and small-scale production institutions which were one of the distinguishing features of the Ottoman era from the rural to the urban areas after World War II. These policies and institutions, which have also been described as populism, were, up to a point, not in contradiction with the model of industrialization through import substitution and the Bretton Woods institutions because the additional income obtained by the broader groups also created additional demand for domestic production, which was strongly protected from foreign competition (Boratav 1986, pp. 117–39; Sunar 1984, pp. 2076–86). After the Bretton Woods order came to an end in the 1970s with the disintegration of the fixed exchange-rate regime and lifting of controls on international capital flows, it would become increasingly difficult to sustain some of these arrangements.

Institutions and State Interventionism

State interventionism certainly contributed to growth in Turkey during the decades after World War II. However, the low rates of total productivity growth and no more than average rates of economic growth also suggest that state interventionism has had a mixed record during this period. In addition, state interventionism often served the interests of narrow groups, reproduced existing inequalities, and created new inequalities. The evolution of state interventionism and the mixed results it generated during the 1960s and 1970s necessitates a closer examination of the roles played by formal and informal institutions in the implementation of interventionism. The success and failure of state interventionism has been due not only to the content of the policies but also the specific sets of institutions that were chosen or designed to implement these policies. One important reason why government interventionism produced mixed results was the weaknesses of the two main actors—the bureaucracy and the private sector—and their inability to cooperate. Institutions of cooperation, organization, and conflict resolution were critically important not only for the state but also for social actors to function effectively in the defense of their interests. Institutions could contribute but also impede the cohesion and strength of different social actors.

The absence of a cohesive and stable bureaucratic structure and a poorly organized private sector often dependent on the public sector as well as the politicians made it very difficult to develop regularized ties and institutions of consultation and cooperation between them. The weaknesses of the public sector, the cleavages and weaknesses of the private sector, and the difficulties of cooperation between the two are best understood in historical terms, in terms of the persistence of key institutions. Despite the tradition of a strong state going back to the nineteenth century and even earlier, the public sector often lacked the cohesion and autonomy from both the politicians and the private sector to implement coherent, rules-based policies. It is not surprising that the model of strong, cohesive, and autonomous public agency directing industrialization and guiding the private sector during the 1960s did not survive very long. The public sector became increasingly more fragmented during the political instability and short-lived coalition governments of the 1970s as political parties divided the ministries and tried to maximize the electoral gains. There were frequent changes in the higher echelons of the bureaucracy. The economic bureaucracy thus lost the cohesion and capacity necessary for the implementation of a coherent program of interventionism in favor of industrialization.

The private sector was also fragmented and poorly organized. Cleavages have often made it difficult for different groups to come together and negotiate and cooperate. As a result, individual or small group interests organized around informal networks have often taken precedence over larger collective interests. The business organizations were dominated by politicians. The major national organization bringing together representatives of the private sector, Union of the Chambers and Commodity Exchanges, was established by law in 1951 and was controlled by the government. Industrialists were not always the most powerful group within the private sector. Governments paid a good deal of attention to the demands of large-scale merchants. Leading industrial groups began to organize during this period around holding companies or conglomerates controlled by families. Examples of cooperation within business groups existed, but companies and individual businessmen often preferred to engage in bilateral lobbying. A large part if not most of lobbying remained focused on particular and narrow benefits (Öncü 1980, pp. 455–80; Bianchi 1984; Biddle and Milor 1997, pp. 277–309).

The first voluntary organization of the private sector consisting mostly of the owners and managers of the largest conglomerates was established in 1971. The Turkish Industry and Business Association (TUSIAD) was not able to shed its image as the club for the rich, however. It also lacked the capacity to design and enforce well-defined rules of interaction with the public sector for its members. Members and their companies continued to engage in bilateral lobbying. Politicians and state elites often found it expedient to encourage and take advantage of these cleavages by playing one group against the other. In fact, rather than well-defined, transparent channels and well-observed rules, both the private sector and the politicians often preferred bilateral and opaque ties and particularistic relations.

More broadly, the success of the institutions and policies of state interventionism have been closely related to the relations between the competing elites and the state in Turkey. State elites, the bureaucracy, and the military have also played important roles in this process as they pursued their own interests by themselves or in cooperation with some of the other elites. The configurations between the competing elites, between the private and the state elites, and between the secular and conservative elites have changed over time, but the cleavages and weak state capacity have persisted. When the distribution of benefits from an existing institution or a new institution was not consistent with the existing distribution of power in society, the various elites could mobilize, bargain, and put pressure on others as well as the state to try to change the formal institutions or reverse the policies. For this purpose, the competing elites often made use of informal institutions including identity-based networks and patron-client relations. In other words, although it may often be difficult to distinguish between interests and culture as the ultimate cause, many of the patterns and outcomes that appear to be to the result of beliefs, norms, customs, and more generally culture may in fact be explained by interests and power.

Countries in East Asia had success with state interventionism but they had very different balances between the state and the elites and different institutions. While the state actively interacted with society, it also maintained a high degree of autonomy when confronted with the short-term interests of different groups. The formal and informal institutions that facilitated the consultation and cooperation of the public and private sectors played key roles in the successful outcomes in these East Asian countries. State policies supported by these institutions not only changed the behavior of the private sector, but they also enabled new institutions to emerge and made it easier for the new institutions promoting industrialization to become stronger over time. The institutional structure created during the industrialization process thus gained permanence over time and continued to influence behavior in later periods. The East Asian state and its relationship with the private sector was the product of unique historical circumstances, however, and it has not been easy to replicate the success of East Asian countries with interventionism in other countries even though the same formal institutions and similar strategies of support for export-oriented manufacturing have been adopted. The problem has not been just that state capacity or the capabilities of the formal agencies charged with enforcement duties was weak. The state in Turkey could not harness the different powers and capacities of the elites and deal with various collective-action problems. The distribution of benefits from the enforcement of the new institutions and policies of interventionism has not been not in line with the existing distribution of power in society. Various elites often chose to develop formal and informal institutions different from those defined by the state that will better serve their interests.

Human Development

Measures of both health and education, the two basic dimensions of human development, began to show more rapid improvement in Turkey after World War II. In comparison to the nineteenth century, mortality rates especially among infants and children had begun to decline and life expectancy had begun to rise more rapidly during the Interwar period, but the increases accelerated significantly after World War II. Life expectancy at birth rose from 44 years in 1950 (45 for women, 42 for men) to 59 years (61 for women, 57 for men) in 1980. In other words, life expectancy rose by one year every two years in Turkey during the decades after World War II (see figure 2.3 in chapter 2 and table 10.2).

Two broad causes were responsible for the decline in mortality and the increases in life expectancy. First, economic growth meant rising income levels and better nutrition, especially for the poor in both the urban and rural areas. Economic growth also led to increases in the resources of the state and more generally increases in state capacity. As public revenues and expenditures increased and links between rural and urban areas were strengthened, medical facilities, health-care services, as well as basic infrastructure such as clean drinking water were made more readily available across the country, particularly in rural areas. Urbanization made it easier for a rising share of the population to access health-care services. The fights against malaria, tuberculosis, and other contagious diseases were helped by these improvements. Second, growing knowledge and new ways of doing things such as the discovery of penicillin and other antibiotics, and routine vaccinations, brought about more effective ways to fight diseases and reduce mortality around the world and in Turkey. It is difficult to measure the contribution of each, but they both contributed strongly to the rise of life expectancy at birth. The changing institutions, both formal and informal, also played important roles in the rise of life expectancy at birth. Not only the increase in state capacity and government policies but the acceptance and growing willingness on the part of the population, especially the rural population, to make use of these services mattered (Hacettepe Üniversitesi Nüfus Etütleri Enstitüsü 2008, pp. 12–20; Akder 2010, pp. 224–31).

The second important and related cause of the increases in life expectancy at birth was the slow decline in infant mortality which accounted for a large share of total deaths. Infant mortality declined from about 250 per thousand in 1950 to 125 per thousand in 1980 as diseases, particularly diarrheal, respiratory, and other infectious diseases, persisted among rural children. Infant mortality remained high and declined slowly also because of the low education levels of women in rural areas, as well as the large social and economic inequalities between regions. As a result, large differences in infant mortality rates between rural and urban areas and the west and the east of the country persisted during these decades. The highest rates of infant mortality occurred in rural areas in the mostly Kurdish southeast where both income per capita and levels of education, especially rural women's education, lagged well behind national averages.

Gains in life expectancy as well as access to health care were also distributed unevenly between urban and rural areas, between regions of the country, men and women, as well as the rich and the poor. The most rapid increases in life expectancy occurred in the urban areas and in the western and coastal regions, where incomes were higher and health services were more readily available. While we do not have detailed estimates for the earlier period, it is clear that women benefited more than men from the declines in mortality, as the life expectancy at birth between women and men expanded from 2 to 4 years during the post–World War II decades.

Life expectancy at birth rose strongly in most developing countries during the decades after World War II. In fact, all developing regions of the world with the exception of Sub-Saharan Africa experienced convergence in life expectancy toward the levels of developed countries, as the gains due to the declines in infant mortality in the developing countries was greater than the gains in life expectancy due to declines in adult mortality in developed countries. It may be useful to assess how Turkey fared in terms of life expectancy at birth in relation to other developing countries, and more specifically, in relation to developing countries with similar levels of GDP per capita. Samuel Preston has identified a relationship between GDP per capita and life expectancy at birth but has also shown that this curve has shifted upward over time due to growing knowledge and new ways of doing things. For its level of GDP per capita, life expectancy at birth in Turkey during the decades after World War II remained close to but slightly below the levels expected on the basis of its rising GDP per capita. In other words, Turkey was placed close to but slightly below the Preston Curve as the latter shifted upward over time. High rates of infant mortality, low levels of education for women, and high levels of regional inequality were among the leading reasons why life expectancy in Turkey lagged behind other developing countries with similar levels of GDP per capita during these decades (Zijdeman and de Silva 2014, pp. 106–12; Riley 2001, pp. 1–57; Deaton 2013, pp. 101–64).

As for education, numbers of students at all levels began to rise more rapidly in the decades after World War II along with more rapid economic growth, higher government spending, and rapid urbanization. The literacy rate increased from 33 percent in 1950 (19 percent for women and 46 percent for men) to 68 percent in 1980 (55 percent for women and 80 percent for men) (see table 10.2). Graduation rates from elementary schools rose from 30 percent of the age group in 1950 to 85 percent in 1980. Similarly, graduation rates for secondary schools increased from 4 percent of the age group in 1950 to 22 percent in 1980, and graduation rates for four-year universities increased from 1 percent of the age group in 1950 to about 6 percent in 1980. However, because of the slow increases in resources allocated to education as well as low levels of income and the reluctance of some families to send their daughters to school, Turkey continued to lag behind other developing countries with similar GDP per capita levels in basic indicators of education.

Moreover, as in health, the increases in student numbers and years of schooling did not lead to decline in inequalities. Differences in educational attainment remained strongly linked to rural-urban, regional, gender, and income differences. While literacy rates increased among the rural population, average years of schooling increased faster in the urban areas. Literacy and years of schooling also rose faster in the more developed western and coastal regions than in the east and southeast. In addition, differences in the quality of education between rural and urban areas, between the more and less developed regions, and between income groups persisted and may have even increased, further contributing to the regional inequalities. Nonetheless, higher levels of public spending on education and rising numbers of students helped make education an important vehicle for social mobility, especially among the urban population during this period (Tansel 2002, pp. 455–70; Tansel and Güngör 1997, pp. 541–47).

Gender differences also remained high and declined only slowly at all levels of schooling during these decades. While numbers of female students increased from 60 percent to 80 percent of those of male students among elementary students, among high school and university students, numbers of female students increased only slightly, from 25 percent to 32 percent of those of male students between 1950 and 1980. Average years of schooling for all adult women increased from about 42 percent to 60 percent of those for men during the same period. The gender differences were lower in the urban areas, in the more developed western regions, and among middle- and higher-income groups, but higher in rural areas, in the less developed east and southeast, and among lower-income groups.

Average formal schooling received by adults over fifteen years of age increased from 1.2 years in 1950 to 4.2 years in 1980 in Turkey, while the world averages increased from 3.2 years to 5.3 years during the same period. This put education levels in Turkey not only well below the developed countries of Western Europe and the United States but also below the averages for Eastern Europe, Latin America, and China, but above those of Egypt, and South and Southeast Asia and Sub-Saharan Africa (van Leeuwen and van Leeuwen-Li 2014, pp. 93–98). In other words, Turkey lagged behind countries with similar levels of GDP per capita in Latin America and East Asia when it came to education during the decades after World War II, making it more difficult for manufacturing to move up toward higher technology, higher value-added goods, and sectors requiring higher skills.

Demographic Transition

Like the majority of developing countries, Turkey experienced the demographic transition or the transition from high birth rates and high mortality rates to low birth and low mortality rates during the twentieth century and mostly after World War II. Even though mortality rates had begun to decline, the fertility rates had remained high in the Interwar period .[1] As a result, the demographic transition began in earnest after World War II, but it proceeded

---

1. Duben and Behar have shown that the fertility rate was quite low in Istanbul during the second half of the nineteenth century and before World War I. However, this was not necessarily true of the other urban areas or the rural areas for which we have little information (Duben and Behar 1991). In fact, it is likely that the fertility rate for Turkey as a whole during the nineteenth century was not very different from what it was during the Interwar period.

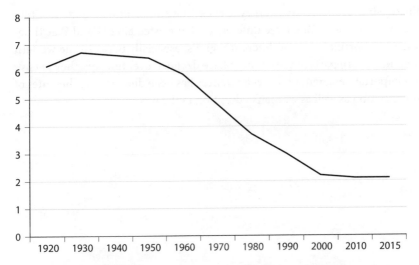

FIGURE 10.4. Fertility Rate in Turkey, 1925–2015 (average numbers of live births per woman). Sources: Hacettepe Üniversitesi Nüfus Etütleri Enstitüsü 2008, pp. 12–20; Turkey, Devlet İstatistik Enstitüsü (State Institute of Statistics), 1995.

very rapidly. Along with mortality rates, birth rates declined sharply. The fertility rate, which reflects the average number of live births per woman during child-bearing years, declined from 6.5 in the 1950s to 3.8 in the 1980s, and 2.1 in the 2010s (figure 10.4). That is, the decline in the mortality rate was the main reason for the high rates of population growth during the decades following World War II. As the decline in mortality rates began to slow down, the rapid decrease in the total fertility rate emerged as the main cause behind the decline in population growth rates, from 2.9 percent per year in the 1960s to 1.1 percent in the 2010s.

Urbanization contributed strongly to the decline in both mortality and fertility rates after World War II. The greater availability of health-care services in the urban areas led to significant declines in both infant and adult mortality rates. As infant deaths decreased, families began to have fewer children. More importantly, as women began to gain more education in the urban areas and to work outside the home, albeit in limited numbers, the transition to a family structure with fewer children that offered each of the children better educational opportunities gained momentum. The fertility rate always showed large differences between rural and urban areas. In 1950, while the total fertility rate in rural areas was 6.8, it was 4.3 in other cities, and in Istanbul and İzmir it was only 2.7. The same rates declined to 4.0, 2.8, and 2.2, respectively, by 1990 (Shorter and Macura 1983, pp. 66–101; Hacettepe Üniversitesi Nüfus Etütleri

Enstitüsü 2008, pp. 12–47; Turkey, Devlet İstatistik Enstitüsü [State Institute of Statistics] 1995). The large differences that existed after World War II between the fertility rates of different regions, especially between the western and the eastern parts of the country, have declined over time but they persist. An important element of these differences has been due to the higher rates of urbanization as well as women's education in the west.

11

Neoliberal Policies and Globalization

THE GLOBAL RECESSION THAT FOLLOWED the OPEC-led increase in oil prices in 1973 brought about the end not only of a long period of expansion but also of Keynesian-style macroeconomic management and welfare state policies in the developed countries. The shift to neoliberal policies around the world began in the 1970s as the Bretton Woods system was disintegrating and the developed economies on both sides of the Atlantic Ocean were searching for policies to deal with the combination of stagnation and inflation. The Thatcher government in the United Kingdom and the Reagan administration in the United States led the movement toward greater emphasis on markets in both macro- and microeconomic policy. The new policies began to reduce the barriers in the way of trade and even more importantly the controls on international capital flows. These changes ushered in a new era known as the second wave of globalization after the first wave during the century before World War I (Rodrik 2011, pp. 89–206; Eichengreen 2008, pp. 134–227).

The large trade surpluses of the oil-exporting countries created new liquidity and lower interest rates in the international markets during the 1970s. Rather than slow down their economies in response to the increase in oil prices, many developing countries attempted to take advantage of the new liquidity and borrowed large amounts in order to extend the ISI-related boom. This strategy could not be sustained for long, however. The rapid escalation of the outstanding debt and growing difficulties of servicing and repayment in many developing countries gave the IMF and the World Bank renewed power to bring about long-term structural changes in these economies and their linkages with the world economy (Haggard and Kaufman 1992, pp. 3–37).

While obstacles to international capital movements were removed in many countries, both developed and developing, the obstacles in the way of international labor movements remained in place. At the same time, legal and technological changes weakened the labor unions and more generally the bargaining capacity of labor in many countries. As a result, the benefits of economic growth in the new era were distributed unequally between capital and labor. In addition, the growing volume of international capital movements introduced a new source of instability, not only to national economies, but for the entire global economy as well. The Asian crisis at the end of the 1990s created difficulties for many developing countries and demonstrated the risks associated with financial globalization. The global economic crisis that began in 2008 led to a sharp decline in output followed by slow recovery in the developed countries. GDP per capita levels for the developed countries as a whole were lower in 2015 than they were in 2007. The impact of the crisis on developing countries was more limited, however.

Turkey's encounter with neoliberal policies and globalization began with the new policy package launched in January 1980 in response to the severe economic crisis at the end of the 1970s. But the initial changes in formal policies and institutions were only part of the story. The distribution of benefits from the enforcement of the new policies and institutions was not always in line with the distribution of power and changing politics. The new policies and institutions interacted with existing institutions, the changing distribution of power, as well as domestic politics, and changed over time. The end result was rather different than what the original policies and institutions were supposed to achieve. Of the new policies, trade liberalization, the emphasis on exports, and lifting of restrictions on international capital flows remained mostly intact. Perhaps the most important area where major differences emerged between what the new economic policies intended in theory and what actually happened in practice concerned the role of the state in the economy. The market-oriented economic policies were supposed to reduce the interventionism of the state in the economy. More than three decades later, the role of the state in the economy remained strong. While some important changes occurred in the relationship between the state and the private sector, the government continued to have power and discretion to decide the winners in the new era.

This chapter and the next will examine the era since 1980 in terms of four subperiods (table 11.1). This chapter will begin with global and national political developments and examine how they led to changes in economic policies and institutions in Turkey as well as the consequences of these changes. The next chapter will review Turkey's record in economic growth, income distribution, and human development in both absolute and relative terms. It will also evaluate the role of institutions and institutional change in economic development since 1980.

In the first subperiod, which covers 1980–87, the new economic policies aimed to replace the interventionist and inward-oriented model that prevailed since the 1930s with one that relied more on markets and was more open to

TABLE 11.1. A Periodization of Economic Trends, 1980–2015

Subperiod	Population	GDP	Agriculture	Manufacturing	GDP per capita	Level of GDP per Capita at the End of Subperiod 1980 = 100
		Average Annual Growth Rates				
1980–1987	2.4	5.6	0.7	8.7	3.1	124
1988–2002	1.7	3.2	1.4	4.0	1.5	155
2003–2007	1.4	6.9	0.4	8.1	5.4	202
2008–2015	1.4	3.3	2.5	2.8	1.9	234
1980–2015	1.6	4.1	1.1	5.6	2.5	234

Source: Author's calculations based on the official national income series in Turkey, Türkiye İstatistik Kurumu (Turkish Statistical Institute), 2014.

international trade and capital flows. With the help of the military regime, which reduced wages and agricultural incomes, significant increases were achieved in exports of manufactures during this period. The achievements of the new policies in other areas were limited, however. The second subperiod, 1987–2001, was characterized by a great deal of political and economic instability. The repression of domestic politics during the military regime had led to fragmentation on both the right and left of the political spectrum. As a result, the 1990s witnessed rivalries between large numbers of parties and series of short-lived coalitions. One important outcome of political instability was the loss of fiscal discipline and the sharp rise in budget deficits, leading to very high rates of monetary expansion and inflation as well as high levels of public borrowing and debt accumulation. Macroeconomic instabilities were exacerbated by the decision to fully liberalize the capital account in 1989. As a result, large fiscal deficits combined with financial globalization resulted in stop-go cycles of international capital flows for more than a decade.

Turkey's experience with neoliberal policies entered a new phase with the economic program of 2001 and the rise to power of the Justice and Development Party (JDP) the following year. The new program prepared in the aftermath of a severe economic crisis differed from earlier programs reflecting the Washington Consensus. It explicitly recognized the role played by institutions and independent regulating agencies and was supported by a series of reforms and new legislation. The 2001 program also placed a great deal of emphasis on fiscal discipline and macroeconomic stability which were embraced by the JDP. It would be best to divide the JDP era into two, however. The earlier years through 2007 were characterized by improvements in both political and economic institutions supported by Turkey's candidacy for EU membership as well as growing liquidity and low interest rates in global financial markets. In the more recent period since 2008, in contrast, the JDP and its leader, Recep Tayyip Erdoğan, moved to consolidate their power and establish an increasingly authoritarian regime. Along with growing political polarization, political as well as economic institutions deteriorated steadily. The ensuing decline in both the domestic and international investments significantly reduced the growth rates (Şenses 2012, pp. 11–31).

Washington Consensus Policies

In the face of a great deal of political instability during the 1970s, coalition governments in Turkey had tried to avoid dealing with the root causes of the economic problems by relying on the remittances from workers in Western Europe and short-term borrowing with unfavorable terms. By the end of the decade, the political difficulties were compounded by a severe economic crisis. Against the background of import and output contraction, commodity shortages, and strained relations with the IMF and international banks, the newly installed center-right minority government of Süleyman Demirel announced a comprehensive and unexpectedly radical policy package of stabilization and liberalization in January 1980. Turgut Özal, a former chief of the State Planning Organization, was to oversee the implementation of the new package. While the Demirel government lacked the political support necessary for the implementation of the package, the military regime that came to power after the coup in September of the same year endorsed the new program and made a point of appointing Özal as deputy prime minister responsible for the economy. Özal thus made his mark on Turkey's economy during the 1980s, first as the architect of the January 24 decisions, later as deputy prime minister during military rule, and as prime minister after his party won the elections in 1983. With the experience he had acquired at the World Bank during the 1970s, he had first-hand knowledge of the new economic policies and, once in power, made radical decisions toward opening the economy.

The aims of the new policy package were threefold: to improve the balance of payments and to reduce the rate of inflation in the short term and to create a market-based, export-oriented economy in the longer term, thus putting the economy on an outwardly oriented course, a sharp turn from the previous era of inwardly oriented growth and industrialization. The package began with a large devaluation of the lira followed by continued depreciation of the currency in line with the rate of inflation, greater liberalization of trade and payments regimes, elimination of price controls, substantial price increases for the products of the state economic enterprises, elimination of many of the government subsidies, freeing of interest rates, subsidies, and other support measures for exports, and promotion of foreign capital (Arıcanlı and Rodrik 1990a, pp. 1343–50; Arıcanlı and Rodrik 1990b).

Bringing about reductions in real wages and the incomes of agricultural producers in order to improve fiscal balances and competitiveness in international markets was an important part of the new policies. The parliamentary government of Demirel had little success in dealing with the labor unions as strikes and other forms of labor resistance, often violent, became increasingly common in the summer of 1980. After the coup, the military regime prohibited labor union activity and brought about large reductions in labor incomes. The government's purchase programs for agricultural crops were also scaled back and agricultural prices remained significantly lower during military rule.

From the very beginning, the January 1980 program benefited from the close cooperation and goodwill of the international agencies, especially the IMF and the World Bank as well as the international banks. One reason for this key support was the increasingly strategic place accorded to Turkey in the aftermath of the Iranian Revolution. Another reason was the close relations between Özal and the international agencies and the special status accorded to Turkey. For most of the decade Turkey was portrayed by these agencies as a shining example of the validity of the stabilization and structural adjustment programs they promoted and enjoyed their goodwill. In economic terms, this support translated into better conditions in the rescheduling of the external debt and substantial amounts of new credit.

After the shift to a restricted parliamentary regime in 1983, Özal was elected prime minister as the leader of the new Motherland Party he had formed. He launched a new wave of liberalization of trade and payments regimes including reductions of tariffs and quantity restrictions on imports. These measures opened domestic industry further to the competition from imports especially in consumer goods. However, the frequent revisions in the liberalization lists, the arbitrary manner in which these were made, and the favors provided to groups close to the government created a good deal of uncertainty regarding the stability and durability of these changes. The response of the private sector to import liberalization was mixed. While export-oriented groups and sectors supported the new measures, the ISI industries, especially the large-scale conglomerates whose products included consumer durables and automotives, continued to lobby for protection of their industries. As the new regime gained permanence and the protectionism of the earlier era was dismantled in the following years, however, industry turned increasingly toward exports.

One of the more important new policies was the liberalization of the financial sector and opening it to the outside world. The exchange regime underwent fundamental changes and many transactions involving foreign exchange that previously were the monopoly of the Central Bank were opened to commercial banks. In addition, the government allowed all citizens to open and maintain accounts in foreign currency in the domestic banks. This new policy aimed at and succeeded in drawing the large foreign currency balances of the public from "under the mattress" into the banking system. In the longer term, however, this move made currency substitution away from the lira or "dollarization" easier. Because of the decline in the effectiveness of monetary policy, it became harder to deal with inflation in later years.

The liberalization of the financial markets took place gradually. In the earlier era, the nominal interest rates on domestic deposits had been determined by the Central Bank, usually below the rate of inflation. The transition toward the determination of interest rates by markets was complicated and involved a number of crises. From 1985 onward, important changes aimed at deepening the financial markets were also undertaken. Through auctions, the Treasury started selling bonds to banks and private individuals. In later years, the government would begin to make extensive use of this facility, thus straying further away from fiscal discipline. In addition, with the new flexibility gained in the exchange-rate regime, private banks were able to secure new credit from international sources, both private and public. These innovations, in a country where the savings rate had always remained low and an important share of investments was financed through external sources, created important opportunities on the one hand, but also introduced new risks (Arıcanlı and Rodrik 1990a, pp. 1343–50; Arıcanlı and Rodrik 1990b).

The most notable success of the new policies was the increase in exports. From very low levels of $2.3 billion and 2.6 percent ratio of GDP in 1979, export revenues rose to $8 billion in 1985 and $13 billion or 8.6 percent of GDP in 1990 (figures 11.1 and 11.2). Most of the increases were caused by the rise in exports of manufactures whose share in total exports rose from 36 percent in 1979 to 80 percent in 1990. Textiles, clothing, and iron and steel products ranked at the top of the list of exports (Turkey, Turkish Statistics Institute, 2014). The growth in exports was achieved primarily by reorienting the existing capacity of ISI industries toward external markets. In the early years, the exporters were supported by a steady policy of exchange-rate depreciation, by credits at preferential rates, tax rebates, and foreign exchange allocation schemes. The latter mechanisms amounted to a 20–30 percent subsidy on unit value, although their magnitudes gradually declined during the second half of the decade. In the early stages, the export drive also benefited from the war between Iraq and Iran as Turkey exported to both countries. After the end of the war, however, the European Community's share in Turkey's exports returned to 50 percent and remained at that level until the end of the century (Barlow and Şenses 1995, pp. 111–33; Waterbury 1991, pp. 127–45; Arslan and van Wijnbergen 1993, pp. 128–33; also see figure 11.6 below).

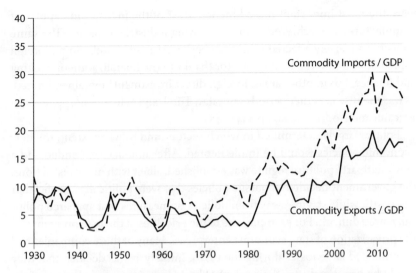

FIGURE 11.1. Share of Foreign Trade, 1929–2015 (Ratios of Commodity Imports and Commodity Exports to GDP in percent). Source: Official series from Turkey, Turkish Statistical Institute 2014.

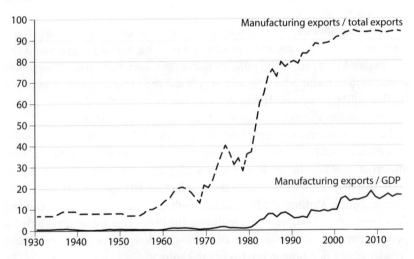

FIGURE 11.2. Shares of Manufacturing Exports in Turkey, 1930–2015 (percent). Source: Official series from Turkey, Turkish Statistical Institute 2014.

Aside from the export performance, however, the impact of the new policies on the real economy was rather mixed. Most importantly, the new policies were not able to mobilize high levels of private investment. In the manufacturing industry, high interest rates, steady depreciation of the currency which raised the cost of imported capital, and the unstable political environment were the most important impediments. Most of the increase in exports of manufactures was achieved with the existing industrial capacity. The same concerns adversely affected foreign direct investment as well. Some foreign capital flowed into the banking sector thanks to the liberalization of banking and finance, but in other areas, foreign direct investments remained limited, as was the case in earlier periods (Boratav, Türel, and Yeldan 1996, pp. 373–93; Arıcanlı and Rodrik 1990a, pp. 1347–48).

Politics largely determined in which sectors, and to what extent, the new economic policies would be implemented. After military rule ended and a new multiparty political regime was established, albeit with many restrictions, the government decided to pursue policies that were politically beneficial or less costly, while staying away from policies or measures that appeared politically more difficult. For example, one of the priorities of the 1980 program was the privatization of state economic enterprises. Many of these companies had accumulated large losses during the 1970s. Initially, it was decided that they would be privatized after their balance sheets were improved. The privatization process was littered with technical, legal, and political obstacles, however. Those standing against privatization did not just include the workers, but also the politicians who had no intention of abandoning the control they exercised over these firms.

Reducing labor and agricultural incomes was one of the most fundamental elements of the January 1980 program. Both the military regime and the Motherland Party followed policies that kept wages and agricultural prices low until 1987, taking advantage of the political and other restrictions imposed by the military regime. The burden of the new policies was thus placed squarely on the shoulders of groups that could not make their voices heard and were not sufficiently organized. The closure of the unions by the military government and the introduction of new laws that eroded their power played important roles in the decline of wages. The agricultural sector, which provided employment and income to about half of the labor force, was also all but ignored by the Motherland Party. As a result, the agricultural sector showed the lowest rates of output increase during the postwar era, averaging only 1.4 percent per year for the decade and failing to keep pace with population growth for the first time in the twentieth century.

The new policies were thus given support from two corners during the 1980s—repression of labor and agricultural incomes by the military and generous foreign capital inflows by the international financial institutions. Despite the decline in wages and agricultural prices paid by the government as well as the volume of price support programs, however, public sector deficits, high rates of monetary expansion and inflation continued. The annual rate of inflation declined from 90 percent in 1980 to 30 percent in 1983 but remained around 40 percent in the following years (Rodrik 1990, pp. 323–53).

One investment program that was pursued energetically by the government was the large Southeast Anatolia Project originally planned in the 1960s. It envisaged the building of a number of interrelated dams on the Euphrates River, including hydroelectric plants and irrigation of 1.6 million hectares in the plain of Harran, which would double the irrigated area under cultivation in Turkey. This large and expensive project stood apart from all other rural development schemes since the end of World War II. For a long time, however, the project was designed and implemented without sufficient understanding or concern for the needs of the local population. In response to the rise of Kurdish nationalism in the region, governments in Ankara attempted to redefine the project as an integrated regional development program seeking to improve the social and economic fabric of a large and poor region. The project then began to include large investments in a wide range of development-related sectors, including transportation, urban and rural infrastructure, as well as agriculture and energy. The absence of a shared vision between the planners and the intended beneficiaries, the local Kurdish communities, has seriously limited its benefits, however (Mutlu 1996, pp. 59–86; Çarkoğlu and Eder 2005, pp. 167–84).

Along with trade and capital account liberalization in the new era, governments also began to support the tourism sector as an important foreign exchange earner and employment provider. Beginning in the 1980s, allocation of state lands and long-term loans with low interest rates from public banks attracted large-scale investments in the sector by domestic entrepreneurs. As tourism evolved further in the 1990s, these private companies began to adopt the low-cost, labor-intensive, all-inclusive holiday packages organized by international tour operators as the leading product in the sector. These packages were offered by hundreds of hotels and holiday villages of various sizes along the southern and southwestern coastline. Turkey received 40 million tourists and ranked sixth in the world in 2014. Total international tourism receipts were close to $30 billion, about 3 percent of GDP, and ranked eleventh in the world in the same year (World Tourism Organization 2016, pp. 8–11). Tourism thus provided significant amounts of full-time and part-time employment at different skill levels but remained vulnerable to global or regional economic downturns as well as international and domestic political events, including terrorism.

Return of Political and Economic Instability

The restrictions the military regime placed on the politicians of the 1970s were lifted after a referendum and they returned to active politics in 1987. With the transition to a more open electoral regime, the opposition began to criticize both the deterioration of income distribution and the arbitrary manner in

which Özal and his Motherland Party implemented the new policies. The protests and resistance movements that began among public sector workers and
continued with the miners of Zonguldak in 1989 showed that the period of
repression imposed by the military government was being left behind. In the
longer term, the fragmentation on both the center-right and center-left of the
political spectrum between the old and new politicians fueled a good deal of
instability. Under short-lived coalition governments, budget deficits soared
and public sector debt accumulated. Between 1987 and 2002, Turkey thus
went through a very difficult period, marked by intertwined political and economic crises. Like the other military coups launched ostensibly to restore
political stability, the 1980 coup thus became the cause of long-lasting political
and economic instability.

In response to the more competitive political conditions after 1987, the
Motherland Party government and the coalition governments that replaced it
beginning in 1991 responded with populist policies. They sharply raised wages
in the public sector as well as the prices of agricultural products and broadened the scope of the state's purchase programs for agricultural crops. Through
public banks, they extended cheap credits to small businesses as well as agricultural producers. In addition, the prices of products sold by state economic
enterprises began to lag behind inflation. These policies rapidly widened the
budget deficit. In addition, state economic enterprises including public banks
began to record huge losses. The expanding war with the Kurdish PKK which
began in 1984 in the southeast continued to place new burdens on the budget
(Kirişci and Winrow 1997; Aydin and Emrence 2015).

In August 1989, as macroeconomic balances began to deteriorate, Özal and
the Motherland Party decided to further liberalize the exchange-rate regime
and remove the restrictions on inflows and outflows of capital including foreign borrowing by the Treasury. With the infamous decree number 38, financial globalization acquired a legal framework. The basic aim of the decree was
to ease the difficulties that the public sector was facing with financing its budget deficits, even if only in the short term, and to widen the room for maneuver of the government. After the decree, high domestic interest rates and a
pegged exchange-rate regime attracted large amounts of short-term capital
inflows. Private banks rushed to borrow from abroad in order to lend to the
government at high rates of interest. Public sector banks were directed by the
governments to finance part of the deficits. In the longer term, the decision to
liberalize the capital account without achieving macroeconomic stability and
creating a strong regulatory infrastructure for the financial sector proved to be
very costly. As the economy became increasingly vulnerable to external
shocks and sudden outflows of capital, the 1990s turned into the most difficult
period in the post–World War II era (Akyüz and Boratav 2003, pp. 1549–66;

Demir 2004, pp. 851–69; Gemici 2012, pp. 33–55). Turkey's economy continued to struggle with large current account deficits and macroeconomic stability in later periods as well. In fact, one can argue that full liberalization of the capital account or financial globalization has not interacted very well with Turkey's domestic institutions.

Another method used to finance the rapidly widening budget deficit, as was the case in earlier periods, was printing money. As the money supply began to increase, inflation, which was brought under control only partially during the 1980s, began to pick up pace again. Annual rates of inflation rose at the end of the 1980s and fluctuated between 50 percent and 100 percent during the 1990s (figure 11.3). One important factor that reinforced the link between public sector deficits and inflation was the introduction of foreign exchange deposit accounts in 1984 as part of the policies of financial liberalization. By reducing the demand for domestic money, this measure increased the inflationary impact of the public sector deficits.

It was not easy to follow the rise of public sector deficits and outstanding debt from the official series at the time since large parts of the deficits and losses were transferred to the balance sheets of the public sector enterprises during this period. Moreover, the full cost to the public of the pillaging of the assets of the public banks could be estimated only after the 2001 crisis. It is now possible to put together an approximate account of the rise of the outstanding debt of the public sector in relation to the size economy. Figure 11.4 shows that the total domestic and foreign debt of the public sector rose dramatically from about 40 percent of GDP in 1990 to 90 percent in 2001.

Along the way, measures that would have increased the resilience of the economy to internal and external shocks were pushed aside. Virtually no progress was made in the privatization of the state economic enterprises. Both workers and politicians remained opposed to privatization. Moreover, attempts to sell some of the large state enterprises were accompanied by scandals involving leading politicians. The sale of some of the smaller public sector banks resulted in large losses for the state sector as these banks were stripped of their assets by the well-connected buyers, and the full guarantees on bank deposits made the public sector responsible for their large losses. These large losses were all added to outstanding public debt after 2001 (Tükel, Üçer, and Rijckeghem 2006, pp. 276–303; Akın, Aysan, and Yıldıran 2009, pp. 73–100).

The large public sector deficit and the rapidly rising public sector debt made the economy very vulnerable to external as well as internal shocks. A negative event in the global economy or politics or the perception that the public sector deficit was becoming unsustainable could trigger large outflows of short-term capital, raise interest rates, depreciate the currency, and lead to a recession. These stop-go cycles of capital flows were repeated four

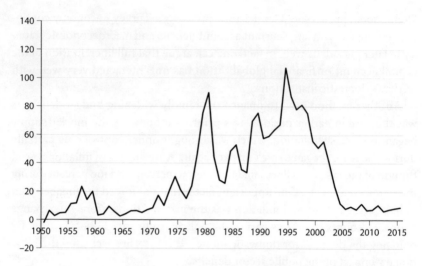

FIGURE 11.3. Annual Rate of Inflation in Turkey, 1950–2015 (percent).
Source: Official series from Turkey, Turkish Statistical Institute 2014.

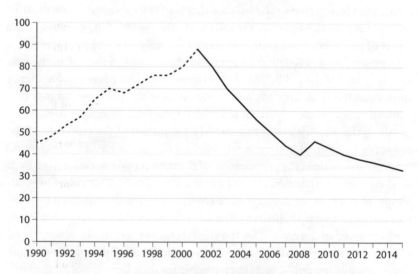

FIGURE 11.4. Public Sector Debt Stock / GDP, 1990–2015 (percent).
Source: Based on official series from Turkey, Ministry of Development 2017.

times, in 1991, 1994, 1998 and 2000–2001, the last of which was the most severe. Even though GDP per capita continued to rise during these years, the trend rate was significantly lower than both the earlier and later periods (figure 11.5).

High rates of inflation and high real interest rates made income distribution increasingly more unequal during the 1990s. The more organized groups

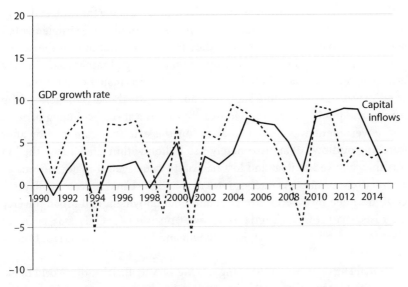

FIGURE 11.5. Capital Inflows and GDP Growth, 1990–2015 (as percentage of GDP).
Source: Official series from Turkey, Ministry of Development 2017.

were able to develop some protection and shield themselves to some extent. Organized workers benefited from collective wage agreements, agricultural producers from support purchases, and small business owners from low-interest credit. Middle classes relied on bank accounts in foreign currency and those with larger cash assets lent to the government at high rates of interest. Not all sections of society were equally successful against inflation, however. With the added impact of the war in the Southeast and forced migration of large numbers of Kurds from rural to urban areas, income distribution deteriorated sharply (Yükseker 2009, pp. 262–80).

Crisis and Another Program

By the end of 1999 it was clear that the macroeconomic balances were not sustainable. Negotiations with the IMF led to a new stabilization program with a pegged exchange-rate regime as the key anchor to bring down inflation. Stability programs supported by the IMF were launched several times during the 1990s, but their implementation was soon abandoned in each case. There were major questions about the design and implementation of the new program. While the program included a plan to reduce the large deficits in public finances and deal with the large losses accumulated by public banks as well as the problems of the private banks, it remained to be seen whether these measures would be adopted by the government.

Even though some progress was made toward reducing the budget deficit, many of the measures envisaged in the program could not be implemented because the coalition government led by Ecevit could not muster the necessary political will. The IMF's insistence on a managed rather than floating exchange rate also contributed to the crisis. After a smaller crisis at the end of 2000 was met with some support from the IMF, the large deficits of the private and public banks resulted in a major crisis at the beginning of 2001. The government was forced to abandon the exchange-rate anchor after watching outflows of approximately $20 billion within a few days. The lira was then allowed to float and lost half of its value against major currencies within a few months. As interest rates rose and the banking sector collapsed, GDP declined by 6 percent in 2001 and unemployment and urban poverty increased sharply (Akyüz and Boratav 2003, pp. 1549–66; Öniş 2003, pp. 1–30; Kazgan 2005, pp. 231–54; Van Rijckeghem and Üçer 2005, pp. 7–126; Özatay 2009, pp. 80–100).

Kemal Derviş, who was working as a high-level official at the World Bank, was invited to Turkey in early 2001 to prepare a new program and secure international support for it as minister in charge of the economy. The new program, prepared with the support of the IMF, contained stabilization measures as well as long-term structural and institutional reforms. For long-term macroeconomic stability, the program aimed to build budget surpluses for years to come in order to reduce the large outstanding public sector debt. It also aimed to insulate the public sector enterprises and especially the banks legally and administratively against the encroachment of the governments. Furthermore, instead of trying to control the inflation by managing the exchange rate and limiting the depreciation of the lira, a strategy that turned out to be very costly in the previous period, the new program adopted a floating exchange-rate regime.

The 2001 program also contained elements that differed significantly from those in the previous programs prepared with IMF support after 1980. In fact, it has been argued that the program reflected the post–Washington Consensus principles (Öniş and Şenses 2005, pp. 263–90). Instead of establishing the macro balances and leaving the rest to the markets, it accepted that the markets, left to their own devices, could produce undesirable outcomes and needed to be regulated. The program thus envisaged a new division of labor between markets and the state. The regulation and supervision of specific markets was being delegated to newly established institutions, which were intended to be independent from the government. For this reason, the program needed to be supported by a series of structural reforms and new laws. Some of the other legislative changes were designed to prevent governments from using for its short-term goals the public sector, particularly the public banks, and more generally increase the autonomy of the Central Bank. To what extent these regulations would be effective and whether and to what extent the new institutions would be independent from the political authorities would be determined more by how the laws would be implemented over time, rather than by the laws themselves (Sönmez 2011, pp. 145–230).

The new program also sought to restructure the banking sector after all the turbulence it experienced during the 1990s. Both public and private sector banks that had gone bankrupt would be dismantled and the outstanding debts of the public banks would be assumed by the public sector and spread out over time. In addition, contrary to the lax practices of the 1990s, the program envisaged closer supervision of the banking sector. A Banking Regulation and Supervision Agency which was to function independently of the government was set up for this purpose (Tükel, Üçer, and Rijckeghem 2006, pp. 276–303; Akın, Aysan, and Yıldıran 2009, pp. 73–100). After the Justice and Development Party (JDP) came to power on its own following the elections of 2002, it decided to continue to implement the new program with the support of IMF.

Customs Union and the EU Candidacy

Turkey's relations with the European Union go back to the Ankara Agreement of 1963, which had anticipated eventual membership in what was then called the Common Market. The Common Market and later the European Community was Turkey's most important trading partner, accounting for approximately 50 percent of its exports and more than 60 percent of its imports during those decades (figure 11.6). Little progress was made toward membership, however. During the military regime and its aftermath, Turkey remained far from fulfilling the political criteria for membership and the application for candidacy made by Prime Minister Özal was rejected in 1987. The coalition governments of the 1990s thus sought to at least take economic relations one step closer by signing the Customs Union agreement in 1994. With the agreement, the two sides eliminated the customs duties in the trade of manufactured goods between Turkey and the EU and aligned customs tariffs on imports from third countries with the levels applied by the EU. Trade in agricultural goods was left outside the customs union.

The EU share in Turkey's foreign trade did not increase after the signing of the customs union agreement because the tariff levels between Turkey and the EU had been declining since the 1980s and they were quite low in the early 1990s. Nonetheless, the EU remained Turkey's largest trading partner by a substantial margin. As economic stability returned after 2001, Turkey began to expand its external trade, including trade with the EU. Turkey's exports to

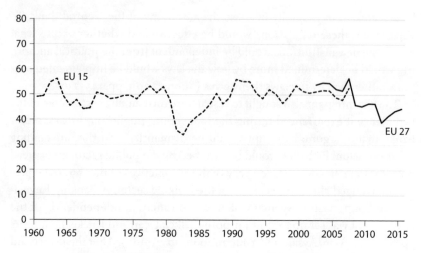

FIGURE 11.6. EU's Share in Turkey's Exports, 1960–2015 (percent).
Source: Official series from Turkey, Turkish Statistical Institute 2014.

the EU began to rise rapidly and multinational companies producing in Turkey, especially in the automotive industry, began to use Turkey as a production base for export both to the EU and other countries. In the more labor-intensive sectors such as textiles, exports to the EU also increased initially but they declined after the EU lifted restrictions imposed on China.

The customs union arrangement brought important benefits to Turkey's economy and especially to its manufacturing sector. At the time the customs union agreement was signed, the government and the political establishment thought that Turkey would soon become a member of the EU and would be included in the decision-making. However, as Turkey continued to remain outside the decision-making structures of the EU in later years, the inability to influence tariffs related to imports from third countries, especially those from East Asia, it began to impose costs and limit the benefits of the Customs Union arrangement (Yilmaz 2011, pp. 235–49; Antonucci and Manzocchi 2006, pp. 157–69).

The public saw the benefits of EU membership more in economic than in political terms and expected that after membership, per capita incomes would rise rapidly toward EU averages. The economic difficulties of the 1990s and the crisis of 2000–2001 thus served as a powerful reminder of the economic benefits of EU membership and created considerable pressure on the politicians to proceed with political reforms. The coalition governments thus gathered a good deal of political will around the turn of the century and stood behind the reforms, including important political and social amendments to the military regime constitution of 1982. As a result, the EU brought up, for the first time, the possibility of formally accepting Turkey as a candidate for membership.

Early JDP Years

While the secular parties struggled with rising political and macroeconomic instability as well as the many demands of a rapidly urbanizing society during the 1990s, the Islamist political parties focused on local organization and local government delivering urban services. They were often set back by the military and the judiciary but returned with perseverance. In the process, they moderated their policies and improved their political skills. The emergence of an Islamic bourgeoisie seeking economic integration with the West also helped them reshape their political goals and ideology.

The depth of the economic crisis in 2001 generated strong reactions from the public, not only against the political parties in power, but against all the parties that had been in charge of the economy during the previous decade. In the general elections held in 2002, all of them were voted out of the parliament. While those parties paid dearly for more than a decade of political and economic instability, the Justice and Development Party, formed by a group of politicians who had split from the Islamist movement, was able to exploit this opportunity and came to power by itself with only 34 percent of the national vote. The weaknesses of the secularists and the strengths of the Islamist movement thus precipitated JDP's ascent to government.

At the time JDP won the elections, Turkey's relations with the EU were making significant progress. The new party had been established by politicians who had pursued Islamist policies in parties led by Necmettin Erbakan and opposed Turkey's membership in the EU for many years. Before the elections of 2002, however, the new party began to differentiate itself from Erbakan's positions. Once in power, JDP continued to support Turkey's membership in the EU and the political reforms. Turkey was formally accepted by the EU as a candidate for membership in 2004. The IMF and the EU emerged in this period as the two external anchors reinforcing the stabilization of the economy and the long-term transformation of the institutional framework (Öniş and Bakır 2007, pp. 1–29; Yılmaz 2011, pp. 235–49).

In its early years in power, JDP appeared to pursue democratization and the Westward-oriented goals of Republican modernization. The party hoped to expand the room for Islam and religious freedoms more generally with its goals of democratization and EU membership. With this agenda, it was able to build a broad coalition. In its first five years in power, JDP also pursued policies that were more pro-private sector than any of the earlier governments. As a result, it received the support of major businesses and industrialists in

Istanbul as well as the more conservative businesses and industrialists across the country.

The JDP governments led by Recep Tayyip Erdogan also embraced the 2001 program supported by the IMF. Fiscal discipline, which was a key element of that program, became a key priority for JDP governments for achieving macroeconomic stability. Indirect taxes on gasoline and consumer goods were raised sharply. Another important contribution to lowering the public sector deficits came from privatizations. Earlier attempts at privatization had not made much progress because of legal and political obstacles, but JDP pursued them even at the cost of abandoning goals such as long-term productivity, efficiency, competition, and protecting the interests of the consumer (Atiyas 2009, pp. 101–22; Ökten 2006, pp. 227–51). As a result, the government was able to maintain large public sector surpluses before debt payments which averaged 6 percent of GDP until the global crisis of 2008–2009. Thanks to these surpluses, the ratio of public sector debt to GDP was reduced from approximately 80 percent in 2002 to 40 percent in 2008 (figure 11.4).

These large budget surpluses enabled the JDP government to bring inflation under control and below 10 percent annually for the first time since the 1960s (figure 11.6). The restoration of macroeconomic balances and the start of accession negotiations with the EU also paved the way for significantly higher levels of foreign direct investment. Also supported by growing global liquidity, foreign direct investments, which had remained very low since the 1920s, rose sharply from less than $3 billion annually before 2004 to $20 billion annually during 2005–2007. Because an important share of these investments took the form of acquisitions of existing local companies, however, their contribution to job creation remained limited.

Macroeconomic stability combined with strong increases in exports as well as the favorable global economic environment of growing liquidity and low interest rates led to large increases in GDP per capita. The accumulation of excess capacity and pent-up demand during the previous fifteen years of low economic growth also helped economic performance during the early JDP years. From 2003 through 2007, GDP increased at an annual rate of 6.9 percent and by a total of 40 percent. GDP per capita increased at an annual rate of 5.4 percent and by a total of 30 percent (table 11.1). Both of these annual rates were well above the long-term trend rates for Turkey and for developing countries as a whole since the end of World War II. Economic growth and lower debt payments thanks to declining public sector debt soon enabled the government to raise spending on infrastructure investment, health care, and education. JDP was thus able to deliver significant material benefits to its constituents not only through the increases in incomes but also higher levels of government spending in these areas. These benefits continued to support JDP at election time in later years.

While the economy recovered and incomes increased, the economic policies of JDP did not evolve beyond the institutional regulations and the fiscal discipline included in the 2001 program. The JDP governments did not develop their own long-term perspective on industrialization, growth, and employment creation (Taymaz and Voyvoda 2012, pp. 83–111). As a result, the economy had already begun to slow down before the onset of the global crisis. An important cause of the slowdown was the considerable appreciation of the Turkish lira due to short-term capital inflows and the loss of competitiveness of domestic production in international markets. Rising levels of global liquidity and the appreciation of the lira also encouraged importation of more inputs rather than their production locally, and even encouraged some firms to shift their production abroad to lower cost locations. Combined with a declining savings rate, the balance-of-payments deficit began to widen. Nonetheless, the economic recovery and growth achieved in its first five years in power allowed JDP to increase its share of the vote to more than 46 percent and secure a larger majority in parliament in the 2007 elections (Akçay and Üçer 2008, pp. 211–38; Öniş 2009, pp. 21–40).

Political and Economic Deterioration after 2007

The global crisis of 2008–2009 caught Turkey's economy on a slowly declining trend. Because the previous crises were still fresh in everyone's minds, the first impact of the crisis proved severe. In the initial months, large declines were recorded not just in exports, but also in investments and consumption. However, the banking sector had behaved more cautiously after the 2001 crisis, and the supervision and monitoring of the sector had been well managed. As a result, the banking sector remained resilient and the impact of the crisis was short-lived. In addition, the tight fiscal policies followed in the previous years had reduced the public sector debt ratio. Both monetary and fiscal policy could be relaxed for a few years to soften the impact of the crisis, an option not available to many other countries. By 2010, production and employment had returned to their pre-crisis levels, even if that was not yet the case for exports. However, as the economic problems faced by the European Union, which accounted for 50 percent of Turkey's exports, and the political problems in the Middle East deepened in the following years, Turkey's exports began to stagnate as well (figure 11.1).

Even more importantly, the formal negotiations for Turkey's membership in the EU began in 2005. At about the same time, however, center-right governments came to power in Germany and France and they soon began to openly oppose Turkey's membership. This shift in the positions of the two key countries was an important turning point in Turkey's relations with the EU. The EU anchor had underpinned important political reforms after 1999 and had also contributed to the economic recovery after 2001. As that anchor began to weaken and the goal of EU membership became increasingly uncertain, JDP's willingness to continue with the political reforms as well as long-term changes in economic institutions began to wane.

Domestically, the secular elites in the judiciary and the military attempted to close down JDP in 2007 at a time when it was actually in government. The final vote in the Constitutional Court was close and JDP avoided closure by a single vote. After the national elections in 2007, defeating its rivals and consolidating its power became the single most important goal for JDP and its leader, Prime Minister Erdoğan. Many of the earlier alliances were dismantled as he pursued an increasingly narrow path toward greater power in later years. Using a good deal of fabricated evidence and the network of the Muslim cleric Fethullah Gülen inside the judiciary and the police, the JDP then launched a wave of court cases against the military, accusing its leadership of plotting against the government and putting them on the defensive. The government soon began to control large segments of the media and curtail civil liberties. It moved to dispose of the checks and balances in the political system and undermine the separation of powers between the executive, legislature, and judiciary. A referendum in 2010 presented as legal reforms for EU membership allowed JDP and Erdoğan to undermine and eventually eliminate the independence of the judiciary. While society and politics were becoming increasingly polarized, the rising levels of employment and incomes as well as the increases in the access to health care, education, and other government services during the early JDP years helped the party maintain its popular support.

Turkey's slide toward authoritarianism continued after Erdoğan was elected president by popular vote in 2014. As he struggled to change the constitution and move from a parliamentary to a presidential system, the civil war in Syria and the return of military conflict in the Kurdish areas added to the political and economic difficulties. In foreign policy, the JDP had attempted to be more active in the Middle East. Peaceful relations with its neighbors in the region appeared to provide economic as well as political benefits. However, unrealistic expectations about a leadership role in the Middle East after the Arab Spring backfired badly, drawing Turkey into a ruinous civil war in Syria. One result was the arrival of three million Syrian refugees shortly after 2011. Another reversal of policy with major consequences took place on the Kurdish issue. For many years during the JDP era, the Kurdish conflict had edged toward a peaceful resolution. After the PKK refused to support Erdo-ğan's plans for a presidential system, however, tensions escalated very quickly in 2015. Once again, the southeast turned into a zone of conflict as the security forces and the PKK inflicted large casualties on each other as well as the civilian population. Tourism, which had emerged as an important sector of the economy since the 1980s, was deeply hurt by the outbreak of these conflicts and the associated incidents of terrorism inside Turkey.

Since 2007, politics and the drive to consolidate power have been the main priorities for JDP and Erdoğan. After the strong performance in the earlier years, the economy has been seriously damaged by the growing political conflict as well as the slide toward authoritarian rule. As the JDP government moved to control the economy more closely after 2007, the regulatory agencies established as part of the 2001 program came under increasing pressure and their autonomy was soon eliminated. Similarly, the Central Bank was forced to adjust its stance under pressure from the government. It soon abandoned its goal of lowering the inflation rate further and began to pursue more accommodative monetary policy. The annual rate of inflation which had declined to 6 percent in the aftermath of the global crisis thus began to edge up toward 10 percent (Gürkaynak and Sayek-Böke 2012, pp. 64–69; Acemoglu and Üçer 2015). Because the JDP governments maintained fiscal discipline even after the stand-by agreement with the IMF came to an end in 2008, they were able to avoid the economic crises like those of the 1990s. Fiscal stability was not sufficient to maintain the high rates of growth, however.

As JDP moved to consolidate its rule, supporting business groups close to the party and the government emerged as a leading goal of economic policy after 2007 and especially after 2010. Business groups close to JDP were increasingly favored in tenders launched by the central government as well as the local governments, in large-scale energy, infrastructure and housing projects, in the allocation of credit by public and private banks and other areas. For example, the procurement law which sought transparency and competitiveness and passed with the support of the World Bank in 2002 was amended more than 150 times during JDP rule in order to adapt it closely to the needs of the government and the public agencies. In addition, an increasing number of industries and activities were exempted from the law over time (Çeviker Gürakar 2016; Buğra and Savaşkan 2014, pp. 76–81). As the political fight between the JDP and the network of the Islamist cleric Gülen intensified after 2012, property rights of the political opponents of the government declined, rapidly raising questions about how far the slide toward authoritarianism would continue and which other groups may be threatened in the future.

Rising political tensions and steady deterioration of the institutional environment after 2010 sharply reduced private investment. The stagnation in

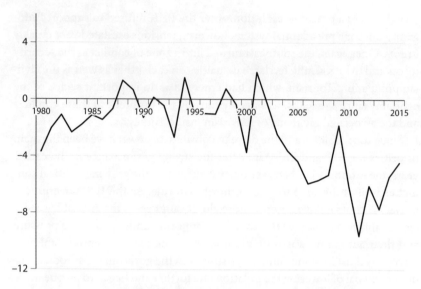

FIGURE 11.7. Current Account Balance, 1980–2015 (as percentage of GDP).
Source: Official series from Turkey, Ministry of Development 2017.

European markets, the civil war in Syria, terrorism, and the sharp decline in tourism revenues have also contributed to the economic slowdown. As a result, annual growth rates of GDP declined from an average of 6.9 percent during 2003–2007 to 3.2 percent during 2012–2015. The unemployment rate in the urban economy increased from 10.5 percent at the end of 2011 to 12.3 percent at the end of 2015.

Another important long-term economic problem has been the steady decline in the savings rate from 24 percent of GDP in 1998 to 18 percent in 2007 and 13 percent in 2015. Current account deficits widened as a result and the private sector had to secure large sums from abroad every year in order to finance its investments (figure 11.7). Foreign direct investments, most of which came from the EU countries, could finance only a fraction of the deficits. Foreign direct investments, which increased to $20 billion per year or more than 3 percent of GDP along with Turkey's EU candidacy during 2005–2007 declined during the global crisis and with the fading of Turkey's candidacy. They averaged $13 billion or about 1.5 percent of GDP during 2010–2015. Thanks to the high levels of liquidity in the international markets in the aftermath of the global crisis, financing the rest of the current account deficits was not a problem early on. The banking sector was able to borrow record amounts from the international banks and direct most of these funds to the private sector and use the rest to finance private consumption. As quantitative easing by the Federal Reserve began to end, however, Turkey's economy looked increasingly vulnerable. During the difficult 1990s, the large public sector deficits had been the major problem for the economy. Economic policy during the JDP era eliminated the public sector deficits but shifted them, in effect, to the private sector. Large current account deficits as well as the rising levels of indebtedness of the private sector thus made Turkey's economy increasingly fragile during the later years of the JDP era.

In response to lower rates of growth and rising levels of unemployment, the government tried to keep interest rates low and support the construction sector as well as private consumption. Given the high rates of urbanization and growing demand for real estate, the construction sector appeared especially attractive to the government for creating domestic demand. In addition, changing the existing rules on urban plans and allowing higher densities of construction was usually a safe and low-tech method for ensuring that specific firms and individuals would benefit directly and quickly. Accommodative monetary policy kept the construction boom going. The shopping malls and the growing number of housing and office building projects rising in big cities thus became symbols of an economic model based on consumption and construction funded by external borrowing.

Agriculture in the Neoliberal Era

During the ISI era after World War II, Turkish agriculture was regulated by support price policies, subsidies for agricultural inputs, commodity boards, and a protectionist trade regime. Commodity boards and other public agencies were also expected to develop quality standards for food and agricultural products and ensure that the growers and producers complied with them. As a result, farmers enjoyed considerable security and managed to remain relatively immune to market fluctuations. Along with the neoliberal restructuring of the economy under the auspices of the IMF and the World Bank, various measures were introduced with the aim of reducing government support programs and more generally government interventionism in agriculture and liberalizing food markets. Although its pace was slow due to political instability during the 1990s, restructuring gained momentum during the JDP era with the enactment of an economic reform package with strong terms for further liberalization of the farming sector. The agreements signed with the IMF and the World Bank after the crisis of 2001, Turkey's candidacy for EU membership, and the commitments made by the government for WTO membership played key roles in this shift. As a result, agricultural support policies for many commodities were largely discontinued, subsidies for agricultural inputs and credits were generally removed, most of the state agricultural enterprises were privatized, and the trade regime in agriculture was liberalized to a significant degree. This restructuring had the effect of shifting power and responsibility in marketing and quality management of agricultural products from public bodies to private institutions. It also increased the power and profile of the large international companies in domestic markets. The scope of this deregulation process has been wider and its intensity has been stronger in Turkey than in many other developing countries (Aydın 2010, pp. 149–87; Keyder and Yenal 2011, pp. 60–86).

In addition, relaxation of import controls has led to swift commercialization and internationalization not only in the seed sector but also in other input markets such as fertilizers, chemicals, and pesticides. On the output side, big international retailers and food manufacturing firms have been heavily engaged in organizing flexible procurement networks that stretch across Turkey as well. The role played by retailing and wholesaling firms, market brokers, and supermarket chains, all of which acted as intermediaries between the direct producer and the consumer, have thus increased in recent decades. These firms have better access to relevant information networks and have been more flexible in their procurement and marketing strategies.

These far-reaching changes have presented new opportunities as well as challenges for the small and medium-sized farmers. For the grain, pulses, and sugar beet farmers of the Anatolian interior, the options have been limited. Their crops were not labor-intensive and the sunk costs made it harder to switch. These farmers also had relatively stable family populations and there was not much excess labor to employ in additional household income-earning strategies. In contrast, in the coastal regions, especially in Mediterranean and Aegean villages, opportunities from market-oriented, labor-intensive agriculture were often combined with employment and incomes elsewhere. The farming of fresh vegetables and fruits has become the most dynamic agricultural activity in these regions in recent decades, contributing to the rise in the value added. The annual value of fresh produce has recently exceeded one-quarter of the total value of crop production. Turkey is currently among the top ten producers of tomatoes, cucumbers, eggplants, and onions in the world. Vegetables and fruits began to lead agricultural exports as well. More than half of Turkey's agricultural exports have been in fruits and vegetables in the last decade. The European Union countries, Russia, and some Middle Eastern countries have been the main markets for vegetable and fruit exports. Small and medium-sized producers in the more commercialized regions have combined income from these often labor-intensive agricultural activities with employment opportunities provided by tourism and seasonal employment in other sectors (Keyder and Yenal 2011, pp. 60–86).

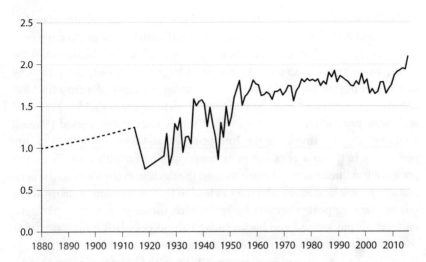

FIGURE 11.8. Agricultural Value Added per Population in Turkey, 1880–2015 (index in constant prices; 1880 = 1,0). Source: Based on national income and population series discussed in chapter 2 for the Ottoman era; national income accounts and population series from Turkey, Turkish Statistical Institute 2014 for the period since 1923.

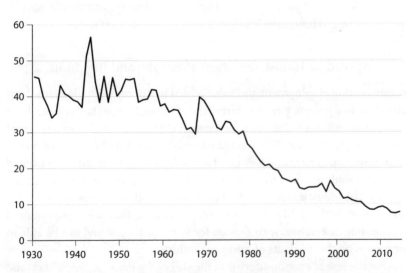

FIGURE 11.9. Share of Agriculture in GDP, 1930–2015 (in current prices and percent). Source: Based on national income accounts from Turkey, Turkish Statistical Institute 2014.

Turkey was a relatively underpopulated country and had plenty of uncultivated land during the nineteenth century and until the 1960s. As a result, it was not very difficult or expensive to increase agricultural production until the 1970s. These increases in output ensured that agricultural output could grow faster than population and meet the increasing per capita demand for food and also account for a large share of total exports (figure 11.8). However, land and labor productivity increased rather slowly during that period (Pamuk 2008, pp. 375–96; Imrohoroglu, Imrohoroglu, and Murat Üngör 2014, pp. 998–1017). In the new era since 1980, the adoption of neoliberal policies, the pressure from international agencies, and the decline in the share of the agricultural population have combined to lead to the elimination of many of the government support programs for agriculture. Increases in the value of agricultural output slowed and began to lag behind population increases after 1980. With the introduction of more labor-intensive crops, however, total agricultural output began to increase once again in the last decade (figure 11.8). Share of agriculture in total employment declined from 50 percent in 1980 to less than 20 percent in 2015. Most of these men and women are employed as unpaid workers in the more than 3 million small and medium-sized family farms. Share of agriculture in GDP similarly declined from about 25 percent in 1980 to less than 8 percent in 2015 (figure 11.9). Average incomes in agriculture continued to remain well below those in the urban economy.

Spread of Industrialization after 1980 and Its Limits

Manufacturing employment and value added in Turkey expanded rapidly, at rates close to 9 percent per year during the 1960s and 1970s (tables 9.1 and 11.1; figures 11.10 and 11.11). The manufacturing sector had a number of important shortcomings, however. It remained inward-oriented, and exports of manufactures remained very low. Geographically, industry remained concentrated in the Istanbul region, and more generally, in the northwest corner of the country. The industrial elites of that era remained strongly dependent on the government, seeking subsidies and tariff protection. They were also opposed to economic integration with Europe for fear that they would not be able to compete with the products of European industry.

After the severe economic crisis at the end of the 1970s, more market- and export-oriented economic policies were adopted beginning in 1980. The balance sheet of Turkey's policies during the era of globalization is rather mixed, however. Perhaps the most successful aspect of the new policies was the drive for exports of manufactures. Total exports increased from less than $3 billion in 1980 to $13 billion in 1990, $28 billion in 2000, and $160 billion in 2015. This rise is in part due to the decline in the value of the dollar against other leading currencies, but it also reflects a major expansion in the volume of exports. The ratio of commodity exports to GDP rose from less than 3 percent in 1980 to 16 percent in 2010. The increase was achieved almost entirely because of exports of manufactured products. Share of manufactured goods in total exports rose from 35 percent in 1980 to more than 95 percent in 2010. Equally important, a large share of Turkey's exports were directed to the European Union during this period. The share of the EU in Turkey's total exports has been above 50 percent since 1980 (figures 11.1, 11.2, and 11.5).

These increases in exports of manufactures were accompanied by the rise of new industrial centers after 1980. Industrialization thus gained momentum in provinces like Tekirdağ, Kırklareli, Sakarya, Balıkesir, Eskişehir, Manisa, and İçel because of their proximity to the centers of the import-substitution period such as Istanbul, Bursa, Kocaeli, İzmir, and Adana. In addition, manufacturing value added, employment, and labor productivity also increased faster in the new industrial centers of Denizli, Konya, Kayseri, Gaziantep, Kahramanmaraş, and Malatya than in the centers of the earlier era (Filiztekin and Tunalı 1999, pp. 77–106). The share of these new centers in Turkey's manufacturing exports has also been rising, although it is not easy to determine their exports from the official statistics. Nonetheless, the rate of growth of manufacturing value added has remained below 6 percent per year in the era since 1980, distinctly lower than the earlier period.

The industrial enterprises in these emerging centers were mostly small to medium-sized family firms with limited capital. They began production in the low-technology and labor-intensive industries such as textiles and clothing, food processing, metal industries, wood products, furniture, and chemicals. From the early stages, they have taken advantage of the low wages to turn to exports in the new centers. They also have been been employing workers with little or no social security or health benefits while local and national governments looked the other way. Low technology, the emphasis on labor-intensive industries, and low wages were all reflected in the productivity levels. Labor productivity in manufacturing in the new districts remained below the averages not only for the more established industrial areas such as the Istanbul region but also below the averages for the country as a whole.

The small and medium-sized enterprises in the new districts relied mostly on their own capital and informal networks. They often did not borrow from banks but tended to grow primarily through the reinvestment of profits, which perhaps explains their resilience in the face of the recurring boom and bust cycles especially during the 1990s. With time, these companies became increasingly more conscious of the importance of new technology. The more succesful enterprises, especially the larger companies, have been attempting to produce higher technology goods by adopting more up-to-date

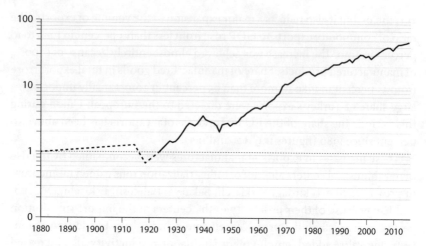

FIGURE 11.10. Manufacturing Value Added per Population in Turkey, 1880–2015 (index in constant prices; 1880 = 1,0). Source: Based on national income and population series discussed in chapter 2 for the Ottoman era; national income accounts from Turkey, Turkish Statistical Institute 2014 for the period since 1923.

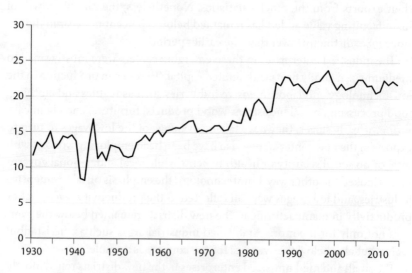

FIGURE 11.11. Share of Manufacturing Industry in GDP, 1930–2015 (in current prices and percent). Source: Based on national income accounts from Turkey, Turkish Statistical Institute 2014.

technologies. The extent to which or how rapidly these firms would be able to move on to the production of goods with higher value added, making use of a better educated labor force with new skills and to achieve increases in labor productivity, remained a key question. Without significant increases in labor productivity and shift to goods with higher skill content and higher value added, these companies were soon forced to compete in the international markets, and even in the domestic market, with the manufactures from China and from other developing countries with lower wages.

The JDP governments after 2002 did not provide a new vision or develop long-term policies of support for these manufacturing enterprises. After the rapid economic recovery and export growth of the early years, the JDP governments led by prime minister and later president Erdoğan chose to focus on politics and consolidating their power. Creating a new stratum of businessmen close to the party became a leading goal of economic policy. For these political goals, greater emphasis on large scale housing and infrastructure projects seemed a more attractive alternative. The construction sector rather than manufacturing industry emerged as the most popular means for enriching the business groups close to the government and the party.

The limits of the new centers of manufacturing activity thus need to be emphasized as well. Three decades after the adoption of the new policies and greater export orientation of the economy, the new industrial centers remained limited in number, and their shares in the total industrial production, industrial employment, and exports have remained rather low compared to Istanbul and the Marmara region. In 2010, 64 of the top 100 companies and 360 of the top 1,000 companies in terms of sales were still located in the old industrial centers of the import-substitution period, such as Istanbul, Kocaeli, Bursa, Ankara, and İzmir. In contrast, only 7 of the top 100 companies and 120 of the top 1,000 companies were located in the new industrial centers. The rather slow rise of the new centers was also connected to the less than stellar performance of manufacturing in Turkey in recent decades. Turkey was also hurt in recent decades by what Dani Rodrik has called "premature deindustrialization," a tendency for manufacturing industry in developing countries to begin experiencing declining shares in employment and GDP at lower levels of GDP per capita than did today's developed countries decades earlier (Rodrik 2015). Share of value added of manufacturing industry in GDP in current prices rose above 20 percent for the first time in the 1980s but has not increased further, fluctuating around 22 percent since (figure 11.11). The term "Anatolian tigers" used frequently in the 1990s in connection with the new centers thus appears to be an exaggeration in retrospect. Nonetheless, the social and political implications of these new industrial centers deserve further attention.

What a small number of Anatolian cities experienced in the decades after 1980 was a good example of industrial capitalism emerging in a predominantly rural and merchant society. The new industrialists were latecomers, both in their own regions and nationally. They were eager to establish themselves and take some power away from the earlier generation of business elites. In earlier years they had supported the Islamist parties led by Necmettin Erbakan, which were inward looking on economic issues and did not look beyond the Islamic world for international alliances. As Turkey's export-oriented industrialization proceeded and the customs union agreement established the EU as the leading market for Turkey's manufactures, their views began to change. After a group of politicians led by Recep Tayyip Erdogan broke off from Erbakan and moved to establish a new political party in 2001, the new industrialists offered critical support to JDP for its more moderate, outward-looking positions. The power of the big Istanbul industrialists was limited at the ballot box. In contrast, support coming from the owners and managers of small and medium enterprises from different corners of Anatolia proved to be more important on election day.

During its first term in office until 2007, JDP followed moderate policies and remained on track toward EU integration. It appeared friendly to large segments of the private sector and was supported by them in turn. Its export-oriented policies also received much-needed support across Anatolia from the business elites of these emerging regional centers. It thus appeared that an emerging middle class which benefited from globalization had played an important role in the rise of JDP as well as its market-oriented and pro-EU policies. Since 2007, however, both the political and the economic pictures have taken a turn for the worse. As the EU accession process ran into trouble and JDP moved to consolidate its power, few of the new or the old industrialists or other businessmen raised their voices in response to the deterioration of the institutional environment and the rise of authoritarianism. Along with the stagnation in exports, share of manufacturing industry in GDP has continued to stagnate. The new industrial centers were also not able to make much progress toward higher-technology, higher value-added products.

12

Economic Development and Institutional Change, 1980–2015

Economic Growth

There are important differences in the patterns of growth between the Bretton Woods era after World War II and the more recent period of neoliberal policies and globalization. The Bretton Woods era had provided more stable growth with limited fluctuations for most developed and developing economies. In contrast, with the significant exceptions of China and India, the long-term rates of growth for the developed and developing regions have been distinctly lower and fluctuations have increased for most countries since 1980. For the developed economies of Western Europe, the United States, and Japan, average annual rates of increase of per capita GDP were close to 3 percent from the end of World War II until the 1970s. In contrast, the same growth rates remained below 2 percent since 1980. In addition, the growing volume and fluctuations of international capital movements added a new source of instability, not only for national economies, but for the entire global economy as well. The Great Recession that began in 2008 led to a sharp decline in output followed by slow recovery in the developed countries. Moreover, even though the differences in average incomes between the developed countries have been declining, the distribution of income within most of the developed countries has become more unequal since the 1970s.

Most parts of the developing world did reasonably well and the variation of the growth rate between the developing regions of the world was limited before 1980. In contrast, while average, population-weighted rates of annual increase of GDP per capita in developing countries have exceeded 3 percent since 1980, there has been much greater variation between regions of the developing world in the new era. The averages of developing countries were pulled upward by the very high growth rates of South and East Asia, which include the world's most populous countries. In China, per capita incomes

TABLE 12.1. GDP per Capita in the World and in Turkey, 1980–2015

	GDP Per Capita		Annual Rate of Increase (percent)
	1980	2015	
Western Europe	13150	21000	1.6
United States	18600	30400	1.7
Japan	13400	22350	1.7
Developed Countries	14900	24700	1.7
Eastern Europe excl. Russia	5800	8600	1.3
Italy	13150	22700	1.6
Spain	9200	18350	2.0
China	1050	7500	6.7
India	940	3250	4.2
South Korea	4100	20000	5.4
Asia excl. Japan	1500	5900	4.7
Africa	1500	1950	0.8
Egypt	2100	4450	2.2
Iran	4000	6500	1.4
South America	5450	7150	0.9
Developing Countries	1920	5300	3.4
World	**4500**	**8100**	**2.0**
Turkey	**4750**	**11200**	**2.5**

Sources: Maddison 2007, pp. 375–86; Bolt and Van Zanden 2014, pp. 627–51; Pamuk 2006, pp. 809–28 for Turkey.

Note: GDP per capita are given in purchasing power parity (PPP) adjusted 1990 US dollars. For details, see chapter 2.

increased by more than 6 percent a year, while in the second largest country, India, the growth rate exceeded 4 percent. In Asia, excepting Japan, the average growth rate reached 4.7 percent. In contrast, in many countries of Central and South America, Africa, and the Middle East, the average growth rates of GDP per capita were 1 percent a year, or even lower (table 12.1 and figure 12.1). In addition, the Asian crisis at the end of the 1990s and the global financial crisis that began in 2008 created difficulties for many developing countries.

Turkey's long-term rates of increase of GDP per capita during the three decades after World War II had been close to but higher than the averages for the developing countries. In contrast, Turkey's average rates of increase of GDP per capita since 1980 have been close to but lower than the population-weighted averages for the developing countries as a whole. In the new era since 1980, Turkey's long-term growth rates have been higher than those of Latin America, Africa, and the Middle East but have lagged well behind those of the more successful and more populous countries in East, Southeast, and South Asia including China and India (table 12.1 and figure 12.1).

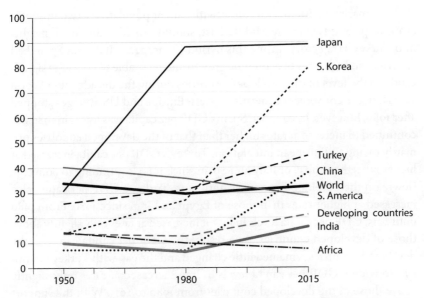

FIGURE 12.1. GDP Per Capita in the World and in Turkey, 1950–2015 (PPP adjusted and as percentage of Western Europe and the United States). Sources: Maddison 2007, pp. 375–86; Bolt and Van Zanden 2014, pp. 627–51; Pamuk 2006 for Turkey.

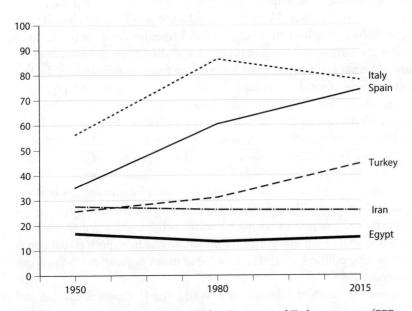

FIGURE 12.2. GDP per Capita in Four Other Countries and Turkey, 1950–2015 (PPP adjusted and as percentage of Western Europe and the United States). Sources: Maddison 2007, pp. 375–86; Bolt and Van Zanden 2014, pp. 627–51; Pamuk 2006 for Turkey.

A comparison with four countries with similar populations, two in southern Europe and two in the Middle East, should provide additional insights into Turkey's trajectory during this period (figure 12.2). Italy and Spain had experienced high rates of economic growth and were able to converge significantly to the level of the developed countries during the decades after World War II. Italy's convergence toward Western Europe and US averages stopped after 1980, however. In contrast, Spain's GDP per capita was lower in 1980 but continued to increase at rates higher than that of the developed countries primarily owing to European integration. Turkey's GDP per capita increased at higher rates than those of Italy and Spain since 1980, continuing to converge slowly on the developed countries until 2015. Turkey's GDP per capita also increased at higher rates than those of Egypt and Iran since 1980. From 1980 until 2015, GDP per capita levels in Egypt increased at rates only slightly above those of developed countries. As a result, the GDP per capita gap with the developed countries remained little changed and the gap with Turkey continued to widen. GDP per capita levels in Iran increased at rates only slightly above those of the developed countries from 1980 to 2015. With the support of oil revenues, Iran's GDP per capita had remained above that of Turkey during the decades after World War II but has fallen behind since 1980.

The proximate causes of growth will provide important insights for understanding the long-term trends in economic growth in the new era since 1980. In the decades after World War II, Turkey had attained unprecedented rates of growth by raising both its savings and investments rates from 11 percent of GDP in the early 1950s to 22 percent of GDP in the late 1970s. Investments in plant and equipment as well as education were financed primarily by domestic savings, even though as per capita incomes continued to rise after 1980, the savings rate did not rise. In fact, the savings rate, which averaged above 20 percent of GDP during the 1980s and the first half of the 1990s, then declined, first because of the public sector deficits and then because of the decline in the savings rate of the private sector to less than 15 percent of GDP for 2005–2014. As a result, the investment/GDP ratio of about 20 percent of GDP which was achieved in the earlier period could only be sustained by borrowing abroad after 1980. The growing dependence on short-term foreign capital inflows caused a significant increase in macroeconomic instability. The fluctuations in short-term movements of capital, arising from both global trends and domestic political instability, have led to major fluctuations in the economy since 1980.

As was the case in the decades after World War II, capital deepening and the shift of the labor force to urban areas have been the main sources of labor productivity growth since 1980. Urbanization and the shift of the labor force from the agricultural sector where they worked with lower productivity to the

TABLE 12.2. Basic Economic and Social Indicators for Turkey, 1980–2015

	1980	2015
Population (millions)	44.7	79.0
Urbanization Rate (%)		
Centers above 10,000 / Total Population	44	78
Life Expectancy at Birth (years)	59 (M: 57; W: 61)	76 (M: 73; W: 79)
Literacy Rate (%)	68 (M: 80; W: 55)	94 (M: 98; W: 90)
Average Years of Schooling		
of Adult Population over age 15	4.2	7.2
Share of Agriculture in Labor Force (%)	50	22
Share of Agriculture in GDP (%)	25	9
Share of Manufacturing Industry in GDP (%)	17	22
Exports / GDP (%)	4	15
Imports / GDP (%)	11	23
Investment / GDP (%)	22	20
Revenues of Central Government / GDP (%)	13	23

Source: Turkey, Türkiye İstatistik Kurumu (Turkish Statistical Institute), 2014 and 2016.

urban economy where they worked with higher levels of physical capital and were more productive had been one of the leading causes of productivity increases and economic growth in Turkey in the three decades after World War II. As the share of urban population increased from 44 percent in 1980 to more than 75 percent in 2015, the contribution of this sectoral shift to economic growth continued. It is estimated that as much as a third of the growth rate since 1980 has been due to this shift effect. However, the share of the labor force in agriculture has gone below 20 percent in recent years. Since the shift of labor from agriculture to the urban economy that began after World War II will be slowing down, this effect will inevitably decline in importance in the coming decades. In contrast, increases in total factor productivity continued to remain below 1 percent annually. In other words, most of the total increase and increase in per capita production was achieved not by increasing production per unit of input but through new investments and the accumulation of inputs, as has been the case in most developing countries (Atiyas and Bakış 2013; Saygılı, Cihan, and Yurtoğlu 2005; Altuğ, Filiztekin, and Pamuk 2008, pp. 393–430).

Low rates of total productivity growth during recent decades have gone hand in hand with the low education and skill levels of the labor force and the low technology content of manufactures. While some progress has been made since the nineteenth century, Turkey continues to trail world averages and the averages of countries with similar GDP per capita levels in terms of years of schooling as well as skills (figures 2.7 and 2.8 in chapter 2). The shortcomings of the education system have caused serious difficulties in the transition to an economy that can use and develop more advanced technologies. This pattern goes back more than a half century. When Turkey embarked on a new industrialization drive under the guidance of the State Planning Organization during the 1960s, the more difficult and higher technology branches of production were left aside under pressure from the large-scale manufacturers of the private sector. Instead of boosting research activities and developing the capacity to produce new technologies, partnerships were formed with multinationals in sectors that used higher technologies, and the technology was imported often entirely, as in the example of the automotive industry. The manufacturing industry has been reluctant to invest in branches of production that involve higher technology and require higher skills as they turned to export markets after 1980. As a result, manufactures with standard technologies continued to dominate the exports in the new era (Taymaz and Voyvoda 2012, pp. 83–111).

Income Distribution

Institutional changes at both the global and national levels played key roles in the evolution of the distribution of income since 1980. The rising influence of neoliberal economics supported by the governments of the developed countries and the international agencies tended to raise the power of capital and reduced the power of labor at the global level. Institutional changes that increased the mobility of capital while keeping in place the obstacles against the mobility of labor have worked in the same direction. Similarly, the extensive changes in political and economic institutions in Turkey that began with the military regime in the early 1980s and continued in later periods seriously eroded the power of labor as well as small and medium-sized agricultural producers and reduced their share in national income in comparison to the earlier era (Berik and Bilginsoy 1996, pp. 37–64). Growing imports of labor-intensive manufactures from East Asia have also put downward pressure on labor incomes in recent decades.

I will examine the distribution of income at the national level in this period in three stages: first, the distribution within the agricultural sector; then, the inequalities between agriculture and the urban economy; and finally, the inequalities within the urban economy. It needs to be emphasized at the outset that because of urbanization, share of agriculture was declining and share of the urban economy was rising rapidly during these three decades. The share of agriculture in the labor force declined from 50 percent in 1980 to less than 25 percent in 2015. Share of agriculture in GDP declined from 25 percent to 9 percent during the same period. In other words, while the distribution within agriculture had dominated the distribution of income at the national level during earlier periods, the differences between agriculture and the urban economy and the distribution within the urban economy mattered more with each passing decade. In this most recent period since 1980, the share of agriculture has declined further and the urban economy and the rising inequalities within it began to dominate the countrywide picture of income distribution.

In the absence of other evidence, especially for earlier periods, the key indicator for the distribution of income within the agricultural sector is the distribution of land. A relatively stable Gini coefficient around 0.6 suggests that the distribution of land did not change significantly since the 1960s. The inequality of the distributions by holdings and by ownership also changed little. While some large plots were being cultivated by small and medium-sized tenants, some of the small plots have been consolidated into larger holdings with the prevalence of tractors and other machinery in agriculture. The consumption surveys for rural households that have become available in recent years suggest a more equal distribution of consumption, but the limitations and problems associated with these household surveys need to be taken into account.

Differences in per capita income between agriculture and the urban economy have shown considerable fluctuations since 1980 due to political as well as economic causes. The large decline in the volume of price support programs and subsidies as well as the prices paid by the government during the military regime after 1980 and the Özal years that followed sharply increased the per capita income differences between the two sectors. After the return to a more competitive political regime and during the period of coalition governments until 2002, however, price support programs expanded once again and agricultural incomes recovered to some extent. The JDP governments since 2002 have once more reduced the use of price support programs, but the agricultural sector has been buoyed by the favorable movements in sectoral terms of trade going back to the end of the 1990s. Equally significant, the acceleration of rural to urban migration since the mid-1990s, in part as a response to the decline in agricultural support programs, has also played an important role in preventing the rural-urban differences in per capita income from rising. Despite the considerable migration flows, however, the urban-rural differences in average incomes have remained high (Boratav 1990, pp. 199–229; Boratav 2005; Keyder and Yenal 2011, pp. 60–86).

Large regional inequalities have been an important part of the income distribution in Turkey. Until recent decades, the private sector led industrialization concentrated mostly in the western third of the country. Market orientation of agriculture and development of tourism also proceeded further in the western and coastal regions. In addition to lower incomes, the eastern third of the country has also been lacking in infrastructure and services provided by the government, especially education and health. The rise of Kurdish insurgency in the southeast after 1984 further increased the large regional disparities, adding to the pressures for rural-to-urban as well as east-to-west migration. Many families of Kurdish origin, who fled the war or were forced to leave their villages, first migrated to cities in the region, and later to the cities in the southern and the western regions (Yükseker 2009, pp. 262–80; Aydın and Emrence 2015). The decline in the intensity of the conflict after 1999 helped the region recover economically, but the large-scale energy and irrigation projects that had been expected to turn the southeast into an important growth pole have so far fallen short of tinitial expectations. The resumption of the hostilities once again in 2015 suggests that economic development in that part of the country and the decline of the significant regional disparities hinges, above all, on a political resolution of the Kurdish question.

In the absence of other series on the distribution of income within the urban economy for the entire period since 1980, one basic indicator to begin is the ratio of urban wages to GDP per capita or average income in the urban economy. The available series indicate that after rising significantly during the decades following World War II, this ratio has been declining and urban wages have been lagging behind the increases in average income in urban areas since 1980 (figure 10.3 in chapter 10). While real GDP per capita in the urban economy approximately doubled from 1980 to 2015, the purchasing power of wages increased but by less than half during the same period. Around this broad trend of declining share of wage income in the urban economy, there were large medium-term fluctuations. The purchasing power of wages declined by about 30 percent during the military regime and the era of restricted politics that followed. With the arrival of a more competitive political regime and growing demands from workers at the end of the 1980s, wages recovered most of these losses only to decline again during the highly inflationary 1990s and the frequent economic crises. During the JDP era since 2002, urban wages increased, but they lagged well behind the increases in average income in the urban economy.

Since the 1990s a new source of data has become available for studying income distribution at the national level. These are the household consumption surveys conducted by the government agency, Turkish Statistical Institute (TurkStat). These surveys ask households the same set of questions as in other countries and follow a similar methodology in analyzing the responses. They indicate that in the 2000s, the top 20 percent group had an income eight times greater than that of the lowest 20 percent income tier. On the basis of the household responses to the surveys, TurkStat calculates a Gini coefficient of 0.4, suggesting that the household distribution of income and consumption in Turkey in recent years has been more unequal than those in western European countries but more equal than those in Latin America countries such as Mexico, Brazil, and Chile, or South Africa, and roughly similar to those in Iran, Portugal, Russia, and the United States. The results of the annual surveys also suggest that inequalities in the distribution of income in Turkey have decreased somewhat between the 1990s and the 2000s.

As is the case with the household surveys in many other countries, especially developing countries, however, one needs to evaluate these results with caution. One important reason is that all incomes and consumption expenditures are understated by the respondents in these surveys and this tendency is much greater amongst the higher income households. Households with highest incomes often refuse to participate in these surveys. In fact, there is growing evidence for Turkey as well as other developing countries that the household surveys do not accurately capture higher incomes. Since many recent studies emphasize that the share of the highest income groups is often the most important factor for determining how unequal income distribution is at the national level, underestimating that share can be a serious problem. It is highly likely that existing household surveys underestimate the degree of income inequality. As the recent studies have shown, it is also possible to estimate the share in total income of the highest income groups in the developed countries by studying their annual income tax statements. This option is not available in Turkey and in many other developing countries, however, because of the many loopholes legally provided to high-income groups as well as the poor or lax methods often used in the auditing of tax statements (Palma 2011, pp. 87–153; Milanovich 2016, pp. 46–117; Bourguignon 2015, pp. 47–73; Piketty 2014, pp. 237–429).

Another explanation for the apparent discrepancy between the decline in the share of wage incomes in urban areas and the more optimistic picture offered by the household surveys of consumption expenditures may be the government transfers to low- and middle-income groups. Various transfer programs were first launched in the 1980s by the conservative Prime Minister Özal and the Motherland Party governments in response to rising poverty in urban areas. With high inflation, recurring macroeconomic crises, and the armed conflict in the Kurdish region in the southeast, urban poverty probably reached its peak during the crisis of 2001. JDP governments after 2002 approached the issue with a combination of market-friendly measures and a conservative approach to charity. JDP governments preferred to direct assistance to poor families through civil society groups, local party organizations, and local authorities controlled by the party, as well as by religious networks and brotherhoods. Instead of well-defined formal programs, priority was given to informal networks and personal relations (Buğra and Keyder 2006, pp. 221–28; Buğra 2007, pp. 33–52). By reducing the budget deficit and the need for debt and interest payments, the JDP was also able to free up a large part of the national budget for education, health care, and infrastructure expenditures.

Role of Institutions and Institutional Change

Turkey's formal political and economic institutions as well as the global economic institutions underwent major changes after 1980. The military regime after the coup in 1980, the subsequent struggles toward a more open and inclusive political system, relations with the European Union, and the rapid slide to authoritarianism after 2008 all played important roles in shaping the formal political institutions. The formal economic institutions of the new era were initially shaped by the embrace of Washington Consensus principles and market-oriented policies. The new formal institutions introduced in 1980 were only the beginning and part of the story, however. In the following years, the formal political and economic institutions of the new era changed and evolved as a result of domestic politics and the changing distribution of power. Moreover, the extensive changes in formal institutions in the new era did not crowd out informal institutions but continued to interact and coexist with them. In fact, informal institutions played key roles in both politics and economic development during these decades, in rural and urban areas as well as in state interventionism. For a more nuanced assessment of the role of institutions in economic development since 1980, how new institutions emerged, and how they contributed to or hindered long-term economic development, it is thus necessary to examine both the formal and informal institutions as well as their interaction with domestic politics and changing distribution of power.

Turkey's democracy and political institutions have remained under pressure ever since the shift to a multiparty political system in 1950. The military coups in 1960 and 1971 gave the armed forces significant power over the regime and veto power on many issues. The coup of 1980 further boosted the power of the military. The 1982 Constitution brought in broad restrictions on freedom of thought and association and cast a long shadow on the political system that would last for decades. By prohibiting the prominent politicians of the 1970s from returning to politics, the military regime also caused a great deal of political instability. As a result, the 1990s witnessed a series of short-lived coalition governments in which both center-right and center-left parties competed primarily against parties occupying the same positions on the political spectrum rather than against those across the spectrum. The repeated dismantling of the main political parties by the military helped the rise of the

Islamist parties and resulted after 2002 in the consolidation of the rule of Justice and Development Party, which had Islamist roots. Even though civil society organizations began to get stronger, the internal structure and functioning of political parties continued to display hierarchical characteristics in the post-1980 environment of prohibitions and restrictions. Internal party democracy did not develop, and the power of party leaders continued undiminished thanks to both written and unwritten rules. From 1999 until 2005, when Turkey was formally accepted as a candidate for EU membership, major improvements were brought about in the political regime as political parties across the spectrum responded with major amendments to the 1982 Constitution, significantly broadening political and civil rights, including some basic rights for the Kurdish minority. Agreement on a new constitution proved elusive, however. After the EU essentially withdrew its promise of membership, however, Turkey's politics began to deteriorate. The rule of JDP became increasingly authoritarian, especially after it defeated the military and began to control the judiciary in 2010.

The military regime after 1980 was especially harsh on the Kurds, which made up an estimated 15 percent of the total population, most of whom lived in the southeastern part of the country. In response, an armed organization, Kurdistan Workers' Party (PKK), has been fighting since 1984, at times for autonomy and at times for independence. The historical roots of Kurdish nationalism and demands for autonomy go back to the Ottoman centralization drive in the nineteenth century. Kurds contributed to the struggle for a new nation-state after World War I, but they were suppressed violently when they sought greater autonomy during the Interwar period. Since the 1980s, Kurdish political parties began to be represented in parliament and the intensity of the fighting varied over time, but it did not stop entirely. The military conflict has had serious economic consequences not only in the rural and urban areas of the southeast but also across the country, as many Kurds were forced to migrate in the 1990s and violence often spread to other urban areas. Three decades of war with the PKK has led to the deaths of close to 40,000 people on both sides and has created a large fiscal burden as well (Kirişci and Winrow 1997; Aydın and Emrence 2015).

Global forces and institutions have also played important roles in shaping Turkey's formal economic institutions since 1980. The embrace of Washington Consensus principles and the adoption of new economic policies and institutions proceeded in two waves. Turkey's domestic politics and related economic crises rather than global developments determined the timing, with the first wave beginning in 1980 and the second in 2001. In each round, new policies as well as new economic institutions were adopted at a time of severe economic crisis and with the support of the IMF. Trade liberalization, the emphasis on exports, new exchange-rate policies, liberalization of the capital account, privatization, and other new policies and institutions all had important consequences for long-term economic growth and income distribution.

Initial changes in formal institutions were only part of the story, however. How the new policies and institutions interacted with existing institutions as well as domestic politics often held the key to understanding how and to what extent institutions changed and what kinds of new institutions emerged. The end result in both waves turned out to be rather different from what the original policies and institutions were supposed to achieve. In addition, the distribution of benefits from the enforcement of the new institutions and policies was not always in line with the existing distribution of power and changing politics. As a result, in many situations, powerful groups, including new governments and the central bureaucracy, resisted institutional changes or exerted pressure to ensure that an institution operated in a way that was different from the intended aim. The problem in these circumstances was not only that the enforcement capabilities of the state were weak but also that the new institutions were not consistent with the underlying power balances in society.

Of the new policies, trade liberalization, the emphasis on exports, and lifting of restrictions on international capital flows remained mostly intact since 1980. Perhaps the most important area where major differences emerged between what the new economic policies intended in theory and what actually happened in practice concerned the role of the state in the economy. The market-oriented economic policies were supposed to reduce the interventionism of the state in the economy. More than three decades later, the role of the state remained strong. While some important changes occurred in the relationship between the state and the private sector, government interventionism and discretion continued to decide the winners in the economy in the new era.

In the interventionist model of the import-substituting industrialization era, the state had played a central role in the economy, allocating scarce resources such as foreign exchange and often deciding on the winners. The disintegration of the system of protectionism and incentives and the emergence of retail relations between the state and the private sector in the 1970s had been much criticized, and it was then emphasized that this situation was an inevitable outcome of the model of industrialization through import substitution. With the adoption of the Washington Consensus policies in 1980, it was claimed that the role of the state in the economy would shrink and its old interventionist role would disappear. Under the new model, most of the ISI measures of support for industrial activity including sector-based policies were in fact scaled down and dismantled. Obstacles to foreign trade and controls over international movements of capital were lifted to a large extent.

The actual implementation of the new policies led to a different picture, however. The role of the central and local governments in deciding the recipients of subsidies, tax exemptions, as well as public sector contracts was not actually reduced. Many informal institutions that had been used in the earlier era continued to be used after 1980 to boost the private sector and benefit groups among those close to the government. Moreover, even when taking some of the most radical decisions, Prime Minister Özal often sprung into action without thinking much about the legal and institutional infrastructure that was necessary for the new policies. Since the new economic policies had not been tied to long-term rules, personal decisions and arbitrary behavior emerged in their implementation, instead of lasting and long-term rules. The new provisions were managed with a personal style and there were frequent changes of direction. Short-term political requirements emerged at the forefront as decisions were made. With the return to active politics in 1987 of the politicians banned by the military regime, Özal abandoned his reformist and innovative traits and embraced the most blatant examples of short-term measures designed to save the day. The arbitrary and individual decisions that were launched, as well as the favors and privileges that were distributed during this period, paved the way for far worse practices in the 1990s when political instability increased greatly and fiscal discipline collapsed (Öniş 2004, pp. 113–34).

Even though the role of government interventionism may have declined in theory and even though some of the earlier mechanisms for government support may have faded, government support for the private sector continued and the government remained central to deciding the winners in the economy in the new era. While protectionism and allocation of scarce foreign exchange, the much sought-after benefits of government largesse in the previous era, disappeared, low-interest credit from public sector banks, various tax exemptions, and subsidies continued. Privatization auctions and winning infrastructure and public procurement contracts from the government, both national and local, remained key mechanisms in the new era.

The new program devised after the economic crisis in 2001 represented a second stage in new economic policies. In addition to fiscal discipline, the program envisaged a new division of labor between markets and the state, at least in theory. The regulation and supervision of specific markets was delegated to newly established institutions, which were intended to be independent from the government (Öniş and Şenses 2005, pp. 263–90; Sönmez 2011). In its early years, when the goal of EU membership was still on the table, the JDP government chose to pursue a more rule-based style and tried to avoid favoritism among the business groups. Economic policies and their implementation were equally open to all groups in the private sector. The government also did not meddle with the institutional provisions of the 2001 program (Atiyas 2012, pp. 57–81).

As JDP began to consolidate its power after the 2007 elections, however, it abandoned economic policies that supported the private sector as a whole in favor of more discriminatory practices. While fiscal discipline was maintained as a key component of economic policy, the government began to undermine the independence of, and eventually controlled, the regulatory agencies established under the 2001 program. In an environment of growing authoritarianism, partisanship in bureaucratic appointments and the awarding of an increasing number of government contracts and other forms of support on the basis of political affiliations made clear to all that remaining close to the government mattered. In fact, promoting a new layer of conservative businessmen loyal to the party became a leading priority.[1]

Conservative business groups close to the JDP thus began to attain privileged positions in tenders launched by local authorities or the central government, as well as in the distribution of credits by public and private banks. Government influence over public sector banks and over the credit they provided increased in this period. In other words, in the era of neoliberal policies, when state interventionism was alleged to have become more limited, the capacity of the political power to decide who would profit in the economy, and how they would, was not reduced. In fact, the role of the central government and local authorities in selecting who would win and who would lose in the economy became steadily stronger. In an environment of growing authoritarianism, partisanship in bureaucratic appointments and the awarding of increasing number of government contracts and other forms of support on the basis of political affiliations made clear to all that remaining close to the government mattered. Attributing state and local authority tenders to progovernment companies are practices well known in Turkey. But the much

1. This broad trajectory of the content and quality of institutions is in line with the surveys and evaluations by various international organizations. International indexes designed to measure the quality of political and economic institutions have ranked Turkey close to or below the averages for developing countries in recent decades. In most of these indexes, Turkey's score and international rank improved from the 1990s to the late 2000s, but they have declined significantly since. The most recent indexes compiled by The Freedom House for 2016 indicate that after the Central African Republic, Turkey has experienced the second most extensive deterioration in basic freedoms during the previous ten years (Freedom House 2016). Also see the Democracy Index prepared by the Economist Intelligence Unit; Freedom Index prepared by Freedom House; World Governance Indicators prepared by the World Bank; the Rule of Law Index prepared by the World Justice Project; Corruption Perception Index is prepared by Transparency International; and the Competitiveness Index by World Economic Forum. Many of these indexes have components that provide additional scores and rankings.

longer tenure in power of the JDP, compared to the earlier periods, has caused much more extensive relationships to be formed between the government and the new business groups (Atiyas 2012, pp. 57–81; Buğra and Savaşkan 2014, pp. 76–176).

Institutions also played key roles in enhancing the ability of different social groups to solve their collective-action problems and pursue their common interests. Institutions of cooperation, organization, and conflict resolution are necessary not only for the state but also for social actors to function effectively in the defense of their interests. However, institutions can both contribute to and also impede the cohesion and strength of different social actors. The private sector in Turkey, especially since the end of World War II, has had a mixed record in organizing and defending its collective interests. It has been hampered by divisions along the lines of large versus small, secular versus conservative, and the pursuit of more narrow interests by these smaller groups. These cleavages have often made it difficult for different groups to come together and negotiate and cooperate. As a result, individual or small group interests organized around informal networks have often taken precedence over larger collective interests (Bianchi 1984; Heper 1991; Biddle and Milor 1997, pp. 277–309).

Along with rising political and social polarization, cleavages inside the private sector intensified. Fragmentation of the private sector between politically connected big business and the smaller companies, but also on the basis of social preferences, increased. The first voluntary organization of the private sector, TÜSİAD, consisting mostly of the owners and managers of the largest conglomerates, was established in 1971. However, TÜSİAD lacked the capacity to design and enforce well-defined rules of interaction with the public sector for its members. Both politicians and the well-connected large business groups distrusted pluralistic channels and prefered particularistic, clientelistic relations.

While the secular elites of large-scale businesses that had been favored in the previous era were being pushed out, the newly emerging conservative groups connected to the JDP benefited from government support. Beginning in the 1990s, new employers' associations like MÜSİAD and later TÜSKON sought to play the same role among conservative business groups that TÜSİAD had played as an umbrella organization for large-scale business groups since the 1970s. The new association of conservative businessmen, MÜSİAD, became increasingly powerful as its members gained the inside track on many government contracts, both national and local. It is not surprising that particularistic relations rather than rules-based support flourished under these conditions (Buğra 1998a, pp. 521–39; Buğra and Savaşkan 2014, pp. 109–49).

One of the key areas which tended to lose from these conditions was technology and industries with higher technological components. Individuals and firms often found it more expedient and easier to use their resources to stay close to and seek favors from the government rather than invest in education, skills, and technology to improve competitiveness in domestic and international markets. Such behavior certainly has led to some economic growth, but there were also limitations to the economic growth created under this model.

In comparison to earlier stages, later stages of industrialization required a different kind of state intervention and different kind of interaction between the state and the private sector. Later stages of industrialization put greater emphasis on skills, higher technology content, at least some innovation, and higher value added. In turn this stage necessitated higher capacity and stronger cohesion and organization on the part of both the state and the private sector as well as greater coordination and cooperation and greater information sharing between the public and private sectors. The interaction between the public and private sectors needed stronger and better-designed institutions. Similarly, the support for the manufacturers needed to be more selective and for selective activities rather than enterprises. A better educated, more skilled labor force was also an important condition. Without rules-based interventionism and due to informal channels of interaction between the public and private sectors, quality of both investment and output as well as the rates of increase in total factor productivity has remained low. In other words, while state interventionism has contributed to extensive growth in Turkey, it has been less successful in generating intensive growth.

Interaction between Formal and Informal Institutions

As rural to urban migration kept pace after 1980, many of the informal networks as well as power relations continued to flourish in the urban areas. As was the case in the earlier period, patronage, religious and regional solidarity networks as well as many other informal institutions developed further, interacting with formal institutions and creating new institutions in the urban areas. These informal relations played key roles for the recent migrants in securing housing, urban services, and employment. They also played prominent roles in the business activities of a rapidly growing private sector in the urban areas. With the rise in the political organization and power of the recent migrants, the role and power of the informal networks expanded as well. For winning smaller or medium-sized contracts from local or even central governments, for example, the support of these networks became an important asset (Erder 1999, pp. 161–72).

With increasing urbanization and the continuation of a competitive political regime, political patronage networks also continued to spread in the urban
areas. Political patronage responded to the needs of the poor, especially the
recent migrants, and of politics, and in the short term it also contributed to
economic development. The power and persistence of patronage relations
also prevented the emergence and development of more powerful institutions, however. All political parties tried to make use of political patronage,
but some were more successful than others. The JDP was especially skillful in
developing extensive networks among the recent migrants in the urban areas.
The in-kind aid distributed to voters by foundations, municipalities and civil
society organizations aligned with the local party organizations as well as by
charitable organizations close to the government, replaced the macro-
populism of the pre-1980 period. In addition, JDP developed programs in education, health, and mass housing aimed at low-income groups and the poor
(Sayarı 2014, pp. 660–63).

Overlapping to some extent with the networks based on localism were the
networks formed by religious ethnic communities, Sunni, Alevi, and Kurdish.
Heterogeneous in terms of class background, these networks reflected the
demands as well as the frustrations of the newly urbanized who suffered various kinds of inequalities, especially at the level of access to municipal services.
The use of networks of religious communities for economic purposes began
to gain strength in the 1980s when local and national governments began to
direct contracts to them. Individuals in the networks did not limit their activities to other people and companies in the same network. However, being part
of the same network created mutual trust and made economic relations easier.
In time, being part of these networks began to lead to significant advantages
in tenders launched by local authorities and the central government, as well
as in credit relations. By contrast, especially in small centers, individual or
companies that did not join these networks found it harder to survive.

Not all networks were equally successful in this competition, however.
Alevi and Kurdish organizations and networks have often been excluded or
have lagged behind. They have not had the same access to the central government even if they controlled some local governments. In contrast, the Sunni
groups have been generally more successful in securing access to national as
well as local governments. The Islamist parties were much better organized at
the grassroots level. The informal networks played crucial roles in the rise of
JDP to power. Many of the politicians who founded JDP came from these
networks and these relationships. From the first years of JDP government,
networks based on brotherhoods and religious communities gained more
prominence in the economy. The JDP era also saw increasing formalization of

some of the religious networks as they established their own holding companies involving large numbers of firms, banks, media companies, foundations,
and even labor unions. Most powerful among these was the Gülen network,
which remained the most powerful ally of JDP until a bitter fight for power
broke out among them in 2013.

Growth, Urbanization, and the Environment

From the 1960s, with economic growth as well as rapid urbanization industrialization, environmental problems began to increase in Turkey. The pressures
on the ecological system that built up in the following years were not limited
to the problems caused by urbanization and the industrial sector. With the use
of large amounts of chemicals and pesticides in agriculture, the pollution of
water sources above and underground, and the pollution of the soil, the ero-
sion, the salinization due to excessive water use, the deforestation or the opening of forests for settlement, the decline in biological diversity, the activities
of the tourism sector paying no heed to nature and the environment, fossil
fuel–based energy policies, and the rapidly growing emissions of greenhouse
gas, environmental problems grew deeper every year. Although air pollution,
which had become a very severe problem, particularly in the urban areas, was
overcome to a large extent thanks to the use of natural gas, the problem persisted in areas where industrial production was concentrated (Adaman and
Arsel 2005, pp. 1–11, 293–98; Aksoy 2005; Adaman, Akbulut, and Arsel 2017).

Partly under pressure from international agencies, comprehensive and detailed laws on environmental issues were prepared, and a large national bureaucracy began to be established in the 1970s. However, these formal institutions did not work by themselves but interacted with other formal and
informal institutions as well as interests and power relations. When it came to
enforcement, the national government and the local authorities were largely
indifferent to the implementation of the laws. As economic growth resumed
and large infrastructure investments and other construction projects were
launched in the JDP era, environmental problems gained urgency both in the
urban and rural areas. These problems were made more severe as JDP sided
with growth and the private sector in these conflicts. The increasingly authoritarian tendency of JDP in later years was reflected in environmental issues as
well. Instead of trying to deal with environmental issues and conflicts through
negotiation and compromise, the JDP opted to change the laws that it viewed
as obstacles. Various powers were transferred from local governments and
agencies and to Ankara in order to reduce or eliminate controls on the private
sector, remove obstacles, and overcome the opposition that developed against
infrastructure and commercial investment projects. In international negotia-

tions, instead of supporting the Kyoto Protocol, which sought to develop international cooperation on climate change and to set national quotas, the government tried to stay out of the process for as long as possible. Turkey signed the Protocol four years later in 2009 as the 185th party (Adaman and Arsel 2005, pp. 1–11, 293–98; Adaman, Akbulut, and Arsel 2017).

International indexes and comparisons show that, as a result of infrastructure investments, Turkey has made some improvements in recent years on issues falling under the heading of "environmental health," such as clean water, reduction of air pollution, sanitary cleanliness, garbage management, and waste treatment. The same international indexes also show that Turkey has regressed significantly in international rankings on biological diversity, the protection of ecosystems, the impact on the environment of inputs and technologies in the agricultural sector, and the development of clean and renewable energy sources. The numerous dams built on waterways, the large-scale energy projects, and the devastation wrought upon nature by tourism investments, and the removal of marsh and coastal areas from the zones under protection, are among the main reasons why Turkey has been lagging in international rankings on environmental issues. In the Environmental Performance Index prepared by Yale University for 2016, Turkey occupied ninety-ninth place among 180 countries (Environmental Performance Index 2016).

An important and related issue concerns the appropriation of urban land and rents created by rapid urbanization and economic growth since the end of World War II. Specific historical circumstances, most importantly the availability of large amounts of state-owned lands in urban areas, led to a sui generis solution to the housing problem for the migrants during the decades after World War II in Turkey. The migrants built their own modest houses, or gecekondus, on state-owned lands and eventually acquired formal property rights to these lands as well as obtaining from the local governments the infrastructure and other services to their rapidly growing districts. As a result, large segments of the population were able to claim at least a modest share of the urban lands rents and the growing economic pie. As state lands available for gecekondu production were being exhausted in the decades after 1980, the existing gecekondu owners were allowed to build bigger structures on their plots. The expanding urban rents were thus shared between small and medium-sized construction companies and the local residents. Formal rules regarding urban zoning and construction existed, but they were usually not enforced and were changed periodically to reflect and keep up with the changing conditions on the ground. When it came to enforcement, the national government and the local authorities were largely indifferent to the implementation of these laws. Formal institutions usually did not work by themselves in these settings but interacted with other formal and informal institutions as well as interests and power relations (Karpat 1976; Öncü 1988, pp. 38–64; Buğra 1998b, pp. 303–17).

Since 2002, JDP has carried the organization and distribution of urban rents to a new level. The Mass Housing Administration, a state agency that was established in 1984 to build low-cost housing, was given extra powers by legislation during the JDP era. The agency's operations expanded dramatically and became more opaque as it took over public lands or exchanged public lands for valuable private lands for building. Frequent changes were made in laws and regulations and zoning, and other regulatory powers of the local governments and local agencies were transferred to the agency and the central government in Ankara. In cooperation with large and medium-sized construction groups close to the government, the agency coordinated the construction of more than a half-million housing units until 2015, mostly for medium and higher income groups. Urban construction thus emerged as the most popular means for enriching the big business groups close to the government. Extensive networks of patronage relations characterize the relations between the government and the construction companies. Business groups not well connected to the government were excluded from these projects (Keyder 1999; Buğra and Savaşkan 2014, pp. 81–95, 109–49).

Human Development

Rapid increases in life expectancy at birth and years of schooling that began after World War II continued after 1980. Life expectancy at birth, which increased at the pace of one year every two years during the decades after World War II, continued to rise at about the same pace until 2015, increasing from 59 years in 1980 (61 for women and 57 for men) to 76 years in 2015 (79 for women and 73 for men). The continuing decline in infant mortality especially in rural areas played an important role in this trend. Nationwide, the infant mortality rate dropped from 125 per thousand in 1980 to 12 per thousand in 2015. In addition, adult mortality continued to decline in all age groups (table 12.2). Turkey thus began to make the transition from a society where a large share of the deaths were among infants due to infectious diseases, to a society where most deaths are among older people due to chronic illnesses such as heart disease and cancer. Because infant mortality has declined to low levels, increases in life expectancy will be slower and will depend more on the decreases in adult mortality in the coming decades (Deaton 2013, pp. 218–67). Economic growth, increases in the share of the national budget allocated to health care, urbanization, improvements in knowledge and health-care practices, and the increases in state capacity associated with these trends have all contributed to this outcome.

At the same time, however, access to health care remained uneven and the gains in life expectancy were distributed unevenly between age groups, urban and rural areas, regions of the country, as well as the rich and the poor. During the decades after World War II, most rapid declines in infant mortality and most rapid increases in life expectancy had occurred in the urban areas and more developed western regions. In the period since 1980, there has been some catching up by the rural areas and less developed regions in the east and southeast. In addition, rural to urban migration continued to bring down the national averages in infant mortality. Nonetheless, highest rates of infant and adult mortality continued to occur in rural areas in the mostly Kurdish southeast where both income per capita and levels of education, especially rural women's education, lagged well behind national averages. More than one-third of the population, especially those in the rural areas, most of the poor and unemployed had little access to health care. Those who went to public sector hospitals with limited medical staff and resources often faced long waits and could obtain only limited and poor-quality service. The AKP health-care initiative launched in 2003 made health care services more accessible and more widely available to lower income groups. Even though the new regime did not significantly improve the quality of health care, it earned AKP a great deal of political support, especially among the poor and lower income residents of the urban areas (Yılmaz 2017, pp. 149–66).

Life expectancy at birth rose strongly in most developing countries since 1950. In fact, not only Turkey but all developing regions with the exception of Sub-Saharan Africa experienced convergence in life expectancy toward the levels of developed countries as the gains due to the declines in infant mortality in the developing countries were greater than the gains in life expectancy due to declines in adult mortality in developed countries during these decades. For its level of GDP per capita, life expectancy at birth in Turkey during the decades after World War II was close to but slightly below the levels expected on the basis of its GDP per capita (Zijdeman and de Silva 2014, pp. 106–12). In the decades since 1980, however, life expectancy in Turkey increased slightly more rapidly than what would be expected on the basis of the increases in its GDP per capita. High levels of infant mortality in the earlier period and their decline since 1980 is probably the most important cause of this pattern.

Basic quantitative indicators of education such as years of schooling and graduation rates also continued to rise slowly in Turkey after 1980. The large gender differences in education that were so striking during the earlier periods began to decline as well. Nonetheless, because of the slow increases in the resources allocated to education and the persistence of many of the related institutions, Turkey continued to lag behind other developing countries with

similar GDP per capita in the basic indicators that measure inputs in education as well as educational outcomes such as reading and math scores.

The literacy rate in Turkey increased from 80 percent to 98 percent for men
and from 55 percent to 90 percent for women between 1980 and 2015 (table
12.2). Enrollment numbers and graduation rates have also increased for
school-age groups and for the population as a whole. By 2015, almost all of the
people in the related age group were enrolled in primary school, 60 percent
were enrolled in high school, and about 28 percent were enrolled in higher
education. Around 1980, 22 percent of the population in the age group graduated from high school and about 6 percent graduated from a four-year university. By 2015, more than 60 percent of the population in the same age group
graduated from high school and about 24 percent graduated from four-year
institutions of higher learning. Average formal schooling received by adults
over fifteen years of age increased from about 4.2 years in 1980 to 7.6 years in
2012. As world averages increased from 5.3 years to 8.0 years during the same
period, average schooling in Turkey remained well behind not only the developed countries but also the averages for Eastern Europe, Latin America, and
China, about the same level of those of Southeast Asia but above those of
Egypt, India, and Sub-Saharan Africa (van Leeuwens and van Leeuwen-Li
2014, pp. 87–97).

Unfortunately, most of the evidence on education is about the quantity of
inputs such as years of schooling and graduation rates rather than the outcomes in terms of what the students actually learn. As a result, we do not
know very much about the changes in the quality of schooling. Nonetheless,
some evidence has been emerging in recent years on the outcomes, thanks to
the reading and math scores in PISA tests administered by the OECD. These
tests indicate that the scores of students from Turkey lag behind not only
those from higher income countries but also those from developing countries with similar levels of income. In other words, while inputs have been
rising and more people are spending longer periods in school at all levels,
improvements in educational outcomes have not been very strong in Turkey
(OECD 2015).

One important reason for this pattern has been the low rates of investment
in education in Turkey compared to other countries. Public and private investment in educational institutions in Turkey have edged up from about 1.5
percent of GDP in 1980 to about 3 percent of GDP in 2015, but rates have been
well below not only those of developed countries but also those of developing
countries with similar levels of per capita income. Another reason for the poor
outcomes and slow improvements in skills has been the emphasis on quantity
such as classroom or enrollment numbers and the absence of a strategy based
on quality or outcomes. With the rise of the Islamist parties and growing po-

litical and social polarization in recent decades, the education system has been viewed as an ideological battle front and the curriculum at all levels has been changed frequently in recent decades. The JDP governments made several systematic efforts after 2010 to overhaul and Islamize the country's education system and introduce more Islamic content in science as well as social science and humanities topics at both elementary and secondary levels.

Moreover, increases in the quantity of schooling did not proceed evenly since 1980. Levels of educational attainment remained strongly linked to rural-urban, regional, gender, as well income differences. While average years of schooling increased among the rural population, they increased faster in the urban areas. Years of schooling also rose faster in the more developed western and coastal regions than in the east and southeast. In addition, differences in the quality of education between rural and urban areas, between more and less developed regions, and between income groups persisted and may have even increased, contributing further to the regional inequalities. The migration of the younger and generally more educated people from the rural to the urban areas gradually led to the rise in the average age of those that stayed behind, further widening the education gap between rural and urban areas. Those remaining in the rural areas thus tended to be somewhat older and less educated. In contrast, the most educated segments of the population tended to concentrate in the urban areas, especially in the largest metropolitan areas (Tansel and Güngör 1997, pp. 541–47; Kırdar and Saracoglu 2008, pp. 545–66; Kırdar 2009, pp. 297–333).

The quantitative indicators also show that the large gender inequalities of the earlier periods began to narrow since 1980, a trend that is observed in other developing countries as well. The numbers of female students increased from 80 percent of male students toward parity among elementary school students between 1980 and 2015. More strikingly, numbers of female students increased from 32 percent to 85 percent of male students among high school students and from 32 percent to more than 90 percent of male students among university graduates. As a result, average years of schooling for all adult women increased from 60 percent to 85 percent of those for men between 1980 and 2015. In other words, gender differences in education have diminished significantly among the young population but they persist among the middle-aged and elderly. The gender differences in schooling also persist in rural areas, in the less developed east and southeast regions, and among lower income households, and they remain an important cause of the relatively high infant death rates (Tansel 2002, pp. 455–70).

Inequalities in access to education have also been a result of differences in income levels, and access to good education continues to depend on income levels. In the decades after World War II, when public expenditures on education were still low, those who were able to proceed beyond elementary school mostly belonged to middle and higher income groups in urban areas. Nonetheless, public education still provided a strong means for social mobility for those from rural areas and low- and middle-income groups in urban areas. Both public and private expenditures on education have been rising since 1980, and the numbers of students receiving education beyond elementary school have been rising rapidly. However, demand for education has increased more rapidly than the public resources allocated to education in recent decades. Families began to supplement the education provided in public institutions with private expenditures and turned to private preparatory schools for help, especially for gaining a seat in the public universities. The educational expenditures of the various income groups thus began to diverge rapidly. It is estimated that in recent decades households in the top 20 percent income group have spent three times more on education than the next 20 percent income group, and thirteen times more than the households in the bottom 20 percent income group. The slow rise of public education expenditures and the growing disparities in private spending have thus led to growing inequalities in the access to quality education which, in turn, has reduced the role of education as a factor reducing intergenerational income inequalities (Tansel 2002, pp. 455–70).

The human development indexes calculated by the United Nations offer additional insights into Turkey's comparative human development performance in recent decades. These indexes also show that Turkey achieved improvements in both health and education but continued to lag behind countries with similar levels of GDP per capita. In 1980, Turkey ranked 55th among 125 countries in GDP per capita rankings but ranked 129th among 187 countries in health and 100th among 140 nations in education. Turkey was in 64th place among 107 countries in the 1980 rankings for human development, which included GDP per capita as well as health and education. A similar pattern emerges in the calculations and rankings made in 2010. Turkey was ranked 70th out of 187 countries in GDP per capita but stood at 77th and 120th place out of 187 countries for health and education respectively. Turkey was in 94th place among 187 countries in the HDI rankings for 2010 (table 2.2 in chapter 2).

Turkey's international ranking in human development improved between 1980 and 2010 primarily because of the rapid decline in infant deaths, which had been quite high for its income per capita levels, which also improved its ranking in health. In contrast, no significant improvement can be observed in the education rankings. One important reason for the low rankings in education is the inequalities between women and men. Even though women's enrollment ratios have risen significantly toward parity with men at all levels of education in recent decades, gender differences for the educational levels of adult population as a whole are still significant. Another important reason for Turkey's low rankings in health and education are the large regional inequalities and the low levels of health and education as well as per capita income in the southeast region, where the majority of the population is Kurdish. One of the recent country reports for Turkey prepared by United Nations Development Program shows, for example, that the top ten (out of 81) most developed provinces including Istanbul which are located in the western and northwestern parts of the country had HDI values close to those of East-Central European countries such as Croatia or Slovakia. In contrast, the poorest ten provinces located in the mostly Kurdish southeastern part of the country had average HDI values that were close to those of Morocco or India in the same year (UNDP 2004).

Gender Inequalities

Inequalities between women and men have political and social, as much as economic, dimensions. For example, the gender equality index prepared by the United Nations, aside from the inequalities in health and education, also pays attention to inequalities in membership in national and local parliaments as well as other public offices. In the United Nations gender inequality rankings for 2010, Turkey was placed in the middle in world rankings, in 77th place among 146 countries. As in the case of the human development index, this puts Turkey below the average of countries in its own income group (UNDP 2011).

As with other inequalities, there is strong persistence in gender inequality as well. I have shown earlier in the book that the roots of inequality between women and men in the field of education also go way back. Rates of literacy as well as schooling among women, especially Muslim women, remained very low, well below 5 percent during the nineteenth century. By 1950, when the literacy rate among men had risen to 47 percent, it was only 19 percent among women. The female literacy rate rose in the second half of the twentieth century and it reached 90 percent in 2015. Nonetheless, large gender inequalities at all levels of schooling persisted until recently. In 1950, the numbers of females that attended elementary school were 60 percent of the numbers for males and the same ratio was only 25 percent for high school and university graduates. In 1980, the numbers of females that graduated from elementary school were higher than 80 percent of the numbers of males, but the same ratio was still around 30 percent for high school and university graduates. Not surprisingly, most of the gender differences in schooling were among the rural and low-income urban households. In recent decades, however, the same gender ratio for elementary school students has approached parity, while the numbers of females that graduate from high school now exceed 80 percent of those for men and the numbers of females that graduate from university exceed 90 percent of those for men (Tansel 2001; Tansel 2002, pp. 455–70).

Before the nineteenth century, it was very rare for women to seek employment outside the home or the family farm. As production for market began to spread in the nineteenth century, women in urban areas started to work more outside the home. They were seen mainly as a cheap source of labor, especially for seasonal activities, and their wages remained much lower than those of men (Quataert 1993b, pp. 255–70). Nonetheless, differences in labor force participation rates between men and women remained limited until the second half of the twentieth century, as most women worked in agriculture. With the acceleration of rural to urban migration after World War II, however, rates of labor force participation of women began to decline. Most of the women who moved to the urban areas stayed at home, and only a small share of them started working outside the home. As a result, low labor force participation rates for women in the urban economy has emerged as one of the most striking dimensions of gender inequality in Turkey in recent decades. In 1990, less than 20 percent of women in the urban areas worked outside the home. In 2010, while the labor force participation rate was 70 percent among men in urban areas, it was only 30 percent among women in urban areas (figure 12.3).

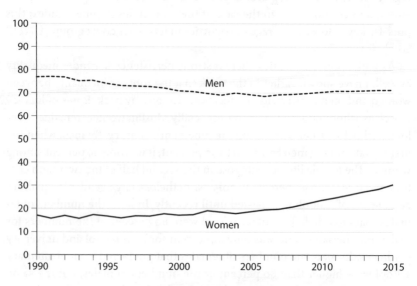

FIGURE 12.3. Labor Force Participation Rates in the Urban Economy, 1990–2015 (percent). Source: Official series from Turkey, Turkish Statistical Institute 2014.

The women's labor force participation rate in Turkey is not only lower than European countries, it stands below that of Middle Eastern countries with mostly Muslim populations. Low rates of labor force participation for women should not be seen only as personal choice. Many obstacles, some of them in the family, stand in the way of greater participation of women in the labor force. The causes should also be sought outside the home, in the fact that the economy has not been generating large numbers of jobs and the urban unemployment rate has been above 10 percent in recent decades, and governments at the national and local levels have not done enough to support female employment. In addition, these obstacles as well as opportunities of employment are distributed unequally. Participation in the work force is significantly higher among women with higher education. As the education level declines, so does the labor force participation rate (White 1994).

Institutions play a major role in the reproduction of gender inequalities as in the case of other inequalities. Moreover, yesterday's inequalities are strengthening the institutions that are creating and reproducing today's inequalities, as the latter are paving the way for tomorrow's inequalities. Institutions matter, but formal institutions are only part of the story. Formal institutions usually do not work by themselves but interact or work together with constellations of other formal and informal institutions. Moreover, some formal institutions can change very rapidly while others change slowly. How the reforms interacted with and adapted to other institutions often held the key to the outcomes. Educated urban women have been organizing and fighting for women's rights, and governments in Turkey have been adopting laws to address gender inequalities since the Young Turk Revolution in 1908. Primary education was made compulsory for girls in 1913. The public schools and some areas in civil service and the professions were opened in greater numbers to urban, middle-class women. In 1930 the political leaders of the secular republic granted women the right to partake in municipal elections. In 1934, women gained the right to elect and be elected to the national parliament. Educated urban women's participation in the professions rose significantly during the Interwar period and after World War II (Arat 2008, pp. 388–418). Yet the diffusion of formal political and other rights to the rural areas has been slow. The large differences in the literacy and schooling rates as well as opportunities between men and women persisted, especially in the rural areas. As rural to urban migration accelerated after World War II, these gender inequalities added to the existing inequalities in the urban areas.

The inequalities between women and men are not just creating inequality today, but by preventing a large part of the population from developing their skills, they are also preventing economic development. The contribution to the economy of a very large part of the population is limited to activities at home. Over time, as women become more educated, and especially if and when the pace of job creation picks up, urban women are expected to start working outside the home in larger numbers. In fact, available data suggest such a trend, albeit weak, has emerged in recent years. Nonetheless, the difference in the rate of labor force participation of men and women is still quite high (figure 12.3).

13

Conclusion

MOST COUNTRIES AROUND THE WORLD have experienced significant increases in per capita income and improvements in human development during the last two centuries. Turkey's performance in economic growth and human development has been close to and a little above developing-country and world averages during this period. In this book, I have established, for the first time, Turkey's record in a comparative perspective. I have also tried to explore why Turkey's performance in economic growth and human development has not been significantly better than the averages by examining both the proximate and deeper causes. Some of the answers may lie in Turkey's special circumstances, but others are relevant for many other developing countries.

Contours of Economic Development since 1820

For thousands of years, per capita production and incomes around the world had remained at low levels. Even if a society managed to raise incomes, these increases could not be sustained for long. That has changed with the Industrial Revolution that began in Great Britain in the second half of the eighteenth century. Economic growth has since become the key process that determines the wealth and poverty of nations. This book has examined economic growth and human development in Turkey during the last two centuries from a comparative global perspective. I have examined in both absolute and comparative terms Turkey's record in economic growth and human development. I have also attempted to provide an assessment of the causes.

I have shown that Turkey's rates of economic growth have been close to world averages in each of the four periods defined in the book and for the last two centuries as a whole. GDP per capita in the area within Turkey's current borders has increased approximately fifteenfold since 1820. The rates of economic growth were very different before and after 1950, however. Long-term rates of increase of per capita income remained below 1 percent per year until 1950. While Turkey did slightly better than the averages for the developing countries, the gap with developed countries widened significantly. The most basic reason for this pattern was the relatively rapid industrialization in Western Europe and North America, while Turkey as well as other developing countries stayed mostly with agriculture. Turkey experienced a spurt of industrialization and high rates of growth during the 1930s, but those gains were reversed during and after World War II.

As is the case for most developing countries, long-term rates of growth have been significantly higher since the end of World War II. As urbanization and industrialization picked up, annual rate of increase of per capita income rose above 3 percent, and per capita income increased more than sixfold between 1950 and 2015. Consequently, Turkey has closed the gap with the developed countries from about 1:4 in 1950 to almost 1:2 in 2015. Turkey's long-term growth rates have been higher than the averages for South America and Africa since 1950. However, the two large developing countries, China and India, and more generally East, Southeast, and most recently South Asia, have experienced significantly higher rates of growth than Turkey since 1980. While Turkey has not been among the top performers, neither has it been among the worst performers in any of the four periods during the last two centuries.

The improvements in health and education in Turkey since 1820 have been closely correlated with but not identical to that in GDP per capita. Improvements in health and education were slow in the nineteenth century but they picked up pace after World War I and especially after World War II. Life expectancy at birth in the eras within present-day borders of Turkey increased slowly until 1950 and much more rapidly since. As a result, the gap with the developed countries that widened until 1950 has closed significantly since, a pattern that is close to the averages for the developing countries as a whole. Turkey's experience with education shows a broadly similar pattern of slow improvements during the nineteenth century and more rapid improvements during the twentieth century, especially since the end of World War II. However, the basic indicators point out that Turkey has lagged behind not only the world averages but also the averages for the developing countries as well as the countries with similar levels of GDP per capita for most if not all of the last two centuries. One important cause of this poor performance has been the large and persistent gender inequalities. Another important reason for Turkey's low rankings in health and education are the large regional inequalities and the low levels of health and education as well as per capita income in the southeast region, where the majority of the Kurdish population live.

The most important proximate cause of the large divergence in per capita incomes between Western Europe and much of the rest of the world during the nineteenth century was the very different rates of adoption of the new technologies of the Industrial Revolution. A large part of the slow increases in per capita GDP in Turkey until World War I was due to the expansion of agricultural production for domestic and export markets. Rural households specialized more in agriculture by increasing their labor time and cultivating more land to produce more cash crops for markets. Technological change in agriculture remained slow, however. Mechanization in agriculture remained limited to small pockets of export-oriented production. Rising but low levels of state expenditures as well as the slow diffusion of new technologies also led to slow improvements in health and education during the nineteenth century.

A decade of wars beginning in 1912 led not only to the end of the Ottoman Empire but to a loss of close to 20 percent of the population within present-day borders of Turkey and a good deal of physical destruction with long-term economic as well as political consequences. After the Great Depression led to the collapse of agricultural prices, an important shift took place in economic strategy. Industrialization was embraced as the new engine of economic growth, and protectionism was adopted as the key economic policy for this purpose. Rates of investment mostly in manufacturing and more generally in the urban economy, financed almost entirely with domestic savings, averaged 10 percent of GDP during the 1930s. Share of state revenues and expenditures in GDP as well as state capacity continued to rise slowly. Agriculture, which continued to employ close to 80 percent of the population, turned inward and remained insulated until after World War II.

One proximate cause for the rise in the long-term growth rate after World War II was the beginning of rapid urbanization and the shift of the labor force from agriculture to the urban economy, where they worked, on average, with higher levels of physical capital and higher productivity. More than a third of all the increases in labor productivity and per capita income achieved in Turkey since 1950 have been due to the shift of labor from the low-productivity agricultural sector to the more productive urban economy. Share of agriculture in total employment declined from 75–80 percent in 1950 to less than 20 percent in 2015. Share of agriculture in GDP similarly declined from 42 percent in 1950 to 8 percent in 2015. Shares of the manufacturing industry in both employment and GDP rose during the decades after World War II. Since 1990, however, shares of manufacturing industry stagnated while shares of services in total employment and GDP continued to rise. Another reason for the higher rates of growth after 1950 has been the higher rates of investment in physical capital, which increased from about 10 percent in 1950 to more than 20 percent until the 1970s. Most of this investment was financed with domestic savings. In the more recent period since 1980, however, the aggregate savings rate did not rise any further and declined significantly since the turn of the century. As a result, a rising share of investments began to be financed mostly with short- and medium-term foreign capital inflows, which emerged as an important source of macroeconomic instability.

Another potential source for the increases in productivity in both agriculture and the urban economy was the more efficient use of the existing resources, in other words, increases in total factor productivity. As was the case in most developing countries during this period, however, total factor productivity increases remained limited in Turkey since World War II, at around 1 percent annually. In other words, a large part of the productivity increases since 1950 have been due to the accumulation of more inputs, especially physical and to a lesser extent human capital. While rates of physical capital formation in Turkey since World War II have been close to the averages of other countries with similar levels of per capita income, rates of human capital formation lagged behind. The technology and skills content of Turkey's exports and more generally production also remained low in comparison to other non-oil countries with similar levels of per capita income.

Role of Institutions

There is growing recognition in recent decades that rates of investment and rates of productivity are not exogenous but are determined by the social, political, and economic environments as well as historical causes. While research is still at early stages, institutions or rules and their enforcement are now considered to be more fundamental determinants of economic development and of long-term differences in per capita GDP between countries than rates of physical and human capital accumulation or research and development themselves. There is increasing agreement that more complex and advanced forms and innovations that lead to increases in productivity can only emerge if institutions in a society encourage and support activities in that direction.

At its broadest, the new literature is an attempt to shed light on how economic behavior and outcomes are mediated by the institutional setting in which they take place. The interaction between institutions and economic change, technology, politics, social structure, distribution of power, beliefs, ideologies, and expectations work both ways. Institutions influence the others but are also influenced by them. Similarly, institutions shape behavior and relations among the various actors and, in turn, are shaped by them. The emphasis on the role of institutions also should not deny the role of broad political and social forces such as classes or groups and individual actors that shape the outcomes. Institutions thus influence behavior, but they are not the sole cause of outcomes. As a result, however, it is not easy to isolate the effect of institutions on economic development. The analysis of the role of institutions is more complicated and the case for attributing economic growth to institutions alone is weaker because institutions are endogenous and are influenced by economic change as well as the other variables. Nonetheless, to acknowledge that institutions are influenced by the other variables does not imply that institutions do not matter or that they have only limited impact on economic performance.

One recurring explanation focuses on Islam as the key to societies in the Middle East and the primary cause of economic stagnation in the region. As part of this tradition, recently it has been argued that even though Islamic law initially provided the Middle Eastern societies with effective legal regimes that encouraged trade and economic development, some features of Islamic law prevented more complex, impersonal, and flexible organizational forms in later centuries. There are many examples where Islam and Islamic law appear to have played an important role in the shaping of institutions in the Middle East. However, Islamic law was not an unchanging and autonomous sphere in the Ottoman Empire. The society and the government played a prominent role in shaping the law. There is a large body of evidence indicating that, when the need or demand was present and when power relations allowed, Islamic societies often circumvented or adapted those religious rules that appear to prevent change, including economic change. Moreover, others have argued that it is not the unique aspects of Islam that are ultimately responsible for the unfavorable political and economic outcomes. In fact, it has been politics that tends to dominate and use Islam. Rulers in Muslim countries have tried to manipulate the many interpretations of Islam in order to acquire political support. When rulers tried to use Islam for political support, they were more likely to adopt policies against change.

While not denying the role of culture, this book has focused on an interest-based explanation instead. I have argued that for understanding the role of institutions in economic development in Turkey, it is necessary to understand how the formal and informal institutions interacted and created pressures for institutional configurations that contributed to or prevented economic development. This interaction has not been one-sided: formal institutions exercised causal pressures on informal institutions, and the latter, often built from the bottom up, influenced the path of formal institutions. Moreover, both formal and informal institutions have also interacted with economic development and social structure.

There was some popular support and also support among the elites, but a large part of the formal institutional changes Turkey experienced during the last two centuries, especially those in the earlier period, have been top-down. The reform program called Tanzimat was launched not by the civilian or economic elites but by the Ottoman central government. These institutional changes remained selective and reflected, above all, the interests and priorities of the state and the state elites. Top-down institutional changes were continued after the end of the Ottoman Empire and the emergence of Turkey as a new nation-state following World War I. The radical modernizing reforms of the new republic were built upon the secularization of state, law, and education begun one century earlier. As urbanization began to gain momentum after World War II, the political elites opened politics to greater participation and competition with the transition to a multiparty system. Yet, a series of military coups in the following decades ensured that the military and civilian state elites closely controlled the political system, guarding secularism and restricting political freedoms including the rights of the Kurdish minority. More recently, a new political party led by Islamist elites defeated the military, but rather than opening the system to the participation of other segments of society including the economic elites, it moved increasingly toward authoritarian and personal rule.

Turkey's formal economic institutions and economic policies also experienced a great deal of change during the last two centuries. The formal economic institutions as well as economic policies adopted by the governments have been influenced by international political developments as well as international or global rules such as free trade, the Bretton Woods system, and Washington Consensus principles. Proximity to Europe meant not only that the Ottoman Empire maintained close economic relations with Europe, but it also began to experience the impact of the Industrial Revolution early. When the Ottoman elites decided to respond to European military and economic advances, they adopted a program of institutional changes along European lines. In exchange for the support of the European states for the reforms, the government agreed to pursue laissez-faire policies and kept the economy open to foreign trade and foreign investment. The economic institutions of this period were shaped to a large extent by the bargaining between the central government and the European states.

The influence of international political developments and international economic institutions on domestic economic institutions and policies continued in the twentieth century. The global conditions after World War I allowed the new nation-state under a new leadership to try to create a national economy within the new borders. Protectionist and inward-looking policies continued after World War II as industrialization began to be led increasingly by the Muslim-Turkish private sector. After 1980, economic policies and institutions of the inward-looking industrialization era were abandoned in favor of Washington Consensus principles, most importantly, greater emphasis on markets, liberalization of external trade, and finance and privatization. Turkey's close relations with Europe continued after World War II. In the 1980s, governments in Turkey began to express the desire to join the European Union by completing a long list of political and economic reforms. The customs union agreement in 1994 facilitated greater economic integration with the European Union. Negotiations for membership formally began in 2005 but Turkey's candidacy faded after governments in France and Germany turned against it.

These extensive changes in formal political and economic institutions played important roles in bringing about significant increases in per capita income as well as major improvements in health and education during the last two centuries. Changes in the formal institutions were only part of the story, however. For understanding the role of institutions, it was necessary to understand how the formal and informal institutions interacted and how new formal institutions adapted to informal institutions and what kinds of new institutions emerged. In addition, it was necessary to examine how the institutions interacted with economic change, social structure, distribution of power, and expectations to determine whether the institutional configurations that emerged were growth-enhancing or growth-inhibiting.

The informal institutions arrangements continued to coexist with and often substituted for the new formal institutions during the nineteenth century and the first half of the twentieth century. With more rapid urbanization and economic growth after World War II, the fiscal, administrative, and legal capacities of the state also increased. But these developments did not mean the disappearance of the informal institutions. On the contrary, regional solidarity, patronage, and religious networks, as well many other informal institutions, developed further and flourished in the urban areas since 1950. Examples provided in the book from various areas ranging from the spread of education in rural areas to efforts to secure housing and access to local government services by recent migrants in urban areas to the organization of the private sector to the relations between the private sector and the government and more generally the workings of state interventionism in the economy have made clear that the informal institutions continued to play important roles in the economy. These examples also illustrated why formal and informal institutions continued to coexist and showed the long-term consequences of their interaction. They proved not only that the informal institutions continued to play important roles in the economy but also that the new formal institutions functioned differently as they interacted with the informal institutions as well as with social structure and the distribution of power.

There is a good deal of evidence that informal institutions have made important contributions to economic growth and human development. It is also true, however, that many informal institutions are typically based on social networks with clearly defined borders. In later stages of economic development, when more complex organizations are necessary to further increase value added and per capita income, some of those informal institutions designed to serve small groups and often the elites of smaller groups have become obstacles in the way of further economic development by preventing greater integration between different groups and making it more difficult to bring together the resources and skills of people from different backgrounds. Some informal institutions have also added to the cleavages between different groups and contribute to political instability rather than bringing about greater cooperation and integration. As a result, raising value added per person and achieving higher levels of total factor productivity have often become more difficult, especially at higher stages of economic development.

Cleavages

The changes in formal and informal institutions have brought about a good deal of economic growth and development. By themselves, however, they cannot explain the overall pattern of economic growth and development during the last two centuries. This is because of the two-way interaction between institutions and economic growth as well as the two-way interaction between institutions and social structure. Formal and informal institutions have influenced economic outcomes and, in turn, economic outcomes have influenced the institutions. The two-way interaction between social structure and institutions has also been important. Institutions have shaped social structure not only through their influence on the economic outcomes but also directly through their influence on the behavior of various actors as well as the relations among these actors. In turn, the social structure made up of many groups with diverging interests, with cooperation as well as cleavages between them, influenced the institutions. When these differences were not handled well, the result has often been political and economic instability with significant implications for economic development.

In Turkey since the nineteenth century, class cleavages have always mattered, and their intensity varied over time. Equally important and at times more important have been the identity cleavages between the social groups and also between their elites. Exact configurations have changed over time but coalitions and cleavages have continued between Muslims and non-Muslims, between secular and conservative elites, between Turks and Kurds since the Tanzimat reforms of the nineteenth century to the present. In each period, the interests of the various elites as well as the alliances and the cleavages were also influenced by the global institutions and the economic models and policies allowed by the global economic system. I have examined in the book how these coalitions and cleavages have been influenced by the formal institutions, and, in turn, how they have shaped not only the formal institutions but also the informal institutions as well as the pattern of economic growth and development.

The identity cleavages made it more difficult for alliances and coalitions to emerge between the different elites. The cleavages also had negative consequences for state capacity and the ability of the state to enforce the formal institutions. Reaching an understanding if not consensus between the different elites, including the state elites, and harnessing their different powers and capacities as well as dealing with various collective-action problems were critical for the successful enforcement of the new institutions not only at the macro level but also at the micro level. If the distribution of benefits from an existing institution or a new institution was not consistent with the existing distribution of power in society, the various elites could mobilize, bargain, and put pressure on others as well as the state to try to bring formal and informal institutions back into line. In these conflicts, the competing elites often made use of informal institutions including identity-based networks and patron-client relations.

Even though the exact configurations between the various elites and their relation to state elites changed over time, the weakness of the economic elites and their dependence on the state elites dating back to the Ottoman era persisted. The centralizing reforms of the nineteenth century were designed and initiated mostly by the state elites. Some elites in the provinces supported the reforms, but many others opposed them. The reforms were also supported by European states who demanded an open economy specializing in agriculture and offering privileges to European companies. The main beneficiaries of these changes were the state elites, European states and companies, and the non-Muslim merchants who lived in the port cities. In contrast, the urban notables and other elites in the provinces who had gained power by keeping a large share of the tax revenues in the earlier centuries experienced a decline in their wealth as well as political power. As a result, the reforms were met with resentment by the Muslims who dominated the agricultural towns in the interior with growing commercialization of agriculture and the spread of private landownership. The Muslims in the interior began to unite in response to the growing economic cleavages, often by making use of religious networks and other informal institutions. The centralizing reforms and the growing presence of the central government were also resisted by the Kurdish tribal leaders in Eastern Anatolia. In other words, the centralizing reforms and the opening of the economy to globalization were accompanied by the rise of identity cleavages. The emerging center-periphery duality in the nineteenth century thus had economic roots and was not a purely cultural phenomenon.

The end of the Ottoman Empire and the formation of a nation-state under new leadership after World War I led to important changes in political and economic institutions, but the cleavages between the elites persisted. The War of Independence from 1920 to 1922 was supported by a broad coalition of the provincial notables, merchants, landowners, and religious leaders. After abolition of the sultanate and the caliphate and the proclamation of the Republic, however, Mustafa Kemal and his close associates began to eliminate the opposition and adopted a narrower secular line. The prohibition of the activities of religious orders and networks suppressed but did not entirely eliminate their activities in the provinces. The uprisings by the Kurds in southeastern Turkey were also defeated. The state elites of the new republic responded to the Great Depression and the fall in agricultural prices by adopting protectionism and the state-led industrialization strategy. Rising inequalities between the countryside and the urban areas where the new elites lived reinforced the use of religion and cultural values in opposition. The embrace of Islam and the spread of informal networks in response to the centralizing reforms of the secularist elites that began in the nineteenth century thus continued in the Interwar era. Although a number of the notables were integrated into the ranks of the Republican People's Party, the cultural as well as economic disconnect between the conservative peasantry and the secularizing policies of the new regime at Ankara persisted.

With the transition to a multiparty parliamentary system and competitive elections after World War II, it became possible not only for big landowners, merchants, and industrialists, but also for the large numbers of small and medium-sized agricultural producers, to make their preferences heard. With rapid rural to urban migration, patronage, regional and religious networks, as well as many other informal institutions which already existed in the urban areas developed further and flourished, interacting with formal institutions and creating new institutions. Political parties such as the Democrat Party and its successor, the Justice Party, benefited from the skillful use of patronage networks and successfully carried these relationships and the existing cultural and economic cleavages to the urban areas, mobilizing conservative rural population and migrants against the secular elites and the bureaucracy. The minority Alevis and Kurds also began to organize, but the majority Sunni religious networks were more effective during these decades. Informal networks based on Sunni religious communities played key roles in the rise of new political parties with Islamist roots.

While these cleavages and the competition between different elites undermined state capacity, the state elites, both the military and the bureaucracy, remained key players as they pursued their own interests by themselves or in cooperation with other elites. The military coups in 1960, 1971, and 1980 returned power to the secular military elites and the bureaucracy and made them leading partners in the ruling coalition with veto powers on many key issues. Periods of military rule also served as reminders of the continuing cleavages between the urban secular elites and the conservative rural elites. The secular business elites were the main beneficiaries of government interventionism as the private sector began to lead the economy under protectionism and domestic market–oriented industrialization.

Turkey's formal political and economic institutions as well as the global economic institutions underwent major changes after 1980. The coup of 1980 and its new constitution brought in broad restrictions on basic freedoms and further boosted the power of the military. By prohibiting the prominent politicians of the earlier era from returning to politics, the military regime caused the fragmentation of the party system and added to political instability. The rise of Kurdish nationalism and the ongoing military conflict in the Kurdish southeast region after 1984 also contributed to the political cleavages. Along with the rise of political Islam after the military coup, cleavages inside the private sector not only between politically connected big business and the smaller companies but also on the basis of social preferences intensified. After a severe economic crisis, a new party with Islamist origins came to power, promising to bridge the divide between the secularists and the conservatives as well as the Turks and the Kurds. Religious networks and other informal institutions played key roles in the JDP's rise to power.

Politicians always used Islam to gain support among the voters, but in the period after 1980 and especially after they began to control the government in 2002, the Islamist politicians carried this method to new levels. Along with rising political and social polarization, cleavages inside the private sector deepened further not only between politically connected big business and the smaller companies but also on the basis of social preferences. While the secular business elites that had been favored in the previous era were pushed out, the newly emerging conservative groups connected to the JDP benefited from government support. Supported by an electoral majority, the JDP moved against the military and the judiciary in later years and began to change the political institutions in order to create a powerful executive branch. In the process, the party and especially its leader used and exaggerated the identity cleavages in order to consolidate and tighten their grip on power.

The frequent military coups and the recent slide to authoritarianism suggest that Turkey's political institutions and the multiparty political system since 1950 have not been able to handle these cleavages very well. The persistence of the cleavages and recurring periods of political instability, in turn, have had adverse consequences for economic development both in the short and the longer term. In the absence of an understanding if not consensus between the elites, including the state elites, different powers and capacities of the state remained weak. The problem has not been just that state capacity or the capabilities of the formal agencies charged with enforcement duties was weak. Political order, which depends on the degree of understanding and consensus between different groups in society regarding basic rights, how to resolve conflicts, and the behavior of the state about the rules and their enforcement, is a necessary condition for political and economic development. In the absence of such an understanding if not consensus, the competition between elites and their relations with the state could always threaten the political order. By changing the expectations and beliefs, increasing political instability and political disorder could cause political and economic actors to behave very differently.

State Interventionism

The role of institutions and the key role played by the interaction between formal and informal institutions were also evident in the success and limitations of state interventionism, and more specifically, state interventionism in support of industrialization in Turkey. State interventionism has certainly contributed to economic growth during the twentieth century, especially since 1929. The low rates of total factor productivity growth and no more than average rates of economic growth in the long term suggest, however, that state interventionism has had a mixed record in Turkey. Formal and informal institutions played key roles in enhancing or limiting the ability of different social groups to solve their collective-action problems and pursue their common interests. Institutions could contribute and also impede the cohesion and strength of different social actors. Institutions of cooperation, organization, and conflict resolution were necessary not only for the state but also for social actors to function effectively in the defense of their interests.

Despite the tradition of a strong state going back to the nineteenth century and even earlier, the public sector often lacked the cohesion and autonomy from both the politicians and the private sector to implement coherent, rules-based policies. With the adoption of etatism, new institutions were created to support a Muslim-Turkish private sector during the Interwar period. As this private sector began to take control of the economy after World War II, the institutions of state interventionism expanded. The absence of a cohesive and stable bureaucratic structure and a poorly organized private sector often dependent on the public sector and the politicians have made it very difficult to develop regularized ties and institutions of consultation and cooperation between them. In the absence of consultation and cooperation, the public-private sector ties have been pushed into ad hoc and personalized rather than institutionalized channels. Informal networks and institutions as well as bilateral relations persisted. Without rules-based interventionism and due to individualized channels of interaction between the public and private sectors, quality of investment and output as well as the rates of increase in total factor productivity have remained low.

More broadly, the degree of success of state interventionism has been closely related to the relations between the competing elites and the state in Turkey. The configurations between the competing private and the state elites have changed over time, but the cleavages and weak state capacity have persisted. The problem has not been just that state capacity or the capabilities of the formal agencies charged with enforcement duties was weak. Reaching an understanding if not consensus between the elites including the state elites and harnessing their different powers and capacities were critical for the successful enforcement of the new institutions both at the macro and micro levels. When the distribution of benefits from an existing institution or a new institution was not consistent with the existing distribution of power in society, the various elites could mobilize, bargain, and put pressure on others as well as the state to try to change the formal institutions or reverse the policies. They often chose to develop formal and informal institutions different from those defined by the state that will serve their interests better, including identity-based networks and patron-client relations.

As has been the case in most developing countries, total factor productivity increases in Turkey have remained below 1 percent annually since the end of World War II. Moreover, a large part of the increases in total factor productivity have been due to urbanization and the shift of labor from low-productivity agriculture to the higher-productivity urban sector. In other words, most of the total increase and increase in per capita production was achieved not by increasing production per unit of input but through new investments and the accumulation of inputs. Analysis of the role of institutions has helped us understand not only why long-term economic growth in Turkey has been above zero but also why it has not been much higher than the long-term averages. The persistence of cleavages between elites, recurring periods of political instability, the use of informal networks designed for small groups, and often the elites of small groups as well as the mixed outcomes associated with state interventionism have made it more difficult to bring together the resources and skills of people from different backgrounds and develop more complex organizations using more advanced technologies. In addition, while some progress has been made since the nineteenth century, Turkey continues to lag behind world averages and the averages of countries with similar GDP per capita levels in terms of years of schooling as well as skills acquired at different levels of schooling. The shortcomings of the education system have also made it more difficult to move up the ladder toward the production of goods with higher technology content and toward higher technology sectors with higher value added. As a result, many individuals and firms continue to find it more expedient to use their resources to stay close to and seek favors from the government and the state elites rather than invest in education, skills, and technology and pursue long-term gains in value added and productivity.

Turkey and Other Developing Countries

This book has examined economic development in Turkey during the last two centuries from a comparative global perspective. I constructed long-term GDP per capita and other series and established for the first time Turkey's record in economic growth and human development in both absolute and relative terms. Turkey is one of the larger developing countries. It had many features common with other developing countries, including a similar trajectory of economic development during the last two centuries. Early in the nineteenth century, when the Industrial Revolution began to gain momentum in northwestern Europe, significant differences in per capita incomes already existed between Turkey and northwestern Europe. Industrialization did not really begin in Turkey until the 1930s. In each of the four historical periods I have examined in the book, governments in Turkey pursued economic policies consistent with the most common strategy of economic development at the time. Like other developing countries, Turkey's institutions and economy have received their share of influences from the outside. Moreover, Turkey's long-term economic performance has been close to both the world and developing country averages during the last two centuries. For these reasons, one could argue that in contrast to the more successful and better known developing countries, Turkey is a more representative case and offers more insights into the experiences of other developing countries.

The case of Turkey during the last two centuries had many things in common with other developing countries. It also had a number of important special features. Turkey was not particularly rich in mineral reseources or oil. Aside from brief occupation of parts of the country after World War I, Turkey did not experience colonial rule. The area within the present borders of Turkey was part of a large, multiethnic empire until the end of World War I. As a result, Turkey's institutions and economy were not subjected to wholesale institutional change by an outside power. Formal institutional changes were introduced from within, mostly by governments and elites. Turkey's institutions during the last two centuries were shaped by the interaction between the new institutions and those that existed, including the Islamic-Ottoman institutions of the earlier era.

I have also tried to evaluate the deeper causes of Turkey's record of economic development. The case of Turkey has shown that the proximate causes consisting mostly of economic variables are necessary for understanding long-term economic development, but they do not tell the whole story. Long-term economic development cannot be fully understood without taking into account the social and political environment as well as the historical causes. Our knowledge about how institutions work and how they support or hinder economic development is still evolving, but I have tried to show how economic outcomes in Turkey have been mediated by institutions, including global institutions. As in the case of many other developing countries, formal institutions designed by elites or by global powers or global agencies were only part of the story. To understand how they contributed to economic development, it was also necessary to examine how they interacted with the existing formal and informal institutions and which new institutions emerged.

The case of Turkey also showed that institutions mattered but they were not the only thing that mattered. In addition to the interaction between the new and existing institutions, there was interaction between the institutions, on the one hand, and economic change, technology, politics, social structure, interests, distribution of power, ideas, beliefs, and expectations, on the other. Institutions influenced the others but were also influenced by them. Institutions shaped behavior and relations among the various actors and, in turn, were shaped by them. Formal as well as informal institutions have also been shaped by social structure and politics, including the cleavages between the various groups and their elites. In other words, institutions have certainly influenced the outcomes, but they have not been the sole cause of outcomes. Not only the influence of formal and informal institutions but also the influence of social structure and politics help explain why economic growth and development have remained close to the developing-country averages. For these reasons as well, the case of Turkey also offers important insights into the experiences of other developing countries during the last two centuries.

REFERENCES

Abramowitz, Moses. 1986. "Catching Up, Forging Ahead and Falling Behind." *Journal of Economic History* 46(2): 385–406.

Acemoglu, Daron. 2003. "Why Not a Political Coase Theorem? Social Conflict, Commitment and Politics." *Journal of Comparative Economics* 31(4): 620–52.

Acemoglu, Daron, and James Robinson. 2012. *Why Nations Fail: The Origins of Power, Prosperity and Poverty*. New York: Crown.

Acemoglu, Daron, Simon Johnson, and James Robinson. 2001. "The Colonial Origins of Comparative Development: An Empirical Investigation." *American Economic Review* 91(6): 1369–1401.

———— 2005a. "Institutions as the Fundamental Cause of Long-Run Growth." In *Handbook of Economic Growth*, ed. Philippe Aghion and Steve Durlauf, 385–471. Amsterdam: Elsevier.

———— 2005b. "The Rise of Europe: Atlantic Trade, Institutional Change and Economic Growth." *American Economic Review* 95(3): 546–79.

Acemoglu, Daron, and Murat Üçer. 2015. "The Ups and Downs of Turkish Growth, 2002–2015: Political Dynamics, The European Union and the Institutional Slide." *NBER Working Papers*, No. 21608. Cambridge, MA: National Bureau of Economic Research.

Adaman, Fikret, Ayça Akarçay Gürbüz, and Kıvanç Karaman. 2015. "Yeni kurumsal iktisadın penceresinden toplumsal düzenin tesisi: Geç Osmanlı–Türkiye Cumhuriyeti tarihine alternatif bir yaklaşım." *Toplum ve Bilim* 133: 166–85.

Adaman, Fikret, Bengi Akbulut, and Murat Arsel. 2017. *Neoliberal Turkey and Its Discontents, Economic Policy and the Environment Under Erdoğan*. London and New York: I.B. Tauris.

Adaman, Fikret, and Murat Arsel. 2005. "Introduction" and "Conclusion." In *Environmentalism in Turkey: Between Democracy and Development*, ed. Fikret Adaman and Murat Arsel, 1–11 and 293–98. London: Routledge.

Agir, Seven. 2013. "The Evolution of Grain Policy, the Ottoman Experience." *Journal of Interdisciplinary History* 43(4): 571–98.

———— 2018. "The Rise and Demise of Gedik Markets in Istanbul, 1750–1860." *Economic History Review* 71(1): 133–56.

Agoston, Gabor. 2003. "A Flexible Empire: Authority and Its Limits on the Ottoman Frontiers." *International Journal of Turkish Studies* 9(1–2): 15–31.

Ahmad, Feroz. 1977. *The Turkish Experiment in Democracy, 1950–1975*. London: C. Hurst for the Royal Institute of International Affairs.

———— 1988. "War and Society under the Young Turks, 1908–1918." *Review (Fernard Braudel Center)* 11(2): 265–86.

Ahmad, Feroz. 1995. "The Development of Class Consciousness in Republican Turkey, 1923–45." In *Workers and the Working Class in the Ottoman Empire and the Turkish Republic, 1839–1950*, ed. Donald Quataert and Erik Jan Zürcher, 75–94. London and New York: I.B. Tauris.

——— 2010. "Military and Politics in Turkey." In *Turkey's Engagement with Modernity, Conflict and Change in the Twentieth Century*, ed. Celia Karslake, Kerem Öktem, and Philip Robins, 92–116. Houndmills, Basingstoke: Palgrave Macmillan.

Akarlı, Engin. 1976. "The Problem of External Pressures, Power Struggles and Budgetary Deficit under Abdulhamid II, 1876–1909: Origins and Solutions." PhD dissertation, Princeton University.

Akçay, Cevdet, and Murat Üçer. 2008. "A Narrative on the Turkish Current Account." *Journal of International Trade and Diplomacy* 2(2): 211–38.

Akder, Halis. 2010. "Forgottten Campaigns: A History of Disease in Turkey." *Turkey's Engagement with Modernity, Conflict and Change in the Twentieth Century*, ed. Celia Karslake, Kerem Öktem, and Philip Robins, 210–35. Houndmills, Basingstoke: Palgrave Macmillan.

Akgüngör, Sedef, Ceyhan Aldemir, Yeşim Kuştepeli, Yaprak Gülcan, and Vahap Tecim. 2012. *Türkiye'de Demiryolları ve Karayollarının Ekonomik ve Sosyal Etkileri: 1856–2008 Dönemi için Bir İnceleme*. İzmir: Dokuz Eylül Üniversitesi Yayınları.

Akın, G. Gülsün, Ahmet Faruk Aysan, and Levent Yıldıran. 2009. "Transformation of the Turkish Financial Sector in the Aftermath of the 2001 Crisis." In *Turkey and the Global Economy: Neo-Liberal Restructuring and Integration in the Post-crisis Era*, ed. Ziya Öniş and Fikret Şenses, 73–100. London: Routledge.

Aksoy, Zühre. 2005. "Biodiversity and Biotechnology in the Agricultural Sector." In *Environmentalism in Turkey, between Democracy and Development?*, ed. Fikret Adaman and Murat Arsel, 235–48. Aldershot: Ashgate.

Aktar, Ayhan. 2000. *Varlık Vergisi ve "Türkleştirme" Politikaları*. Istanbul: İletişim Yayınları.

Akyıldız, Ali. 1996. *Osmanlı Finans Sisteminde Dönüm Noktası: Kâğıt Para ve Sosyo-Ekonomik Etkileri*. Istanbul: Eren Yayıncılık.

Akyüz, Yılmaz, and Korkut Boratav. 2003. "The Making of the Turkish Financial Crisis." *World Development* 31(9): 1549–66.

Al, Hüseyin. 2007. *Uluslararası Sermaye ve Osmanlı Maliyesi, 1820–1875*. Istanbul: Osmanlı Bankası Arşiv ve Araştırma Merkezi.

Alesina, Alberto, and Paola Giuliano. 2015. "Culture and Institutions." *Journal of Economic Literature* 53(4): 898–944.

Alkan, Mehmet Ö. 2000. *Education Statistics from the Tanzimat to the Republic, 1839–1924*. Ankara: State Institute of Statistics.

Allen, Robert C. 2001. "The Great Divergence in Wages and Prices from the Middle Ages to the First World War." *Explorations in Economic History* 38(4): 411–47.

——— 2011. *Global Economic History. A Very Short Introduction*. Oxford and New York: Oxford University Press.

Altuğ, Sumru, Alpay Filiztekin, and Şevket Pamuk. 2008. "Sources of Long-Term Economic Growth for Turkey, 1880–2005." *European Review of Economic History* 12(3): 393–430.

Amsden, Alice H. 1989. *Asia's Next Giant, South Korea and Late Industrialization*. Oxford and New York: Oxford University Press.

Antonucci, Daniele, and Stefano Manzocchi. 2006. "Does Turkey Have a Special Trade Relation with the EU?: A Gravity Model Approach." *Economic Systems* 30(2): 157–69.

Arat, Yeşim. 2008. "Contestation and Collaboration, Women's Struggles for Empowerment in Turkey." In *Turkey in the Modern World, Volume 4, The Cambridge History of Turkey*, ed. Reşat Kasaba, 388–418. Cambridge and New York: Cambridge University Press.

Arı, Kemal. 1995. *Büyük Mübadele / Türkiye'ye Zorunlu Göç (1923–1925)*. Istanbul: Tarih Vakfı Yurt Yayınları.

Arıcanlı, Tosun, and Dani Rodrik. 1990a. "An Overview of Turkey's Experience with Economic Liberalization and Structural Adjustment." *World Development* 18(10): 1343–50.

———— 1990b. *The Political Economy of Turkey: Debt, Adjustment and Sustainability*. New York: St. Martin's Press.

Arslan, İsmail, and Sweder van Wijnbergen. 1993. "Export Incentives, Exchange Rate Policy and Export Growth in Turkey." *Review of Economics and Statistics* 75(1): 128–33.

Artunç, Cihan. 2015. "The Price of Legal Institutions: The *Beratli* Merchants in the Eighteenth-Century Ottoman Empire." *Journal of Economic History* 75(3): 720–48.

Atiyas, İzak. 2009. "Recent Privatization Experience of Turkey: a Reappraisal." *Turkey and the Global Economy: Neo-Liberal Restructuring and Integration in the Post-crisis Era*, ed. Ziya Öniş and Fikret Şenses, 101–22. London: Routledge.

———— 2012. "Economic Institutions and Institutional Change in Turkey during the Neoliberal Era." *New Perspectives on Turkey* 47, 57–81.

Atiyas, İzak, and Ozan Bakış. 2013. "Aggregate and Sectoral TFP Growth in Turkey: A Growth Accounting Exercise." *TÜSİAD—Sabancı University Competitiveness Forum Working Paper* No. 2013–1.

Aydın, Ayşegül, and Cem Emrence. 2015. *Zones of Rebellion, Kurdish Insurgents and the Turkish State*. Ithaca, NY: Cornell University Press.

Aydın, Zülküf. 2010. "Neo-liberal Transformation of Turkish Agriculture." *Journal of Agrarian Change* 10(2): 149–87.

Aytekin, Atila. 2009. "Agrarian Relations, Property and Law: An Analysis of the 1858 Land Code in the Ottoman Empire." *Middle Eastern Studies*: 45(6): 935–51.

Bailey, F. E. 1940. "The Economics of British Foreign Policy, 1825–50." *Journal of Modern History* 12(4): 449–84.

Balla, Eliana, and Noel D. Johnson. 2009. "Fiscal Crisis and Institutional Change in the Otoman Empire and France." *Journal of Economic History* 69(3): 809–45.

Banerjee, Abhijit, and Lakshimi Iyer. 2005. "History, Institutions and Economic Performance: the Legacy of Colonial Land Systems in India." *American Economic Review* 95(4): 1190–1213.

Barkan, Ömer Lütfi. 1953–54. "H. 933–934 (M. 1527–1528) Mali Yilina Ait Bir Bütçe Örnegi." *Istanbul Üniversitesi Iktisat Fakültesi Mecmuasi* 14(3): 251–329.

Barkey, Karen. 1994. *Bandits and Bureaucrats: The Ottoman Route to State Centralization*. Ithaca, NY: Cornell University Press.

Barlow, Robin, and Fikret Şenses. 1995. "The Turkish Export Boom: Just Reward or Just Lucky?" *Journal of Development Economics* 48(1): 111–33.

Baskıcı, Mehmet Murat. 2005. *1800–1914 Yıllarında Anadolu'da İktisadi Değişim*. Ankara: Turhan Kitabevi.

Baten, Joerg, and Matthias Blum. 2014. "Chapter 7: Human Heights since 1820." In *How Was Life? Global Well Being Since 1820*, ed. Van Zanden, Baten et al., 117–37. Paris: OECD Publishing and International Institute of Social History.

Behar, Cem. 1996. *Osmanlı İmparatorluğu'nun ve Türkiye'nin Nüfusu, 1500–1927*. Ankara: Tarihi İstatistikler Dizisi, Devlet İstatistik Enstitüsü.

———. 2006. "Demographic Developments and Complementarities: Ageing, Labor and Migration." *Turkish Studies* 7(1): 17–31.

Berend, Ivan. 2006. *An Economic History of Twentieth-Century Europe, Economic regimes from Laissez–Faire to Globalization*. Cambridge and New York: Cambridge University Press.

———. 2013. *An Economic History of Nineteenth-Century Europe, Diversity and Industrialization*. Cambridge and New York: Cambridge University Press.

Berik, Günseli, and Cihan Bilginsoy. 1996. "The Labor Movement in Turkey: Labor Pains, Maturity, Metamorphosis." In *The Social History of Labor in the Middle East*, ed. Ellis Jay Goldberg, 37–64. Boulder, CO: Westview.

Berkes, Niyazi. 1964. *The Development of Secularism in Turkey*. Montreal: McGill University Press.

Besley, Tim, and Torsten Persson. 2010. "State Capacity, Conflict and Development." *Econometrica* 78(1): 1–34.

———. 2011. *Pillars of Prosperity: The Political Economics of Development Clusters*. Princeton, NJ: Princeton University Press.

Bianchi, Robert. 1984. *Interest Groups and Political Development in Turkey*. Princeton, NJ: Princeton University Press.

Biddle, Jesse, and Vedat Milor. 1997. "Economic Governance in Turkey: Bureaucratic Capacity, Policy Networks and Business Associations." In *Business and the State in Developing Countries*, ed. Sylvia Maxfield and Ben Ross Schneider, 277–309. Ithaca, NY: Cornell University Press.

Birdal, Murat. 2010. *The Political Economy of Ottoman Public Debt*. London and New York: I.B. Tauris.

Birtek, Faruk. 1985. "The Rise and Fall of Etatism in Turkey, 1932–1950." *Review (Fernand Braudel Center)* 8(3): 407–38.

Birtek, Faruk, and Çağlar Keyder. 1975. "Türkiye'de Devlet-Tarım İlişkileri, 1923–1950." *Birikim* 22: 31–40.

Blaisdell, Donald C. 1929. *European Financial Control in the Ottoman Empire: A Study of the Establishment, Activities, and Significance of the Administration of the Ottoman Public Debt*. New York: Columbia University Press.

Bolt, Jutta, Robert Inklaar, Herman de Jong, and Jan Luiten van Zanden. 2018. "Rebasing 'Maddison': New Income Comparisons and the Shape of Long-Run Economic Development." GGDC Research Memorandum, 174, University of Groningen, Groningen Growth and Development Center.

Bolt, Jutta, and Jan Luiten Van Zanden. 2014. "The Maddison Project. Collaborative Research on Historical National Accounts." *Economic History Review* 67(3): 627–51.

Boogert, Maurits H. van den. 2005. *The Capitulations and the Ottoman Legal System: Qadis, Consuls and Beratlis in the 18th Century*. Leiden: Brill.

Boratav, Korkut. 1981. "Kemalist Economic Policies and Etatism." In *Atatürk: Founder of a Modern State*, ed. Ali Kazancıgil and Ergun Özbudun, 165–90. London: C. Hurst.

———— 1982. "Anadolu Köyünde Savaş ve Yıkım." *Toplum ve Bilim* 15–16: 61–75.

———— 1986. "Import Substitution and Income Distribution Under a Populist Regime: The Case of Turkey." *Development Policy Review* 4(1): 117–39.

———— 1990. "Inter-class and Intra-class Relations of Distribution Under Structural Adjustment: Turkey During the 1980s." In *The Political Economy of Turkey: Debt, Adjustment and Sustainability*, ed. Tosun Arıcanlı and Dani Rodrik, 199–229. London: Macmillan.

———— 2005. *1980'li Yıllarda Türkiye'de Sosyal Sınıflar ve Bölüşüm*. Ankara: İmge Kitabevi.

———— 2009. *Bir Krizin Kısa Hikâyesi*. Ankara: Arkadaş Yayınevi.

———— 2011. *Türkiye İktisat Tarihi, 1908–2009*. Istanbul: İmge Kitabevi Yayınları.

Boratav, Korkut, Gündüz A. Ökçün, and Şevket Pamuk. 1985. "Ottoman Wages and the World Economy, 1839–1913." *Review (Fernand Braudel Center)* 8(3): 379–406.

Boratav, Korkut, Oktar Türel, and Erinç Yeldan. 1996. "Dilemmas of Structural Adjustment and Environmental Policies under Instability: Post-1980 Turkey." *World Development* 24(2): 373–93.

Boratav, K., A. E. Yeldan, and A. H. Köse. 2000. *Globalization, Distribution and Social Policy: Turkey, 1980–1998*. CEPA Working Paper Series, No. 20.

Bourguignon, François. 2015. *The Globalization of Inequality*. Princeton, NJ: Princeton University Press.

Bourguignon, François, and C. Morrisson. 2002. "The Size Distribution of Income among World Citizens." *American Economic Review* 92(4): 727–44.

Bozarslan, Hamit. 2008. "Kurds and the Turkish State." In *Turkey in the Modern World, Volume 4, The Cambridge History of Turkey*, ed. Reşat Kasaba, 333–54. Cambridge and New York: Cambridge University Press.

Braudel, Fernand. 1979. *Civilization and Capitalism, 15th–18th Century, vol. III, The Perspective of the World*. New York: Harper & Row.

Broadberry, Stephen, Bruce Campbell, Alexander Klein, Mark Overton, and Bas Van Leeuwen. 2015. *British Economic Growth, 1270–1870*. Cambridge and New York: Cambridge University Press.

Broadberry, Stephen, and Mark Harrison. 2005. *The Economics of World War I*. Cambridge and New York: Cambridge University Press.

Broadberry, Stephen, and Kevin H. O'Rourke, eds. 2010. *The Cambridge Economic History of Modern Europe, Volume 1:1700–1870* and *Volume 2: 1870 to the Present*. Cambridge and New York: Cambridge University Press.

Buğra, Ayşe. 1994. *State and Business in Modern Turkey: A Comparative Study*. Albany: State University of New York Press.

———— 1998a. "Class, Culture and State. An Analysis of Interest Representations by Two Turkish Business Associations." *International Journal of Middle East Studies* 30(4): 521–39.

———— 1998b. "The Immoral Economy of Housing in Turkey." *International Journal of Urban and Regional Research* (22): 303–17.

———— 2007. "Poverty and Citizenship: An Overview of the Social Policy Environment in Republican Turkey." *International Journal of Middle East Studies* 39(1): 33–52.

Buğra, Ayşe, and Çağlar Keyder. 2006. "The Turkish Welfare Regime in Transformation." *Journal of European Social Policy* 16(3): 211–28.

Buğra, Ayşe, and Osman Savaşkan. 2014. *New Capitalism in Turkey: The Relationship Between Politics, Religion and Business.* Cheltenham: Edward Elgar.

Bulutay, Tuncer. 1995. *Employment, Unemployment and Wages in Turkey.* Ankara: International Labour Office.

Bulutay, Tuncer, Yahya S. Tezel, and Nuri Yıldırım. 1974. *Türkiye Milli Geliri (1923–1948).* Ankara: Ankara Üniversitesi Siyasal Bilgiler Fakültesi Yayınları.

Çağaptay, Soner. 2006. *Islam, Secularism and Nationalism in Modern Turkey. Who Is a Turk?* London and New York: Routledge.

Çarkoğlu, Ali, and Mine Eder. 2005. "Development alla Turca: The Southeastern Anatolia Development Project (GAP)." In *Environmentalism in Turkey, between Democracy and Development?,* ed. Fikret Adaman and Murat Arsel, 167–84. Aldershot: Ashgate.

Celasun, Merih, and Dani Rodrik. 1989. "Debt, Adjustment, and Growth: Turkey." In *Developing Country Debt and Economic Performance. Vol. III: Country Studies—Indonesia, Korea, Philippines, Turkey,* ed. J. D. Sachs and S. M. Collins, 615–808. Chicago: University of Chicago Press.

Çeviker Gürakar, Esra. 2016. *Politics of Favoritism in Public Procurement in Turkey, Reconfigurations of Dependency Networks in the AKP Era.* New York: Palgrave Macmillan.

Cezar, Yavuz. 1986. *Osmanlı Maliyesinde Bunalım ve Değişim Dönemi: XVIII. Yüzyıldan Tanzimat'a Mali Tarih.* Istanbul: Alan Yayıncılık.

Chang, H. J. 2002. *Kicking Away the Ladder: Development Strategy in Historical Perspective.* London: Anthem Press.

Çizakça, Murat. 1995. "Cash Waqfs of Bursa, 1555–1823." *Journal of the Economic and Social History of the Orient* 38(3): 313–54.

———— 1996. *A Comparative Evolution of Business Partnerships: The Islamic World and Europe.* Leiden: Brill.

Clark, E. C. 1974. "Ottoman Industrial Revolution." *International Journal of Middle East Studies* 5(1): 65–76.

Clay, Christopher. 1994. "The Origins of Modern Banking in the Levant: The Development of a Branch Network by the Imperial Ottoman Bank, 1890–1914." *International Journal of Middle East Studies* 26(4): 589–614.

———— 1998. "Labour Migration and Economic Conditions in Nineteenth-Century Anatolia." *Middle Eastern Studies* 34(4): 1–32.

———— 2000. *Gold for the Sultan: Western Bankers and Ottoman Finance, 1856–1881.* London and New York: I.B. Tauris.

Coşar, Nevin. 1995. "Denk Bütçe–Sağlam Para Para Politikası ve Devletçilik (1924–1938)." In *Türkiye'de Devletçilik,* ed. Nevin Coşar, 259–92. Bağlam Yayınları.

Coşgel, Metin M. 2011. "The Political Economy of Law and Economic Development in Islamic History." In *Law and Long-Term Economic Change,* ed. Jan Luiten van Zanden and Debin Ma, 158–77. Stanford, CA: Stanford University Press.

———— 2015. "The Fiscal Regime of an Expanding State: Political Economy of Ottoman Taxation." In *Fiscal Regimes and the Political Economy of Premodern States,* ed. Andrew Monson and Walter Scheidel, 404–28. Cambridge and New York: Cambridge University Press.

Coşgel, Metin M., and Bogaç Ergene. 2016. *The Economics of Ottoman Justice, Settlement and Trial in the Sharia Courts*. Cambridge and New York: Cambridge University Press.

Coşgel, Metin, Thomas J. Miceli, and Jared Rubin. 2012. "The Political Economy of Mass Printing: Legitimacy and Technological Change in the Ottoman Empire." *Journal of Comparative Economics* 40 (August): 357–71.

Courbage, Youssef, and Philippe Fargues.1997. *Christians and Jews under Islam*. London and New York: I.B. Tauris.

Crafts, Nick. 1996. "The Golden Age of Economic Growth in Europe, 1950–1973." *Economic History Review* 48(3): 429–47.

——— 1997. "The Human Development Index and Changes in Standards of Living: Some Historical Comparisons." *European Review of Economic History* 1(3): 299–322.

——— 2002. "The Human Development Index, 1870–1999: Some Revised Estimates." *European Review of Economic History* 6(3): 395–405.

Davison, Roderic. 1963. *Reform in the Ottoman Empire, 1856–1876*. Princeton, NJ: Princeton University Press.

Deaton, Angus. 2013. *The Great Escape: Health, Wealth and the Origins of Inequality*. Princeton, NJ: Princeton University Press.

Deaton, Angus, and Alan Heston. 2010. "Understanding PPPs and PPP-national Accounts." *American Economic Journal: Macroeconomics* 2(4): 1–35.

Dell, Melisa. 2010. "The Persistent Effects of Peru's Mining *Mita*." *Econometrica* 78(6): 1863–1903.

Demir, F. 2004. "A Failure Story: Politics and Financial Liberalization in Turkey. Revisiting the Revolving Door Hypothesis." *World Development* 32(5): 851–69.

Derviş, Kemal, and Sherman Robinson. 1980. "The Structure of Income Inequality in Turkey in Turkey, 1950–1973." In *The Political Economy of Income Distribution in Turkey*, ed. Ergun Özbudun and Aydın Ulusan, 83–122. New York: Holmes and Meier.

Diaz Alejandro, Carlos. 1984. "Latin America in the 1930s." In *Latin America in the 1930s. The Role of the Periphery in the World Crisis*, ed. Rosemary Thorp, 17–49. London: Macmillan.

Di Maggio, Paul. 1992. "Culture and Economy." In *The Handbook of Economic Sociology*, ed. Neil J. Smelser and Richard Swedberg, 27–57. Princeton, NJ: Princeton University Press.

Duben, Alan, and Cem Behar. 1991. *Istanbul Households: Marriage, Family and Fertility, 1880–1940*. Cambridge and New York: Cambridge University Press.

Eichengreen, Barry. 2008. *Globalizing Capital: A History of the International Monetary System, Second Edition*. Princeton, NJ: Princeton University Press.

Eldem, Edhem. 1999. *A History of the Ottoman Bank*. Istanbul: Ottoman Bank Historical Research Center and History Foundation.

Eldem, Vedat. 1970. *Osmanlı İmparatorluğu'nun İktisadi Şartları Hakkında Bir Tetkik*. Istanbul: İş Bankası Yayınları.

——— 1994. *Harp ve Mütareke Yıllarında Osmanlı İmparatorluğu'nun Ekonomisi*. Ankara: Türk Tarih Kurumu.

Elmacı, Mehmet Emin. 2005. *İttihat-Terakki ve Kapitülasyonlar*. Istanbul: Homer Kitabevi.

Emrence, Cem. 2006. *99 Günlük Muhalefet, Serbest Cumhuriyet Fırkası*. Istanbul: İletişim Yayınları.

Engerman, Stanley L., and Kenneth L. Sokoloff. 2005. "Institutional and Non-Institutional

Explanations of Economic Differences." In *Handbook of New Institutional Economics*, ed. Claude Menard and Mary M. Shirley, 639–66. Dordrecht, Netherlands: Springer.

Environmental Performance Index. 2016. Yale University, https://epi.envirocenter.yale.edu.

Epstein, S. R. 2000. *Freedom and Growth, The Rise of States and Markets in Europe, 1300–1750*. London: Routledge.

Erder, Sema. 1999. "Where Do You Hail From? Localism and Networks in Istanbul." In *Istanbul, Between the Global and the Local*, ed. Çağlar Keyder, 161–72. Lanham, MD: Rowman & Littlefield.

Erdilek, Asım. 1982. *Direct Foreign Investment in Turkish Manufacturing*. Tübingen: Mohr.

Erickson, E. J. 2001. *Ordered to Die: A History of the Ottoman Empire in the First World War*. Westport, CT: Praeger.

Evans, Peter. 1995. *Embedded Autonomy: States and Industrial Transformation*. Princeton, NJ: Princeton University Press.

Evered, Kyle T., and Emine O. Evered. 2011. "Governing Population, Public Health and Malaria in the Early Turkish Republic." *Journal of Historical Geography* 37(1): 470–82.

Faroqhi, Suraiya. 1984. *Towns and Townsmen of Ottoman Anatolia: Trade, Crafts and Food Production in an Urban Setting*. Cambridge and New York: Cambridge University Press.

———— 2009. *Artisans of Empire: Crafts and Craftspeople Under the Ottomans*. London and New York: I.B. Tauris.

Filiztekin, Alpay, and İnsan Tunalı. 1999. "Anatolian Tigers: Are They for Real?." *New Perspectives on Turkey* 20: 77–106.

Findlay, Ronald, and Kevin O'Rourke. 2007. *Power and Plenty, Trade, War and the World Economy in the Second Millennium*. Princeton, NJ: Princeton University Press.

Findley, Carter. 1980. *Bureaucratic Reform in the Ottoman Empire: the Sublime Porte 1989–1922*. Princeton, NJ: Princeton University Press.

Fogel, Robert W. 2004. *Escape from Hunger and Premature Death, 1700 to 2010: Europe, America and the Third World*. Cambridge and New York: Cambridge University Press.

Fortna, Benjamin C. 2010. "The Ottoman Educational Legacy." In *Turkey's Engagement with Modernity, Conflict and Change in the Twentieth Century*, ed. Celia Karslake, Kerem Öktem, and Philip Robins, 15–26. Houndmills, Basingstoke: Palgrave Macmillan.

———— 2011. *Learning to Read in the Late Ottoman Empire and the Early Turkish Republic*. Houndmills, Basingstoke: Palgrave Macmillan.

Freedom House. 2016. *Freedom in the World 2016*; https://freedomhouse.org/report/freedom-world/freedom-world-2016.

Gatrell, Peter. 2005. "Poor Russia, Poor Show: Mobilising a Backward Economy for War, 1914–1917." In *The Economics of World War I*, ed. Stephen Broadberry and Mark Harrison, 235–75. Cambridge and New York: Cambridge University Press.

Gedikli, Fethi. 1998. *Osmanlı Şirket Kültürü: XVI.–XVIII. Yüzyıllarda Mudarabe Uygulaması*. İstanbul: İz Yayıncılık.

Gemici, Kurtuluş. 2012. "Rushing toward Currency Convertibility." *New Perspectives on Turkey* 47: 33–55.

Genç, Mehmet. 1989. "Osmanlı İktisadi Dünya Görüşünün İlkeleri." *İstanbul Üniversitesi Edebiyat Fakültesi Sosyoloji Dergisi*, 175–85. Istanbul: Istanbul University.

———— 1995. "Esham." *İslam Ansiklopedisi*, 11, 376–380. Ankara: Türk Diyanet Vakfı.

———— 2000. *Osmanlı İmparatorluğunda Devlet ve Ekonomi*. Istanbul: Ötüken Yayınları.

Gerber, Haim. 1987. *The Social Origins of the Modern Middle East*. Boulder, CO: Lynne Rienner.

———— 1994. *State, Society and Law in Islam: Ottoman Law in Comparative Perspective*. New York: State University of New York Press.

Gerschenkron, Alexander. 1962. *Economic Backwardness in Historical Perspective*. Cambridge, MA: Belknap Press.

Gilbar, Gad. 2003. "The Muslim Big Merchants–Entrepreneurs of the Middle East, 1860–1914." *Die Welt des Islams* 43(1): 1–36.

Gordon, Robert J. 2016. *The Rise and Fall of American Growth, The U.S. Standard of Living since the Civil War*. Princeton, NJ: Princeton University Press.

Granovetter, Mark. 1985. "Economic Action and Social Structure: The Problem of Embeddedness." *American Journal of Sociology* 91(3): 481–510.

Grant, Jonathan. 1999. "Rethinking the Ottoman 'Decline': Military Technology Diffusion in the Ottoman Empire, Fifteenth to Eighteenth Centuries." *Journal of World History* 10(1): 179–201.

Greenwood, Antony. 1988. "Istanbul's Meat Provisioning: A Study of the Celepkesan System." Ph.D. dissertation, University of Chicago.

Greif, Avner. 1994. "Cultural Beliefs and the Organization of Society: A Historical and Theoretical Reflection on Collectivist and İndividualist Societies." *Journal of Political Economy* 102(5): 912–50.

———— 2006. *Institutions and the Path to the Modern World Economy: Lessons from Medieval Trade*. Cambridge and New York: Cambridge University Press.

Guiso, Luigi, Paola Sapienza, and Luigi Zingales. 2006. "Does Culture Affect Economic Outcomes?" NBER Working Paper 11999. Cambridge, MA: National Bureau of Economic Research.

Güran, Tevfik. 1997. *Agricultural Statistics of Turkey during the Ottoman Period, 1909–1914*. Ankara: State Institute of Statistics.

———— 1998. *19. Yüzyıl Osmanlı Tarımı*. Istanbul: Eren Yayınları.

———— 2003. *Ottoman Financial Statistics, Budgets, 1841–1918*. Ankara: Devlet İstatistik Enstitüsü.

Gürkaynak, Refet, and Selin Sayek–Böke. 2012. "AKP döneminde Türkiye Ekonomisi." *Birikim* 296(1): 64–69.

Hacettepe Üniversitesi Nüfus Etütleri Enstitüsü. 2008. *Türkiye'nin Demografik Dönüşümü, 1968–2008*. Ankara: Hacettepe Üniversitesi Nüfus Etütleri Enstitüsü.

Haggard, Stephan, and Tobert R. Kaufman. 1992. *The Politics of Adjustment: International Constraints, Distributive Conflicts and the State*. Princeton, NJ: Princeton University Press.

Hall, Peter A., and David Soskice. 2001. *Varieties of Capitalism: The Institutional Foundations of Comparative Advantage*. Oxford and New York: Oxford University Press.

Hall, Robert E., and Charles I. Jones. 1999. "Why Do Some Countries Produce So Much More Output Per Worker Than Others?" *Quarterly Journal of Economics* 114(1): 83–116.

Hansen, Bent. 1991. *Egypt and Turkey: The Political Economy of Poverty, Equity and Growth*. Oxford and New York: Oxford University Press for the World Bank.

Helpman, Elhanan. 2004. *The Mystery of Economic Growth*. Cambridge, MA: Harvard University Press.

Heper, Metin. 1991. *Strong State and Economic Interest Groups. The Post-1980 Turkish Experience*. Berlin and New York: Walter de Gruyter.

Hershlag, Z. Y. 1968. *Turkey: The Challenge of Growth*. Leiden: Brill.

Hillman, Henning. 2013. "Economic Institutions and the State: Insights from Economic History." *Annual Review of Sociology* 39: 251–73.

Hirsch, Eva, and Abraham Hirsch. 1963. "Changes in Agricultural Output Per Capita of Rural Population in Turkey, 1927–1960." *Economic Development and Cultural Change* 11 (4): 372–94.

———— 1966. "Changes in Terms of Trade of Farmers and Their Effect on Real Farm Income Per Capita of Rural Population in Turkey, 1927–1960." *Economic Development and Cultural Change* 14(4): 440–57.

Hirschman, Albert O. 1968. "The Political Economy of Import-Substituting Industrialization in Latin America." *Quarterly Journal of Economics* 82(1): 1–26.

Hobsbawm, Eric. 1968. *Industry and Empire: From 1750 to the Present Day. The Pelican Economic History of Britain*. Hammondsworth, Middlesex: Penguin Books.

Hourani, Albert. 1966. "Ottoman Reform and the Politics of Notables." In *The Modern Middle East*, ed. Albert Hourani, Philip S. Khoury, and M. C. Wilson, 83–110. London and New York: I.B. Tauris.

Imber, Colin. 2002. *The Ottoman Empire, 1300–1650. The Structure of Power*. Houndmills, Basingstoke: Palgrave Macmillan.

Imrohoroglu, Ayşe, Selahattin Imrohoroglu, and Murat Üngör. 2014. "Agricultural Productivity and Growth in Turkey." *Macroeconomic Dynamics* 18(5): 998–1017.

İnalcık, Halil. 1969. "Capital Accumulation in the Ottoman Empire." *Journal of Economic History* 29(1): 97–140.

———— 1970. "The Ottoman Economic Mind and Aspects of the Ottoman Economy." In *Studies in the Economic History of the Middle East*, ed. M. A. Cook, 207–18. Oxford and New York: Oxford University Press.

———— 1971. "İmtiyazat: the Ottoman Empire." *Encyclopedia of Islam*, second edition. Leiden: Brill, Vol. 3, pp. 1179–89.

———— 1973. "Applications of the Tanzimat and Its Social Effects." *Archivum Ottomanicum* 97–128.

———— 1980. "Military and Fiscal Transformation in the Ottoman Empire, 1600–1700." *Archivum Ottomanicum* 6, 283–337.

———— 1992. "The Ottoman Market in Cotton Fabrics, India and England: The Role of the Cost of Labor in Commercial Rivalry." In *The Middle East and the Balkans Under the Ottoman Empire, Essays on Economy and Society*, ed. H. Inalcik, 254–306. Bloomington: Indiana University Press.

———— 1994. "The Ottoman State: Economy and Society, 1300–1600." In *An Economic and Social History of the Ottoman Empire, 1300–1914*, ed. Halil İnalcık and Donald Quataert, Part I, 11–409. Cambridge and New York: Cambridge University Press.

İnalcık, Halil, and Mehmet Seyitdanlıoğlu. 2006. *Tanzimat: Değişim Sürecinde Osmanlı İmparatorluğu*. Ankara: Phoenix Yayınevi.

İslamoğlu, Huri. 2004. *Constituting Modernity: Private Property in the East and West*. London and New York: I.B. Tauris.

İsmihan, Mustafa, and Metin Özcan Kıvılcım. 2006. "Türkiye Ekonomisinde Büyümenin Kaynakları, 1960–2004." *İktisat, İşletme ve Finans* 21(241): 74–86.

Issawi, Charles. 1980. *The Economic History of Turkey, 1800–1914*. Chicago: University of Chicago Press.

——— 1981. "Egypt, Iran and Turkey, 1800–1970: Patterns of Growth and Development." In *Disparities in Economic Development Since the Industrial Revolution*, ed. Paul Bairoch ve Maurice Levy-Leboyer, 65–77. New York: St. Martin's Press.

——— 1982. *An Economic History of the Middle East*. New York: Columbia University Press.

Jennings, Ronald C. 1973. "Loans and Credit in Early 17th Century Ottoman Judicial Records." *Journal of the Economic and Social History of the Orient* 16(2/3): 168–216.

Johnson, Noel D., and Mark Koyama. 2017. "States and Economic Growth: Capacity and Constraints." *Explorations in Economic History* 64: 1–20.

Karakışla, Yavuz Selim. 1995. "The Emergence of the Ottoman Industrial Working Class." In *Workers and the Working Class in the Ottoman Empire and the Turkish Republic, 1839–1950*, ed. Donald Quataert and Erik Jan Zürcher, 19–34. London and New York: I.B. Tauris.

Karakoç, Ulaş, Şevket Pamuk, and Laura Panza. 2017. "Industrialization in Egypt and Turkey, 1870–2010." In *The Spread of Modern Industry to the Periphery since 1871*, ed. Kevin Hjortshoj O'Rourke and Jeffrey Gale Williamson, 142–65. Oxford and New York: Oxford University Press.

Karaman, Kıvanç, and Şevket Pamuk. 2010. "Ottoman State Finances in Comparative European Perspective, 1500–1914." *Journal of Economic History* 70(3): 593–627.

Karaömerlioğlu, Asım. 1998. "The Village Institutes Experience in Turkey." *British Journal of Middle Eastern Studies* 25(1): 47–73.

——— 2006. *Orada Bir Köy Var Uzakta / Erken Cumhuriyet Döneminde Köycü Söylem*. Istanbul: İletişim Yayınları.

Karpat, Kemal. 1976. *The Gecekondu, Rural Migration and Urbanization*. Cambridge and New York: Cambridge University Press.

——— 1985a. *Ottoman Population: 1830–1914, Demographic and Social Characteristics*. Madison: University of Wisconsin Press.

——— 1985b. "The Ottoman Emigration to America." *International Journal of Middle East Studies* 17(2): 175–209.

——— 2001. *The Politicization of Islam. Reconstructing Identity State, Faith and Community in Late Ottoman State*. Oxford and New York: Oxford University Press.

Kasaba, Reşat. 1988. *The Ottoman Empire and the World Economy: The Nineteenth Century*. Albany: State University of New York Press.

——— 2008. *Turkey in the Modern World, Volume 4, Cambridge History of Modern Turkey*. Cambridge and New York: Cambridge University Press.

——— 2009. *A Movable Empire: Ottoman Nomads, Migrants and Refugees*. Seattle and London: University of Washington Press.

Kazgan, Gülten. 1977. "Türk Ekonomisinde 1927–35 Depresyonu, Kapital Birikimi ve Örgütleşmeler." İktisadi ve Ticari İlimler Akademisi Derneği Istanbul Şubesi. *Atatürk Döneminin Ekonomik ve Toplumsal Sorunları*, 231–74. Istanbul: Murat Matbaacilik.

Kazgan, Gülten. 2005. *Türkiye Ekonomisinde Krizler (1929–2001)*. Istanbul: İstanbul Bilgi Üniversitesi Yayınları.

Kazgan, Haydar. 1980. "İkinci Sultan Mahmut Devrinde Enflasyon ve Darphane Amiri Kazaz Artin." *Toplum ve Bilim* 11: 115–30.

———— 1995. *Osmanlıda Avrupa Finans Kapitali*. Istanbul: Yapı Kredi Yayınları.

Kemp, Tom. 1983. *Industrialization in the Non-Western World*. London and New York: Longman.

———— 1993. *Historical Patterns of Industrialization*. London and New York: Longman.

Keyder, Çağlar. 1979. "Osmanlı Ekonomisi ve Osmanlı Maliyesi, 1881–1914." *Toplum ve Bilim* 8, pp. 37–48.

———— 1981. *The Definition of a Peripheral Economy: Turkey, 1923–1929*. Cambridge and New York: Cambridge University Press.

———— 1987. *State and Class in Turkey. A Study in Capitalist Development*. London and New York: Verso.

———— ed. 1999. *Istanbul, Between the Global and the Local*. Lanham, MD: Rowman & Littlefield.

Keyder, Çağlar, Eyüp Özveren, and Donald Quataert. 1993. "Port Cities in the Ottoman Empire." *Review (Fernand Braudel Center)*, 10: 519–58.

Keyder, Çağlar, and Faruk Tabak. 1991. *Landholding and Commercial Agriculture in the Middle East*. Albany: State University of New York Press.

Keyder, Çağlar, and Zafer Yenal. 2011. "Agrarian Change Under Globalization: Markets and Insecurity in Turkish Agriculture." *Journal of Agrarian Change* 11(1): 60–86.

Kindleberger, Charles. 1986. *The World in Depression, 1929–1939*. Berkeley and Los Angeles: University of California Press.

Kingston, Christopher, and Gonzalo Caballero. 2009. "Comparing Theories of Institutional Change." *Journal of Institutional Economics* 5(2): 151–80.

Kıray, Emine Z. 1988. "Foreign Debt and Structural Change in 'The Sick Man of Europe'— The Ottoman Empire, 1850–1875." PhD dissertation, Massachusetts Institute of Technology.

Kırdar, Murat. 2009. "Explaining Ethnic Disparities in School Enrollment in Turkey." *Economic Development and Cultural Change* 57(2): 297–333.

Kırdar, Murat, and Şirin Saraçoglu. 2008. "Migration and Regional Convergence: An Empirical Investigation for Turkey." *Papers in Regional Science* 87(4): 545–66.

Kirişci, Kemal. 2008. "Migration and Turkey: The Dynamics of State, Society and Politics." In *Turkey in the Modern World, Volume 4, The Cambridge History of Turkey*, ed. Reşat Kasaba, 175–98. Cambridge and New York: Cambridge University Press.

Kirişci, Kemal, and Gareth Winrow. 1997. *The Kurdish Question and Turkey. An Example of a Trans-State Ethnic Conflict*. London and Portland, OR: Frank Cass.

Knight, Jack. 1992. *Institutions and Social Conflict*. Cambridge and New York: Cambridge University Press.

Kocabaşoğlu, Uygur. 2001. *Türkiye İş Bankası Tarihi*. Istanbul: İş Bankası Kültür Yayınları.

Kuran, Timur. 2011. *The Long Divergence: How Islamic Law Held Back the Middle East*. Princeton, NJ: Princeton University Press.

Kurmuş, Orhan. 1974. *The Role of British Capital in the Economic Development of Western Anatolia 1850–1913*. PhD thesis, University of London.

———— 1983. "The 1838 Treaty of Commerce Re-examined." In *Economie et Société dans l'Empire Ottoman*, ed. J.-L. B. Grammont and Paul Dumont, 411–17. Paris: CNRS.

———— 1987. "The Cotton Famine and Its Effects on the Ottoman Empire." In *The Ottoman Empire and the World Economy*, ed. Huricihan Islamoglu-Inan, 160–69. Cambridge and New York: Cambridge University Press.

Kurt, Mustafa, Kemalettin Kuzucu, Baki Çakır, and Kemal Demir. 2016. "19. Yüzyılda Osmanlı Sanayileşmesi Sürecinde Kurulan Devlet Fabrikaları, Bir Envanter Çalışması." *OTAM, Ankara Üniversitesi Osmanlı Tarihi Araştırma Merkezi Dergisi* 40: 245–77.

Kuruç, Bilsay. 2011. *Mustafa Kemal Döneminde Ekonomi, Büyük Devletler ve Türkiye*. Istanbul: Istanbul Bilgi Üniversitesi Yayınları.

Kuznets, Simon. 1955. "Economic Growth and Income Inequality." *American Economic Review* 45(1): 1–28.

———— 1966. *Modern Economic Growth*. New Haven, CT: Yale University Press.

Leonard, Carol, and Jonas Ljungberg. 2010. "Population and Living Standards, 1870–1914." In *The Cambridge Economic History of Modern Europe, Volume 2: 1870 to the Present*, ed. Stephen Broadberry and Kevin H. O'Rourke, 232–63. Cambridge and New York: Cambridge University Press.

Lewis, W. A. 1954. "Economic Development with Unlimited Supplies of Labour." *Manchester School* 22(2): 139–91.

Lindert, Peter H. 2004. *Growing Public: Social Spending and Economic Growth since the Eighteenth Century*, 2 volumes. Cambridge and New York: Cambridge University Press.

Livi-Bacci, Massimo. 2017. *A Concise History of World Population*, Sixth Edition. Oxford: Wiley Blackwell.

Maddison, Angus. 1985. *Two Crises, Latin America and Asia: 1929–38 and 1973–83*. Paris: OECD Development Studies Center.

———— 2003. *The World Economy: Historical Statistics*. Paris: OECD Development Studies Center.

———— 2007. *Historical Statistics for the World Economy, 1–2005*. Paris: OECD Development Studies Center.

Makal, Ahmet. 1999. *Türkiye'de Tek Partili Dönemde Çalışma İlişkileri, 1923–1946*. Ankara: İmge Yayınevi.

———— 2002. *Türkiye'de Çok Partili Dönemde Çalışma İlişkileri, 1946–1963*. Ankara: İmge Yayınevi.

Mandaville, J. E. 1979. "Usurious Piety: The Cash Waqf Controversy in the Ottoman Empire." *International Journal of Middle East Studies* 10(3): 289–308.

Mardin, Şerif. 1973. "Center-Periphery Relations: A Key to Turkish Politics?" *Deadalus* 102(1): 169–90.

McCarthy, Justin. 1983. *Muslims and Minorities: The Population of Ottoman Anatolia and the End of the Empire*. New York: New York University Press.

———— 2002. *Population History of the Middle East and the Balkans*. Istanbul: Isis Press.

Metinsoy, Murat. 2007. *İkinci Dünya Savaşında Türkiye: Savaş ve Gündelik Yaşam*. Istanbul: Homer Kitabevi.

Milanovich, Branko. 2005. *Worlds Apart: Measuring International and Global Inequality*. Princeton, NJ: Princeton University Press.

Milanovich, Branko. 2016. *Global Inequality: A New Approach for the Age of Globalization.* Cambridge, MA: Belknap Press of Harvard University Press.

Milor, Vedat. 1990. "The Genesis of Planning in Turkey." *New Perspectives on Turkey* 4: 1–30.

Mokyr, Joel. 2009. *The Enlightened Economy: An Economic History of Britain, 1700–1850.* New Haven, CT: Yale University Press.

————— 2017. *A Culture of Growth: The Origins of the Modern Economy.* Princeton, NJ, and Oxford: Princeton University Press.

Mutlu, Servet. 1996. "The Southeastern Anatolia Project (GAP) in Turkey." *Orient* 37: 59–86.

Nordhaus, William D. 1997. "Do Real-Output and Real-Wage Measures Capture Reality? The History of Lighting Suggests Not." In *The Economics of New Goods*, Studies in Income and Wealth, Vol. 58, ed. Timothy F. Breneshan and Robert J. Gordon, 29–70. Chicago: University of Chicago Press for NBER.

North, Douglass C. 1981. *Structure and Change in Economic History.* New York and London: Norton.

————— 1990. *Institutions, Institutional Change, and Economic Performance.* Cambridge and New York: Cambridge University Press.

North, Douglass C., John Josep Wallis, and Barry R. Weingast. 2009. *Violence and Social Orders: A Conceptual Framework for Interpreting Recorded Human History.* Cambridge and New York: Cambridge University Press.

Nunn, Nathan. 2009. "The Importance of History for Economic Development." *Annual Review of Economics* 1: 65–92.

O'Brien, Patrick. 2011. "The Nature and Historical Evolution of an Exceptional Fiscal State and Its Possible Significance for the Industrialization of the British Economy." *Economic History Review* 64(2): 408–46.

OECD. 2015. PISA 2015 Key Findings for Turkey; http://www.oecd.org/turkey/pisa-2015 -turkey.htm.

Ogilvie, Sheilagh. 2011. *Institutions and European Trade: Merchant Guilds, 1000–1800.* Cambridge and New York: Cambridge University Press.

Ogün, Tuncay. 1999. *Kafkas Cephesinin I. Dünya Savaşı'ndaki Lojistik Desteği.* Ankara: Atatürk Araştırma Merkezi.

Ökçün, Gündüz A. 1968. *Türkiye İktisat Kongresi, 1923–İzmir, Haberler, Belgeler, Yorumlar.* Ankara: Ankara Üniversitesi Siyasal Bilgiler Fakültesi Yayınları.

————— 1970. *Osmanlı Sanayii, 1913–1915 Yılları Sanayi İstatistiki.* Ankara: Tarihi İstatistikler Dizisi, Devlet İstatistik Enstitüsü.

————— 1982. *Tatil-i Eşgal Kanunu, 1909, Belgeler-Yorumlar.* Ankara: Ankara Üniversitesi Siyasal Bilgiler Fakültesi Yayınları.

————— 1983. *Tarımda Çalışma ve Ekme Yükümlülüğü, 1914–1922.* Ankara: Ankara Üniversitesi Yayınları.

Ökte, Faik. 1951. *Varlık Vergisi Faciası.* Istanbul: Nebioğlu Yayınevi.

Ökten, Çiğdem. 2006. "Privatization in Turkey: What Has Been Achieved?" In *The Turkish Economy: The Real Economy, Corporate Governance and Reform*, ed. Sumru Altuğ and Alpay Filiztekin, 227–51. London: Routledge.

Okyar, Osman. 1987. "A New Look at the Problem of Economic Growth in the Ottoman Empire, 1800–1914." *Journal of European Economic History* 16(1): 7–49.

Olson, Mancur. 1965. *The Logic of Collective Action, Public Goods and the Theory of Groups*. Cambridge, MA: Harvard University Press.

Öncü, Ayşe. 1980. "Chambers of Industry in Turkey, An Inquiry into State-Industry Relations as a Distributive Domain." In *The Political Economy of Income Distribution in Turkey*, ed. Ergun Özbudun and Aydin Ulusan, 455–80. New York: Holmes and Meier.

——— 1988. "The Politics of the Urban Land Market in Turkey: 1950–1980." *International Journal of Urban and Regional Research* 12(1): 38–64.

Öniş, Ziya. 1991. "The Logic of the Developmental State." *Comparative Politics* 24 (1): 109–26.

——— 2003. "Domestic Politics Versus Global Dynamics: Towards a Political Economy of the 2000 and 2001 Financial Crises in Turkey." *Turkish Studies* 4(2): 1–30.

——— 2004. "Turgut Özal and His Economic Legacy: Turkish Neo-Liberalism in Critical Perspective." *Middle Eastern Studies* 40(4): 113–34.

——— 2009. "Conservative Globalism at the Crossroads: The Justice and Development Party and the Thorny Road to Democratic Consolidation." *Mediterranean Politics* 14(1): 21–40.

Öniş, Ziya, and Canan Bakır. 2007. "Turkey's Political Economy in the Age of Financial Globalization: The Significance of the EU Anchor." *South European Society and Politics* 12(2): 1–29.

Öniş, Ziya, and Fikret Şenses. 2005. "Rethinking the Emerging Post–Washington Consensus." *Development and Change* 36(2): 263–90.

——— 2007. "Global Dynamics, Domestic Coalitions and a Reactive State: Major Policy Shifts in Post–War Turkish Economic Development." *METU Studies in Development* 34: 251–86.

——— 2009. *Turkey and the Global Economy: Neoliberal Restructuring and Integration in the Post-crisis Era*. London: Routledge.

Ortaylı, İlber. 1983. *İmparatorluğun En Uzun Yüzyılı*. Istanbul: Hil Yayınları.

Osterhammel, Jürgen. 2014. *The Transformation of the World: A Global History of the Nineteenth Century*. Princeton, NJ: Princeton University Press.

Owen, Roger. 1969. *Cotton and the Egyptian Economy, 1820–1914*. Oxford and New York: Oxford University Press.

——— 1981. *The Middle East in the World Economy 1800–1914*. London and New York: Methuen.

Özatay, Fatih. 2009. *Finansal Krizler ve Türkiye*. Istanbul: Doğan Kitap.

Özbek, Nadir. 2003. "Kemalist Rejim ve Popülizmin Sınırları. Büyük Buhran ve Buğday Alım Politikaları, 1931–1937." *Toplum ve Bilim* 96: 219–38.

——— 2012. "The Politics of Taxation and the 'Armenian Question' during the Late Ottoman Empire, 1876–1908." *Comparative Studies in Society and History* 54(4): 770–97.

——— 2015. *İmparatorluğun Bedeli, Osmanlı'da Vergi, Siyaset ve Toplumsal Adalet (1839–1908)*. Istanbul: Boğaziçi Üniversitesi Yayınları.

Özbudun, Ergun. 1996. "The Continuing Ottoman Legacy and State Tradition in the Middle East." In *Imperial Legacy: The Ottoman Imprint on the Balkans and the Middle East*, ed. L. Carl Brown, 133–57. New York: Columbia University Press.

Özel, Işık, and Şevket Pamuk. 1998. "Osmanlı'dan Cumhuriyet'e Kişi Başına Üretim ve Milli Gelir, 1907–1950." In *75 Yılda Para'nın Serüveni*, ed. Mustafa Sönmez, 83–90. Istanbul: Tarih Vakfı Yayınları.

Özmucur, Süleyman, and Şevket Pamuk. 2002. "Real Wages and Standards of Living in the Ottoman Empire, 1489–1914." *Journal of Economic History* 62(2): 292–321.

Öztürk, Nazif. 1995. *Türk Yenileşme Tarihi Çerçevesinde Vakıf Müessesesi*. Ankara: Türkiye Diyanet Vakfı Yayınları.

Özvar, Erol. 2003. *Osmanlı Maliyesinde Malikâne Uygulaması*. Istanbul: Kitabevi Yayınları.

Özyüksel, Murat. 2011. "Rail and Rule, Railway Building and Railway Politics in the Ottoman Empire." In *Comparing Empires: Encounters and Transfers in the Long Nineteenth Century*, ed. J. Leonhard and U. von Hirschhausen, 109–36. Göttingen: Vandenhoeck & Ruprecht.

——— 2016. *The Berlin Baghdad Railway and the Ottoman Empire: Industrialization, Imperial Germany and the Middle East*. London and New York: I.B. Tauris.

Paine, Suzanne. 1974. *Exporting Workers: The Turkish Case*. Cambridge and New York: Cambridge University Press.

Palma, Jose Gabriel. 2011. "Homogeneous Middles vs. Heterogeneous Tails, and the End of the Inverted-U: It Is All About the Share of the Rich." *Development and Change* 42(1): 87–153.

Pamuk, Şevket. 1987. *The Ottoman Empire and European Capitalism, 1820–1913: Trade, Investment and Production*. Cambridge and New York: Cambridge University Press.

——— 1991. "War, State Economic Policies and Resistance by Agricultural Producers in Turkey, 1939–1945." In *Peasant Politics in the Modern Middle East*, ed. John Waterbury and Farhad Kazemi, 125–42. Gainesville: University Press of Florida.

——— 2000. *A Monetary History of the Ottoman Empire*. Cambridge and New York: Cambridge University Press.

——— 2004. "Institutional Change and the Longevity of the Ottoman Empire, 1500–1800." *Journal of Interdisciplinary History* 35(2): 225–47.

——— 2005. "The Ottoman Economy in World War I." In *The Economics of World War I*, ed. Stephen Broadberry and Mark Harrison, 112–36. Cambridge and New York: Cambridge University Press.

——— 2006. "Estimating Economic Growth in the Middle East since 1820." *Journal of Economic History* 66(3): 809–28.

——— 2008. "Agricultural Output and Productivity Growth in Turkey since 1880." In *Agriculture and Economic Development in Europe since 1870*, ed. P. Lains and V. Pinilla, 375–96. London and New York: Routledge.

——— 2009. "Estimating GDP per Capita for the Ottoman Empire in a European Comparative Framework, 1500–1800." Paper presented at the 15th World Economic History Congress, August, Utrecht.

——— 2012. "The Evolution of Fiscal Institutions in the Ottoman Empire, 1500–1914." In *The Rise of Fiscal States. A Global History*, ed. Bartolome Yun-Casalilla, Patrick O'Brien, and Francisco Comin Comin, 304–31. Cambridge and New York: Cambridge University Press.

Pamuk, Şevket, and Jeffrey G. Williamson. 2011. "Ottoman De-Industrialization 1800–1913: Assessing the Magnitude, Impact and Response." *Economic History Review* 64(1): 159–84.

Panza, Laura. 2014. "De-industrialization and Re-industrialization in the Middle East: Reflections on the Cotton Industry in Egypt and in the Izmir Region." *Economic History Review* 67(1): 146–69.

Panza, Laura, and Jeffrey G. Williamson. 2015. "Did Muhammad Ali Foster Industrialisation in 19th Century Egypt?" *Economic History Review* 68(1): 79–100.

Panzac, Daniel. 1985. *La peste dans L'empire Ottoman, 1700–1850*. Leuven: Editions Peeters.

Parvus, Efendi. 1977. *Türkiye'nin Mali Tutsaklığı*. Istanbul: May Yayınları.

Piketty, Thomas. 2014. *Capital in the Twenty-First Century*. Cambridge, MA: Belknap Press.

Platteau, Jean–Philippe. 1994. "Behind the Market Stage Where Real Societies Exist—Part I: The Role of Public and Private Order Institutions." *Journal of Development Studies* 30(3): 533–77.

——— 2000. *Institutions, Social Norms and Economic Development*. Amsterdam: Harwood Academic.

——— 2011. "Political Instrumentalization of Islam and the Risk of Obscurantist Deadlock." *World Development* 39(2): 243–60.

——— 2017. *Islam Instrumentalized: Religion and Politics in Historical Perspective*. Cambridge and New York: Cambridge University Press.

Prest, Alan Richmond. 1948. *War Economics of Primary Producing Countries*. Cambridge and New York: Cambridge University Press.

Preston, Samuel. 1975. "The Changing Relationship Between Mortality and the Level of Economic Development." *Population Studies* 29(2): 231–48.

Prichett, Lant. 1997. "Divergence, Big Time." *Journal of Economic Perspectives* 11(3): 3–17.

Przeworski, Adam. 2004. "The Last Instance: Are Institutions the Primary Cause of Economic Development?" *European Journal of Sociology* 45(2): 165–88.

Puryear, Vernon J. 1969. *International Economics and Diplomacy in the Near East*. Stanford, CA: Archon Books.

Quataert, Donald. 1975. "Dilemma of Development: The Agricultural Bank and Agricultural Reform in Ottoman Turkey, 1888–1908." *International Journal of Middle East Studies* 6(2): 210–27.

——— 1977. "Limited Revolution: The Impact of the Anatolian Railway on Turkish Transportation and the Provisioning of Istanbul, 1890–1908." *Business History Review* 51(2): 139–59.

——— 1983. *Social Disintegration and Popular Resistance in the Ottoman Empire, 1881–1908: Reactions to European Economic Penetration*. New York: New York University Press.

——— 1992. *Manufacturing and Technology Transfer in the Ottoman Empire, 1800–1914*. Istanbul: Isis Press.

——— 1993a. *Ottoman Manufacturing in the Age of Industrial Revolution*. Cambridge and New York: Cambridge University Press.

——— 1993b. "Women, Households and Textile Manufacturing, 1800–1914." In *The Modern Middle East*, ed. Albert Hourani, Philip S. Khoury, and Mary C. Wilson, 255–70. London and New York: I.B. Tauris.

——— 1994. "The Age of Reforms." In *An Economic and Social History of the Ottoman Empire, 1600–1914*, ed. Halil İnalcık and Donald Quataert, 761–933. Cambridge and New York: Cambridge University Press.

Quataert, Donald, and Erik Jan Zürcher. 1995. *Workers and the Working Class in the Ottoman Empire and the Turkish Republic, 1839–1950*. London and New York: I.B. Tauris.

Reinhart, Carmen M., and Kenneth Rogoff. 2009. *This Time Is Different: Eight Centuries of Financial Folly*. Princeton, NJ: Princeton University Press.

Richards, Alan, and John Waterbury. 2008. *A Political Economy of the Middle East*. Third Edition. Boulder, CO: Westview Press.

Riley, James C. 2001. *Rising Life Expectancy: A Global History*. Cambridge and New York: Cambridge University Press.

Rodrik, Dani. 1990. "Premature Liberalization, Incomplete Stabilization. The Özal Decade in Turkey." In *Lessons of Economic Stabilization and Its Aftermath*, ed. Michael Bruno, Stanley Fischer, and Elhanan Helpman, 323–53. Cambridge, MA: MIT Press.

———. 2011. *The Globalization Paradox*. New York: Norton.

——— 2015. "Premature Deindustrialization." NBER Working Paper 20935. Cambridge, MA: National Bureau of Economic Research.

Rodrik, Dani, Arvind Subramanian, and Francesco Trebbi. 2004. "Institutions Rule: The Primacy of Institutions over Geography and Integration in Economic Development." *Journal of Economic Growth* 9(2): 131–65.

Roland, Gerard. 2004. "Understanding Institutional Change: Fast-Moving and Slow-Moving Institutions." *Studies in Comparative International Development* 38(4): 109–31.

Rothermund, Dietmar. 1996. *The Global Impact of the Great Depression, 1929–1939*. London: Routledge.

Rubin, Jared. 2011. "Institutions and the Rise of Commerce and the Persistence of Laws: Interest Restrictions in Islam and Christianity." *Economic Journal* 121 (557): 1310–39.

——— 2017. *Rulers, Religion and Riches: Why the West Got Rich and the Middle East Did Not*. Cambridge and New York: Cambridge University Press.

Salzman, Ariel. 1993. "An Ancien Regime Revisited: Privatization and Political Economy in the Eighteenth-Century Ottoman Empire." *Politics and Society* 21(4): 393–423.

Sayarı, Sabri. 1977. "Political Patronage in Turkey." In *Patrons and Clients in Mediterranean Societies*, ed. Ernest Gellner and John Waterbury, 103–13. London: Duckworth.

——— 2014. "Interdisciplinary Approaches to Political Clientelism and Patronage in Turkey." *Turkish Studies* 15(4): 655–70.

Saygılı, Şeref, Cengiz Cihan, and Hasan Yurtoğlu. 2005. *Türkiye Ekonomisinde Sermaye Birikimi, Büyüme ve Verimlilik, 1972–2003*. Ankara: Devlet Planlama Teşkilatı.

Schoenberg, Philip Ernest. 1977. "The Evolution of Transport in Turkey under Ottoman Rule, 1856–1918." *Middle Eastern Studies* 13(3): 359–72.

Sen, Amartya. 1981. *Poverty and Famines*. Oxford and New York: Oxford University Press.

——— 2001. *Development as Freedom*. Oxford and New York: Oxford University Press.

Şenses, Fikret. 2012. "Turkey's Experience with Neoliberal Policies since 1980 in Retrospect and Prospect." *New Perspectives on Turkey* 47: 11–31.

Shaw, Stanford J. 1962. *The Financial and Administrative Development of Ottoman Egypt, 1517–1798*. Princeton, NJ: Princeton University Press.

——— 1971. *Between the Old and the New: The Ottoman Empire under Selim III, 1789–1807*. Cambridge, MA: Harvard University Press.

——— 1975. "The Nineteenth Century Ottoman Tax Reforms and Revenue System." *International Journal of Middle East Studies* 6(4): 421–59.

——— 1978. "The Ottoman Census System and Population, 1831–1914." *International Journal of Middle East Studies* 9(3): 325–38.

Shorter, Frederic C. 1985. "The Population of Turkey after the War of Independence." *International Journal of Middle East Studies* 17(4): 417–41.

Shorter, Frederic C., and Miroslav Macura. 1983. *Türkiye'de Nüfus Artışı (1935–1975), Doğurganlık ve Ölümlülük Eğilimleri*. Ankara: Yurt Yayınları.

Sokoloff, Kenneth L., and Stanley L. Engerman. 2000. "History Lessons: Institutions, Factors Endowments and Paths of Development in the New World." *Journal of Economic Perspectives* 14(3): 217–32.

Somel, Selçuk Akşin. 2001. *The Modernization of Public Education in the Ottoman Empire, Islamization, Autocracy and Discipline, 1839–1908*. Leiden: Brill.

Sönmez, Ümit. 2011. *Piyasanın İdaresi, Neoliberalizm ve Bağımsız Düzenleyici Kurumların Anatomisi*. Istanbul: İletişim Yayınları.

Srinivasan, T. N. 1994. "Human Development: A New Paradigm or Reinvention of the Wheel." *American Economic Review* 84(2): 238–43.

Starr, June. 1979. *Law and Social Transformation in Aegean Turkey*. New Delhi: Skinnycats.

Starr, June, and Jonathan Pool. 1974. "The Impact of a Legal Revolution in Rural Turkey." *Law and Society Review* 8(4): 533–60.

Stiglitz, Joseph, Amartya Sen, and Jean-Paul Fitoussi. 2010. *Mismeasuring Our Lives: Why GNP Doesn't Add Up*. New York: New Press.

Stiglitz, Joseph, and Justin Yifu Lin, eds. 2013. *The Industrial Policy Revolution: The Role of Government Beyond Ideology*. New York: Palgrave Macmillan.

Sunar, İlkay. 1990. "Populism and Patronage: The Democrat Party and Its Legacy in Turkey." *Il Politico* 55 (4): 745–57.

Tabellini, Guido. 2010. "Culture and Institutions: Economic Development in the Regions of Europe." *Journal of the European Economic Association* 8(4): 677–716.

Tansel, Ayşe. 2001. "Economic Development and Female Labor Force Participation in Turkey: Time Series Evidence and Cross-Province Estimates." *Economic Research Forum*, Cairo, Working Paper, No. 124.

Tansel, Aysıt. 2002. "Determinants of School Attainment of Boys and Girls in Turkey, Individual, Household and Community Factors." *Economics of Education Review* 21 pp. 455–70.

Tansel, Aysıt, and Nil Demet Güngör. 1997. "The Educational Attainment of Turkey's Labor Force: A Comparison Across Provinces and Over Time." *METU Studies in Development* 24(4): 531–47.

Taymaz, Erol, and Ebru Voyvoda. 2012. "Marching to the Beat of a Late Drummer: Turkey's Experience of Neoliberal Industrialization since 1980." *New Perspectives on Turkey* 47: 83–111.

Tekeli, İlhan, and Selim İlkin. 1977. *1929 Dünya Buhranında Türkiye'nin İktisadi Politika Arayışları*. Ankara: Orta Doğu Teknik Üniversitesi.

——— 1982. *Uygulamaya Geçerken Türkiye'de Devletçiliğin Oluşumu*. Ankara: Orta Doğu Teknik Üniversitesi.

——— 1993. *Osmanli İmparatorluğunda Eğitim ve Bilgi Üretim Sisteminin Oluşumu ve Dönüşümü*. Ankara: Türk Tarih Kurumu Basımevi.

——— 2004a. "Osmanlı İmparatorluğu'nun Birinci Dünya Savaşı'ndaki Ekonomik Düzenlemeleri içinde İaşe Nezareti ve Kara Kemal Bey'in Yeri." *Cumhuriyetin Harcı, c. II: Köktenci Modernitenin Ekonomik Politikasının Gelişimi*, ed. İlhan Tekeli and Selim İlkin, 1–44. Istanbul: İstanbul Bilgi Üniversitesi Yayınları.

Tekeli, İlhan, and Selim İlkin. 2004b. "Savaşmayan Ülkenin Savaş Ekonomisi: Üretimden Tüketime Pamuklu Dokuma." *Cumhuriyetin Harcı, c. II: Köktenci Modernitenin Ekonomik Politikasının Gelişimi*, ed. İlhan Tekeli and Selim İlkin, 409–64. Istanbul: İstanbul Bilgi Üniversitesi Yayınları.

―――― 2004c. "Cumhuriyetin Demiryolu Politikalarının Oluşumu ve Uygulanması." *Cumhuriyetin Harcı, vol. III: Modernitenin Altyapısı Oluşurken*, ed. İlhan Tekeli and Selim İlkin, 271–324. Istanbul: İstanbul Bilgi Üniversitesi Yayınları.

―――― 2004d. "Türkiye'de Demiryolu Öncelikli Ulaşım Politikasından Karayolları Öncelikli Ulaşım Politikasına Geçiş (1923–1957)." *Cumhuriyetin Harcı, vol. III: Köktenci Modernitenin Ekonomik Politikasının Gelişimi*, ed. İlhan Tekeli and Selim İlkin, 369–432. Istanbul: İstanbul Bilgi Üniversitesi Yayınları.

―――― 2014. *İktisat Politikaları ve Uygulamalarıyla İkinci Dünya Savaşı Türkiyesi*. Istanbul: İletişim Yayinlari.

Tekin, Ali. 2006. "Turkey's Aborted Attempt at Export-Led Strategy: Anatomy of the 1970 Economic Reform." *Middle Eastern Studies* 42(1): 133–63.

Temin, Peter. 1996. *Lessons from the Great Depression*. Cambridge, MA: MIT Press.

Tezcan, Baki. 2010. *The Second Ottoman Empire: Political and Social Transformation in the Early Modern World*. Cambridge and New York: Cambridge University Press.

Tezel, Yahya S. 1986. *Cumhuriyet Döneminin İktisadi Tarihi (1923–1950)*. Ankara: Yurt Yayınları.

Thobie, Jacques. 1977. *Interests et imperialisme dans l'empire ottoman (1895–1914)*. Paris: Publications de la Sorbonne.

Thornburg, Max Weston. 1949. *Turkey: An Economic Appraisal*. New York: Twentieth Century Fund.

Toksöz, Meltem. 2010. *Nomads, Migrants and Cotton in the Eastern Mediterranean: The Making of the Adana-Mersin Region*. Leiden and Boston: Brill.

Toniolo, Gianni. 2013. *The Oxford Handbook of the Italian Economy Since Unification*. Oxford and New York: Oxford University Press.

Toprak, Zafer. 1982. *Türkiye'de Milli İktisat (1908–1918)*. Ankara: Yurt Yayınları.

―――― 2016. *Türkiye'de İşçi Sınıfı*. Istanbul: Tarih Vakfı Yurt Yayınları.

Tören, Tolga. 2007. *Yeniden Yapılanan Dünya Ekonomisinde Marshall Planı ve Türkiye Uygulaması*. İstanbul: Sosyal Araştırmalar Vakfı.

Tükel, Ali, Murat Üçer, and Caroline Van Rijckeghem. 2006. "The Banking Sector. From Crisis to Maturation." In *The Turkish Economy: The Real Economy, Corporate Governance and Reform*, ed. Sumru Altuğ and Alpay, 276–303. London: Routledge.

Tunçer, Ali Coşkun. 2015. *Sovereign Debt and International Financial Control: the Middle East and the Balkans*. Houndmills, Basingstoke: Palgrave Macmillan.

Türegün, Adnan. 2016. "Policy Response to the Great Depression of the 1930s: Turkish Neomercantilism in the Balkan Context." *Turkish Studies* 17(4): 666–90.

Türkcan, Ergun. 2010. *Atilla Sönmez'e Armağan: Türkiye'de Planlamanın Yükselişi ve Çöküşü*. Istanbul: Istanbul Bilgi Üniverstesi Yayınları.

Turkey, Devlet İstatistik Enstitüsü (State Institute of Statistics). 1995. *Türkiye Nüfusu, Demografi Yapısı ve Gelişimi, 1923–1994*. Ankara: Devlet İstatistik Enstitüsü.

Turkey, Kalkınma Bakanlığı (Ministry of Development). 2017. *Ekonomik ve Sosyal Göstergeler*. http://www.kalkinma.gov.tr/Pages/EkonomikSosyalGostergeler.aspx.

Turkey, Türkiye İstatistik Kurumu (Turkish Statistical Institute). 2014. *İstatistik Göstergeler-Statistical Indicators, 1923–2013*. Ankara: Turkish Statistical Institute.

Turkey, Türkiye İstatistik Kurumu (Turkish Statistical Institute). 2015. *Turkey's Statistical Yearbook, 2015*.

Udovitch, Abraham L. 1970. *Partnership and Profit*. Princeton, NJ: Princeton University Press.

———— 1988. "Merchants and *Amirs*: Government and Trade in Eleventh-Century Egypt." *Asian and African Studies* 22(1–3): 53–72.

United Nations Development Programme. 2004. *Turkey 2004, Human Development Report*, UNDP, Ankara.

———— 2011. *Human Development Report, 2011*. New York.

Uzun, Ahmet. 2002. *Tanzimat ve Sosyal Direnişler*. Istanbul: Eren Yayınları.

Van Leeuwen, Bas, and Jieli van Leeuwen-Li. 2014. "Chapter 5: Education since 1820." In *How Was Life? Global Well Being Since 1820*, ed. Van Zanden, Jan Luiten, Joerg Baten et al., 87–100. Paris: OECD Publishing, International Institute of Social History.

Van Rijckeghem, Caroline, and Murat Üçer 2005. *Chronicle of the Turkish Financial Crisis of 2000–2001*. Istanbul: Boğaziçi University Press.

Van Zanden, Jan Luiten, Joerg Baten, Peter Foldvari, and Bas van Leeuwen, eds. 2014a. *How Was Life?, Global Well Being Since 1820*. Paris: OECD Publishing, International Institute of Social History.

———— 2014b. "The Changing Shape of Global Inequality 1820–2000: Exploring a New Dataset." *Review of Income and Wealth* series. 60 (2): 279–97.

Wade, Robert. 1990. *Governing the Market: Economic Theory and the Role of Government in East Asian Industrialization*. Princeton, NJ: Princeton University Press.

Waterbury, John. 1991. "Export-Led Growth and the Center-Right Coalition in Turkey." *Comparative Politics* 24(2): 127–45.

Weber, Max. 1978. *Economy and Society. An Outline of Interpretative Sociology*, ed. Guenther Roth and Clasu Wittich. Berkeley and Los Angeles: University of California Press.

White, Jenny B. 1994. *Money Makes Us Relatives: Women's Labor in Urban Turkey*. Austin: University of Texas Press.

Williamson, Jeffrey G. 2006. *Globalization and the Poor Periphery before 1950*. Cambridge, MA: MIT Press.

———— 2011. *Trade and Poverty: When the Third World Fell Behind*. Cambridge, MA: MIT Press.

World Tourism Organization. 2016. *World Tourism Highlights 2016 Edition*; http://www.e-unwto.org/doi/pdf/10.18111/9789284418145.

Yalman, Ahmet Emin. 1934. *Turkey in the World War*. New Haven, CT: Yale University Press.

Yavuz, Erdal. 1995. "Conditions of the Labor Force in Industry, 1923–1940." In *Workers and the Working Class in the Ottoman Empire and the Turkish Republic, 1839–1950*, ed. Donald Quataert and Erik Jan Zürcher, 95–125. London and New York: I.B. Tauris.

Yaycioglu, Ali. 2016. *Partners of the Empire: The Crisis of the Ottoman Order in the Age of Revolutions*. Stanford, CA: Stanford University Press.

Yenal, Oktay. 2003. *Cumhuriyet'in İktisat Tarihi*. Istanbul: Homer Kitabevi.

Yıldırım, Onur. 2006. *Diplomacy and Displacement: Reconsidering the Turco-Greek Exchange of Populations*. New York: Routledge.

Yıldırmaz, Sinan. 2017. *Politics and the Peasantry in Post-War Turkey: Social History, Culture and Modernization*. London and New York: I.B. Tauris.

Yılmaz, Kâmil. 2011. "The EU–Turkey Customs Union Fifteen Years Later: Better, Yet Not the Best Alternative." *South European Society and Politics* 16(2): 235–49.

Yılmaz, Volkan. 2017. *The Politics of Healthcare Reform in Turkey*. London and New York: Palgrave Macmillan.

Yücel, Yelda. 1996. *Macroeconomic Policies in Turkey during the Great Depression, 1929–1940*. Unpublished MA thesis: Istanbul: Boğaziçi University.

Yükseker, Deniz. 2009. "Neoliberal Restructuring and Social Exclusion in Turkey." In *Turkey and the Global Economy: Neo-liberal Restructuring and Integration in the Post-crisis Era*, ed. Ziya Öniş and Fikret Şenses, 262–80. London: Routledge.

Zijdeman, Richard L., and Filipa Ribeiro de Silva. 2014. "Chapter 6: Life Expectancy since 1820." In *How Was Life? Global Well Being Since 1820*, ed. Van Zanden, Jan Luiten, Joerg Baten et al., 101–16. Paris: OECD Publishing and International Institute of Social History.

Zürcher, Erik J. 2004. *Turkey: A Modern History, Third Edition*. London and New York: I.B. Tauris.

INDEX

Note: Figures and tables are indicated by "f" or "t" following a page number. The four historical periods covered in the book are indexed as: contemporary Turkey (1980–2015); Ottoman Empire (1820–1914); post–World War II period (1950-1980); World Wars period (1914–1950)

Deutsche Bank, 119

developed countries: GDP per capita gap with developing countries, 5–6; GDP per capita in, 28

developing countries: GDP per capita gap with developed countries, 5–6; GDP per capita gap within, 27–28; GDP per capita in, 28; life expectancy in, 240–41; responses of, to Great Depression, 156–57; state interventionism in, 70–72, 156–57, 222

Diaz Alejandro, Carlos, 70–71, 157

East Asia, 6, 10, 28, 35, 71–72, 233, 238–39

Eastern Europe, 223

Ecevit, Bülent, 221, 258

economic growth: agriculture and, 138–41; in contemporary Turkey, 257f, 262, 266–67, 276–80, 292–94; culture's influence on, 65–67; environmental effects of, 292–94; historical overview of, 1, 2–7, 32–36, 134–36, 303–6; human development indicators in relation to, 304; informal institutions' influence on, 309–10; institutions' role in, 8–11, 23, 55–60, 306–10, 317; Islam's influence on, 62, 307; in Ottoman Empire, 134–41; in post–World War II period, 219, 222–28; state's role in, 9–10, 246, 286–90; urbanization linked to, 12, 14, 23, 226–27, 279, 292–94; in World Wars period, 158t, 172–73, 184–92; worldwide comparisons of, 25–29. See also deeper causes of economic growth; proximate causes of economic growth

economic institutions: history of, 1–2, 308; in post–World War II period, 206, 214–20, 232; reforms of, 16–17, 97–101, 112–14; World War I and, 160; in World Wars period, 160, 169–73, 195

economic miracles, 28, 35

economic policies: in contemporary Turkey, 248–59, 262–63, 265; history of, 1–2; neoliberal, 245, 246–48, 267–68; political

control of, 252; populist, 212, 254; reforms of, 16–17; in response to Great Depression, 12, 17, 70, 156–57; scope (long-, medium-, short-term) of, 103, 113–14, 132, 145, 214–16, 220–21, 232–34, 287; World War I and, 160; in World Wars period, 157, 160, 170–71, 179–80

economic sectors, 12, 13f, 14

economy: closing of, 174–75, 175f; opening of, 112–14, 144–49

education and educational indicators: in contemporary Turkey, 295–300; curriculum in, 297; historical overview of, 3, 7, 36, 43–46; inequalities in, 7, 44, 46, 155, 202, 241–42, 297–300; investments in relation to, 296; Islamization of, 297; of non-Muslims, 96; Ottoman, 95–97, 154–55; outcomes of, 296–97; in post–World War II period, 228, 241–42; private, 298; productivity linked to, 228, 279–80, 290; reforms of, 95–97, 148; in rural areas, 43, 199, 202–3; secularization of, 16, 168, 201; in World Wars period, 199, 201–3. See also higher education

Egypt: economic growth in, 6, 34f, 35, 138, 187, 188f, 226, 277, 278f; geography of, 149–50; as model for Ottoman reform, 100; monetary policy of, 104; nineteenth-century reforms of, 93, 148–49; opening of economy of, 114, 146, 149–52; Ottoman Empire and, 99–100; Turkey compared to, 149–52, 191–92

Eldem, Vedat, 30, 136

electricity, 209–10, 253

elites: economic, 88–89, 206, 232, 311; institutions in relation to, 56–57; interrelations among, 238, 311–12; provincial, 74–75; state-affiliated, 88, 311–13; the state in relation to, 9–10, 19, 68–69, 72–75, 88; state interventionism and, 315; tax collection by, 85–86. See also provincial notables

emigration, 48, 51–52, 216. See also remittances

313; multiparty system, 1, 16, 205–7, 232, 284, 313; patronage in, 235, 291; in post–World War II period, 205–7, 221; single-party regime, 16, 168, 174, 177, 178, 182–83, 206–7. *See also* political institutions
population: age structure of, 54; demographic transition and, 53–54, 243–44; historical fluctuations in, 11–12; historical overview of, 47–54, 49t; immigration and nineteenth-century growth of, 48–50, 120–21, 123; non-Muslims in, 50–51; in post–World War II period, 243–44; Turkey's share of world's, 47–48, 47t; in twentieth century, 51–54; World War I's effect on, 166–67; in World Wars period, 157, 173, 186f, 189
populism, macroeconomic, 212, 254
post–World War II period (1950–1980), 21; agriculture in, 207–10, 217, 224, 226; balance-of-payments crisis in, 211–12, 220–21, 246; economic and social indicators in, 227t; economic growth in, 219, 222–28; economic institutions in, 206, 214–20; education in, 228, 241–42; emigration in, 51–52; as golden years, 212; health indicators in, 239–41; human development in, 239–44; income distribution in, 228–31; infrastructure in, 208–10; institutions in, 231–39; ISI in, 214–21, 233; military coups in, 211–12, 232–33; overview of, 204–5; periodization of economic trends in, 205t; political institutions in, 232; politics in, 205–7; population in, 51–54, 243–44; regional economic differences in, 230–31; state interventionism in, 236–39; urbanization in, 52–53, 212–14, 226–27, 229–30
poverty, 283
Preston, Samuel, 38, 241
price ceilings, 76
price supports, 210–11, 236, 281
primary schools, 95
printing press, 64
private finance: persistence of, 120; and per-

sonal credit, 63, 80–82; state use of, 81, 83–84
private sector: cleavages in, 237–38, 289; economy guided by, 170–72, 215–16, 232–34; and ISI, 215; JDP and, 265, 288–89; in post–World War II period, 206–7; state relations with, 75–78, 82; in World Wars period, 177–78, 197
privatization, 198, 252, 255, 262
procurement law, 265
productivity. *See* total factor productivity
Progressive Republican Party, 168
protectionism: introduction of, 12, 71; manufacturing aided by, 177; rationale for, 132–33; in World Wars period, 174, 187, 189. *See also* state interventionism
provincial notables: and agriculture, 125; central government vs., 62–63, 74–75, 92, 93, 122; contributions of, 74; and land, 79–80; and Tanzimat reforms, 15; tax collection by, 62–63, 74–75, 85, 122, 143, 171
Provisional Law for the Encouragement of Industry (1913), 133
proximate causes of economic growth: in contemporary Turkey, 277–79; defined, 7, 55; explanatory value of, 1, 7–11, 55–56; historical overview of, 11–15, 304–6; in Ottoman Empire, 138–41; post–Industrial Revolution, 22–23; in post–World War II period, 226–27; urbanization as, 213; in World Wars period, 187, 213
purchasing power parity (PPP) adjustment, 24, 25

Quran schools, 95

railroads: benefits of, 117–18; European construction of, 12, 113, 117–18; nationalization of, 172; in Ottoman Empire, 11–12, 100, 113, 117–18; state investment in, 178; in Turkey, 169; in World Wars period, 172
Reagan, Ronald, 245
Reform Edict (1856), 113

Régie Company, 109
religion. *See* Islam
religious community networks, 291–92
remittances, 217, 218, 248
Republican People's Party, 171, 180, 183, 193,
    197, 200, 203, 207, 208, 214–15, 312
Reşit Pasha, 94, 98
roads and highways, 208–10
Rodrik, Dani, 273
Rubin, Jared, 64, 80
rural areas: agricultural production in, 120–
    21; consumption in, 217; education and
    educational indicators in, 43, 199, 202–3,
    241; health indicators in, 42; income in,
    141–42, 193; informal institutions in, 17;
    manufacturing and crafts in, 128–30; mi-
    gration to urban areas from, 53, 212–14,
    229, 231, 290–91; mortality rates in, 153–
    54; Turkish government in relation to,
    196, 198, 200; in World War I, 162
Russia, Ottoman wars with, 75, 85, 92, 104,
    106, 109

Sabancı group, 216
Salonica, 131
sarrafs (financiers), 105, 118
savings, 13f, 14
schooling, years of, 36, 43–44, 45f, 155, 201–
    3, 242, 296
sectors. *See* economic sectors
secularization: of education, 16, 168, 201;
    rural opposition to, 200; of Turkish na-
    tion, 168
Selim III, 93, 94
Sen, Amartya, 36, 163
sipahis (state employees), 79
social conflict, 67–68
social structure: Egyptian vs. Turkish, in re-
    lation to trade, 150–51; institutions in re-
    lation to, 18–19, 310
Soil Products Office, 175, 210–11
Sokoloff, Kenneth, 61
South America, 33, 135, 223
Southeast Anatolia Project, 253

South Korea, 28, 35, 71
Soviet Union, 205–6
Spain: economic growth in, 5–6, 34f, 35, 87,
    136, 137f, 138, 187, 188f, 225f, 226, 277, 278f;
    economic miracle in, 28, 35; wages in, 86
SPO. *See* State Planning Organization
    (SPO)
state: and agriculture, 122–23; East Asian,
    71–72; elites in relation to, 9–10, 19, 68–
    69, 72–75, 88; formation of Turkish
    nation-state, 168–69; institutions in rela-
    tion to, 9–10, 68–75; and land regime, 78–
    80; as nation-state after War of Indepen-
    dence, 168–69; pre-nineteenth-century,
    73; private sector relations with, 75–78,
    82; role of, in economic growth, 9–10,
    246, 286–90; societal cleavages in rela-
    tion to, 19, 312–14. *See also* state
    interventionism
state interventionism: in Britain, 70; in con-
    temporary Turkey, 286–90; in develop-
    ing countries, 70–72, 156–57, 222; East
    Asian, 10, 71–72, 238–39; elites' role in,
    315; in Europe, 141; and industrialization,
    10, 70–72, 141, 178–81, 196–98, 314–16;
    overview of, 314–16; in post–World War
    II period, 214–20, 236–39; in response to
    Great Depression, 70–72, 156–57, 179–80;
    roles of formal and informal institutions
    in, 237; in World War I, 167; in World
    Wars period, 32, 167. *See also* import-
    substituting industrialization;
    protectionism
State Planning Organization (SPO), 214–16,
    233, 280
strikes, 132, 177, 249
Sümerbank, 177, 198
Sunni community networks, 291, 312
Swiss civil code, 16, 168
Syrian immigration, 51, 264, 267f

Taiwan, 28, 35, 71
Tanzimat Decree, 15, 94, 95, 99, 101, 122,
    307–8

tariffs: introduction of, 12; protectionist, 132–33; in response to Great Depression, 174; in World Wars period, 160, 169–71, 174

taxes: on animals, 170; central administration vs. individuals over collection of, 74–75, 79, 83–85, 93, 101–2, 122, 143; collection of, 83–86; on internal trade, 100; local collection of, 85–86; *timar* system and, 63, 79, 83; in World War I, 164–65; in World Wars period, 170

tax farming, 63, 81, 83–85, 94, 101–2, 122, 143, 196

technology: role of, in economic growth, 11

textiles, 127–29, 129f

Tezcan, Baki, 73

Tezel, Yahya S., 30

Thatcher, Margaret, 245

timar system, 63, 79, 83

Tinbergen, Jan, 214

tithes, 102, 122, 170–71, 189, 196

top-down institutional changes, 1, 15–16, 18, 94, 97, 144–49, 307–8

total factor productivity, 14, 227–28, 279, 306, 309–10, 315

tourism, 253, 265

trade, 127; agricultural, 208, 211; EU involvement in, 259–60, 260f, 272; European involvement in, 16, 77–78, 90–91, 97–99, 112–18, 144–49, 160–62, 195–96; Great Depression's effect on, 173–74; monopolies on, 59, 70, 97, 164; opening of economy to, 112–14, 144–52; Ottoman Empire and, 77–78, 112–14, 144–49; taxes on internal, 100; Turkey, Egypt, and Iran compared, 150t; World War I's effect on, 160–62; in World Wars period, 160–62, 169, 173f, 181. *See also* protectionism

Treaty of Küçük Kaynarca, 92

Turkey, map of, xvi

Turkish Industry and Business Association (TÜSİAD), 238, 289

Turkish language, 96

Turkish Statistical Institute (TurkStat), 30, 31, 282

Turkish Straits, 206

TurkStat. *See* Turkish Statistical Institute

TÜSİAD. *See* Turkish Industry and Business Association

TÜSKON, 289

ulema (religious hierarchy), 73, 81, 94, 95

Union and Progress. *See* Committee of Union and Progress

Union of the Chambers and Commodity Exchanges, 237

United Nations, 36, 298

United Nations Development Program, 299

United Nations series, 29

United States, 205–7

urban areas: economic inequalities in, 230f; educational indicators in, 43, 241; health indicators in, 42; income in, 142–43, 193, 229–30, 282; informal institutions in, 17, 235–36, 290–91; labor force in, 177, 214; manufacturing and crafts in, 130–31; mortality rates in, 153–54; poverty in, 283; in World War I, 162–64; in World Wars period, 187, 189–90

urbanization: agricultural production and, 121; causes of, 53, 213; in contemporary Turkey, 278–79, 290–94; defined, 52, 212; demographic transition linked to, 243; economic growth linked to, 12, 14, 23, 226–27, 279, 292–94; environmental effects of, 292–94; historical overview of, 52f; in post–World War II period, 52–53, 212–14, 226–27, 229–30

usury. *See* interest

vakıfs (pious foundations), 63, 80, 81, 94, 120, 148, 199

Varlık Vergisi (Wealth Levy), 182

Village Institutes, 199, 202–3

wages: of construction workers, 87f; historical overview of, 86–87; in manufacturing

THE PRINCETON ECONOMIC HISTORY
OF THE WESTERN WORLD

Joel Mokyr, Series Editor

A NOTE ON THE TYPE

This book has been composed in Arno, an Old-style serif typeface in the
classic Venetian tradition, designed by Robert Slimbach at Adobe.